AMBASSADORS OF REALPOLITIK

Studies in Contemporary European History

Editors:
Konrad Jarausch, Lurcy Professor of European Civilization, University of North Carolina, Chapel Hill, and a Director of the Zentrum für Zeithistorische Studien, Potsdam, Germany
Henry Rousso, Senior Fellow at the Institut d'histoire du temps présent, CNRS (Centre national de la recherche scientifique, Paris)

Volume 1
Between Utopia and Disillusionment: A Narrative of the Political Transformation in Eastern Europe
 Henri Vogt

Volume 2
The Inverted Mirror: Mythologizing the Enemy in France and Germany, 1898–1914
 Michael E. Nolan

Volume 3
Conflicted Memories: Europeanizing Contemporary Histories
 Edited by Konrad H. Jarausch and Thomas Lindenberger with the Collaboration of Annelie Ramsbrock

Volume 4
Playing Politics with History: The Bundestag Inquiries into East Germany
 Andrew H. Beattie

Volume 5
Alsace to the Alsatians? Visions and Divisions of Alsatian Regionalism, 1870–1939
 Christopher J. Fischer

Volume 6
A European Memory? Contested Histories and Politics of Remembrance
 Edited by Małgorzata Pakier and Bo Stråth

Volume 7
Experience and Memory: The Second World War in Europe
 Edited by Jörg Echternkamp and Stefan Martens

Volume 8
Children, Families, and States: Time Policies of Childcare, Preschool, and Primary Education in Europe
 Edited by Karen Hagemann, Konrad H. Jarausch, and Cristina Allemann-Ghionda

Volume 9
Social Policy in the Smaller European Union States
 Edited by Gary B. Cohen, Ben W. Ansell, Robert Henry Cox, and Jane Gingrich

Volume 10
A State of Peace in Europe: West Germany and the CSCE, 1966–1975
 Petri Hakkarainen

Volume 11
Visions of the End of the Cold War in Europe, 1945–1990
 Edited by Frederic Bozo, Marie-Pierre Rey, N. Piers Ludlow, and Bernd Rother

Volume 12
Investigating Srebrenica: Institutions, Facts, Responsibilities
 Edited by Isabelle Delpla, Xavier Bougarel, and Jean-Louis Fournel

Volume 13
Samizdat, Tamizdat, and Beyond: Transnational Media During and After Socialism
 Edited by Friederike Kind-Kovacs and Jessie Labov

Volume 14
Shaping the Transnational Sphere: Experts, Networks and Issues from the 1840s to the 1930s
 Edited by Davide Rodogno, Bernhard Struck and Jakob Vogel

Volume 15
Tailoring Truth: Politicizing the Past and Negotiating Memory in East Germany, 1945–1990
 Jon Berndt Olsen

Volume 16
Memory and Change in Europe: Eastern Perspectives
 Edited by Małgorzata Pakier and Joanna Wawrzyniak

Volume 17
The Long Aftermath: Cultural Legacies of Europe at War, 1936–Present
 Edited by Manuel Bragança and Peter Tame

Volume 18
Whose Memory? Which Future? Remembering Ethnic Cleansing and Lost Cultural Diversity in East, Central, and East-South Europe
 Edited by Barbara Törnquist-Plewa

Volume 19
Wartime Captivity in the Twentieth Century: Archives, Stories, Memories
 Edited by Anne-Marie Pathé and Fabien Théofilakis

Volume 20
Ambassadors of Realpolitik: Sweden, the CSCE and the Cold War
 Aryo Makko

AMBASSADORS OF REALPOLITIK

Sweden, the CSCE and the Cold War

By Aryo Makko

First published in 2017 by
Berghahn Books
www.berghahnbooks.com

© 2017, 2020 Aryo Makko
First paperback edition published in 2020

All rights reserved. Except for the quotation of short passages for the purposes of criticism and review, no part of this book may be reproduced in any form or by any means, electronic or mechanical, including photocopying, recording, or any information storage and retrieval system now known or to be invented, without written permission of the publisher.

Library of Congress Cataloging-in-Publication Data

Names: Makko, Aryo, author.
Title: Ambassadors of realpolitik : Sweden, the CSCE and the Cold War / by Aryo Makko.
Description: First edition. | New York : Berghahn Books, 2016. | Series: Studies in contemporary European history ; volume 21 | Includes bibliographical references and index.
Identifiers: LCCN 2016025400 | ISBN 9781785332845 (hardback : alk. paper) | ISBN 9781785332852 (ebook)
Subjects: LCSH: Sweden--Foreign relations--Europe. | Europe--Foreign relations--Sweden. | Sweden--Foreign relations--1950- | Cold War--Diplomatic history. | National security--Sweden--History--20th century. | Conference on Security and Cooperation in Europe (Organization)
Classification: LCC D1065.S85 M35 2016 | DDC 327.4850409/045--dc23
LC record available at https://lccn.loc.gov/2016025400

British Library Cataloguing in Publication Data

A catalogue record for this book is available from the British Library

ISBN 978-1-78533-284-5 hardback
ISBN 978-1-78920-517-6 paperback
ISBN 978-1-78533-285-2 ebook

Contents

List of Figures	vi
Acknowledgements	vii
List of Abbreviations	ix
Introduction	1
Chapter 1. 1945–1969: Sweden and Europe in a Changing World	33
Chapter 2. 1969–1971: Doubting Détente	47
Chapter 3 1971–1972: Assuming the Role of the Realist	105
Chapter 4. 1972–1973: Engaging in the Dipoli Tea Party	147
Chapter 5. 1973–1975: Making the Helsinki Final Act	183
Conclusion	247
Appendices	255
Bibliography	261
Index	283

Figures

Figure 0.1	Sweden's foreign policy in the era of détente	13
Figure 0.2	Role theory and foreign policy	18
Figure 0.3	Holsti's NRC typology	20
Figure 3.1	CSCE working structure at the Swedish Ministry for Foreign Affairs after December 1971	139

Acknowledgements

Concluding a book project with a note of acknowledgement brings to mind the sheer number of individuals and institutions that have been involved and offered their supported to such an endeavour. I have tried my best not to leave any of them out.

I am indebted to a number of institutions who have generously supported this book, including the Department of History at Stockholm University, Birgit and Gad Rausing's Foundation for Humanistic Research, Helge Ax:son Johnsons Foundation, E Alfred & Bertha Jansson's Foundation, Foundation Olle Engkvist Byggmästare, the Wallenberg Foundation (through the Royal Swedish Academy of Letters, History and Antiquities) and the Gunvor and Josef Anérs Foundation.

My former supervisors Karl Molin and Hossein Sheiban provided excellent academic guidance and encouraged me to explore the many facets of life in academia. The combination of their extensive knowledge on the history of the Cold War and expertise in historical theory and method has been a highly valuable and much appreciated resource. I am also thankful to Leos Müller, who has become an invaluable peer in recent years. The Department of History at Stockholm University has been the best possible environment for a young researcher. I owe special thanks to Annika Brofelth, Eva Eggeby, Agneta Eiseborn, Elisabeth Elgán, Pär Frohnert, Kjell Lundgren, Tom Silvennoinen, Oskar Schelin and Susanne Stenius for providing outstanding working conditions.

It has also been a great pleasure to work with and learn from colleagues at the department. The constructive criticism and helpful comments of Nevra Biltekin, Fredrik Charpentier Ljungqvist, Ann Hallner, Nikolas Glover, Johannes Heuman, Cecilia Notini Burch, Alf Sjöblom, Ingela Sjögren, Oskar Sjöström, Anna-Carin Stymne and Harry Svensson helped me develop ideas and improve my work. Magnus Petersson and Jens

Ljunggren contributed significantly to the improvement of the book by providing comments with meticulous precision. *Tack allihopa!*

I also owe thanks to Chris Chappell, Jessica Murphy and the whole team at Berghahn Books, whose expertise and kind support greatly facilitated the realisation of this book; and to the anonymous reviewers, whose insightful comments helped me improve the manuscript further.

Large portions of the book were researched and written during my stints as visiting research fellow of the International History Department at the Graduate Institute of International and Development Studies in Geneva and the Department of Politics and International Relations and the Modern European History Research Centre, both at the University of Oxford. In Geneva, Thomas Fischer not only shared his wisdom on the CSCE and neutrality and nonalignment in Europe but also offered important personal advice on various occasions. Over various coffee breaks, lunches and dinners at their home in Berne, Thomas, his wife Barbara and their son Frederik have become much valued friends. In Oxford, I am indebted to Anne Deighton, who offered guidance and support and to Kai Hebel for introducing me to local colleagues and Monday football at the University Club.

I would like to thank my parents Elias and Hasare, my sister Shamiram and my brothers Ninos and Nuhro as well as my extended family for unconditional support of my many years of study. Marco Fiorda has been my close friend since our school days, and I have been fortunate to enjoy his friendship ever since. I am also grateful to the following friends and colleagues in Germany, the Netherlands, Sweden, the United Kingdom and the United States for their support, collaboration and friendship: Stellan Andersson, Matay Arsan, Juhana Aunesluoma, Mano Barmano, Josef Cacan, Önver Cetrez, Sargon Donabed, Özkan Ego, Stefan Ekecrantz, Norbert Götz, Jussi M. Hanhimäki, Tomas Isik, Shamiran Mako, Tomas Meytap, Klaus Misgeld (who, sadly, passed away shortly before the completion of this book), Therese Nordlund Edvinsson, Efrem Rhawi, Abraham Staifo, Ninib Staifo, Mark Tomass, Hannibal Travis and Zeki Yalcin.

Finally, and most importantly, I owe a special thank you to my wife, Rimrama. With numerous archives to research in mind, the greatest discovery came to be her love, support and, equally important, her patience. The birth of our son Leo in September 2014 changed everything for the better; he has been a blessing ever since, teaching me anew what really matters in life. This book is dedicated to them.

ABBREVIATIONS

AA	Auswärtiges Amt (Foreign Ministry of the Federal Republic of Germany)
ADR	Archiv der Republik (Archive of the Republic, Austria)
ARAB	Arbetarrörelsens arkiv och bibliotek (Labour Movement Archives and Library)
BKAF	Bruno Kreisky Archives Foundation
BmfaA	Bundesministerium für auswärtige Angelegenheiten (Foreign Ministry of Austria)
CBM	confidence-building measures
CCD	Conference of the Committee on Disarmament
CDU	Christlich Demokratische Union Deutschlands (Christian Democratic Union of Germany)
CPSU	Communist Party of the Soviet Union
CSCE	Conference on Security and Co-operation in Europe
CSSR	Czechoslovak Socialist Republic
CSU	Christlich-Soziale Union in Bayern (Christian Social Union in Bavaria)
DSFP	Documents on Swedish Foreign Policy
EC	European Communities
ECE	United Nations Economic Commission for Europe
ECSC	European Coal and Steel Community
EDC	European Defence Community
EEC	European Economic Community
EFTA	European Free Trade Association
EPC	European Political Cooperation
EPD	Eidgenössisches Politisches Departement
ERP	Economic Recovery Plan
ESC	European Security Conference
EU	European Union

FCO	Foreign & Commonwealth Office
FD	Försvarsdepartementet (Swedish Ministry of Defence)
FPA	foreign policy analysis
FRG	Federal Republic of Germany
FRUS	Foreign Relations of the United States
GATT	General Agreement on Tariffs and Trade
GDR	German Democratic Republic
IB	Informationsbyrån (Information Bureau)
ICPD	United Nations International Conference on Population and Development and Research on Population and the Environment
IMF	International Monetary Fund
IR	International Relations
KB	Kungliga Biblioteket Stockholm (Royal Library Stockholm)
MAC	mutually acceptable conditions
MBFR	mutual and balanced force reductions
MFA	Ministry for Foreign Affairs
MPT	multilateral preparatory talks
MSEUE	Mouvement Socialiste pour les États-Unis d'Europe
N+N	(Group of) Neutral and Nonaligned States
NATO	North Atlantic Treaty Organization
NORDEK	Nordiskt Ekonomiskt Gemenskap (Nordic Economic Community)
NPT	Nuclear Non-Proliferation Treaty
NRC	national role conception
OECD	Organisation for Economic Co-operation and Development
OEEC	Organization for European Economic Co-operation
OPA	Olof Palme Archives
OSCE	Organization for Security and Cooperation in Europe
ÖStA	Österreichisches Staatsarchiv (Austrian State Archives)
PAAA	Politisches Archiv des Auswärtigen Amtes (Diplomatic Archive of the German Ministry for Foreign Affairs)
SALT	Strategic Arms Limitations Talks
SAP	Sveriges socialdemokratiska arbetarparti (Swedish Social Democratic Workers' Party)
SDP	Suomen Sosialidemokraattinen Puolue (Social Democratic Party of Finland)
SDU	Scandinavian Defence Union
SED	Sozialistische Einheitspartei Deutschlands (Socialist Unity Party of Germany)
SIPRI	Stockholm International Peace Research Institute

SPD	Sozialdemokratische Partei Deutschlands (Social Democratic Party of Germany)
SRPD	Système du règlement pacificique des differences (System of Peaceful Settlement of Disputes)
SSU	Sveriges socialdemokratiska ungdomsförbund (Swedish Social Democratic Youth League)
SUKK	Sverige under kalla kriget (Sweden during the Cold War)
TASS	Telegrafnoye agentstvo Sovetskovo Soyuza (Telegraph Agency of the Soviet Union)
TNA	The National Archives (United Kingdom)
TT	Tidningarnas Telegrambyrå (The Newspapers' Telegram Bureau)
UD	Utrikesdepartementet (Swedish Ministry for Foreign Affairs)
UKAS	Universitetskanslersämbetets arbetsgrupp för fasta studiegångar (Working Group for Fixed Courses of Study at the Swedish Higher Education Authority)
UN	United Nations
UNESCO	United Nations Educational, Scientific and Cultural Organization
WBA	Willy Brandt Archives

Introduction

> *The era of confrontation and division in Europe has ended. We declare that henceforth our relations will be founded on respect and cooperation. Europe is liberating itself from the legacy of the past. The courage of men and women, the strength of the will of the peoples and the power of the ideas of the Helsinki Final Act have opened a new era of democracy, peace and unity in Europe.*
>
> —Charter of Paris for a New Europe, 21 November 1990[1]

When thirty-four heads of states from Europe, the United States and Canada formalized the end of the Cold War and the division between East and West by signing the Charter of Paris, the effects of the Helsinki Final Act of 1975 were declared to have been both part of and catalyst for the chain of events leading towards the fall of the Berlin Wall. According to the charter, the interplay between the 'power of the ideas' and the courage and 'will of the peoples' of Eastern Europe had paved the way for lasting peace. The epic year of the old continent in 1989 had not become one of violence and bloodshed, as feared by many contemporaries. Instead, it entered the history books as a chapter on peaceful revolutions, causing optimists like Francis Fukuyama to proclaim the 'end of history'.[2]

Decision makers all over Europe acknowledged that the bloc-to-bloc confrontations epitomizing the Cold War had been overcome peacefully with the help of the so-called spirit of Helsinki. Ambassador Rolf Ekéus gave a similar verdict in a 2002 Swedish government report. Produced by a task group comprising two ambassadors, several assistant deputy under-secretaries from two ministries, several military experts and numerous researchers, the report shared the sentiments expressed in the Charter of Paris. According to the Ekéus report, the Helsinki Final Act had 'created and shaped thoughts and ideas which through their implicit political and moral relevance eventually led to the collapse of the Soviet Empire and communism'.³ However, the road from Helsinki in 1975 to Paris in 1990 was not a straight one. Nor did the idea of causality, established by the heads of states at Paris and acknowledged by the Swedish officials in the Ekéus report, immediately find its way into the historical narrative.

In January 1977, seventeen months after the grande finale at Helsinki's Finlandia Hall, *TIME* magazine reported on a crackdown campaign carried out by Czechoslovakian authorities against the signatories of Charter 77, a civic movement pushing for human rights as decoded in the Helsinki declaration. Against the background of general defiance of the Final Act's human dimension in communist countries, the *TIME* journalist asked a pointed question: 'Spirit of Helsinki, Where Are You?'⁴ Three years later, this question was answered in another article, with a headline claiming, significantly, that the Kremlin was 'killing the Spirit of Helsinki'. The article argued that diplomats struggled to ensure the survival of the Conference on Security and Co-operation in Europe (CSCE) at the follow-up meeting to the Final Act held in Madrid, while Eastern European dissidents, Jews and human rights groups were targeted more directly than ever before. The hopes of these latter groups, once invested in the Final Act, now lay 'in ruins'.⁵

The lack of faith in the value of the negotiations carried out in Geneva and Helsinki between 1972 and 1975 prevailed widely in both East and West, from the time of ratification of the Final Accords until the second half of the 1980s. Few believed that détente would bring about real change, and reports of repressions carried out by Eastern European regimes seemed to confirm this pessimism.⁶ Only when the citizens of the Soviet Union and its allies experienced the first gentle breezes of what would develop into a stormy wind of change in the form of glasnost and perestroika did opinion start to shift.

These early reassessments of political realities all over Europe were soon followed by the bursting of a dam when the world witnessed the rapid collapse of the Soviet Union and the bipartite system of worldwide political reality after a half-century of all-embracing antagonism between communist one-party rule in the East and liberal democracies in the West.

Over the following decade, attempts to explain the quick collapse of the Soviet empire tended to focus on 'hard power' and the effects of the arms race on the Soviet economy. The result was a triumphalist Western narrative of what had happened, claiming a victory of good over evil.⁷ Eventually, increasing access to archival sources in Eastern Europe resulted in more nuanced accounts of the developments in the late 1980s as multilayered processes with origins in the era of détente.⁸ The history of the Cold War had not been exclusively a superpower game – ideas had indeed mattered.

With the wisdom of hindsight, many Europeans had to come to terms with their recent past. In Sweden, change appeared imminent in February 1985 during a heated parliamentary debate on foreign policy in the Riksdag (the parliament of Sweden) in Stockholm. After decades of rather solid consensus building in the realm of foreign policy established by the Social Democrats, years of controversy surrounding foreign violation of Swedish maritime territory caused the conservative opposition to openly question that policy. To Swedish prime minister Olof Palme, the harsh public criticism was nothing less than an attempt by the opposition to 'demolish bridges' and seek 'confrontation all over the battlefield of security policy matters'.[9] After the end of the Cold War, neutrality itself was put on trial when a controversy broke out on its real nature and practices in the early 1990s.[10]

In October 2000, the Swedish government reacted to the persistent debates on this foreign policy matter when Foreign Minister Anna Lindh appointed Ambassador Ekéus as head of the abovementioned investigation committee that would account for the country's foreign policy during the second half of the Cold War.[11] Ekéus was assigned the task of conducting an in-depth study of Sweden's political and military policies at the time. In its directives, the government defined two explicit tasks to be performed by the 'Inquiry on Security Policy' – its official name.

First, it would give an account of the development of general realities during the Cold War in order to provide an understanding of the world to which decision makers in Stockholm had to adapt. Second, it would give an account and produce an analysis of politicomilitary aspects of Swedish security policy during that period. The report, as mentioned above, emphasized the importance of the CSCE and its final declaration. Yet, regardless of this, academic and public debates on Sweden's role in the Cold War have continued to restrict analysis of the European sphere to the process of European integration and its economic aspects. The relevance of European security and the making of the Final Act of 1975 to Sweden remains excluded from the narrative.

The disregard of the question of European security in the historiography of Cold War Sweden has created two interlinked research gaps. First, Europe has been left out of the narrative of the so-called activation of Swedish foreign policy in the 1960s, with emphasis placed instead on international solidarity about which scholarly consensus prevails.[12] Second, and as a consequence, the country's role has not been fully explored by CSCE scholars, mostly due to the predominant interest in Sweden and Europe from an almost exclusively economic perspective.

This book focuses on the reciprocal relationship between Sweden and the early Helsinki Process, starting with the establishment of a continental security conference on the international agenda through the so-called Budapest Appeal of the Warsaw Pact states in early 1969 until the signing of the Final Act on 1 August 1975. It analyses Sweden's contribution to the making of the Helsinki Final Act of 1975 and the significance of the CSCE to Swedish foreign policy between 1969 and 1975 in general. In consequence, the book considers how a historical re-evaluation of these matters would affect the established paradigm of an active Swedish foreign policy during that period.

This is the first comprehensive analysis on the subject, and it offers a narrative that allows a profound understanding of what influence Sweden had on the making of the Helsinki Final Act, and vice versa, based on the first thorough examination of the Swedish role in the CSCE process. In this analysis I have four fundamental purposes: first, to outline and explain the reasons behind the contribution that Swedish decision makers and diplomats of the Ministry for Foreign Affairs made to the design of the Helsinki Final Act of 1975; second, to assess the significance of Swedish engagement at the CSCE to the established notion of the country's foreign policy as 'active'; third, to summarize public and media reactions to this engagement or explain the lack thereof; and finally, to give an account of how Sweden and Swedish policy at the CSCE were perceived abroad. The result of this analysis forces us to reconsider the activism paradigm.

My interest lies not exclusively in international (diplomatic) history but also in exploring how Swedish foreign policy identity was manifested in international negotiations on a multilateral level as well as in considering its repercussions for the domestic 'lowest levels', that is, in reactions to that policy. The research expounded in the body of the book will thus allow an analysis of how 'Swedish', 'Nordic', 'European' or 'global' Sweden was, or should have been, in the eyes of diplomatic and political elites and other actors at the time.

I argue that Sweden's policy towards Europe must be integrated into the narrative about the country's 'active' role in international politics during the period of détente. Regardless of dissimilarities between Swedish and wider European policy, such as economic and security preferences, and despite the CSCE being a reflection of the Cold War conflict between East and West, whereas European integration was an exclusively Western European process, a similar *Berührungsangst* (fear of contact), as Klaus Misgeld has called it, limited the development of a more European Sweden.[13] Accordingly, Sweden's response to the 'European challenge' was trade facilitation.

The Swedes remained the most passive of all European neutrals during the preparatory phase of the CSCE, perceiving the conference to be a Soviet tool, and therefore refrained from designing or cosponsoring any initiatives.[14] For this they were criticized harshly by Eastern, Western and neutral states alike.[15] Because it was feared that heavy involvement in European affairs could lead to limited freedom of action and a decline of Soviet trust in Sweden's political position, such engagement was consequently refused by the government in Stockholm, with reference to the policy of neutrality. Instead of a controversial but domestically appealing *change-oriented* policy carried out on a global level, the Swedes decided on a conservative approach towards Europe.[16] This paradox, between Sweden's active commitment to global issues and its simultaneous reluctance to engage in European affairs, continues to prompt general questions about the pervasive view expressed in the 'active foreign policy' of the first Palme government.

In the empirical analysis to come we will see that human rights were of low priority in Sweden's European policy and that international solidarity served as a guiding principle exclusively along the North-South axis. In global affairs, Sweden played the role of the advocate of the weak, highlighting human rights and international justice; in Europe, however, the Swedish government advocated realpolitik. As a consequence, Sweden's European policy could not be as active or solidarity based as it was on the global level. My broad analysis of Swedish-European engagement is, then, to see it as one of *European paradox.*

Scholars have considered the dissolution of the Soviet Union in 1991 as 'a turn' leading to the end of the 'short twentieth century'[17] and even, as mentioned above, the end of history itself.[18] The ever-expanding number of declassified files from numerous archives all over the world has provided historians with new source material for fundamental research over the course of the past two decades. Geir Lundestad of the Norwegian Nobel Institute is correct in asserting that we are not yet in the position to give a definitive historical account of the end of the Cold War.[19]

Nevertheless, certain causalities explaining the demise of communism have gained momentum in recent years. Shifting from actor-centred explanations towards greater focus on structure and processes, the CSCE has become one of the most prominent objects of study in this respect. It is mostly praised for its contribution to the demise of communism and has been defined as 'the most evident culmination' of the détente period.[20] In 2001 Daniel Thomas argued that the Final Act sparked off human rights activism and networking in Eastern Europe, the so-called Helsinki Effect.[21] More recently, American historian Sarah Snyder has demonstrated in detail the influence of the transnational network that devoted itself to the implementation of the Helsinki Final Act after 1975.[22]

Over the course of the past three decades, the reception of the CSCE has undergone severe changes. A decade after the ratification of the Final

Act, most contemporaries in the West were still unaware of the implications of the Accords, because Moscow's military power drove the transformation dynamics it had sparked off into the shadows. Many would have signed their agreement to the conclusion of Jonathan Luxmoore's 1986 study, which was characteristic of the time: 'After more than a decade, there is no evidence that world opinion has been moved by the Helsinki process to any significant extent, nor that fear of being held to account by Western diplomats has had any significant or lasting impact upon Soviet policy.'[23] Only a few believed anything positive would come out of Helsinki. One exception was Vojtech Mastny, an American historian of Czech descent, who, as early as 1986, stressed that the institutionalization of human rights as a subject in high-level affairs was of exceptional value in itself.[24]

A few years later, everything changed with the fall of the Berlin Wall and the consequent political and social transformation of Eastern Europe.[25] Naturally, 1989 also came to mark a watershed in the development of the historiography of the Cold War era. Working on new documents from declassified archives, and increasingly cooperating across national boundaries, historians quickly understood that there was much to learn about the years that just had passed, and so they developed a 'new' history of the Cold War (as labelled by Odd Arne Westad as early as 1995).[26] Scholars realized a need for greater focus on the Soviet Union as well as making 'a noteworthy shift from an emphasis on geopolitics to a stress on ideology, from a concern with interests to a preoccupation with culture'.[27]

Recognizing this turn in scholarship, Melvyn Leffler pointed out, 'Not long ago, few of us would have focused on Coke™ and Reeboks, on jazz and rock, on Sesame Street and Donald Duck, but we now know that their appeal perhaps counted for more than the Pershing missiles and the neutron bombs that seemed to dominate the diplomacy of the 1970s.'[28] The reassessment of the years of détente elucidated the idea that soft powers at work in the 1970s had contributed substantially to the course of events in the decade that followed.[29] Swedish historian Alf W. Johansson argues that détente changed the monochrome worldview that had dominated during the 1950s and now turned the Cold War more than ever into a 'struggle about people's hearts and minds'.[30] As part of this, how the CSCE itself was perceived underwent a shift: from being totally disregarded to being considered one of the most essential elements in understanding the history of the Cold War. Some scholars have praised the CSCE as 'revolutionary' and a 'milestone' in international affairs.[31]

In harmony with the structure of the CSCE, three different schools, highlighting the different topics (the so-called baskets), have appeared. Rooted in early emphasis on the Soviet origins of the security conference, the impact of the first basket (in which issues of military security were considered) and the recognition of postwar borders have been seen as the most important outcomes of the CSCE by some scholars. As Swedish historian Wilhelm Agrell writes, 'The central element in the Helsinki Accord was without a doubt the recognition of Europe's post-War borders'.[32] This view is also adopted by Russian historian Vladislav Zubok, who, with regard to the Soviet Union, maintains that:

> The outcome of the détente of the 1970s favoured the Soviets. In 1975, the Helsinki Agreement, despite its 'third' basket, brought the Soviet rulers to fulfilment of their long-time program of European stability with acceptance of Soviet domination in Central Europe, recognition of post-War European borders, and the expansion of Soviet positions in the developed world. Inside the country, the Soviet repressive machine completely suppressed internal dissent, and most dissenters 'agreed' to emigrate.[33]

Finnish historian Jussi M. Hanhimäki has argued that the Final Act should be viewed as the de facto end of the postwar era. Hanhimäki points out that it actually had negative effects on security during the first decade after the conclusion of the CSCE.[34] Acceptance of human rights–related concessions in exchange for territorial security seemed profitable to the Kremlin and initially resulted in the accomplishment of early aims, as hoped for by Leonid Brezhnev and Soviet foreign minister Vyacheslav Molotov. Nevertheless, Hanhimäki argues, economic aspects were essential:

> If Basket III had its unexpected long-term consequences, perhaps even more important in the long term was the role of the economic relations, underlined in Basket II of the Helsinki Accords . . . If the human rights provisions of the CSCE had given a certain legitimacy to Soviet dissidents, Soviet economic mismanagement and the inherent problems of Warsaw Pact Socialism were to provide the socioeconomic background against which the dissidents' voices would resonate loudly in the 1980s.[35]

In recent years, however, the emphasis has shifted towards the third basket, which dealt with human contacts, information, culture and education. In Helsinki, respect for human rights and fundamental freedoms as a basic principle for regulating relations between states was codified in an international agreement for the first time; specifications set out in the third basket added substantially 'to the power of the revolutionary theme itself'.[36] Eventually, Eastern European obligations to effect change outweighed Western acceptance of the status quo.[37] In their speeches at the final session in Helsinki on 1 August 1975, communist leaders Leonid Brezhnev and Erich Honecker celebrated the Final Act, as it seemed to them that the original goal of a surrogate peace conference had been accomplished at a reasonable price. The day after, victory celebrations were followed up with publication of extracts of the Accord in certain Eastern European media, such as *Pravda* and *Neues Deutschland*.

After signing the Final Act, Brezhnev told one of his aids, 'Now, I can die in peace'.[38] In internal debates with politburo hardliners, Brezhnev insisted that the concessions the Soviets made to the West in the third basket lacked real substance. Russian scholar Konstantin Khudoley stresses that Brezhnev and Foreign Minister Andrei Gromyko 'mistakenly believed that the post–World War II borders in Europe had become inviolable in Helsinki'.[39] Yet, the Final Act turned out to be delicate in the long run, as these circulated texts aroused interest among activists and interested citizens in Eastern Europe. Eventually, it was at the grassroots level that the Final Act became a point of reference.[40]

Swiss historian Thomas Fischer has illustrated the catalytic role of the neutral and nonaligned states, known as the 'N+N',[41] confirming with comprehensive evidence the earlier claims that the intellectual entrepreneurship of the neutral states enabled the superpowers to maintain dialogue in periods of crisis.[42] The role played by the N+N was just as disproportionate, and unexpected, as the long-term effects of the third basket, as the Finnish scholar Harto Hakovirta argued as early as 1988. He suggested that the nonalignment of the N+N states had allowed them to contribute to the success of the CSCE through means of their own, such as by bridge-building, mediating, offering services and generating independent ideas, initiatives or proposals.[43]

The grouping of the N+N was not unique. At the CSCE, many like-minded actors merged into groups at different points in time. The most prominent were the Warsaw Pact, NATO and the states of the European Communities (or 'EC Nine' in CSCE terminology). To the EC Nine, the conference was an interesting platform for early steps taken towards a (short-lived) vision of a common European foreign policy, the European Political Cooperation (EPC).[44] Other groups, such as the Berlin Group, the Mediterranean Group and the Nordic states,[45] were less significant.[46]

In recent years, and as a consequence of the emphasis put on the CSCE by the Cold War historians quoted above, the body of literature has grown extensively. National narratives have added to the rapidly growing body of historical literature. As part of a larger research project conducted at the German Institut für Zeitgeschichte, nine researchers have been working on different aspects of the CSCE and the Helsinki Process.[47]

Wanda Jarzabek wrote an account on Poland;[48] Petri Hakkarainen and Tetsuji Senoo carried out their research on West German policy during the 1960s and 1970s, with a focus on Willy Brandt and Egon Bahr, respectively;[49] and, in his doctoral dissertation, Takeshi Yamamoto studied the approaches of France, Great Britain and West Germany to the CSCE between 1969 and 1973.[50] Other studies with particular focus on Great Britain and France are still in the making or have recently been finished.[51] In addition to several more limited scholarly accounts, Finland's role has been described in a book by former diplomat Markku Reimaa.[52] At a nongovernmental level, subjects such as the freedom of religion and the role of churches in the Helsinki Process have been treated.[53]

Sweden's role at the CSCE has been studied by Austrian and American political scientists Michael Zielinski and Janie Leatherman and by Swiss historian Thomas Fischer. However, none of these studies has exclusively focused on Sweden, used sources from Swedish archives, or considered in depth the divergent Swedish approaches to European and global affairs. Leatherman concludes that Sweden 'championed the cause of security measures in the CSCE' and played a dual strategic role of negotiator and intermediary, together with Finland and, eventually, the other neutral and nonaligned states.[54] Accordingly, cooperation between Finland and Sweden was a joint effort to overcome the structural disadvantages of neutrality in a confrontational East-West setting and was forged by the general perception of them as mediators and their own understanding of neutrality as the ideal way of 'maximizing their power resources to achieve their broadest goals in disarmament and human rights'.[55]

Zielinski, for his part, claims that Sweden failed to exert influence on the negotiations concerning confidence-building measures (CBM) and disarmament in the role of *demandeur*. He also argues that Sweden advocated on behalf of the interests of developing countries in the second basket and blended a third-party role with criticism of Western policy in human rights–related questions.[56] Then, in a more recent historical study, Fischer describes Sweden as having been initially passive but then constructive in disarmament negotiations at the conference proper.[57] All of these conclusions are based on official declarations, interviews with contemporaries and, in Fischer's case, archival documents from several European countries. But access to recently declassified Swedish archives now allows us to get at the motives and deliberations *behind* Swedish agency.

Swedish neutrality policy has generally been the subject of intensive study in the past twenty years, which has resulted in a number of overviews of the quickly growing body of literature. In her 1997 research report, Ann-Marie Ekengren noted that there was a shortfall in the number of studies applying a democratic perspective, as most researchers preferred ideological approaches or power-oriented outlooks.[58] Together with Ulf Bjereld, Ekengren also published an updated account of more recent research in the form of a book chapter in Thorsten Olesen's anthology on the state of research in the Nordic countries.[59] Ekengren's survey concludes that although intensive research has been conducted on Cold War Sweden, only a few syntheses have been produced.[60]

The analysis of most works centres on Sweden's foreign policy in relation to specific issues, such as Sweden and the Algerian War, or issue areas (for example, Sweden and international disarmament negotiations). Another topic that has been touched upon by a number of studies is the role of specific individuals in the context of the broader debate on foreign policy. Bjereld and Ekengren have noted a shortage of studies on Sweden from a Nordic or a European perspective and emphasized that the body of the literature is still lacking important perspectives and approaches.

Another detailed overview, authored by historians Magnus Petersson and Olof Kronvall, defines the dichotomies 'deterrence versus reassurance' and 'integration versus screening' as guiding themes of Swedish security policy. The first is used to explain Stockholm's policy towards the Soviet Union and its satellite countries, the latter to describe the behaviour towards NATO and the great powers in the West. Kronvall and Petersson maintain that the early period, up until 1970, is well researched, whereas the last two decades of the Cold War remain less explored.[61] They also highlight that most studies have dealt with Sweden's relations with the United States and other Western states, while those with the Soviet Union and Eastern Europe have been neglected. Two main areas are explicitly pointed out as highly promising for future research in terms of analytical perspectives: first, foreign policy-related bureaucracies; second, the interplay between domestic and foreign policy.[62]

Kjell Engelbrekt divided the post-1991 literature into three schools, following Mikael af Malmborg, who adopted the internationally established labels *traditionalist, revisionist* and *postrevisionist*.[63] Mikael Nilsson, who argues that all three schools are revisionist to some extent, has rejected this categorization. Nilsson instead suggests using the categories *moderate, critical* and *radical*. Accordingly, the moderate school admits the existence of a democratic deficit as a consequence of secret cooperation with NATO, which the Swedish government saw as an *obligation* in order to safeguard the country in case of war. Nevertheless, it never pledged any *binding* commitment.[64]

A useful overview of more up-to-date research can also be found in the relevant chapters of Robert Dalsjö's doctoral dissertation, published in 2006.[65] During the 1990s, a number of journalists and scholars revealed that Sweden had secretly been pursuing cooperation in military matters with the West, and the United States in particular. According to some voices in the ensuing debate, this cooperation implied that Sweden would not have followed its declared policy of neutrality in case of war but, rather, would have sided with NATO and the West. Dalsjö argues that the Swedish government in the 1950s understood that neutrality would fail but hoped to stay out of the initial nuclear exchange.[66] The overall conclusion offered by Dalsjö and journalist Mikael Holmström is that neutrality in itself had been an illusion. In reality, these commentators argued, Sweden had always been a de facto member of NATO.[67] Some would even come to argue that there had been a 'general conflict between the Social Democratic government and the NATO-linked national security elite'.[68]

During the first decade of the post–Cold War era, government commissions investigated such controversial issues regarding the country's recent past in the hope that they could be clarified. Consequently, when the clash between traditionalist and revisionist scholarship resulted in an ever more heated debate by the summer of 1992, the government in Stockholm decided to appoint a commission with the task of examining classified documents on preparations to receive military assistance from the Western bloc during the first two decades of the Cold War. Two years later, results were presented to the public in a report titled *Had There Been a War . . .* The commission found, among other things, that the Swedish defence staff had been involved in intelligence collaboration with Norway and Denmark early on. Later, similar cooperation had developed with Great Britain and with US Army and Air Force units based in Europe. From 1949 onwards, a number of measures had been taken to strengthen military cooperation with Denmark and Norway, both signatories of the North Atlantic Treaty.

These measures included coordination of air surveillance, interceptor control, air force search and rescue, and a joint military weather service. Over the years, interest in inter-Scandinavian cooperation subsided as direct contact evolved between Sweden and the United States. By the beginning of the 1960s, Sweden had established extensive and close cooperation on military technology with the United States. In its concluding remarks, the commission argued that Sweden's political and military leadership, being responsible for the country's survival, simply had to prepare for receiving Western assistance in the event of a Soviet attack.

But none of these preparations implied any commitment to taking sides if a war had broken out in its vicinity. According to the commission report, all actions taken in secret were fully compatible with the definition of the concept of neutrality established in international law.[69] Those who had denied that there was close military contact with the West were thus proven wrong – but so were those who had argued that Sweden really had given away its choice to stay neutral in the case of war, thereby misleading the public.

Research projects conducted by historians Charles Silva, Juhana Aunesluoma, Magnus Petersson or Simon Moores over the past three decades have studied documents from Norwegian, British and American archives and provided further details on the scope of Swedish military contact with members of NATO, corroborating the commission's conclusion that the option to choose the path of neutrality always existed and that Sweden was not a 'secret ally', as has been asserted.[70] Detailed accounts of Swedish-American security relations have been presented in the work of Mikael Nilsson – who, in contrast to the abovementioned authors, argues that these relations limited Stockholm's ability to maintain Swedish neutrality in case of war – and that of Jerker Widén, who argues that the Americans viewed Sweden as guardian, political ombudsman and critic.[71]

Several studies have dealt with Swedish active foreign policy of the 1960s and 1970s. In 2000 Karl Molin offered an interpretation of 'activation' (of Sweden's foreign policy) as a strategy that aimed at counterbalancing the critics who saw a moral deficit of the neutrality policy.[72] Eight years later, Molin published a synoptic volume on Swedish foreign policy during the Cold War together with Ulf Bjereld and Alf Johansson that concluded SUKK (Sverige under kalla kriget [Sweden during the Cold War]), a decade-long research collaboration between the Department of Political Science at the University of Gothenburg, Stockholm University's History Department and the Institute for Contemporary History at Södertörn University.

The authors suggest that Palme's active foreign policy can be interpreted as an attempt to meet the challenge of three basic lines of conflict: between national sovereignty and international dependence; between ideological closeness to the West and nonalignment; and between democratic openness and military readiness.[73] Although Bjereld, Johansson and Molin point to the fact that the designation 'active' is 'somewhat misleading', they choose to hold on to the accepted terminology and do not elaborate on it in their criticism.

Political scientist Douglas Brommesson, quoting Palme's first government declaration in 1970, states that the Swedes saw no space for activism in Europe, due to the Cold War conflict. Brommesson argues that Swedish foreign policy was not simply a reflection of a radical leftist position, as pictured by some scholars. He does not, however, regard this as reason enough to put a general question mark on the widespread description of this foreign policy as active and the outcome of an approach based on international solidarity.[74] Sunniva Engh has claimed that there was a special relationship between European welfare states and international solidarity.

Accordingly, Swedish policy, as proclaimed by Palme, was aimed at supporting the peoples of the Third World in 'choosing their own way', with reference to Sweden's duty to be active in world affairs and criticize other nations' policies.[75] Engh does not, however, discuss why the solidarity approach did not apply to the peoples of Eastern Europe. In his 1999 doctoral thesis, Hans Lödén acknowledges that, through the implementation of its foreign policy, Sweden sought greater security for itself.[76] Nevertheless, he does not regard this as reason enough for a reappraisal of the label 'active'. Following up on the criticism of Bjereld, Johansson and Molin, and by acknowledging the positions of Brommesson, Engh and Lödén, we will see the role that solidarity played – amongst other aspects – and its implications for a historical assessment of Sweden's active foreign policy. In such a reappraisal, Europe takes a central position.

Historian Mikael af Malmborg has argued that Sweden's position during the Cold War era 'cannot be captured with the simple dichotomies of "neutral"/"not neutral", or "aligned"/"nonaligned"'. Rather, if one wishes to reach a comprehensive understanding of the development of Swedish foreign policy during this era, the focus should be on 'interaction, on how neutrality was transformed'.[77] According to af Malmborg's definition, Sweden's foreign policy consisted of four elements during the years of détente treated in this study (as illustrated in Figure 0.1): national neutrality, Nordic cooperation, a commitment to UN collective security and a nascent association with the European community and the CSCE.[78]

National neutrality meant that Sweden would stay away from both NATO and the Warsaw Pact. Nordic cooperation was aimed at maintaining the so-called Nordic balance. Offering a platform for work moving towards collective security, the UN was the most important arena in Swedish foreign policy. Europe, however, did not have a natural place in this concept.[79]

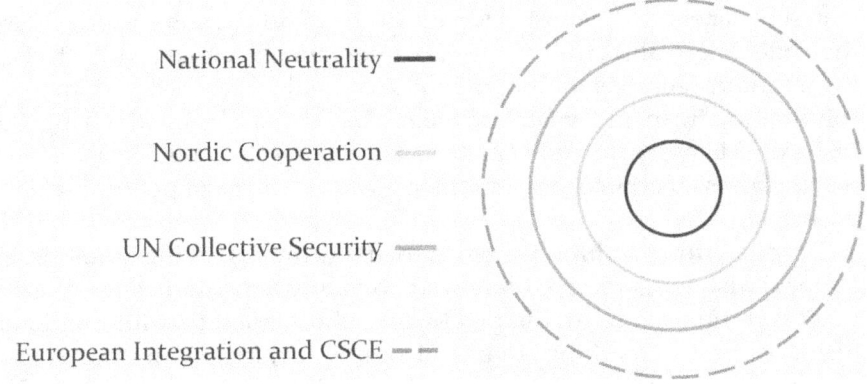

Figure 0.1. Sweden's foreign policy in the era of détente.

The study of Europe, defined as the 'fourth concentric circle' by af Malmborg, has been limited to the subject of European integration. The CSCE remains widely ignored by historians, although it was explicitly regarded as an important part of Swedish foreign policy, as emphasized by Foreign Minister Krister Wickman in the 1972 government declaration.[80] This was also declared to the staff of the Swedish Foreign Ministry in July 1973.[81] Instead, scholarly emphasis has almost exclusively centred on the discussions of whether, and how, Sweden should associate with the EC, overlooking the fact that the idea of a European Security Conference, which would ultimately develop into the CSCE, gained importance among the Foreign Ministry's political strategists almost simultaneously with the ongoing negotiations on Swedish EC membership.[82] It was also during this period that the Swedish government reconsidered EC membership but eventually decided against it on 18 March 1971.[83] In this book, I add to earlier research the missing element of the fourth concentric circle in af Malmborg's conception.

Before proceeding to set out the broader introduction to the analytical framework, the vital question of the use (or lack thereof) and benefits of theory in international history must be addressed.[84] This use has been at the centre of a decade-long debate on the demise of international history in the English-speaking academy but has hardly been discussed with regard to Sweden or Scandinavia.[85]

Starting in the 1960s, expansion and diversification of the discipline and the rise of the French Annales School caused a shift away from the traditional focus on diplomacy and relations between states (or their white male elites) towards social and economic history.[86] Influenced by Marxism, these new trends favoured social science approaches over the classical Rankean exegesis of historical sources and rejected traditional notions of rigorous objectivity and rigid empiricism. Within a short time, diplomatic history would be labelled 'the most arid and sterile of all the sub-histories'.[87] At the same time, realists from the field of international relations (IR) attacked earlier interpretations of how the international system worked, thereby contributing further to what Zara Steiner has called a 'dramatic change' in history.[88] Many traditionalist historians remained puzzled over the new 'wonderlands' of approaches and theories borrowed from political science or sociology.[89]

Despite efforts to broaden their focus in the following years, international historians received renewed and constant critiques from prominent colleagues such as Charles Maier, who argued that international history was still 'marking time' and simply lagging behind theoretical developments elsewhere in the discipline.[90] The cultural turn of the 1990s further compounded the marginalization of international history from history departments everywhere.⁹¹ And, in spite of striking similarities to the international development of the role and evolution of political and diplomatic history, no pertinent debate has appeared in Sweden.⁹² The majority of Swedish historians regard *säkerhetspolitisk historia* as obsolete and theoretically weak. As a result, as observed by Stefan Ekecrantz, it has become monopolized by political scientists.⁹³

More recently, a number of leading historians have started to argue that international history is on the brink of a renaissance, as interest in 'life-and-death governmental decisions for peace or war' is rising again.⁹⁴ A gender and cultural historian, then president of the American Historical Association, Lynn Hunt, discussed this as early as 2002. Viewing the trend towards a revival of international history as problematic, Hunt wondered, 'Where have all the theories gone?' as historians, and their readers, again became all the more concerned with truthfulness and historical objectivity.⁹⁵ Drawing on Hunt's notion of international history as the possible 'next big thing', her successor Michael Hogan elaborated two years later that the field still remained too isolated from postmodern scholarship and needed to keep breaking down disciplinary boundaries through greater incorporation of the cultural turn towards international relations.⁹⁶ Cambridge historian David Reynolds agrees:

> I think there has been a recurrent 'diplomatic twitch' in the saga of international history. And that is because, at its core, this sub-discipline tries to address socially important questions – literally matters of life and death – in a historical way, often near the cutting edge of contemporary events . . . The diplomatic twitch must take full account of the cultural turn. But my hunch is that future generations will keep twitching back to issues of war, peace and decision-making long after our current culture wars have turned into history.⁹⁷

It has also been argued that historians of international relations must not limit their focus to diplomacy but should take into account matters such as human rights, international women's movements and religious movements and should generally be looking beyond the traditional boundaries of the nation-state.⁹⁸ According to the definition of Akira Iriye, the 'history of international relations need not to be the history of government relations, or even the history of individuals and organizations acting on behalf of their governments or in the context of government policy'.⁹⁹ Karl Schweizer and Matt Schumann, for their part, advocate a deeper appreciation of Michel Foucault, Benedict Anderson and Edward Said.¹⁰⁰ Indeed, theoretical awareness is a necessary complement to the thorough study of archival documents, which in itself does not reveal how actors *thought* and *felt*, as Hanhimäki and Westad remind us:

It is important to note, however, that while access to new sources is of crucial importance to historians, it is the accumulation of historical evidence that makes a breakthrough in terms of understanding possible. There has been, and still is, a danger that while we rush to study newly opened archival collections, we fail to put enough emphasis on crucial materials that have been available for decades. Some of these sources include non-archival evidence, and evidence that does *not* come from levels of high diplomacy but rather documents how people in other positions thought, felt, and acted with regard to the Cold War.[101]

Hence, the new international history should certainly draw upon these notions and observations, as a variation in approaches allows the scholar a differentiated and productive (re)interpretation of documents.[102]

The pursuit of such ideals has produced valuable studies on gendered language, in addition to different categories of analysis such as the role of emotion in foreign policy decision-making.[103] In general, theories enable historians to turn implicit understanding into explicit findings. With this background, it is natural to include foreign perceptions within the scope of this study and take a theoretically grounded approach to internal and external actors.

Analytical Framework

The analytical framework of the book is based on the integration of the role of theory in the study of foreign policy. Centred on states as bearers of roles in the international system, it allows an understanding of Swedish agency in the context of the CSCE as an expression of conception(s) of the national role, abbreviated as NRC, as carried out by decision makers and diplomats of the Swedish Ministry for Foreign Affairs (Utrikesdepartementet, UD), as perceived by agents of other states and as reacted to by nonstate actors in Sweden. It integrates these levels of analysis into one expository approach, allowing a deeper understanding of the reasons for and motives behind Swedish decision making in the political and diplomatic process leading to the ratification of the Helsinki Final Act of 1975.

Role theory has been placed in the category of constructivist, reflexive-interpretative approaches.[104] Originally grounded in the sociological and sociopsychological study of human agency, role theory was first introduced into foreign policy analysis (FPA) in a seminal essay by Kalevi Holsti in 1970. Holsti suggested using collective national roles as causal variables in foreign policy decision making and argued that the foreign policy of states can be considered an expression of collective identity, that is, a set of norms and values generally acknowledged by the relevant actors.[105] His work is considered to have broken new ground in the conceptualization of role in foreign policy due to its inductive approach to role conceptions as perceived and defined by decision makers themselves.[106] Holsti's original definition holds:

> A *national role conception* includes the policymakers' own definitions of the general kinds of decisions, commitments, rules and actions suitable to their state, and of the functions, if any, their state should perform on a continuing basis in the international system or in subordinate systems. It is their 'image' of the appropriate orientations or functions of their state toward, or in, the external environment.[107]

His focus on the actor followed an approach introduced to IR in the early 1950s by Richard Snyder, Henry Bruck and Burton Sapin, a circle of theorists based at Princeton University who argued that foreign policy must be studied from levels *below* the nation-state. Ergo, scholars need to look at the human beings who are actually responsible for the actions of states. This important suggestion inspired a new generation of scholars and resulted in the establishment of FPA as an independent subcategory within IR.[108] As a result, focus shifted from the *outcome* of foreign policy towards foreign policy *decision making*.

Political scientists Margaret Sprout and Harold Sprout, also based at Princeton's Wilson Center, elaborated on the suggested actor-oriented focus by arguing that the 'psychomilieu' – that is, how individuals and groups behind foreign policy decisions *perceived* the international and operational environment surrounding them – is a crucial rationale. The Sprouts noted that flawed decisions resulted from incongruence between the real environment and how actors perceived it.[109] James Rosenau, in turn, critically remarked that although a necessary shift in the study of foreign policy had been accomplished, the field still lacked theory that would allow a deeper understanding of the subject.[110] All three studies together created fertile ground for new theories and are considered the 'paradigmatic works' of FPA.[111]

NRCs are based on a collective, or shared, sense of the appropriate position of a nation in the international system that is influenced by two elements, *ego* and *alter*. Although most often applied to elites,[112] even nonstate actors, societal groups and the wider civil society can adopt roles.[113] This is of specific interest to this book, as reactions to the policy carried out by the political and diplomatic elites are considered reflections of a broader perception of what role Sweden was expected to play at the CSCE.

Naomi Wish and Stephen Walker of the first ego-oriented generation of scholars contributed to the validation of Holsti's original model.[114] The second generation of role theorists put stronger emphasis on the integration of the alter. The ego is the actors' collective self-perception vis-à-vis others, based on shared and historically grounded values and norms – in our case, encompassed by notions of Swedish identity and Swedishness.[115] The alter – or *role prescription* – refers to expectations of other actors at the systemic level, that is, agents of other states as well as nonstate actors of foreign countries.[116] German theorists Knut Kirste and Hanns Maull have argued that the actual foreign policy *behaviour*, or *role performance*, of a state is under stronger influence from the ego part than from the expectations of other actors.[117] The role performance consists of repetitive action patterns rather than individual decisions and is defined as '*the* output of foreign policy and *depended variable* in FPA, and *one* input into the international system and *independent variable* in system analysis' (see Figure 0.2).[118]

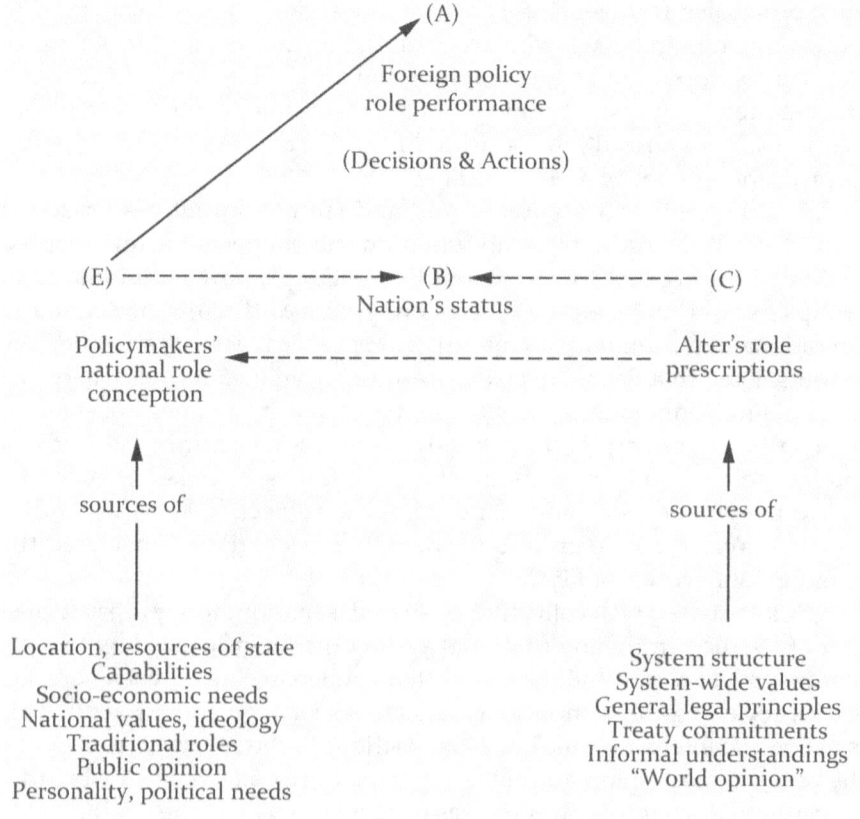

FIGURE 0.2. Role theory and foreign policy.[119]

NRCs affect foreign policy in three ways: they *prescribe* which behaviour and goals are appropriate and *proscribe* which are not; as a result they induce a certain style in foreign policy making.[120] Ulrich Krotz asserts that they are 'products of history, memory and socialization' and that the more integral a part of a country's political culture they become, the stronger they influence its interests and policies. The composition of values, norms, principles and ideals materializes as a certain national political culture. In the context of my own work, I examine this political culture as based on the implications of Swedish neutrality policy. Notions on the meaning of concepts or norms such as 'nonalignment', 'Nordic balance' or 'solidarity' with reference to a certain history or 'traditions' are taken to be key elements of role conceptions that were assembled under the overarching concept of neutrality. In our context, Swedish NRCs and foreign expectations were both bound to neutrality.

Roles are not static but *change* as actors learn and adapt in the context of political and diplomatic processes. States maintain several parallel roles. This holds potential for *conflict*, as roles can be contested in cases when elites fail to enshrine them.[121] Possible sources of such conflict are ambiguities surrounding a role, lack of integration of multiple roles or the fluctuating nature of identity. Change and conflict can occur within a role (*intrarole conflict*) and between roles (*interrole conflict*). Conflict is often the result of contradictions between role performance and identity, or between role and norms, resulting in what has been called *role distance*.[122] Acknowledging the complexity of reality, theorists point to the fact that we must avoid oversimplified analyses. Therefore, role performance must be understood as *role sets* that actors *enact* on the basis of (their national) role conceptions. In conclusion, according to role theory, policy originates in identity construction, and its scope is limited by generally (and implicitly) acknowledged boundaries because roles are *prescriptive* and *proscriptive*.[123]

The NRC typology offered in Holsti's original work (see Figure 0.3) will be applied deductively in the empirical chapters of this book. Several earlier studies have demonstrated that NRCs can also be generated inductively,[124] but I have opted for the earlier method for two main reasons. First, I consider Holsti's typology as particularly useful and authentic, as it is based on an analysis of the international system during the period treated here. Second, the multitude of roles resulting from inductive research makes valid comparisons between different cases more difficult, which subsequently hampers the generalizability of results.

In order to serve the purposes of this study, role theory is applied as a hermeneutic tool,[125] allowing me to typecast state agency in the context of multilateral diplomacy.[126] Methodologically, the application of the

	Role	Definition	Character
1	Bastion of revolution – liberator	'[…] have a duty to organize or lead various types of revolutionary movements abroad'.	active
2	Regional leader	'[…] special responsibilities that a government perceives for itself in its relation to states in a particular region with which it identifies […]'.	active
3	Regional protector	'[…] providing protection for adjacent regions'.	active
4	Active independent	'[…] emphasizes at once independence, self-determination, possible mediation functions, and active programs to extend diplomatic and commercial relations to diverse areas of the world'.	active
5	Liberation supporter	'[…] does not indicate formal responsibilities for organizing, leading, or physically supporting liberation movements abroad'.	active
6	Anti-imperialist agent	'[…] see themselves as agents of 'struggle' against this evil'.	active
7	Defender of the faith	'[…] defending value systems (rather than specified territories) from attack'.	active
8	Mediator-integrator	'[…] perceptions of a continuing task to help adversaries reconcile their differences'.	active
9	Regional-subsystem collaborator	'[…] far-reaching commitments to cooperative efforts with other states to build wider communities, or to cross-cutting subsystems such as the Communist movement'.	active
10	Developer	'[…] special duty or obligation to assist underdeveloped countries'.	active
11	Bridge	'[…] communication function, that is, acting as a "translator" or conveyor of messages and information between peoples of different cultures'.	active
12	Faithful ally	'[…] makes a specific commitment to support the policies of another government'.	active
13	Independent	'[…] the government will make policy decisions according to the state's own interests rather than in support of the objectives of other states'.	passive
14	Example	'[…] promoting prestige and gaining influence in the international system by pursuing certain domestic policies'.	active
15	Internal development	'[…] most efforts of the government should be directed toward problems of internal development'.	passive
16	Isolate	'[…] a minimum of external contacts of whatever variety'.	passive
17	Protectee	'[…] allude to the responsibility of other states to defend them'.	passive

FIGURE 0.3. Holsti's NRC typology

analytical framework consists of establishing a linkage between expressions of motives behind, and behavioural patterns in, decision-making found in archival sources and set out in the definitions of roles as offered in Holsti's typology. Two concrete examples illustrate how role theory will be implemented. References to values and norms made by Swedish actors during negotiations with representatives of other states will be viewed as 'defending value systems . . . from attack' and interpreted as the role performance of a *defender of the faith* (role 7); efforts to restructure proposals offered by opposed parties, for example by combining elements from both sides, will be linked to 'perceptions of a continuing task to help adversaries reconcile their differences', which Holsti gives as the definition of a *mediator-integrator* (role 8).

Foreign policy role analysis and the hermeneutic-deductive approach correspond with the research questions and purpose of my analysis, as they allow a structured, in-depth analysis of sources relating to Sweden and the CSCE. The integration of individuals and the state as actors enables us to contrast new results with both earlier role analyses of official documents and related historical studies.[127]

Sources and Structure

This study is based on multilingual and multiarchival research and draws on documents from eight archives in five countries. The main body consists of about one hundred dossiers of recently declassified files from the Archive of the Swedish Ministry for Foreign Affairs that deal with Sweden's involvement in the CSCE between 1969 and 1976. The series contains a variety of relevant sources, such as diplomatic correspondence, minutes of meetings, political memoranda and strategic papers, and, to a lesser extent, media reports. Similar sources have been consulted in the archives of the foreign ministries of Austria, Germany, Great Britain and Switzerland for the purpose of studying how foreign diplomats perceived Sweden's approach to the CSCE. Archival research has also been conducted in the Olof Palme Archives at the Labour Movement Archives and Library in Stockholm, the Willy Brandt Archive in Bonn and the Bruno Kreisky Archives Foundation in Vienna in order to explore the influence of Prime Minister Olof Palme's personal relations and networks.

These sources have been complemented with memoirs of key actors and official publications, such as *Världspolitikens Dagsfrågor*. Furthermore, this history draws upon interviews with contemporary witnesses, among them politicians, diplomats and scholars, who followed Sweden's policy and the reception of the CSCE in Sweden at the time.

The book comprises seven chapters; along with the introduction and conclusion there are five empirical chapters. The introduction sets out the aims of the study and the research questions as well as providing information on primary sources and previous research. The five empirical chapters of the book form the main body. They deal with the origins and evolution of the Swedish role in the making of the Helsinki Final Act in the years between 1969 and 1975. They have been organized chronologically rather than thematically, as a diachronic narrative is more suitable for a concentrated role analysis. Chapter 1 presents a concise overview of Sweden's foreign policy between 1945 and 1969, with particular focus on Europe. Chapter 2 illustrates early Swedish reactions to the establishment of the conference as part of the agenda of international affairs in 1969–1971. Chapter 3 explains the transformation of the Swedish position from reluctance and passive adjustment to greater flexibility between 1971 and 1972. Chapter 4 discusses Swedish agency at the multilateral preparatory talks (MPT) between November 1972 and June 1973, and the growing interest of public and nonstate actors. Chapter 5 outlines the Swedish policy carried out at the conference proper, mainly in Geneva, between July 1973 and August 1975. A summary and final remarks are presented in the concluding chapter. The appendix comprises a Swedish summary and a register of persons and an index.

Notes

1. Available from www.osce.org/mc/39516 (accessed 14 November 2015).
2. Francis Fukuyama, *The End of History and the Last Man* (New York: Free Press; Toronto: Maxwell Macmillan Canada; New York: Maxwell Macmillan International, 1992).
3. Säkerhetspolitiska utredningen Sverige, *Fred och säkerhet: Svensk säkerhetspolitik 1969–89* (Stockholm: Fritzes offentliga publikationer, 2002), 108. Two years later, a shortened version was published in English as *Peace and Security: Swedish Security Policy 1969–89: Abridged Version and Translation of SOU 2002:108: Report from the Inquiry on Security Policy* (Stockholm: Fritzes offentliga publikationer, 2004).
4. 'HUMAN RIGHTS: Spirit of Helsinki, Where Are You?' *TIME*, 24 January 1977, www.time.com/time/magazine/article/0,9171,945706-2,00.html (accessed 6 October 2015).
5. 'SOVIET UNION: Killing the Spirit of Helsinki', *TIME*, 1 December 1980, www.time.com/time/magazine/article/0,9171,924551,00.html (accessed 6 October 2015).
6. Sarah B. Snyder, '"Jerry, Don't Go": Domestic Opposition to the 1975 Helsinki Final Act', *Journal of American Studies* 44(1), 2010, 67–81.

7. John Lewis Gaddis, *We Now Know: Rethinking Cold War History* (Oxford: Clarendon Press, 1997).
8. For a recent example, see Jussi M. Hanhimäki, 'Conservative Goals, Revolutionary Outcomes: The Paradox of Détente', *Cold War History* 8(4), 2008, 503–12.
9. See minutes of the general debate in the Swedish Parliament on 6 February 1985, www.riksdagen.se/webbnav/?nid=101&dok_id=G80974&bet=1984/85:74 (accessed 22 November 2015).
10. See, for example, Wilhelm Agrell, *Den stora lögnen: Ett säkerhetspolitiskt dubbelspel i alltför många akter* (Stockholm: Ordfront, 1991) and Paul Marion Cole, 'Neutralité du Jour: The Conduct of Swedish Security Policy Since 1945', PhD dissertation (Johns Hopkins University, 1990) for criticism of the Swedish line. For a rejection of this criticism, see Ulf Bjereld, Alf W. Johansson and Karl Molin, *Sveriges säkerhet och världens fred: Svensk utrikespolitik under kalla kriget* (Stockholm: Santérus, 2008).
11. Rolf Ekéus is one of Sweden's most prominent diplomats. He has held a number of diplomatic posts, including chair of the UN Special Commission on Iraq (1991–1997), ambassador to Washington (1997–2000) and High Commissioner on National Minorities at the OSCE (Organization for Security and Cooperation in Europe) (2001–2007).
12. See, for example, Bjereld et al., *Sveriges säkerhet*, 22–25, 224–75; Olof Kronvall and Magnus Petersson, *Svensk säkerhetspolitik i supermakternas skugga 1945–1991* (Stockholm: Santérus, 2012), 11; Ann-Marie Ekengren, *Olof Palme och utrikespolitiken: Europa och tredje världen* (Umeå: Boréa, 2005).
13. Klaus Misgeld, 'Den svenska socialdemokratin och Europa—från slutet av 1920-talet till början av 1970-talet. Attityder och synsätt i centrala uttalanden och dokument', in Bo Huldt and Klaus Misgeld (eds.), *Socialdemokratin och svensk utrikespolitik: från Branting till Palme* (Stockholm: Utrikespolitiska institutet, 1990), 204–5.
14. Thomas Fischer, *Neutral Power in the CSCE: The N+N States and the Making of the Helsinki Accords 1975* (Baden-Baden: Nomos, 2009).
15. Aryo Makko, 'Multilateralism and the Shaping of an "Active Foreign Policy": Sweden During the Preparatory Phase of the CSCE', *Scandinavian Journal of History* 35(3), 2010, 310–29.
16. Scholars have already pointed to the contrast between active global engagement and a cautious and self-serving regional policy. Most often, however, they have defined Scandinavia (or Northern Europe) as a regional space distinct from continental Europe or the whole of Europe. See, for example, Kent Zetterberg, 'Introduktion', in Kent Zetterberg (ed.) *Hotet från öster: tre studier om svensk säkerhetspolitik, krigsplanering och strategi i det kalla krigets första fas 1945–1958* (Stockholm: National Defence College, 1997), 34. For an exception with explicit reference to Europe, see Fredrik Bynander, 'Utrikes- och säkerhetspolitik', in Tom Bryder, Daniel Silander and Charlotte Wallin (eds.), *Svensk politik och den Europeiska unionen* (Stockholm: Liber, 2004), 195–96. See also Aryo Makko, 'Sweden, Europe and the Cold War: A Reappraisal', *Journal of Cold War Studies* 14(2), 2012, 68–97.
17. Eric Hobsbawm, *Age of Extremes: The Short Twentieth Century* (London: Joseph, 1994).
18. For a recent history of the late Cold War period, see Melvyn P. Leffler and Odd Arne Westad (eds.), *The Cambridge History of the Cold War. Vol. III, Endings* (Cambridge: Cambridge University Press, 2010). See also Serhii Plokhy, *The Last Empire: The Final Days of the Soviet Union* (New York: Basic Books, 2014); Geir Lundestad, *East, West, North, South: Major Developments in International Politics Since 1945*, rev. 6th ed. (Los Angeles: SAGE, 2010); Frédéric Bozo et al. (eds.), *Europe and the End of the Cold War: A Reappraisal*

(London: Routledge, 2008); Andrei Grachev, *Gorbachev's Gamble: Soviet Foreign Policy & the End of the Cold War* (Cambridge: Polity Press, 2008); Norman A. Graebner, Richard D. Burns and Joseph M. Siracusa (eds.), *Reagan, Bush, Gorbachev: Revisiting the End of the Cold War* (Westport, CT: Praeger Security International, 2008); Melvyn P. Leffler, *For the Soul of Mankind: The United States, the Soviet Union, and the Cold War* (New York: Hill and Wang, 2007); Vladislav M. Zubok, *A Failed Empire: The Soviet Union in the Cold War from Stalin to Gorbachev* (Chapel Hill: University of North Carolina Press, 2007), chaps. 9 and 10; Olav Njølstad (ed.), *The Last Decade of the Cold War: From Conflict Escalation to Conflict Transformation* (London: Frank Cass, 2004).

19. Lundestad, *East, West, North, South*, 102. Some argue that there cannot be such a thing as a 'definitive record', as historical knowledge is necessarily the result of questions addressed by the asker. For a response to John Lewis Gaddis's triumphant record related to the Nordic Cold War context, see Nikolaj Petersen, '"We now know". The Nordic Countries and the Cold War', in Thorsten Borring Olesen (ed.), *The Cold War—and the Nordic Countries: Historiography at a Crossroads* (Odense: University Press of Southern Denmark, 2004).

20. Jussi M. Hanhimäki, 'Détente in Europe, 1962–1975', in Melvyn P. Leffler and Odd Arne Westad (eds.), *The Cambridge History of the Cold War. Volume II. Crises and Détente* (Cambridge: Cambridge University Press, 2010), 199. For further reading on détente, see Jussi M. Hanhimäki, *The Rise and Fall of Détente: American Foreign Policy and the Transformation of the Cold War* (Washington, DC: Potomac Books, 2013); Wilfried Loth and Georges-Henri Soutou (eds.), *The Making of Détente: Eastern and Western Europe in the Cold War, 1965–75* (London: Routledge, 2008); Wilfried Loth, *Overcoming the Cold War: A History of Détente* (Basingstoke: Palgrave, 2002); Raymond L. Garthoff, *Détente and Confrontation: American-Soviet Relations from Nixon to Reagan* (Washington, DC: Brookings Institution, 1994); and John van Oudenaren, *Détente in Europe: The Soviet Union and the West since 1953* (Durham, NC: Duke University Press, 1991). For a rather controversial hypothesis on détente as reaction to global unrest, see Jeremi Suri, *Power and Protest: Global Revolution and the Rise of Détente* (Cambridge, MA: Harvard University Press, 2003).

21. Daniel C. Thomas, *The Helsinki Effect. International Norms, Human Rights, and the Demise of Communism* (Princeton, NJ: Princeton University Press, 2001).

22. Sarah B. Snyder, *Human Rights Activism and the End of the Cold War: A Transnational History of the Helsinki Network* (Cambridge: Cambridge University Press, 2011).

23. Jonathan Luxmoore, *The Helsinki Agreement: Dialogue or Delusion?* (London: Alliance Publishers, 1986), Preface.

24. Vojtech Mastny, *Helsinki, Human Rights, and European Security: Analysis and Documentation* (Durham, NC: Duke University Press, 1986), 12.

25. Mary Elise Sarotte, *The Collapse. The Accidental Opening of the Berlin Wall* (New York: Basic Books, 2014) and *1989: The Struggle to Create Post-Cold War Europe* (Princeton, NJ: Princeton University Press, 2009).

26. Odd Arne Westad, 'A "New", "International" History of the Cold War?' *Journal of Peace Research* 32(4), 1995, 483–87.

27. Melvyn P. Leffler, 'Bringing It Together: The Parts and the Whole', in Odd Arne Westad (ed.), *Reviewing the Cold War: Approaches, Interpretations, Theory* (London: Frank Cass, 2000), 43.

28. Ibid., 46.

29. The concept of power in international politics has often been applied to US foreign policy. For an introduction of 'hard power', 'soft power' and 'smart power', see

Inderjeet Parmar and Michael Cox (eds.), *Soft Power and U.S. Foreign Policy: Theoretical, Historical and Contemporary Perspectives* (London: Routledge, 2010); Joseph S. Nye Jr., *The Powers to Lead* (Oxford: Oxford University Press, 2008); *Soft Power: The Means to Success in World Politics* (New York: Public Affairs, 2004); Felix Berenskoetter and Michael J. Williams (eds.), *Power in World Politics* (London: Routledge, 2007); Kurt M. Campbell and Michael E. O'Hanlon, *Hard Power: The New Politics of National Security* (New York: Basic Books, 2006).
30. Alf W. Johansson, 'Kampen om hjärtan och sinnen. Nyare forskning om kalla kriget', in Ragnar Björk and Alf W. Johansson (eds.), *Samtidshistoria och politik: vänbok till Karl Molin* (Stockholm: Hjalmarson & Högberg, 2004), 195–216.
31. William Korey, *The Promises We Keep: Human Rights, the Helsinki Process, and American Foreign Policy* (New York: St. Martin's Press, 1993), 2–3, 7.
32. Wilhelm Agrell, *Fred och fruktan: Sveriges säkerhetspolitiska historia 1918–2000* (Lund: Historisk Media, 2000), 194.
33. Vladislav M. Zubok, 'Why Did the Cold War End in 1989? Explanations of "The Turn"', in Westad, *Reviewing the Cold War,* 359.
34. Jussi M. Hanhimäki, 'Ironies and Turning Points: Détente in Perspective', in Westad, *Reviewing the Cold War,* 327. See also 330–32.
35. Ibid., 336–37.
36. Korey, *Promises,* xxi.
37. Loth, *Overcoming the Cold War,* 130.
38. Vladislav Zubok, 'The Soviet Attitude Towards the European Neutrals', in Michael Gehler and Rolf Steininger (eds.), *Die Neutralen und die europäische Integration=The Neutrals and the European Integration* (Vienna: Böhlau, 2000), 40.
39. Konstantin Khudoley, 'Soviet Foreign Policy during the Cold War: The Baltic Factor', in John Hiden, Vahur Made and David J. Smith (eds.), *The Baltic Question during the Cold War* (London: Routledge, 2008), 65.
40. Ibid., 1–10.
41. Fischer, *Neutral Power.*
42. Janie Leatherman, *From Cold War to Democratic Peace: Third Parties, Peaceful Change, and the OSCE* (Syracuse, NY: Syracuse University Press, 2003), 13, 156.
43. Harto Hakovirta, *East-West Conflict and European Neutrality* (Oxford: Clarendon Press; New York: Oxford University Press, 1988), 88, 212, 223–45.
44. Michael E. Smith, *Europe's Foreign and Security Policy: The Institutionalization of Cooperation* (Cambridge: Cambridge University Press, 2004), 87, 113–14 and 137–57; Daniel Möckli, *European Foreign Policy during the Cold War: Heath, Brandt, Pompidou and the Short Dream of Political Unity* (London: I.B. Tauris, 2009); 'The EC Nine, the CSCE, and the Changing Pattern of European Security', in Andreas Wenger, Vojtech Mastny and Christian Nuenlist (eds.), *Origins of the European Security System: The Helsinki Process Revisited, 1965–75* (London: Routledge, 2008), 145–63; Angela Romano, *From Détente in Europe to European Détente: How the West Shaped the Helsinki CSCE* (Brussels: P.I.E. Peter Lang, 2009).
45. For recent literature on Nordic cooperation, see Norbert Götz, *Deliberative Diplomacy: The Nordic Approach to Global Governance and Societal Representation at the United Nations* (Dordrecht: Republic of Letters, 2011); Norbert Götz and Heidi Haggrén (eds.), *Regional Cooperation and International Organizations: The Nordic Model in Transnational Alignment* (London: Routledge, 2009).
46. John J. Maresca, an American negotiator who produced a valuable account in the mid-1980s, even points to the Executive Secretariat as a group, although its role was

limited by the Blue Book. See John J. Maresca, *To Helsinki: The Conference on Security and Cooperation in Europe 1973–1975* (Durham, NC: Duke University Press, 1985), 18–22. Another detailed account made by a contemporary witness is that of Italian ambassador Ferraris. See Luigi Vittorio Ferraris (ed.), *Report on a Negotiation: Helsinki—Geneva—Helsinki 1972–1975* (Alphen aan den Rijn: Sijthoff & Noordhoff, 1979).

47. Matthias Peter, *Die Bundesrepublik im KSZE-Prozess: Die Umkehrung der Diplomatie, 1975–1983* (Berlin: De Gruyter Oldenbourg, 2015); Yuliya von Saal, *Die KSZE-Prozess und Perestroika in der Sowjetunion: Demokratisierung, Werteumbruch und Auflösung 1985–1991* (Munich: Oldenbourg, 2013); Benjamin Gilde, *Österreich im KSZE-Prozess 1969–1983: Neutraler Vermittler in humanitärer Mission* (Munich: Oldenbourg, 2013); Philip Rosin, *Die Schweiz im KSZE-Prozeß 1972–1983: Einfluß durch Neutralität* (Munich: Oldenbourg, 2013); Anja Hanisch, *Die DDR im KSZE-Prozess 1972–1985: Zwischen Ostabhängigkeit, Westabgrenzung und Ausreisebewegung* (Munich: Oldenbourg, 2012). Results from the other projects (Veronika Heyde, 'Die Französische Politik im Rahmen der KSZE in den 70er Jahren: Entspannung, Sicherheitsordnung, Menschenrechte und nationale Unabhängigkeit'; Gunter Dehnert, 'Die Folgen des KSZE-Prozesses in Polen: Selbstorganisation der Gesellschaft—Solidarnosc, Bürgerkomitees und der lange Weg zur Demokratie'; Benjamin Müller, 'Die Folgen des KSZE-Prozesses in der Tschechoslowakei: Von Helsinki über Prag auf dem Weg zum neuen Europa. Die Entwicklung der tschechoslowakischen Oppositionsbewegung zwischen 1975 und 1989'; Ernst Wawra, 'Die Folgen des KSZE-Prozesses in der Sowjetunion: Von Helsinki nach Gor'kij. Die Entwicklung der sowjetischen Bürgerrechtsbewegungen und Helsinkigruppen zwischen 1975 und 1982') were published together with conference proceedings in two edited volumes: Matthias Peter and Hermann Wentker (eds.), *Die KSZE im Ost-West-Konflikt: Internationale Politik und gesellschaftliche Transformation* (Munich: Oldenbourg, 2012); Helmut Altrichter and Hermann Wentker (eds.), *Der KSZE-Prozess: vom Kalten Krieg zu einem neuen Europa 1975 bis 1990* (Munich: Oldenbourg, 2011).

48. Wanda Jarzabek, 'Hope and Reality: Poland and the Conference on Security and Cooperation in Europe, 1964–1989', Washington, DC: Cold War International History Project, 2008.

49. Petri Hakkarainen, *A State of Peace in Europe: West Germany and the CSCE, 1966–1975* (New York: Berghahn Books, 2011); Tetsuji Senoo, *Ein Irrweg zur deutschen Einheit? Egon Bahrs Konzeptionen, die Ostpolitik und die KSZE, 1963–1975* (Frankfurt a.M.: Peter Lang, 2011).

50. Takeshi Yamamoto, 'The Road to the Conference on Security and Cooperation in Europe, 1969–1973: Britain, France and West Germany', PhD dissertation (London School of Economics and Political Science, 2007).

51. These are the unpublished doctoral dissertation of Kai Hebel, 'Britain's Contribution to Détente: The Conference on Security and Cooperation in Europe, 1972–1975', PhD dissertation (University of Oxford, 2012), and Nicolas Badalassi, *En finir avec la guerre froide: la France, l'Europe et le processus d'Helsinki* (Rennes: Presses universitaires de Rennes, 2014), respectively.

52. Markku Reimaa, *Helsinki Catch* (Helsinki: Edita, 2008); Seppo Hentilä, 'Finland and the Two German States: Finland's German Policy in the Framework of European Détente', in Wilfried Loth and Georges-Henri Soutou (eds.), *The Making of Détente: Eastern and Western Europe in the Cold War, 1965–75* (London; New York: Routledge, 2008), 183–200.

53. Katarina Kunter, *Die Kirchen im KSZE-Prozeß 1968–1978* (Stuttgart: Kohlhammer, 2000); Alexander Hollerbach, 'Religions—und Kirchenfreiheit im KSZE-Prozeß', in Eckart

Klein (ed.), *Grundrechte, soziale Ordnung und Verfassungsgerichtsbarkeit: Festschrift für Ernst Benda zum 70. Geburtstag* (Heidelberg: Müller, 1995), 117–33.
54. See Janie Leatherman, 'Engaging East and West beyond the Bloc Divisions: Active Neutrality and the Dual Role Strategy of Finland and Sweden in the CSCE', PhD dissertation (University of Denver, 1991), 432–81.
55. Ibid., 429, 425.
56. Michael Zielinski, *Die neutralen und blockfreien Staaten und ihre Rolle im KSZE-Prozess* (Baden-Baden: Nomos, 1990), 215–18; see also 59–69, 136–37.
57. Fischer, *Neutral Power*.
58. The Swedish categories were democracy (*demokratiperspektivet*), ideology (*ideologiperspektivet*) and power (*maktperspektivet*); see Ann-Marie Ekengren, *Sverige under kalla kriget 1945–1969: en forskningsöversikt* (Gothenburg: Grafikerna i Kungälv, 1997). For a recent discussion of research trends and potential areas of research, see Cecilia Notini Burch, Karl Molin and Magnus Petersson (eds.), *Svensk säkerhetspolitik under det kalla kriget–öppen för olika tolkningar?* (Stockholm: Stockholm University, 2011).
59. Ulf Bjereld and Ann-Marie Ekengren, 'Cold War Historiography in Sweden', in Olesen, *Historiography*, 143–75.
60. Magnus Petersson, who points to comparable Nordic research, has also emphasized this more recently in Notini Burch et al., *Svensk säkerhetspolitik*, 26.
61. Sweden's forty-year rule on secret records is one important reason for this.
62. Kronvall and Petersson, *Svensk säkerhetspolitik*, 168–78.
63. Kjell Engelbrekt, 'Den sjuttonde alliansmedlemmen?', *Internationella Studier*, 4, 1999, 61–72; 'En bättre återförsäkring än vi anade?' *Internationella Studier*, 1, 2003; Mikael af Malmborg, 'Sweden—NATO's Neutral "Ally"? A Post-Revisionist Account', in Gustav Schmidt (ed.), *A History of NATO—The First Fifty Years* (Basingstoke: Palgrave, 2001), 295.
64. Mikael Nilsson, *Tools of Hegemony. Military Technology and Swedish-American Security Relations, 1945–1962* (Stockholm: Santérus Academic Press, 2007), 43–46; see also 46–56.
65. Robert Dalsjö, *Life-Line Lost: The Rise and Fall of 'Neutral' Sweden's Secret Reserve Option of Wartime Help from the West* (Stockholm: Santérus Academic Press, 2006).
66. Robert Dalsjö, 'The Hidden Rationality of Sweden's Policy of Neutrality during the Cold War', *Cold War History*, 14(2), 2014, 175–94.
67. For a recent account of this position, see Mikael Holmström, *Den dolda alliansen: Sveriges hemliga NATO-förbindelser* (Stockholm: Atlantis, 2011).
68. Ola Tunander, 'The Uneasy Imbrication of Nation-State and NATO: The Case of Sweden', *Cooperation and Conflict*, 34(2), 1999, 169–203. For a critical response to the latter, see Olof Kronvall, Magnus Petersson, Charles Silva and Kjetil Skogrand, 'Comments on Ola Tunander's Article "The Uneasy Imbrication of Nation-State and NATO: The Case of Sweden"', *Cooperation and Conflict*, 35(4), 2000, 417–29.
69. Sverige, Säkerhetspolitiska utredningen, Neutralitetspolitikkommission, *Om kriget kommit . . . Förberedelser för mottagande av militärt bistånd 1949–1969 (SOU 1994:11)* (Stockholm: Fritzes offentliga publikationer, 1994).
70. Charles Silva, 'Keep Them Strong, Keep Them Friendly: Swedish-American Relations and the Pax Americana, 1948–1952', PhD dissertation (Stockholm University, 1999); Juhana Aunesluoma, *Britain, Sweden and the Cold War, 1945–54: Understanding Neutrality* (Basingstoke: Palgrave Macmillan, 2003); Magnus Petersson, *'Brödrafolkens väl': svensk-norska säkerhetsrelationer 1949–1969* (Stockholm: Santérus, 2003); Simon Robert Moores and Jerker Widén, 'Sverige under det kalla kriget—den amerikanska underrättelsetjänstens perspektiv, mars 1952', *Kungliga Krigsakademiens handlingar och*

tidskrift, 5, 2003, 78–92; Simon Robert Moores, '"Neutral on Our Side": US-Swedish Military and Security Relations during the Eisenhower Administration', PhD dissertation (London School of Economics and Political Science, 2005).
71. Nilsson, *Tools of Hegemony*, 409–14; Jerker Widén, *Väktare, ombud, kritiker: Sverige i amerikanskt säkerhetstänkande 1961–1968* (Stockholm: Santérus Academic Press Sweden, 2009).
72. Karl Molin, 'The Central Issues of Swedish Neutrality Policy', in Michael Gehler and Rolf Steininger (eds.), *The Neutrals and the European Integration, 1945–1995* (Vienna: Böhlau, 2000), 261–75.
73. Bjereld, Johansson, Molin, *Sveriges säkerhet*, 27–34.
74. Douglas Brommesson, *Från Hanoi till Bryssel: Moralsyn i deklarerad svensk utrikespolitik 1969–1996* (Stockholm: Santérus, 2007), 78–81.
75. Sunniva Engh, 'The Conscience of the World? Swedish and Norwegian Provision of Development Aid', *Itinerario*, 33(2), 2009, 65–82.
76. Hans Lödén, *'För säkerhets skull': ideologi och säkerhet i svensk aktiv utrikespolitik 1950-1975* (Stockholm: Nerenius & Santérus, 1999).
77. Mikael af Malmborg, *Neutrality and State-Building in Sweden* (Basingstoke: Palgrave, 2001), 148–53.
78. Af Malmborg, *Neutrality and State-Building*, 151.
79. The 'Nordic balance' was a widespread notion developed into a theoretical concept by Norwegian political scientist Arne Olav Brundtland in 1961. He argued that Northern Europe reached stability through balance between the Nordic states' relations with East and West. In this model, the NATO membership of Denmark, Iceland and Norway, together with Sweden's status as a neutral country, outbalanced Finland's special relationship with the Soviet Union. Maintaining this balance would guarantee that the region remained an area with reduced tension and with no foreign troops on Nordic soil. See Arne Olav Brundtland, 'The Nordic Balance. Past and Present', *Cooperation and Conflict*, 1(4), 1965, 30–65.
80. Sweden Ministry for Foreign Affairs, *Documents on Swedish Foreign Policy 1972* (Stockholm: 1973), 22–32.
81. 'It is the opinion of the foreign minister that our CSCE commitment is an important part of Swedish foreign policy at this point and that we, considering Sweden's neutral position and based on our interest in a comprehensive European cooperation, can and should target an active effort in Geneva by presenting a number of concrete proposals among others'. See Sverker Åström, 'Inför ESK 2', 9 July 1973, File 43, Vol. 40, HP (Politiska ärenden 1953–1974), HP79 (Konferenser och kongresser 1953–1974), 1920 års dossiersystem 1920–1974, Utrikesdepartementet [UD], Riksarkivet [RA].
82. The body of the literature on European integration is vast; see, for example, Erik Magnusson, 'Den egna vägen: Sverige och den europeiska integrationen 1961–1971', PhD dissertation (Uppsala University, 2009); Maria Wijk Gussarsson, *Europeiska visioner och nationellt egenintresse: framväxten av den europeiska unionen 1945–2000* (Lund: Studentlitteratur, 2005); 'Realpolitik, ideologi, samarbete: Sveriges EEC-ansökningar 1961 och 1967 ur tre olika tolkningsperspektiv', in Ragnar Björk and Alf W. Johansson (eds.), *Samtidshistoria och politik: vänbok till Karl Molin* (Stockholm: Hjalmarson & Högberg, 2004), 123–43; 'The Swedish Social Democracy, the Plans on West European Economic Cooperation, and International Party Cooperation, 1955–58', *Journal of European Integration History*, 11(1), 2005, 85–101; Jacob Westberg, 'Den nationella drömträdgården. Den stora berättelsen om den egna nationen i svensk och brittisk Europadebatt', PhD dissertation (Stockholm University, 2003), 159–84; Sieglinde Gstöhl, *Reluctant Europeans: Norway, Sweden, and Switzerland in the Process of Integration*

(Boulder: Lynne Rienner, 2002), 133; Jakob Gustavsson, 'The Politics of Foreign Policy Change: Explaining the Swedish Reorientation on EC Membership', PhD dissertation (Lund University, 1998).
83. Sweden is by no means an exception. British historian Piers Ludlow has highlighted the problematic relationship between national historiographies of European integration and the Cold War. According to Ludlow, 'European integration and the Cold War were separate but intertwined', but nevertheless 'have been studied in near total isolation from one another, the subject of separate journals, academic conferences and books, and the primary interest of two distinct groups of specialist scholars who have rarely exchanged ideas'. Ludlow explains the divergence between the two histories by stating the fact that political and military cooperation did not become part of the success story of European integration. Instead, the European Economic Community (EEC) has been the 'dominant manifestation of European integration'. See Piers Ludlow, 'European Integration and the Cold War', in Leffler and Westad, *Crises and Détente*, 179.
84. The term has become popular in recent years. Many American historians still prefer the term 'diplomatic history' over 'international history', although the latter evolved from the former as new elements such as economics, strategy, domestic sources of foreign policy and propaganda, and ideology and intelligence were added to diplomacy and statecraft in the study of the relations between states. See Patrick Finney, 'International History', www.history.ac.uk/makinghistory/resources/articles/international_history.html (accessed 23 October 2015). As I wish to address the distinction mentioned above, I will myself refer to the field as 'international history,' although it has been criticized as 'so broad a term that it loses its usefulness' by Thomas G. Paterson, 'Defining and Doing the History of American Foreign Relations: A Primer', *Diplomatic History*, 14(4), 1990, 585. The Swedish equivalents are, due to the rather strict focus on Sweden, *utrikespolitisk historia* (history of foreign relations) and *säkerhetspolitisk historia* (security policy history).
85. The notable exception is a debate following the publication of a six-volume history of Norwegian foreign policy. See Tor Ergil Førland, 'En empirisk bauta, et intellektuelt gjesp. Kritisk blikk på Norsk utenrikspolitikks historie 1–6', *Historisk Tidsskrift*, 78(2), 1999, 214–36; Iver B. Neumann, 'Norsk utenrikspolitikks historie—en kritikk', *Kungliga Krigsakademiens handlingar och tidskrift*, 5, 1999, 119–44 and 6, 1999, 147–74.
86. Zara Steiner, 'On Writing International History: Chaps, Maps and Much More', *International Affairs*, 73(3), 1997, 531.
87. For an excellent introduction, see Patrick Finney, 'Introduction: What Is International History?' in Patrick Finney (ed.), *Palgrave Advances in International History* (Houndmills; New York: Palgrave Macmillan, 2005), 1–35.
88. Steiner, 'International History', 532. On the relation between historians and political scientists in the study of foreign policy and international relations, see Colin Elman and Miriam Fendius Elman, 'Diplomatic History and International Relations Theory: Respecting Difference and Crossing Boundaries', *International Security*, 22(1), 1997, 5–21; John Lewis Gaddis, 'History, Theory, and Common Ground', *International Security*, 22(1), 1997, 75–85; Alexander L. George, 'Knowledge for Statecraft: The Challenge for Political Science and History', *International Security*, 22(1), 1997, 44–52; Stephen H. Haber, David M. Kennedy and Stephen D. Krasner, 'Brothers under the Skin: Diplomatic History and International Relations', *International Security*, 22(1), 1997, 34–43; Jack S. Levy, 'Too Important to Leave to the Other: History and Political Science in the Study of International Relations', *International Security*, 22(1), 1997, 22–33; Paul W. Schroeder,

'History and International Relations Theory: Not Use or Abuse, but Fit or Misfit', *International Security*, 22(1), 1997, 64–74; Gordon A. Craig, 'The Historian and the Study of International Relations', *American Historical Review*, 88(1), 1983, 1–11.
89. Edward Ingram, 'The Wonderland of the Political Scientist', *International Security*, 22(1), 1997, 54.
90. Charles S. Maier, 'Marking Time: The Historiography of International Relations', in Michael G. Kammen (ed.), *The Past Before Us: Contemporary Historical Writing in the United States* (Ithaca, NY: Cornell University Press, 1980), 355–87.
91. David Reynolds, 'International History, the Cultural Turn and the Diplomatic Twitch', *Cultural and Social History*, 3(1), 2006, 75–91.
92. Some information on the changes is provided in Rolf Torstendahl, 'Thirty-Five Years of Theories in History. Social Science Theories and Philosophy of History in the Scandinavian Debate', *Scandinavian Journal of History*, 25(1–2), 2000, 1–26.
93. Stefan Ekecrantz, *Hemlig utrikespolitik: Kalla kriget, utrikesnämnden och regeringen* (Stockholm: Santérus, 2003), 13–14.
94. Reynolds, 'International History', 75.
95. Lynn Hunt, 'Where Have All the Theories Gone?' *Perspectives*, 40(3), 6–7. Available online at www.historians.org/perspectives/issues/2002/0203/0203pre1.cfm (accessed 22 November 2015).
96. Michael J. Hogan, 'SHAFR Presidential Address: The "Next Big Thing": The Future of Diplomatic History in a Global Age', *Diplomatic History*, 28(1), 2004, 12–17.
97. Reynolds, 'International History', 91.
98. The emphasis on the nation and its boundaries as problematic was also the theme of the 2011 Meeting of Swedish Historians in Gothenburg.
99. Akira Iriye, 'Internationalizing International History', in Thomas Bender (ed.), *Rethinking American History in a Global Age* (Berkeley: University of California Press, 2002), 47–62.
100. Karl W. Schweizer and Matt J. Schumann, 'The Revitalization of Diplomatic History: Renewed Reflections', *Diplomacy & Statecraft*, 19(2), 2008, 172.
101. Jussi M. Hanhimäki and Odd Arne Westad (eds.), *The Cold War. A History in Documents and Eyewitness Accounts* (Oxford: Oxford University Press, 2003), xiii. Emphasis in the original.
102. In early 2012 a 'network for the New Diplomatic History' was founded by a group of young scholars from different European countries. Its declared aim is to add perspectives and methodologies such as prosopography, the sociology of knowledge, gender theory and network analysis to the established political and economic approaches. See www.newdiplomatichistory.org (accessed 22 November 2015).
103. Robert J. McMahon, 'Toward a Pluralist Vision: The Study of American Foreign Relations as International History and National History', in Michael J. Hogan and Thomas G. Paterson (eds.), *Explaining the History of American Foreign Relations*, 2nd ed. (Cambridge: Cambridge University Press, 2004), 47.
104. Ibid., fn. 8; Kirste and Maull, 'Zivilmacht und Rollentheorie', 285.
105. Originally, a typology of seventeen different national role conceptions was presented based on vast quantitative data. Kalevi J. Holsti, 'National Role Conceptions in the Study of Foreign Policy', *International Studies Quarterly*, 14(3), 1970, 233–309.
106. Lisbeth Aggestam, 'Role Conceptions and the Politics of Identity in Foreign Policy', available at www.deutsche-aussenpolitik.de/resources/seminars/gb/approach/document/wp99_8.htm (accessed 5 October 2015); see also *European Foreign Policy and the Quest for a Global Role: Britain, France and Germany* (London: Routledge, 2012).

107. Holsti, 'National Role Conceptions', 245–46; emphasis in the original. Another influential definition by Judith Goldstein and Robert Keohane describes role conceptions as 'a set of norms expressing expected foreign policy behaviour and action orientation' (*Ideas and Foreign Policy: Beliefs, Institutions, and Political Change* [Ithaca, NY: Cornell University Press, 1993], 3–31).
108. It was first published as a small, stand-alone monograph at Princeton University in 1954 and reprinted as part of an edited volume eight years later. I have used the commemorative edition of 2002: Richard C. Snyder, HW Bruck and Burton Sapin, 'Decision-Making as an Approach to the Study of International Politics', in Richard C. Snyder, HW Bruck and Burton Sapin; with new chapters by Valerie M. Hudson, Derek H. Chollet and James M. Goldgeier, *Foreign Policy Decision-Making (Revisited)* (New York: Palgrave Macmillan, 2002), 21–152.
109. Originally a 1956 working paper at Princeton titled 'Man-Milieu Relationship Hypotheses in the Context of International Politics', it was published nine years later as Harold Sprout and Margaret Sprout, *The Ecological Perspective on Human Affairs: With Special Reference to International Politics* (Princeton, NJ: Princeton University Press, 1965).
110. James Rosenau, 'Pre-theories and Theories of Foreign Policy', in RB Farrell (ed.), *Approaches to Comparative and International Politics* (Evanston, IL: Northwestern University Press, 1966), 217–21.
111. For an account of the history of foreign policy analysis, see Valerie Hudson, 'The History and Evolution of Foreign Policy Analysis', in Steve Smith, Amelia Hadfield and Tim Dunne (eds.), *Foreign Policy: Theories, Actors, Cases* (Oxford: Oxford University Press, 2008), 11–29.
112. Examples of such recent case studies are Bülent Aras and Aylin Gorener, 'National Role Conceptions and Foreign Policy Orientation: The Ideational Bases of Justice and Development Party's Foreign Policy Activism in the Middle East', *Journal of Balkan and Near Eastern Studies*, 12(1), 2010, 73–92; Lisbeth Aggestam, 'Role Theory and European Foreign Policy', in Ole Elgström and Michael Smith (eds.), *The European Union's Roles in International Politics: Concepts and Analysis* (London: Routledge, 2006), 11–29.
113. Kirste and Maull, 'Zivilmacht und Rollentheorie', 308.
114. Naomi Wish, 'Foreign Policy Makers and National Role Conceptions', *International Studies Quarterly*, 24(4), 1980, 532–54. For further discussion on the evolution of the theory, see Sebastian Harnisch, 'Role Theory: Operationalization of Key Concepts', in Sebastian Harnisch, Cornelia Frank and Hanns W. Maull (eds.), *Role Theory in International Relations: Approaches and Analyses* (London: Routledge, 2011), 7–15.
115. Christine Agius, *The Social Construction of Swedish Neutrality: Challenges to Swedish Identity and Sovereignty* (Manchester: Manchester University Press, 2006).
116. Harnisch, 'Role Theory', 8. See also Knut Kirste and Hanns W. Maull, 'Zivilmacht und Rollentheorie', *Zeitschrift für internationale Beziehungen*, 3(2), 1996, 289. On the current state of research, see Marijke Breuning, 'Role Theory Research in International Relations: State of the Art and Blind Spots', in Harnisch, Frank and Maull, *Role Theory*, 16–35.
117. Kirste and Maull, 'Zivilmacht und Rollentheorie', 292.
118. Holsti, 'National Role Conceptions', 307; emphasis in the original.
119. Kalevi J. Holsti, 'National Role Conceptions in the Study of Foreign Policy', in Stephen G. Walker (ed.), *Role Theory and Foreign Policy Analysis* (Durham, NC: Duke University Press, 1987).
120. Ulrich Krotz, 'National Role Conceptions and Foreign Policies: France and Germany Compared', unpublished manuscript (Cambridge, MA: Minda de Gunzburg Center for European Studies, Harvard University, 2002), 8–9.

121. Ibid., 6–7.
122. Dirk Nabers, 'Identity and Role Change in International Politics', in Harnisch, Frank and Maull, *Role Theory*, 74–92; Harnisch, 'Role Theory', 8.
123. Krotz, *National Role Conceptions*, 9.
124. See, for example, Widén, *Väktare, ombud, kritiker* and Zielinski, *Die neutralen und blockfreien Staaten*.
125. 'Hermeneutic' designates the process of the interpretation of sources. For an introduction, see Philip Gardner, *Hermeneutics, History and Memory* (Abingdon: Routledge, 2010), 36.
126. This definition has been offered by Zielinski, *Die neutralen und blockfreien Staaten*, 171.
127. In Holsti's original essay, Sweden is mainly described as *mediator-integrator*, switching to the roles of *regional-subsystem collaborator, independent* and *developer* when necessary. See Holsti, 'National Role Conceptions', 276. Other roles performed by Sweden, to a lesser extent, were *bastion of revolution-liberator, regional leader, regional protector, active independent, liberation supporter, anti-imperialist agent, defender of the faith, bridge, faithful ally, example, internal development, isolate* and *protectee*. Ibid., 260–71. On the earlier role analyses of Leatherman and Zielinski, see pp. 22–23.

CHAPTER ONE

1945–1969: Sweden and Europe in a Changing World

Early Postwar Neutrality

The unconditional surrender of Nazi Germany and the end of World War II meant no *Stunde Null* (zero hour) for Sweden. In contrast to its neighbours, Scandinavia's largest nation managed to escape the brutalizing and impoverishing effects of war. Instead, with the Third Reich as the most important trade partner, Sweden's economic well-being improved during the six years of the war. As a consequence of provisioning the Nazi war machine, Sweden's industrial capacity increased approximately 15–20 per cent during the war years, and manufacturing and production outpaced the prewar levels.

The fall of Hitler's empire caused a substantial economic vacuum in the Swedish economy, and sustaining levels of trade and commerce became the predominant foreign policy goal following the collapse of Nazi Germany. In an effort to resuscitate the economy, the Swedish government decided to support the Allied reconstruction efforts in the bombed-out regions in Europe.[1] In the military sector, it had been forging ahead with rearmament since 1942. Due to the reorganization of the European continent, Sweden had to pursue a strategic reorientation in foreign and security policy and choose between neutrality and solidarity as its guiding principle.[2]

The standards for Sweden's early postwar security and foreign policy were set by a small inner circle of decision makers led by Foreign Minister Östen Undén (in office between 1945 and 1962), a law professor at Uppsala University and former League of Nations diplomat.[3] Undén's belief in collective security had been shaken by the collapse of the League, yet he disagreed with his predecessor in the Foreign Ministry, Christian Günther, on the opportunities for global organization and argued for Swedish UN membership in 1946, believing that a new global organization would contribute to world peace.[4]

According to Undén, Swedish neutrality had to be developed along the lines of three principles: resisting and avoiding becoming a part of any bloc, supporting a collective security system through membership in the United Nations and developing and strengthening Nordic cooperation.[5] The overall goal of Sweden's foreign policy quickly became to maintain neutrality in the case of future war and strengthen the credibility (*trovärdighet*) of this policy abroad, in particular among the rulers in the Kremlin. Leading figures such as Undén, Prime Minister Per Albin Hansson, his successor Tage Erlander, Finance Minister Ernst Wigforss and Trade Minister Gunnar Myrdal struggled to maintain a friendly relationship with the Soviet Union, which they considered essential, despite the rise of anticommunism in Sweden.

Initially, the Swedish government opted for a policy of bridge building between East and West.[6] However, after the Czech coup d'état, and due to the emerging division of Europe in 1948, this course was reversed. After failed negotiations with its Nordic neighbours Norway and Denmark on a Scandinavian Defence Union (SDU) in 1948 and 1949, Stockholm finally settled for a more rigid neutrality policy based on nonalignment between the blocs.[7] By the mid-1950s, the Swedish government had managed to establish a passive but watchful line of armed isolationism.

This approach was confirmed in the formulation of a policy of 'nonalignment in peace aiming at neutrality in war', formalized publicly in a government communiqué on 13 October 1956. Soon widely known as *Undénlinjen* (the Undén line), this formula would define and completely dominate Sweden's foreign policy for three decades.[8] Based on myths that attributed the success of the Swedish welfare policy and the 'Swedish model' to long-standing neutrality, the policy of Undén became hegemonic within a decade.[9] Any trade policy proposed from then on would have to accomplish growth and prosperity without disturbing this overall doctrine.

But the government's launch of a trade policy initiative aimed at stimulating potential new trader partners in Europe between 1945 and 1947 turned out to be misguided, creating a heavy surplus of imports followed by a dollar shortage and rapid economic decline. In 1947, strongly affected by the outbreak of the new conflict between east and west, the Swedish government decided to join the newly initiated Marshall Plan (officially, the Economic Recovery Plan, or ERP), which was designed by the United States to rebuild and create a stronger economic foundation for the countries of Europe. In 1948, in order to restrengthen its financial system, Sweden also joined the Organization for European Economic

Co-operation (OEEC), which emerged from the Marshall Plan and the Conference of Sixteen (otherwise known as the Conference for European Economic Co-operation) and sought to establish a permanent organization to continue the work of joint recovery in Europe, particularly the distribution of aid.

As a result of these inclusionary efforts, and despite the signing of a highly controversial trade agreement with the Soviet Union, Sweden quickly integrated with the greater Western European economy.[10] However, despite this economic convergence, and the right wing's call for further ideological and political commitment to the West, the government emphasized that Sweden's neutrality doctrine must remain untouched.[11] Stockholm advocated economic cooperation but refrained from becoming part of the 'United States of Europe', primarily because 'our historical traditions, our people's psychological state, and our geographical situation all argue in favour of a neutrality policy', as Swedish representative Kaj Björk put it in a statement to the congress of the Mouvement Socialiste pour les États-Unis d'Europe (MSEUE) in Paris in July 1947.[12]

Still, the Riksdag voted almost unanimously in favour of becoming one of the ten founding members of the Council of Europe in 1949.[13] Sweden also signed the General Agreement on Tariffs and Trade (GATT) on 30 April 1950[14] and joined both the International Monetary Fund (IMF) and the World Bank on 31 August 1951.[15] This was in stark contrast with other comparable European neutrals, such as Switzerland, whose government in Berne generally maintained greater isolationism in accordance with rejection of European integration, a policy which it had in common with the Swedes.[16]

Although reconsidered critically, and carefully weighed against other options after the end of World War II, it was soon generally accepted that Sweden was a neutral country 'by tradition'.[17] With this established notion as a starting point, certain limits and boundaries were set on the future conduct of the country's foreign policy. On the one hand, Sweden declared itself part of the West economically, culturally and ideologically. On the other hand, it refrained from any form of declared *västorienterad neutralitet* (Western-orientated neutrality), particularly in terms of security. Signing the North Atlantic Treaty, and becoming part of the military alliance it eventually created, was, thus, never an option – a refusal based on an interpretation of neutrality backed by consensus not only among high-ranking representatives from politics and business but also among the broader public.[18]

When Sweden stayed away from the Schuman Declaration on the foundation of a supranational community between France and West Germany, which was open to other European states (1950), as well as the treaties of

Paris (1951) and Rome (1957), no calls for membership in the European Coal and Steel Union (ECSC) and the European Economic Community (EEC) were made in Sweden.[19] Swedish decision makers never seriously considered participation in European political integration, making reference to its 'incoherence with Swedish neutrality'.[20] On the contrary, the government discussed a further withdrawal from European involvement when the Eden Plan, which was proposed to confer on the Council of Europe political authority over the European Defence Community (EDC), was tabled.[21] Leading Social Democrats decided to look again at a Nordic solution, instead of following up their earlier efforts to achieve greater European integration.[22]

In 1954, the foreign minister of the Soviet Union, Vyacheslav Molotov, proposed the idea of a pan-European conference on security. The Iron Curtain had fallen across Europe, without the convocation of a peace conference that could have settled the most essential security issues in Central and Eastern Europe. Instead, Europe was left in a state of unrest, facing a future of division and uncertainty. One of the most important matters for Moscow was the unresolved Oder-Neisse border question between East Germany and Poland, which had remained problematic since the end of the war. Encouraged by the Berlin Conference held in the first weeks of 1954, a meeting between the 'Big Four' (the United States, Great Britain, France and the Soviet Union), and early signs of the post-Stalin thaw, Molotov attempted to reach agreement on the issue of continental security and proposed a security conference. The idea was that European states would come together and discuss essential issues of continental security, without the Americans.

Along with Switzerland and Finland, Sweden belonged to the group of neutral states that received the original Molotov proposal in February 1954.[23] Foreign Minister Undén noted in his diary entry dated 15 February 1954 that 'some features are of interest', although the proposal was laughed at in the international press as a clumsy attempt to remove the Americans from discussions about European security.[24] In contrast to Undén, who leaned favourably towards Molotov's proposal in a meeting of the Swedish Utrikesnämnden (Advisory Council on Foreign Affairs) on 19 November 1954, his fellow council members deemed undesirable any participation in a conference on a collective security system in Europe.[25] Most Western and neutral countries shared this opinion. Stalin had only been dead for a year and a half, and there was no stable condition of relaxation between the blocs to allow a conference to take place, despite the thaw.

Still struggling to establish a clear position for itself between the military blocs, the SAP, with its two front figures, Prime Minister Erlander and Foreign Minister Undén, pushed for a strict line of political neutrality, despite domestic and external criticism. The general formula of Stockholm's early postwar foreign policy was spelled out: 'gladly *Norden* [the North] and the world, but rather not Europe'.²⁶

This was particularly accurate with regard to Swedish security policy, from which Europe virtually disappeared after the Hungarian revolution in winter 1956. With the third Eastern European popular uprising in three years crushed (following East Germany in 1953 and Poland in 1956), ambitions for (peaceful) change finally gave space for a shift towards the status quo and the securing of Soviet trust as the most important Swedish goals in the European realm. As had been the case with the Baltic peoples after the end of the war, an 'almost cynical'²⁷ pragmatism filtered through all of Eastern Europe as a consequence of these events.²⁸ In the following years, Stockholm dealt with security on the Nordic and global levels, limiting its European approach to Western European questions of economic character.²⁹

In the view of its political establishment, Sweden could not join 'a NATO club' but, rather, would have to find a 'Third Way' approach.³⁰ This view was, to the surprise of many contemporary historians, not situational but deeply entrenched among Swedish Social Democrats.³¹ Nevertheless, some of Sweden's leading experts in European politics addressed criticisms of the government's strategy when the 'Inner Six' (Belgium, France, Germany, Great Britain, Luxemburg and the Netherlands)³² created the EEC in 1957.³³ Those critics accused the administration of leading the country into isolation and risking negative economic long-term effects due to a policy based on prejudices and pejorative remarks about the Six being a 'Catholic-dominated, reactionary' group, instead of pursuing constructive realpolitik on the basis of national interests.³⁴

In an attempt to face up to criticism, an internal study group at the Swedish Ministry for Foreign Affairs convened to discuss the benefits and drawbacks of joining the EEC. It concluded that membership would likely result in limited freedom of action (*handlingsfrihet*), *the* cornerstone of the country's foreign policy, and would outweigh any possible advantages. A 'split in the accord between government and industry' then occurred, according to Mikael af Malmborg, as industry representatives countered this assessment, arguing instead for the need to join the ECSC.³⁵ In order to secure domestic political stability in the face of this outspoken industry opposition, the government had to consider further alternatives.

Resultant plans for the creation of a common Nordic market, the so-called Nordek (for Nordiskt ekonomiskt gemenskap), or a common market consisting of the Inner Six, Great Britain and any other interested OEEC countries were eventually abolished in favour of instituting the so-called European Free Trade Association (EFTA), founded in Stockholm on 4 January 1960. Formed by the 'Outer Seven' (Austria, Denmark, Great Britain, Norway, Portugal, Sweden and Switzerland), the Swedish government considered the EFTA solution a *'modus vivendi* with a new, fragile and fairly self-centred EEC'.[36] To the Swedes, the EFTA was a compromise between isolationism and EEC membership.[37]

In August 1961 Great Britain applied for EEC membership, with the consequence that other EFTA states also reconsidered EEC membership in light of London's decision. However, articulating Sweden's response in his famous *metalltal* (metal speech), a public speech delivered to the Metal Industry Workers Union on 22 August 1961, Prime Minister Tage Erlander ruled out full EEC membership and declared the process of European integration as 'incompatible with Swedish nonalignment'.[38] Consequently, Sweden applied for association with the EEC, but not full membership, on 15 December 1961.[39] Negotiations regarding British membership (and, in consequence, all EFTA states' applications) were terminated in January 1963 following the veto by Charles de Gaulle, leaving the question open for another four years.[40]

In the 1960s, the rise of détente and decolonization gave ample scope for a more 'active' Swedish neutrality policy. After two decades of armed, isolationistic neutrality, the leadership of the governing SAP decided on a shift towards an active role in the international system, with specific emphasis on internationalist solidarity and a united struggle against international injustices.[41] Confronted with the zeitgeist of a demand for more active participation, the SAP feared a flight of its young members to other parties if it failed to adopt a more radical and progressive policy.[42] Like other Western examples, the terms '1968' and *68orna* ('the 68ers', i.e. the 1968 generation) became widespread labels, marking events and developments such as intense leftist protests against the Vietnam War, proposed university reforms (UKAS),[43] the women's movement's struggle for gender equality and the politicization of culture.[44] In the following years, Sweden established an image as a critical bridge builder, advocating greater justice in international affairs, with pronounced focus on the North-South axis.

According to the new line, neutrality did not prevent this Nordic country from striving for solidarity. This internationalism was in fact part of the SAP's political heritage, as the party had supported a similar policy under the leadership of the iconic Hjalmar Branting during the 1920s. The new policy comprised good offices, development assistance and a blend of active criticism and mediation.[45] The prestige of being an economically well-developed, liberal country par excellence cemented Sweden's role as the foremost friend of the weak, as Sweden made vociferous pleas for justice and praised a visionary 'third way' of democratic socialism. This earned the Swedes the rather sardonic appellation as the 'Third World's darlings' by realist critics, who, well aware of unspoken limits of Swedish solidarity with regard to Eastern Europe, considered Sweden's stance a case of double standards.[46]

At the time, Olof Palme, the ecclesiastical minister, who was considered an internationalist, was one of Prime Minister Tage Erlander's most influential advisors and the rising star in Swedish politics. Together with Foreign Minister Torsten Nilsson, in 1967 and 1968 Palme criticized the US war in Vietnam.[47] In February 1968 he participated in a Stockholm demonstration against the Vietnam War. A year later, Sweden was the first country to recognize North Vietnam. The younger generation, and much of Swedish intelligentsia, celebrated Palme for being 'a hero in Northern Vietnam and a scoundrel in the U.S.', as it was put by the German journal *DER SPIEGEL*, shortly before Palme took office as prime minister in October 1969.[48] With regard to European affairs, however, Sweden maintained the post-1956 status quo approach.

Olof Palme and Willy Brandt took office on 14 October and 21 October 1969, respectively. Many contemporaries saw their coincidental rise to power as a sign of the times. The 1960s had been a tumultuous decade that produced a new type of political leadership in several Western countries. The contrast between Palme and Tage Erlander, twenty-six years his senior, was as clear as the one between Brandt and his conservative predecessors Kurt Georg Kiesinger, Ludwig Erhard and Konrad Adenauer.

The two prominent Social Democrats were also very different from each other in background. Brandt had suffered his whole life from the fact that he was the illegitimate child of a single mother, and he had fled Nazi Germany in 1936 to spend more than a decade in Scandinavian exile. Palme was from a conservative upper-class family and enjoyed a privileged upbringing, sharing similarities with young, progressive politicians like John F. Kennedy, his brother Robert, the leader of the French Parti radical Jean-Jacques Servan-Schreiber and Canadian prime minister Pierre Trudeau, rather than with the new West German chancellor.[49]

Palme began his term in office with a multitude of foreign trips to numerous European countries, the United States and the Soviet Union. He charmed the press in Paris with his fluent French, but it quickly became obvious that he enjoyed the greatest support in West Germany, where he was considered an important partner to Willy Brandt.[50] To Palme, Brandt was not only a partner but also a friend and a mentor. Brandt was fluent in the Scandinavian languages, and Palme had been raised speaking German to his mother. Naturally, Olof Palme was among the first politicians to unreservedly hail Brandt's *Ostpolitik*, stating that it was 'among the most important things that have happened to post-War Europe'.[51] Palme himself was among a small group of leading Social Democrats who advocated and explained Brandt's new approach in talks with decision makers in Moscow and Warsaw. Together with Austrian chancellor Bruno Kreisky, Brandt and Palme would form the inner core of a Social Democratic network which developed growing influence in international political bodies over the course of the 1970s.[52]

Palme and Brandt shared beliefs in matters of international politics and global development. They quickly developed a mutual respect that served as a solid foundation for their continuing political cooperation. Palme sought advice from Brandt, and to a lesser extent from Kreisky, on a regular basis before taking a stance on an issue. Brandt and Kreisky both belonged to the inner circle of individuals who were consulted before the drafting of Palme's 1972 Christmas speech, in which the Swedish prime minister compared the US bombing of Vietnam to Nazi crimes.[53]

Three years later, the three social democratic heads of state published a book comprising letters and conversations about the role of socialism in international affairs. Brandt and Kreisky were both among the speakers when Palme celebrated his fiftieth birthday in 1977.[54] After Brandt left office in 1974 and Palme lost the election two years later, their cooperation continued in other forums, such as the Socialist International and independent commissions which presented reports to the UN about decolonization and disarmament in 1980 and 1982, respectively.[55]

The European Question: EEC/EC Membership and the CSCE

In 1967 history repeated itself: the renewed membership application to the EEC from Downing Street at the beginning of the year provoked requests by other EFTA states like those made in 1961.[56] Denmark, Ireland and Norway applied for full membership, whereas Sweden followed up on its own efforts more cautiously.[57] On 28 July 1967, the Swedish government formulated its *öppna ansökan* (open application) to the European Communities, emphasizing the economic nature of its interest and the inalterability of its foreign policy.[58] This form of application allowed for open-ended negotiations that could have resulted in membership, association or a free trade agreement.[59] However, France's continued rejection of British membership caused further negotiations to stall until the end of the year, when it became clear that there would be no rapprochement between the EFTA states and the Inner Six without a change of government in Paris.[60]

Subsequently, Nordic cooperation and the idea of a common Nordic market, including Denmark, Finland, Iceland, Norway and Sweden, re-entered the stage from January 1968 onwards, and the Swedish government hoped that an economic customs union between the Nordic states would substitute for EC membership.[61] As mentioned above, Nordek was considered both a *reaction* to the problematic EC relations and a *bridge* towards the EC in the event that conditions for renewed EC membership negotiations improved.[62]

This was the case when Georges Pompidou abandoned France's earlier position of resistance to Great Britain's membership after Charles de Gaulle stepped down on 28 April 1969. Up to that point, Nordek consultations had looked promising to the Swedes.[63] This is illustrated by the fact that the section on Nordic cooperation occupied about five times as much text as the one on economic integration in Europe in the Swedish Foreign Ministry's 1969 annual report (*Utrikesfrågor*).[64] A year later, the two topics were of approximately equal importance, as the security conference became a more established subject on the political agenda.[65]

As the Swedes explored the possibility of an economic approach to Europe, the security situation suffered a heavy setback. During the spring of 1968, the Communist Party of Czechoslovakia, under Alexander Dubček, introduced political liberalization as part of its attempt to develop 'communism with a human face'. Growing concerns expressed by Leonid Brezhnev and members of the Soviet politburo about the effects of developments in Czechoslovakia on the general position of the Eastern bloc resulted in growing tension.[66] To the SAP, this was a problematic situation, given that elections were to be held in September. On the one hand, the Swedish peoples' moral expectations had been raised by their government's strong protests and by Palme's participation in a demonstration in Stockholm in February 1968 against the US war in Vietnam; on the other hand, the Kremlin's confidence in Swedish neutrality was a cornerstone of Swedish neutrality policy.

Eventually, the government refused to take a strong stand against the pressure exerted by the Soviets on Czechoslovakia. Instead, friendly overtures were made to them when Alexei Kosygin visited Stockholm in July, and the Swedish-Soviet communiqué of 13 July 1968 stated that cooperation between European states would be based on principles of equality, territorial integrity and noninterference in internal affairs. This provoked severe criticism from the leader of the Liberal Party (Folkpartiet), Sven Wedén, who went public thirteen days after the publication of the above-mentioned communiqué: 'It would be in conformity with the Swedish government's fundamental position on essential international questions with ideological implications if Prime Minister Tage Erlander and his colleagues made a statement in support of the right to self-determination held by the people of Czechoslovakia'.[67]

The government rejected the criticism and castigated Wedén harshly in the (secret) meetings of the Council for Foreign Affairs.[68] The opposition politician was also accused of violating principles essential for national security for the sake of votes. In the aftermath of Wedén's statement and the Soviet invasion, which killed more than a hundred Czechs, Foreign Minister Torsten Nilsson and Prime Minister Tage Erlander referred to a secret diplomatic report as the reason for the government's cautious line.[69] In reality, it was the general limits of idealist internationalism in European affairs that set boundaries for Swedish solidarity with regard to the Czechoslovakian people. Clearly, the government's approach to European affairs was different from its strategy towards the Far East or Africa. Regardless of the extent of this injustice, Europe was too sensitive in terms of geopolitical strategy and security for ministers to protest or demonstrate the way Palme had against Vietnam. But with the European Security Conference, Sweden would soon be offered an opportunity for a change of direction.

Notes

1. Mikael af Malmborg, 'Den ståndaktiga nationalstaten: Sverige och den västeuropeiska integrationen 1945–1959', PhD dissertation (Lund University, 1994), 29–32. See also Örjan Appelqvist, *Bruten brygga: Gunnar Myrdal och Sveriges ekonomiska efterkrigspolitik 1943–1947* (Stockholm: Santérus, 2000). On the role of Eastern Europe in the early postwar years, see Birgit Karlsson, 'Handelspolitik eller politisk handling: Sveriges handel med öststaterna 1946–1952', PhD dissertation (University of Gothenburg, 1992).
2. Bjereld et al., *Sveriges säkerhet*, 65, 68–69; Kronvall and Petersson, *Svensk säkerhetspolitik*, 17–19.
3. Ekecrantz, *Hemlig utrikespolitik*. On Undén and his early career including his first spell as foreign minister in 1924–1926, see Aryo Makko, 'Arbitrator in a World of Wars: The League of Nations and the Mosul Dispute, 1924–1925', *Diplomacy & Statecraft*, 21(4), 2010, 636–45; John Rogers, 'The Foreign Policy of Small States: Sweden and the Mosul Crisis, 1924–1925', *Contemporary European History*, 16(3), 2007, 362–69; Yngve Möller, *Östen Undén: en biografi* (Stockholm: Norstedt, 1986).
4. Bjereld et al., *Sveriges säkerhet*, 68–69.
5. Malmborg, 'Den ståndaktiga nationalstaten', 49.
6. Erik Noreen, *Brobygge eller blockbildning?: de norska och svenska utrikesledningarnas säkerhetspolitiska föreställningar 1945–1948* (Stockholm: Carlsson, 1994). See also Bjereld et al., *Sveriges säkerhet*, 77–82; Kronvall and Petersson, *Svensk säkerhetspolitik*, 19–32.
7. Bjereld et al., *Sveriges säkerhet*, 88–126; Kronvall and Petersson, *Svensk säkerhetspolitik*, 32–37.
8. Ibid., 172–74.

9. Neutrality (since the early nineteenth century), peace and welfare were intertwined and pictured as natural components of Swedish identity by the SAP (itself founded in 1889). See Bo Stråth, *Folkhemmet mot Europa: ett historiskt perspektiv på 90-talet* (Stockholm: Tiden, 1993), 196–206. See also Agius, *Social Construction*, 60–119.
10. Birgit Karlsson, *Att handla neutralt: Sverige och den ekonomiska integrationen i Västeuropa 1948–1972* (Gothenburg: School of Business, University of Gothenburg, 2001); Jakob Gustavsson, 'The Politics of Foreign Policy Change: Explaining the Swedish Reorientation on EC Membership', PhD dissertation (Lund University, 1998), 30–38; Af Malmborg, 'Den ståndaktiga nationalstaten', 63–68, 111–30.
11. Bjereld et al., *Sveriges Säkerhet*, 87–94.
12. Cited in Af Malmborg, 'Den ståndaktiga nationalstaten', 47–48.
13. Jakobsson, *Politics of Foreign Policy*, 29–34; Af Malmborg, 'Den ståndaktiga nationalstaten', 134–38, 153–66.
14. 'The 128 Countries That Had Signed GATT by 1994', www.wto.org/english/theWTO_e/gattmem_e.htm (accessed 23 November 2015).
15. 'World Bank Group Historical Chronology', http://siteresources.worldbank.org/EXTARCHIVES/Resources/Bank%20chronology.pdf (accessed 3 August 2016).
16. Thomas Fischer, *Die Grenzen der Neutralität: Schweizerisches KSZE-Engagement und gescheiterte UNO – Beitrittspolitik im Kalten Krieg, 1969–1986* (Zurich: Chronos, 2004).
17. Sten Ottosson, *Svensk självbild under kalla kriget: en studie av stats- och utrikesministrarnas bild av Sverige 1950–1989* (Stockholm: Utrikespolitiska institutet, 2003), 22–26.
18. Known as *folkstödsargumentet* (the argument of the 'support of the people'), often instrumentalized by the governing SAP. Bjereld et al., *Sveriges säkerhet*, 123–26.
19. Bjereld et al., *Sveriges säkerhet*, 94–111; Nils Andrén, *Maktbalans och alliansfrihet: svensk utrikespolitik under 1900-talet* (Stockholm: Norstedts juridik, 1996), 66–81.
20. Af Malmborg, 'Den ståndaktiga nationalstaten', 200–2, 212–15.
21. Ibid., 261–62.
22. Undén's plans for a Scandinavian Defence Union had failed in 1948–1949; see also Jacob Westberg, 'Den nationella drömträdgården: den stora berättelsen om den egna nationen i svensk och brittisk Europadebatt', PhD dissertation (Stockholm University, 2003), 120–21.
23. Christian Nuenlist, 'Expanding the East-West Dialog beyond the Bloc Division. The Neutrals as Negotiators and Mediators, 1969–75', in Andreas Wenger, Vojtech Mastny and Christian Nuenlist (eds.), *Origins of the European Security System. The Helsinki Process Revisited, 1965–75* (London: Routledge, 2008), 202.
24. Diary entry 15 February 1954 in Östen Undén (edited by Karl Molin), *Anteckningar, 1952–1966* (Stockholm: Kungliga Samfundet för utgivande av handskrifter rörande Skandinaviens historia, Swedish Science Press, 2002).
25. The Utrikesnämnden brought together government representatives with leaders of other parliamentary parties under the utmost secrecy and was formally led by the king of Sweden. It had no formal decision-making power but served well as a platform for the creation of consensus in highly important foreign policy matters. See diary entry 19 November 1954 in Undén, *Anteckningar*.
26. 'The North', i.e., Scandinavia, Finland, Iceland and the associated territories of Greenland, Svalbard, the Faroe Islands and Åland. See Af Malmborg, 'Den ståndaktiga nationalstaten', 29–34. For the Nordic context, see also Juhana Aunesluoma, Magnus Petersson and Charles Silva, 'Deterrence or Reassurance: Nordic Responses to the First Détente, 1953–1956' *Scandinavian Journal of History*, 32(2), 2007, 183–208.

27. Bjereld et al., *Sveriges säkerhet*, 79.
28. Ibid., 72–79.
29. Ibid., 137–223, in particular 170–96 and 205–19; Kronvall and Petersson, *Svensk säkerhetspolitik*, 63–86.
30. Stråth, *Folkhemmet*, 201–7.
31. Misgeld, 'Den svenska socialdemokratin', 197–200.
32. These were the founding members of the European Communities. They were often called 'the Inner Six' or simply 'the Six'.
33. Af Malmborg, 'Den ståndaktiga nationalstaten', 288–93.
34. Gstöhl, *Reluctant Europeans*, 2, 25; Af Malmborg, 'Den ståndaktiga nationalstaten', 298; Stråth and Folkhemmet, 217. In the vernacular, the Inner Six were also labelled the 'four Cs' (capitalism, clericalism, conservatism, cartels). This expression was originally coined by SPD chairman Kurt Schumacher. See Misgeld, 'Den svenska socialdemokratin', 205.
35. Af Malmborg, 'Den ståndaktiga nationalstaten', 321–24.
36. Ibid., ch. X.
37. Karlsson, *Sverige och den ekonomiska*, 52–54; EFTA Commemorative Publications, 40th Anniversary EFTA 1960–2000 (Brussels: EFTA, 2000), 22–27. See also David Arter, *Scandinavian Politics Today* (Manchester: Manchester University Press, 1999), 316–29.
38. Anders Widfeldt, 'Sweden and the European Union: Implications for the Swedish Party System', in Lee Miles (ed.), *The European Union and the Nordic Countries* (London: Routledge, 1996), 101.
39. Jan Hecker-Stampehl, 'A Short Political History of the Nordek Negotiations', in Jan Hecker-Stampehl (ed.), *Between Nordic Ideology, Economic Interests and Political Reality. New Perspectives on Nordek* (Helsinki: Finnish Society of Science and Letters, 2009), 10.
40. Oliver Bange, *The EEC Crisis of 1963: Kennedy, MacMillan, de Gaulle and Adenauer in Conflict* (Basingstoke: Macmillan, 2000); Ekengren, *Olof Palme och utrikespolitiken*, 66–80; Karlsson, *Sverige och den ekonomiska*, 57–67; Andrén, *Maktbalans och alliansfrihet*, 136–39.
41. Bjereld et al., *Sveriges säkerhet*, 23.
42. Ekengren, 'How Ideas Influence Decision-Making: Olof Palme and Swedish Foreign Policy, 1965–1975', *Scandinavian Journal of History*, 36(2), 2011, 125–27.
43. 'UKAS', http://www.ne.se/uppslagsverk/encyklopedi/lång/ukas-(2) (accessed 23 November 2015).
44. See, e.g., Johan Bergman, *Kulturfolk eller folkkultur? 1968, kulturarbetarna och demokrating* (Umeå: Boréa, 2010); Torbjörn Nilsson, *Hundra år av svensk politik* (Malmö: Gleerups utbildning, 2009), 115–16; Bjereld et al., *Sveriges säkerhet*, 230–32.
45. Ulf Bjereld, 'Critic or Mediator? Sweden in World Politics, 1945–90', *Journal of Peace Research*, 32(1), 1995, 23–35.
46. Maurice Keens-Soper, as quoted in Susan L. Holmberg, 'Welfare Abroad: Swedish Development Assistance', in Bengt Sundelius (ed.), *The Committed Neutral. Sweden's Foreign Policy* (Boulder, CO: Westview Press, 1989), 123.
47. On the role of the Vietnam War in Swedish foreign policy, see Yngve Möller, *Sverige och Vietnamkriget: ett unikt kapitel i svensk utrikespolitik* (Stockholm: Tiden, 1992).
48. 'Held und Halunke', *DER SPIEGEL* (Hamburg), 20 January 1969, www.spiegel.de/spiegel/print/d-45849662.html (accessed 15 November 2015).
49. Henrik Berggren, *Underbara dagar framför oss: en biografi över Olof Palme* (Stockholm: Norstedt, 2010), 311–12.
50. Ibid., 443.

51. Ibid., 448.
52. Bernd Rother, 'Willy Brandts Außenpolitik: Grundlagen, Methoden und Formen', in Bernd Rother (ed.), *Willy Brandts Außenpolitik* (Wiesbaden: Springer, 2014).
53. Ibid., 463.
54. Willy Brandt, Bruno Kreisky and Olof Palme, *Briefe und Gespräche 1972 bis 1975* (Cologne: Europäische Verlagsanstalt, 1975).
55. Carsten Holbraad, *Internationalism and Nationalism in European Political Thought* (New York: Palgrave Macmillan, 2003), 82–83. See also, Guliano Garavini, *After Empires: European Integration, Decolonization, and the Challenge from the Global South 1957–1986* (Oxford: Oxford University Press, 2012), 230–40; Peter Merseburger, *Willy Brandt: 1913–1992: Visionär und Realist* (Munich: DVA, 2006), 751–62, 820.
56. Oliver J. Daddow, (ed.), *Harold Wilson and European Integration: Britain's Second Application to Join the EEC* (London; Portland, OR: Frank Cass, 2003).
57. Martin J. Dedman, *The Origins and Development of the European Union 1945–95: A History of European Integration* (London: Routledge, 1996), 118–21.
58. Sweden not only applied for EEC membership but also explicitly declared its openness to negotiations with the European Communities (the EEC, ECSC and Euratom merged into a single institutional structure known as the 'European Communities' when the Merger Treaty of 1965 came into force on 1 July 1967). Nevertheless, the application, signed by Trade Minister Gunnar Lange, was addressed to the EEC only. This explains the sometimes confusing seemingly interchangeable use of 'EC' and 'EEC' in the literature. The original text of the Swedish application can be accessed at www.ena.lu/sweden_application_accession_eec_stockholm_26_july_1967-020401699.html (accessed 23 November 2015).
59. Andrén, *Maktbalans och alliansfrihet*, 140–41; see also, Bjereld et al., *Sveriges säkerhet*, 261; Gstöhl, *Reluctant Europeans*, 111–12.
60. Ekengren, *Olof Palme och utrikespolitiken*, 88. Andrén, *Maktbalans och alliansfrihet*, 141–44.
61. For a wider introduction to the origins and general ideas of Nordek, see Hecker-Stampehl, *Nordic Ideology*; Lasse Sonne, *NORDEK: A Plan for Increased Nordic Economic Co-operation and Integration, 1968–1970* (Helsinki: Finnish Society of Sciences and Letters, 2007).
62. In April 1970, Finland abandoned the Nordek negotiations due to its disagreement with the concept of Nordek as a springboard to the EEC. See Hecker-Stampehl, 'Short Political History'; Andrén, *Maktbalans och alliansfrihet*, 143.
63. Andrén, *Maktbalans och alliansfrihet*, 142.
64. Sweden. Ministry for Foreign Affairs. *Documents on Swedish Foreign Policy 1969* (Stockholm: 1970), 71–96, 247–49.
65. Sverige. Utrikesdepartementet (ed.), *Utrikesfrågor: offentliga dokument m m rörande viktigare svenska utrikesfrågor 1970* (Stockholm: Utrikesdepartementet, 1971), 68–94, 141–64.
66. Günter Bischof, Stefan Karner and Peter Ruggenthaler (eds.), *The Prague Spring and the Warsaw Pact Invasion of Czechoslovakia* (Lanham, MD: Lexington Books, 2010).
67. See §12 in the proceedings of the parliamentary debate on the so-called Wedén affair of 1968: Riksdagens snabbprotokoll 1993/94:116, 7 June 1994; available online at http://www.riksdagen.se/sv/dokument-lagar/dokument/protokoll/riksdagens-snabbprotokoll-199394116-torsdagen_GH09116/html (accessed 3 August 2016).
68. Council for Foreign Affairs, 'Stenografiskt referat av utrikesnämndens sammanträde torsdagen den 15 augusti 1968,' 15 August 1968, Regeringskansliets Arkiv [RegA], 17–35.

69. The report had been sent to the Foreign Ministry in Stockholm by Agda Rössel, Sweden's ambassador in Belgrade on 17 August 1968. Rössel emphasized that the Czechs would have appreciated Western silence on the issue as much as they had appreciated Yugoslavian and Romanian support. It is highly debatable whether Sweden would have been considered 'Western' there. §12 in the proceedings of the parliamentary debate on the so-called Wedén affair of 1968: Riksdagens snabbprotokoll 1993/94:116, 7 June 1994; http://www.riksdagen.se/sv/dokument-lagar/dokument/protokoll/riksdagens-snabbprotokoll-199394116-torsdagen_GH09116/html (accessed 3 August 2016).

CHAPTER TWO

1969–1971: Doubting Détente

> *We believe in a lengthy process of consultations through bilateral contacts before even a preparatory conference can become possible.*
>
> —Wilhelm Wachtmeister, 20 May 1969

> *In this time of political antagonism between Eastern and Western Europe, we regard it as our task to contribute to the overcoming of the existing gap between the blocs and work for a reduction of the mutual distrust, which is the ground of the bloc constellation.*
>
> —Olof Palme, 28 August 1971

How did the Swedish government and the Ministry for Foreign Affairs in Stockholm react when the proposal for a conference on European security became an established fact in the international agenda? This chapter gives an account of Swedish attitudes towards détente in Europe – in particular, but not exclusively, among the decision-making elite. It addresses how the country's policy shifted from determined reluctance towards relative openness through a strategy of adjustment and how this was viewed in other countries. This shift is analysed with the help of Holsti's typology of NRCs and concludes with a synoptic discussion.

1969: The Year After

Only months had passed since the Prague Spring shocked Europe, Richard Nixon achieved a narrow election victory over his Democratic opponent Hubert Humphrey after a nerve-jangling campaign, and the Vietnam War reached its peak in the aftermath of the Tet Offensive. In Western countries, this gave new impetus to protests against the war. While the student protests in Paris and Berlin turned violent, Stockholm experienced nothing comparable but saw only the relatively peaceful 'May Revolution', with house squatting and numerous demonstrations against US Vietnam policy.[1]

Prime Minister Tage Erlander was then approaching his last year in office, and Olof Palme, his minister of education, who had dealt with the four-day occupation of the students' union at Stockholm University, was preparing for the role of his successor. In this climate of general unrest, domestic restabilization was of paramount concern in foreign policy. The Social Democratic government was keen to ensure that while the younger generation was shifting to the left and requesting foreign policy revaluation at the highest political level, the principal goal was to maintain the traditional policy of neutrality.[2] These opposing demands resulted in the expansion of development aid and the notion of Sweden as 'the conscience of the world' alongside a reaffirmation of its neutrality.[3]

Ever since the failure of attempts to establish the Scandinavian Defence Union in the late 1940s, Sweden had conducted a foreign policy outside the constellation of the Western bloc. The guiding principle was, as explained in the previous chapter, to maintain Sweden's 'traditional neutrality' in the setting of the Cold War. Swedish neutrality was not a de jure condition, however. It had not been coded in international law, unlike Swiss neutrality, for instance, which had been enshrined since the Congress of Vienna; nor had Swedish neutrality been included in the country's constitution, as was done in Austria in 1955. Swedish neutrality was a de facto temporary condition chosen by those wielding power that had become permanent only as a result of the country successfully avoiding armed conflicts for more than 150 years.[4] Against this political and historical background, international consensus on substantial matters was possible only with other nonaligned states.

Deliberations on the proposed security conference could, therefore, include scenarios in which Sweden might cooperate with comparable states. But, as pointed out by Swiss historian Thomas Fischer, the starting point for possible group efforts with regard to a security conference in Europe was disunity.[5] Austrian, Finnish, Swedish and Swiss perceptions of the concept of neutrality differed in legal status or political practice. Until the late 1960s, cooperation among neutrals had occurred only in the context of the 'Group of Nine', with Berne refraining from participation, and the making of the UN resolution 2129(XX) on good neighbourly relations in 1965.[6] Austria and, to an even greater extent, Finland were facing constant Soviet pressure due to their geostrategic positions.

Unsurprisingly, both states welcomed any promising effort towards interbloc rapprochement and lasting détente.[7] Switzerland, for its part, was exploring ways out of traditional isolationism.[8] At the same time, Sweden had a clear preference for the UN as the natural arena for its more active foreign policy, which had been in the making for almost a decade. In conclusion, decision makers in Stockholm had fewer reasons to be attracted to any kind of active search for neutrality or collaboration for the sake of a European security conference than did their colleagues in Berne, Helsinki or Vienna.[9]

Budapest and the Breakthrough of the ESC

After several failed attempts, in 1964, 1966 and 1967, a breakthrough in moving towards a European security conference was accomplished by the Budapest Appeal of 17 March 1969, when the foreign ministers of the Warsaw Pact states issued a declaration. It expressed the desire of the Eastern bloc to work towards 'the establishment of good neighbourly relations, of trust and mutual understanding', which, according to their view, depended 'on the willingness and efforts of the peoples and governments in Europe'.[10] With this, the communist states declared that they were willing to follow up on their earlier calls for a security conference and so solve remaining obstacles through negotiations.[11] Relations with Washington, and the situation in Europe, loomed large in Soviet policy, as Moscow had to struggle with tensions at its empire's eastern border following clashes between Soviet and Chinese forces along the Ussuri River. Moscow aspired for strategic parity with the United States and therefore signalled greater readiness for substantial negotiations and concessions in Budapest.[12]

And, for the first time, the West considered the Eastern bloc's call for a security conference a serious commitment. The Western allies were aware of the Soviet Union's growing interest in economic cooperation with the West and the Kremlin's willingness to overcome the aftermath of the Prague Spring. Therefore, the allies ultimately considered seriously the Eastern states' requests, thereby allowing the Warsaw Pact to establish discussions about the ESC on the daily agenda of international affairs. Fifteen years after Molotov's first proposal, a conference on European security seemed feasible.[13]

NATO's positive response was met with general approval in many European capitals, including Stockholm, as shown by the response of diplomats such as Rune Nyström at the Swedish embassy in Moscow. Nyström was an expert on Eastern Europe and would be appointed as Sweden's ambassador to East Berlin in the early 1980s. In his memorandum to the Foreign Ministry in Stockholm dated 21 March 1969, Nyström pointed out that the declaration of the Warsaw Pact was of a 'dual nature', as it called for European stability, but also warned of further destabilization in Europe at the same time. Overall, his evaluation praised the moderate tone and cooperative spirit of the pact, which, according to Nyström, distinguished it from the 1966 Bucharest Declaration, an earlier Eastern call for a security conference. This positive view was in harmony with the perception of most NATO member states.[14]

Other internal analyses at the Ministry for Foreign Affairs in Stockholm deemed the Budapest Appeal a 'spectacular move' by which the Kremlin was trying to reverse the events of the Prague Spring by expressly underlining a continued Eastern policy of stabilization on issues of European security.[15] A thorough analysis was also carried out at the political department of the Swedish Foreign Ministry. The Swedes conceived Poland to be the strongest advocate of the Budapest Appeal, together with the Soviet Union, while Czechoslovakia, Romania, Hungary and Bulgaria were generally positive but still relatively passive about it. Albania and Yugoslavia were considered the most critical of the Eastern Europeans. On the Western side, the most positive response to the Budapest Appeal had come from the Netherlands, Italy, Denmark and Belgium. Sweden perceived the United States and Canada, together with the Federal Republic of Germany, Norway and France, as rather moderate.

Swedish diplomats such as Kaj Falkman observed that many views prevailed but that most countries had not yet defined clear positions. Falkman summarized the Swedish position on a security conference as 'in general positive' so long as it was 'well-prepared' and would be attended by all concerned states, *including* the United States and Canada.[16] But there was considerable resistance within NATO. The majority of the Western Europeans initially viewed the declaration as mere propaganda, and most NATO member states were keen to avoid a bloc-to-bloc approach that would alienate the neutrals.[17] West German foreign minister Willy Brandt was the major exception. In contrast to Chancellor Kurt Georg Kiesinger, Brandt reacted cautiously optimistically, and the diplomats at the Auswärtiges Amt, West Germany's Federal Foreign Office in Bonn, followed suit. Brandt was willing to explore the opportunities the Appeal might offer although it shared the mistrust of its NATO partners against the Soviet motives.[18]

The Swedes knew that Austria and Finland viewed the Budapest Appeal favourably for different reasons.[19] Finnish president Urho Kekkonen and Kurt Waldheim, Austria's foreign minister and later general secretary of the UN, considered the conference an opportunity for smaller states to actively contribute to a decrease of tension in Europe.[20] The Swiss, on the other hand, were rather reserved.[21]

In the following months, the Swedish government reiterated its receptiveness to a well-prepared conference, expressed both in bilateral contacts and in public statements. There were many question marks remaining, however. The matter was not yet of public interest, and there were no calls for a specific Swedish role in the process.[22] Thus, Sweden refused to make any commitments, even when pressured by the Kremlin merely two weeks after the Budapest Appeal.[23] Soviet ambassador Viktor Maltsev made the first Soviet approaches, explaining his government's position to Wilhelm Wachtmeister, the head of the Foreign Ministry's political department, during a dinner at the Soviet embassy in Stockholm on 27 March 1969, and to Foreign Minister Torsten Nilsson during a visit four days later. Moscow believed that it was high time for real progress and that 'someone has to take the initiative', as Maltsev put it. Nilsson avoided making a statement, replying to Maltsev's notion with courteous words that did not substantively respond to what the Soviet ambassador had said.[24]

The same day and in the same vein, a note verbale from Maltsev's Hungarian counterpart, Ambassador Peter, was handed over to Wachtmeister on behalf of all of the signatories of the Budapest Appeal.[25] As Peter asked for an immediate meeting, Wachtmeister stepped in on behalf of Nilsson, who was busy dealing with Maltsev. The letter delivered by Peter urged the Swedish government to support the Eastern call for awareness of a 'common responsibility' to preserve peace and security in Europe.[26] During the ensuing conversation, Peter elaborated on the position of the East, pointing out that the well-known idea of a conference had not been realized simply because nobody had taken the initiative. This was an oversimplification, of course, as this summary completely skipped over the events in Prague. Avoiding touching this sore spot, Wachtmeister reiterated where the Swedes stood. Yes, Sweden looked favourably on the idea of a conference, he explained, provided that there was the expectation that it would be successful.

Furthermore, no one could expect serious talks on European security to be held without the Americans. After all, Stockholm had to face the reality of two power blocs, each led by a superpower. As security issues were mainly the remnants of World War II, it was expected that the powers involved in the war would take responsibility in the first place. For this particular reason, Sweden had traditionally remained restrained over the 'German Question'. Certainly, however, constructive contributions would be made 'once circumstances allowed', Wachtmeister concluded.[27]

The Eastern approaches were the earliest form of a role prescription. The Soviets wished for Sweden to become a bridge[28] and act as translator and conveyer of messages to the Western allies. Although not completely averse to the idea of a conference itself, the Swedes were certainly not willing to perform such a task. In their view, there was no necessity to act at all. Division in Europe and the existence of military blocs and two German states were viewed as comprising a permanent situation and could only be solved by the powers that had created this situation. This was a constant subtext of Swedish CSCE policy throughout. Therefore, Sweden maintained a cautious behaviour, keeping its options open through positive rhetoric. This early position was based on the assessments of the Stockholm-based experts of the Foreign Ministry and reports from Swedish embassies. Two weeks before Torsten Nilsson paid a visit to Bucharest, the political department requested the Swedish ambassadors stationed in eight important Western countries to report on the prevailing opinion on the ESC.[29]

The responses confirmed, to a large extent, the early assessment of the important role played by the Prague Spring and China and NATO's presumption of US participation.[30] During this time, Sweden established a close relationship with the West German Foreign Ministry and Willy Brandt, who dominated the discourse in Bonn together with his advisor Egon Bahr. Information was exchanged continuously in regular meetings, making West Germany an important link to NATO. Hans Ruete, the political director of the Auswärtiges Amt, maintained close ties with Swedish ambassador Nils Montan, assuring him that Sweden was considered 'the leading neutral nation' (in Europe).[31] As mentioned earlier, there was dissent within the West German government because Kiesinger and his advisor Karl Carstens did not approve of Brandt's optimistic position on the security conference. When Tage Erlander met the West German chancellor in Bonn in mid-April, he learned that Kiesinger did not actually believe that the conference would take place at all.[32]

Over the next few weeks, the Foreign Ministry in Stockholm sought to reach a balance between resisting Eastern attempts to push Sweden to play a more active role and avoiding being regarded an opponent of a security conference. Two days before the upcoming NATO summit in Washington, held on 10 and 11 April 1969, the UD accommodated Maltsev's renewed request for a meeting with Torsten Nilsson. At the meeting, Maltsev assured Nilsson of the peaceful intention of the East and reinforced his government's argument that all states interested in ending hostilities ought to support the convocation of such a conference. The Kremlin was interested in thorough preparations, Maltsev insisted, but regarded early consultations on the conference as both realistic and desirable. The Soviet ambassador added that he had been ordered to 'establish close contact with the Swedish government in all questions related to this issue'.

Nilsson was impressed by the particular significance the issue had for the Soviet Union and that the Soviets acknowledged the need for a conference but pointed to the fact that several years of recurring discussions at just such a conference had failed to produce results. He promised to have the matter discussed at the highest level and get back to Moscow regarding Sweden's willingness to engage in preparations. Despite Maltsev's strong and much-repeated emphasis on the similarities between Swedish and Soviet perspectives, disagreement regarding the participation of the United States persisted.[33]

At the NATO summit, voices were raised against such a hastily organized conference.[34] The United States and France were rather critical, whereas the majority of the Western Europeans was willing to explore opportunities.[35] The dissent resulted in the allies adopting a cautious stance, stating that 'secure, peaceful and mutually beneficial relations between East and West remained the political goal', but not without reminding every delegate present of the 'setback to hopes for improvement in East-West relations as a result of Soviet intervention in Czechoslovakia'. The declaration made no explicit reference to the Budapest Appeal but demonstrated a willingness to proceed in the proposed direction:

> They [the NATO ministers] reaffirmed at this Session that the intention of their Governments was to continue the search for real progress towards this objective by contacts and to explore all appropriate openings for negotiations . . . Bearing especially in mind the situation in Eastern Europe, member Governments recall that any lasting improvement in international relations presupposes full respect for the principles of the independence and territorial integrity of states, non-interference in their domestic affairs, the right of each people to shape its own future, and the obligation to refrain from the threat or use of force.[36]

Although the intention to keep the door open was apparent in the NATO declaration, this response to the Budapest Appeal was not enough for the Warsaw Pact leaders. Consequently, the days following the Washington summit were full of rumours of the Soviets gearing up and pressurizing a number of states to form an 'initiative group'.[37] The news on this increase in intensity reached Stockholm from all over Europe. A secretary of the Romanian embassy in Moscow informed Karl Anders Wollter, the Swedish attaché, in strict confidence (as he explicitly emphasized) that the Romanians were working on an action plan towards adopting a UN resolution in favour of pan-European talks.[38]

Wollter learned that Bucharest's interest in the conference had grown and that in consequence the Romanian government actively opposed anti–West German prejudices in Moscow.[39] Shortly afterwards, the Soviets approached Austria; naturally, the Swedes expected themselves to be another target of Soviet pressure. As a consequence, the Swedish government became only more determined to take control of its own destiny.

Therefore, Tage Erlander and Torsten Nilsson used their ensuing tour to West Germany, Switzerland and Romania to make it clear that Sweden refused to be influenced by the Soviets.

The Swedish delegation comprised Erlander, Wachtmeister, Swedish ambassador Klas Böök and diplomats Gunnar von Sydow, Anders Ferm and Bengt Holmquist and met with Swiss president Willy Spühler and leading members of his staff at the Eidgenössisches Politisches Departement (EPD) on 9 April. The Swiss could see either of the two countries play a more active role, possibly by taking the initiative themselves. Erlander responded that he considered preparations for a conference to be the business of the great powers. The Swiss noted with satisfaction that their positions were in harmony with those of Sweden.[40]

In Bucharest, where they met with Romanian premier Ion Gheorghe Maurer, Erlander acknowledged that small states could play a constructive role but primarily highlighted the economic aspects of a European conference, stating, 'The neutral countries such as Sweden, Finland, Austria and Switzerland would certainly be very interested in questions of economic co-operation during eventual preparations of a European security conference'.[41] At the following press conference, the Swedish prime minister pointed out, 'It is not possible for Sweden to contribute with any particular efforts'.

Erlander also elaborated on the subject at the congress of the SPD, West Germany's Social Democratic Party.[42] Nilsson then travelled on to Copenhagen, where he met with his Nordic colleagues. The communiqué of the Nordic foreign ministers, issued on 24 April, was in line with Sweden's position, stating, 'A precondition for conferences on security issues is that they are prepared thoroughly and that their timing provides prospects of success'.[43] This stance was in harmony with an earlier statement of Willy Brandt at the NATO summit.[44]

On 29 April, Poland joined the list of ESC supporters actively approaching Sweden.[45] Nothing new was added to the earlier Hungarian and Soviet advances when Polish ambassador Kajzer praised Stockholm's 'positive attitude'. Ole Jödahl, the Swedish undersecretary for foreign affairs, reiterated the arguments of his government and responded, albeit reluctantly, to a proposed visit to Warsaw in June.[46]

By the end of April 1969, the Budapest Appeal had led to discussions among politicians and diplomats all over Europe. Although even putting the idea on the international agenda had been an achievement in itself, after years of struggle, the Soviets pushed for more, putting growing pressure on the neutral countries from late March onwards. In the Swedish case, all these attempts remained unsuccessful, as Stockholm considered the conference a substantial power issue to which it could only *react*.

Facing a Fait Accompli: The Finnish Initiative

On 5 May 1969 the Finnish government issued an invitation to all states concerned, including both German states, the United States and Canada, to preparatory talks for a conference on security in Europe. Finland proposed a three-stage procedure and offered its capital as the conference venue. According to the memorandum issued by the Finnish Foreign Ministry in Helsinki, interested governments would begin the first stage of the discussion process with bilateral consultations. If sufficient agreement could be reached, technical questions regarding a security conference would be discussed during a second phase. The conference itself would then enter the third and final stage, according to the Finnish scheme.[47]

While Moscow had failed to push Sweden to take any initiative, things went differently when Helsinki rushed ahead. As the Finns naturally found themselves under greater pressure from the neighbouring Soviet Union than did the Swedes, they scrutinized possible tools for improvement. Therefore, the Kremlin's revived interest in the security conference had already been considered an option for activating the Finnish neutrality policy in June 1968, when a first working paper had been drafted at the Finnish Foreign Ministry. Confronted again with the same Soviet pressure as the other European neutrals, in April 1969 Helsinki came to the conclusion that the initiative desired by Moscow would be useful for its own purposes.

However, expectations were modest, as revealed by Finnish officials after the end of the Cold War. Keijo Korhonen, for example, stated, 'It was not planned to be a tree. It just grew into one'. At the most, 'some kind of diplomatic tea party' was what the Finns expected.[48] At that point in time, however, and with the Prague Spring still fresh in their memory, even a 'tea party' was too much to expect in the eyes of their Swedish neighbour.[49]

Due to the close relationship between the Nordic states, the Swedish embassy counsellor Claes Huldtgren received a memorandum on the initiative two days before it was circulated.[50] President Urho Kekkonen, in Stockholm on a visit that weekend, personally delivered the memorandum to Tage Erlander.[51] Despite knowledge of it, the scale of the initiative apparently surprised the staff of the Foreign Ministry, where it was received with scepticism. Finland's foreign minister, Ahti Karjalainen, had not announced his government's plans to his Nordic colleagues in Copenhagen two weeks earlier. The reason was that the decision on the initiative had been taken in a confidential meeting between President Kekkonen and Ambassador Max Jakobson one week after the meeting of the Nordic foreign ministers.[52]

Stockholm was among the first destinations of Ralph Enckell, an experienced Finnish diplomat who campaigned in favour of the conference as roving ambassador in 1970 and 1971.[53] When Enckell met with Ole Jödahl, he started the meeting by elaborating on the origin and nature of the Finnish initiative, describing it as a 'neutral country's contribution' to European détente. Jödahl expressed concerns about the chosen approach and pointed to the German Question and the lasting disagreement between the participants.[54] He stressed that Sweden was keen on its neutral status and saw no reason to rush.

Enckell eventually agreed that his government shared the Swedish view on the need for setting the agenda during the phase of bilateral consultations, and for including the Americans in the right away. Still, he failed to convince Jödahl, who emphasized the uneasiness of the Finnish ambassador's reactions when asked a number of critical questions. In his report, the Swedish diplomat remarked critically that his interlocutor had not been absolutely certain about how decision makers in Helsinki really anticipated the possible outcome of the project. The significance of these consultations is illustrated by the fact that the minutes of the meeting were sent to politicians and dignitaries at all levels, including Erlander, Nilsson and King Gustaf VI Adolf.[55]

During the following days, it was stated explicitly that Sweden would not participate in a security conference if it was poorly prepared and if the United States and Canada would not be attending. Sweden also decided not to respond to the Finnish initiative, although President Urho Kekkonen and his government expected support in their struggle for recognition that the initiative was a Finnish one, rather than the result of Soviet pressure. But Swedish decision makers did not feel like they were in a position to support the initiative. Facing a fait accompli – that is, the sudden establishment of the conference on the international agenda – Sweden first needed to develop a strategy of its own and used the delay in responding to express its dissatisfaction with the Finnish policy.

The Swedes felt that their Finnish colleagues should have prepared them for what was coming, as they did not share Finland's positive view of the opportunities that a security conference offered and had disliked the Soviet approach in April 1969. Early reactions were, therefore, limited to a wait-and-see policy, and Sweden clearly chose to avoid any kind of active behaviour, refraining from any role performance, as Holsti would put it. Foreign Minister Torsten Nilsson, addressing the Council of Europe in London on 6 May 1969, and Prime Minister Erlander, in a press release published in *Svenska Dagbladet* on 8 May, reiterated publicly the 'generally positive' attitude of Sweden towards a conference.[56]

The Soviet Union tried to use such statements from neutral countries in its own favour. According to *TASS*, the official organ of the ruling Communist Party of the Soviet Union (CPSU), Erlander had 'already advocated the calling of such a conference and expressed the wish of Sweden to participate in it'. Where Moscow exaggerated, Helsinki complained. The Finns, for their part, were disappointed at the fact that the Swedish government had issued no official response in favour of their invitation. During the following weeks, the Finnish Foreign Ministry continued to request an official statement from the Swedish government in support of its initiative.[57]

These calls were ignored in Stockholm, where it was decided to wait for reactions from the Western powers before assessing the chance of setting up a security conference and proceeding in any direction. Despite the knowledge of Moscow's attempts during April to activate the neutrals as catalysts, some diplomats, such as Lennart Petri, Sweden's ambassador in Vienna, opposed the belief that Finland was playing the role of the Kremlin's mailman. Instead, the Swedes believed the Finnish initiative of 5 May to be a move by President Urho Kekkonen, an opinion shared by many US State Department officials.[58] Contradicting these views, and based on evaluations of bilateral talks carried out by the political department, a first official assessment at the Swedish Foreign Ministry held, 'There is reason to believe that the purpose of the proposed meeting in Helsinki is, "via a detour", so to say, to accomplish the limited preparatory meeting proposed by the East and through that engage the neutral states from an early stage'.[59]

However, in bilateral talks with the Austrians, Swedish diplomats pretended otherwise and defended Finland. Although it was made clear that Sweden did not expect the conference to succeed, and had no plans to take further initiatives or play an active role, the invitation from Helsinki was called a 'very clever move', as it had obviated a Soviet demand.[60] While looking to the West for general orientation, developments on the eastern side of the Iron Curtain were not neglected in Stockholm. The Swedes had learned that Hungary was disappointed with the Soviets for supporting Helsinki instead of Budapest as the conference venue.

It was in this context that Sandor Kurtán, Hungary's ambassador in Stockholm, stated to Swedish colleagues, 'Even if it comes into existence, one cannot expect a security conference to solve substantial problems'.[61] Another interesting telegram containing information on the atmosphere in the Eastern camp reached the UD from Prague. Agda Rössel, one of Sweden's few female ambassadors at the time, reported that the new foreign minister of Czechoslovakia, Jan Marko, had stressed the fact that his country had made substantial contributions to the Budapest Appeal, which the Czechs believed provided an opportunity to ease tensions in Europe. Rössel reported that Marko had 'urged' her to forward his 'plea' and had stressed 'the importance of this issue to the CSSR'. The telegram was put through both to Foreign Minister Nilsson and Prime Minister Erlander.[62]

Meanwhile, Romania intensified its efforts to secure a UN resolution in 1970 as 'the year of peaceful co-operation and security in Europe'. Bucharest argued that it was a way for 'the Ten' – the group of small states that had proposed the UN resolution five years earlier – to contribute to further diminishment of hostility. As Sweden did not wish to contribute actively to a security conference, the idea did not rouse enthusiasm in Stockholm. Similar declarations had passed earlier without any effect.[63] Eager to uphold the image that Sweden pursued an active foreign policy, Erlander, during a lecture at the Bucharest Institute of International Affairs, had publicly argued that neutrality did not impose silence on his government.[64] Sverker Åström acknowledged that 'we too have indeed assumed that the Swedish government could do nothing but affirm such an initiative' and recommended that Sweden state its interest, although with reservations.[65] Here, we see a concrete example of the influence emanating from the expectations of other actors, or, as Holsti called it, from role prescriptions.

The more subtle and diverse Eastern attempts to engage Sweden became, the harder it was for Stockholm to uphold and justify its complete lack of participation in the process. Still, the most relevant factor affecting the Swedish government at this point was that it had no interest in presenting itself as an ostensible cosponsor of a resolution on deeper cooperation with the Warsaw Pact less than a year after the Prague Spring. It had already faced severe domestic criticism for its silence during the invasion and did not believe in the presumed motives behind the proposed resolution.[66] The situation in Czechoslovakia was highly sensitive, and was treated accordingly by Sweden. Wilhelm Wachtmeister requested the opinion of further diplomats with relevant expertise before it was decided that a resolution would be supported only if it was completely detached from the conference's position.[67] Eventually, Sweden remained true to itself and avoided taking a stand on security, restricting its European policy to economic endeavours.

The Swedes considered the interpretation of the Finnish memorandum made by most Eastern European countries to be distorted by the propaganda of the communist authorities.[68] Their faith in the West, on the other hand, was much greater. It was to the West that Swedish decision makers looked when taking stock of the situation and before agreeing on further steps. Among the Western allies, however, there were differences of opinion regarding the proper response to the Finnish invitation. In Washington, the proposed security conference was not popular. It was generally considered a Soviet project, and US national security advisor Henry Kissinger was reluctant to multilateralize questions of security. Officials of the State Department stated to Swedish ambassador Hubert de Besche that they had little hope for the convocation of a conference within a reasonable timescale and therefore had not replied to the Finns.[69] Great Britain also did not believe that much would come out of the conference but wanted to give the impression that it was ready for any kind of future development.

Thus, London decided to 'take note politely' and tell the Finns, 'We shall bear it in mind'. France was concerned with the effects a security conference would have on international affairs, rather than with its content per se. At the Quai d'Orsay, the French Ministry for Foreign Affairs, a special relationship with the Soviet Union was favoured over multilateral détente. The Netherlands remained passive and issued no official response. Turkey and Italy also suspected the conference to be nothing more than a Soviet tool; Belgium refused it as overhasty. More problematic for Sweden was the reaction of its closest partners. The three Nordic members of NATO looked positively upon the Finnish memorandum, and so did West Germany, as Foreign Minister Willy Brandt regarded the Finnish memorandum favourably despite refraining from making commitments of any kind.[70] Nobody had expected the Finnish initiative, however, and therefore Brandt did not mention it at all when he delivered a speech in Hamburg on 7 May.[71]

In a response to Leif Belfrage, Sweden's ambassador in London, Wilhelm Wachtmeister pointed out:

> Our attitude towards the Finnish initiative is thus generally positive. The intention [of the Foreign Ministry] is, however, not to formally 'respond' [to] the Finnish memorandum. Our view is that the government has expressed our attitude on the conference issue clearly. It now seems appropriate to await the reaction of the Western powers in order to be able to assess the conditions for the realization of the idea of a conference in the near future ... With regard to this, we believe in a lengthy process of consultations through bilateral contacts before even a preparatory conference can become possible.[72]

Sweden received praise for its Western-orientated policy from Washington. Martin Hillenbrand, responsible for the State Department's European desk, told Ambassador de Besche that the Swedish attitude was greatly appreciated by US officials.[73] The Alpine neutrals, Switzerland and Austria, reacted to the memorandum more positively than did the Swedes. Vienna welcomed the Finnish invitation and responded with an official aide-mémoire on 28 May 1969 emphasizing that consensus would have to be reached among relevant states.[74] The same applied to the Swiss, who pointed out that there was no need to hurry. In a conversation with Bengt Holmquist, Sweden's ambassador in Berne, Hans Miesch, the head of the political section at the Swiss Foreign Ministry, expressed his suspicions that the Soviets 'had more than one finger in the [Finnish] pie'.

Berne was also sceptical about the participation of the German Democratic Republic (GDR).[75] The goal for the Swedes was to find a balance between their own reluctance and their traditional support of Finland. Ingemar Hägglöf, the ambassador in Helsinki, defined the task of Sweden as to make some contribution that would keep Finland 'on a straight and realistic course'.[76] One way to do so was Nordic cooperation at the UN. At a meeting between the Nordic UN representatives in New York on 30 May, there was consensus on issuing a recommendation to the foreign departments to adopt a general 'wait-and-see' attitude, decline the Romanian resolution proposal and the idea of a cosponsored conference outside of the UN and refrain from forming a group with regard to the question of a European security conference.[77]

The Swedes collected detailed information from embassies all over the world during the following month. At the same time, the Finns were still awaiting an official statement from Stockholm. Switzerland and Austria had responded immediately to the Finnish initiative, but support from its Swedish neighbour, with which Finland shared historical bonds and close relations, was considered particularly important and was therefore eagerly anticipated. When asked by the Czech ambassador in Stockholm whether the Swedes had responded officially to Finland yet, Wachtmeister referred evasively to the communiqué of the 24 April meeting of the Nordic foreign ministers in Copenhagen. He added that the Finnish memorandum had not explicitly called for a response, nor had it been welcomed in the public statements of Erlander in any case. Wachtmeister also stated that the Swedish position 'might eventually be specified in written form'.[78]

Finally, after more than two months, and as one of the last countries to do so, the Swedish government responded to the Finnish initiative on 10 July 1969, calling it 'a constructive contribution to the work for relaxation in Europe'.[79] Thorough, effective preparations and the inclusion of the United States on the basis of the 1945 Treaty of Potsdam and of Canada from the very beginning of the process, as well as the possibility of bilateral consultations between small states and the superpowers, were defined as preconditions for the convening of a security conference.

The Swedish delayed response was a form of criticism of Kekkonen's line taken in late April and early May 1969. After all, the Kremlin had shown its ugly face less than a year earlier in Czechoslovakia, and nothing indicated that the Soviets would change their view in matters related to the Brezhnev Doctrine, which claimed that the development of a socialist country towards capitalism was the concern of all socialist countries.[80] In consequence, there was not much to commit to yet. In the eyes of the Swedes, Finland had gone out on a limb. They did not fully understand the extent to which Kekkonen was driven by the events of the Prague Spring, which contemporaries described as 'a shock' to him.[81] This is the first of many examples of why Leatherman's idea of a dual role played by Sweden and Finland in the context of the CSCE must be rejected.

During the following period of roughly six months, the diplomats of the UD tried to establish a line that would strike a balance between supporting its Nordic neighbour and resisting the attempts of the Eastern bloc to activate the neutral states. The Swedish approach to the security conference at this early point was *defensive* in nature. It lacked the idealist ambitions epitomized by the architects of Sweden's active foreign policy elsewhere.

From Helsinki to Prague – the Summer of '69

As announced in their response to the Finnish memorandum, the Swedes introduced a period of bilateral consultations during the summer of 1969. West Germany played a central role in Sweden's positioning process. A lengthy bilateral evaluation took place on 15 July, when the West German chargé d'affaires Karl Rowold met with Dag Malm at the Swedish Foreign Ministry. Rowold informed his interlocutor about Bonn's efforts to ensure the material and procedural aspects of the ESC. The West German diplomat had been ordered to investigate Sweden's attitude to the connection between the ESC, the US-Soviet strategic arms limitation talks (SALT) and the German Question. Malm responded that no official position on future agenda points yet existed and that it was unlikely for Sweden to declare such an agenda in the near future. Although voices had been raised in Sweden for the inclusion of disarmament questions, Sweden held that SALT was a bilateral superpower issue directly contributing to a conference, so long as it developed positively.

It would also be important for small states to be given the opportunity to discuss certain issues with the great powers. Rowold concluded the talks, explaining that Bonn would try to use the Eastern interest in the ESC to secure inner-German relaxation.[82] Sweden knew a good deal about the West German approach and was aware of Bonn's hopes for an improved political climate allowing for European détente after the September 1969 elections. The West Germans for their part were well aware about the differences between Sweden's active neutrality in Europe and the Third World: '[The Swedish] Government and public opinion tend to react harshly against measures and events in the Eastern bloc that clash with Swedish ideas of democracy and humanity . . . There is no mistaking, however, that despite all trenchancy, a certain care is exercised when criticism is voiced against measures and shortcomings in the Soviet sphere of interest'.[83]

At that point, the West German government did not want the German Question to become the centre of interest at a conference that would touch upon the political, military and legal status not only of the currently divided but of the whole of a future unified Germany.[84] The special relation between Bonn and Stockholm was not a secret. Often, Eastern European states would approach the Swedes when they needed help with anchoring ideas in Bonn.[85] This was natural, due to the good relations between social democrats in Sweden and West Germany, but was not promoted publicly, as it would not have fit with the domestic strategy of the SAP.

During the summer, it became apparent that the Budapest Appeal and the Finnish invitation had given the conference idea some momentum. Discussions on procedures and content became more concrete as obstacles were approached by way of proposed concessions. Entirely positive reactions to the Finnish initiative had come from Bulgaria, Poland, Romania, Czechoslovakia and the GDR. Their responses were linked to a call for equal rights of participation and acknowledgement of territorial realities.[86]

The Soviet ambassador in Vienna informed his Swedish colleague that Moscow had abandoned its reluctance to US participation in the conference proper.[87] Although these were further steps in the right direction, this was not enough for Sweden, which considered it inevitable that the United States would be actively involved from the very beginning, at the preparatory stage. Such minor concessions, expressed in the form of a modification of the Soviet expectations of Sweden's role, were not enough to prompt the government in Stockholm to abandon its reluctance to an ill-prepared security conference.

In late August, the Swedish Foreign Ministry first compiled a summary of its impressions. The Warsaw Pact states were characterized by the desire they expressed for a special preparatory meeting. Moscow, in particular, argued that such a meeting would allow the overcoming of minor obstacles and catalyse the process, driving it towards a conference. Poland specified the schedule, venue, invitation procedure and agenda as obstacles that would have to be removed through diplomatic endeavours. The Poles held that all European states, regardless of their political system, should be invited with no preconditions early on, while non-European states ought to take part only at the actual conference. Poland was the country with the most explicit position on the necessity of a security conference; it pointed out that territorial and political realities existing in Europe needed to be acknowledged. Therefore, it was natural that the harshest criticism of the cautious Swedish response to the Finnish initiative came from Warsaw.[88]

In a meeting with Poland's deputy foreign minister, Jozef Winiewicz, Director-General for Trade Policy Kaj Björk was confronted with the Polish call for greater Swedish commitment to the ESC. Winiewicz argued that with France lacking a clear line after the change in the presidential office in Paris, and with uncertainty before the election in West Germany, Sweden, as a highly industrialized and neutral country, would have to take greater responsibility in European affairs.

Björk's concerns regarding the Brezhnev Doctrine were dismissed by Winiewicz, who argued that the 'total chaos in Czechoslovakia' had forced necessary action and was to be considered an internal matter for the Warsaw Pact not related to the security conference, which was not intended to be held between the blocs. Björk answered evasively and stated that his country had not been productive until then 'because the initiative has come from outside and [we are] primarily devoting ourselves to asking questions and discussing problems in this respect'. He added that Sweden was not an industrial power, nor did it 'overestimate its capability of influencing European affairs'.[89]

This disparity between Björk's conception of Sweden's role and the role prescription articulated by his Polish interlocutor is particularly interesting, as it touches upon the very essence of this study. After all, Sweden was active, and even controversial, in extra-European issues, despite having an equally limited capability to influence global affairs. Therefore, expecting the Swedes to adopt a similar role in the context of the security conference seemed legitimate. Due to the role of Europe in Sweden's foreign policy, however, this rationale forced Björk to *explicitly* reject Winiewicz's *implicit* equation between the role Sweden could play in global and European affairs. In the view of the Swedes, the time was not yet ripe for more than 'exploring the chances of success', as Foreign Minister Nilsson told his Austrian colleague Kurt Waldheim during a visit to Vienna.[90]

In consultations with the Belgian ambassador in Stockholm, Wilhelm Wachtmeister chose a slightly more positive approach, stating that Sweden agreed with those arguing for the initiation of negotiations between East and West on the least controversial issues. Wachtmeister pointed to the commercial, technological and cultural fields as examples of such matters. He acknowledged that disarmament traditionally was of interest to his government, but he was also clear on the fact that any further steps would have to be postponed until the NATO states had declared their position more carefully at their next summit, in December 1969.[91] Generally, approaches suggesting greater commitment were not looked on favourably, as illustrated by the Swedish reaction to Hungarian calls to suggest Stockholm as the conference venue:

> My Hungarian colleague, a fine little man with a somewhat frightened appearance, visited me today to push for the security conference. The only new thing was that, as he assured me with the utmost seriousness, the Dutch are said to prefer Stockholm or Vienna over Helsinki as a venue. I assured him that I had not heard a word about this and that the Swedish government, which had warmly welcomed the Finnish initiative, as is widely known, found it self-evident that the conference would take place in Helsinki as planned. We had not wasted much thought about trying to bilk our Finnish brothers of their meeting [conference].[92]

There was no real interest in Stockholm, and the Swedes assumed that Hungary, feeling sidelined over the venue question, just wanted to spite the Finns.[93] Sweden had no intention of playing a prominent role in the preparations for a security conference, a fact emphasized in bilateral talks with representatives of the Swiss and Belgian foreign ministries.[94] As a result, Wachtmeister's Swiss counterpart Pierre Micheli reported to Berne the possibility that the two countries might actually 'often take different lines' in the future.[95] Instead, Stockholm strictly maintained its wait-and-see attitude, referring to the NATO summit as the next landmark and ignoring recurring statements to the contrary. This was in harmony with the NATO allies, who also assumed the role of observer, awaiting elections in West Germany and the December summit.[96]

The Western interpretation of 'observing' nevertheless diverged from the Swedish one, as it did not prohibit the discussion of substantial matters such as mutual measures towards military constraints and reductions in the armed forces.[97] Twenty-two out of thirty-two countries had responded positively to the Finnish invitation by mid-September 1969. NATO did not take a collective stance but left it to individual governments to reply to Helsinki. Although much remained to be done, the idea of an ESC was fully established on the political agenda.[98] Sweden also shared NATO's opinion on slowing down the general pace of the process. Therefore, Sweden never considered any initiatives. In contrast, Kurt Waldheim invited the Group of Ten for consultations regarding the ESC.[99]

The Swedish irritation with Finland arose again when Urho Kekkonen publicly discussed ideas on the establishment of a European security system. With this, the Finnish president ignored the Swedish position of the previous months with just days left until the German election and

Tage Erlander's resignation. 'Little by little, we shall certainly see what the point of such long phrases is. If there is one', commented an annoyed Ingemar Hägglöf. Clearly, there was little agreement between Finland and Sweden on how to look at, frame or approach the security conference.[100]

When Kekkonen was confronted with this impasse during a meeting with the Scandinavian ambassadors in Prague, he agreed on the necessity for US and Canadian participation but also praised the new leader of the Communist Party, Gustáv Husák, who had deeply impressed him. Kekkonen defended the Kremlin, arguing that Soviet leaders had feared that the events of Prague, during which the Czechoslovakians had been 'completely crazy', could have led to a third world war. Since May, Kekkonen and the Finns had been playing a new role of great interest to the Swedes, as the ESC had become Moscow's greatest concern in the Nordic sphere by late 1969. The Kremlin was equally in favour of the status quo in Nordic security issues and seemed to have little interest in the ongoing talks concerning Nordek. Ingemar Hägglöf portrayed Finnish-Soviet relations with condescension. He claimed that the Soviets were endorsing the Finnish initiative and tried to link it to the course of the Warsaw Pact 'lock, stock and barrel'.[101]

At that time, five weeks had passed since Olof Palme had entered office. Naturally, this was not the best time for a radical re-evaluation of Sweden's European policy, and thus the Swedish Foreign Ministry was hoping for a calm end to the year. But when the foreign ministers of the Warsaw Pact states gathered in Prague on 30 and 31 October 1969, the Swedes quickly realized that their appeals for a slower pace had been in vain. Claes Wollin, Sweden's ambassador in Warsaw, reported extensively on the ongoing discussions of the first day. Two lines of approach were distinguishable: Poland's maximalist proposal to draft a broad conference programme and the Soviet Union's minimalist idea of requesting a legal treaty on economic and technological cooperation. The Polish line was aimed at forcing the Western Europeans and their American ally to adopt more concrete positions, whereas the Soviets preferred to dangle a carrot before the West.[102]

In the declaration published on the following day, the seven signatories asserted that 'practical possibilities for the convening of the conference and for the achievement of European security through joint efforts in the interest of all states and people of Europe' had been accomplished. Accordingly, the time had come to include two important questions on the agenda of the 'all-European conference'. These were the renunciation of the use or threat of force in mutual relations between states in Europe and the expansion of trade and economic, scientific and technical relations.

If any such 'historic event' could take place, 'other problems' relating to European security could be considered later. With this, the communist states abandoned their earlier demand for a preparatory meeting, hoping for a speedier convening of the conference, which they thought could be held in Helsinki as early as the first half of 1970.[103] The Soviet position in Prague gave rise to questions on Finnish independence in designing the initiative of 5 May. This added to the suspicions of critics who had already deemed the whole project propaganda. Ingemar Hägglöf, the Swedish ambassador in Helsinki, was one of those critics. To him, the Kremlin was just being 'fanciful' about the whole matter.[104]

Now, during the first six months after the Finnish initiative, Sweden was forced to adapt to an unwelcome change in East-West relations. Western interests, particularly those of West Germany, were closely observed, which resulted in growing tension with Finland. As observed elsewhere, it was the European focus of Finnish foreign policy activism that varied greatly from Sweden's universalist orientation.[105] This disagreement was largely concealed in public statements and bilateral contacts. Swedish decision makers wished to avoid illustrating their repugnance for the Finnish stance, which allowed tensions to remain behind the closed doors of the foreign ministries in Stockholm and Helsinki. And, despite the Social Democratic victory in the West German elections and Willy Brandt's appointment to the office of chancellor – which allowed him to realize the ideas of the *Ostpolitik* and led to growing hope for rapprochement in Europe – the Swedish government saw little space for itself to participate in détente.[106]

Position Fixing and Criticism

In the eyes of Swedish diplomats, the Prague summit had altered the situation. In Prague, the Soviets and the East Germans had taken over, to the dissatisfaction of Poland, which argued that the declaration did not go far enough.[107] The declaration had streamlined the Warsaw Pact's earlier position and made Western agreement with the conference more realistic.[108] The Kremlin, having outmanoeuvred Poland, considered the declaration a step towards cooperation and reason enough to expect more substantial contributions from the neutrals. In order to carry out this task, roles were distributed among the Eastern states. Poland was assigned the task of approaching the Nordic countries, Austria, the Netherlands and Belgium for renewed bilateral consultations.[109] Moscow continued along its chosen dominant path and started defining a broader remit for the conference, adding cooperation to security. This evolution was made public in two *Pravda* articles written by two separate prominent journalists, Igor Troyanovsky and Yuri Zhukov, two weeks later.[110]

However, the Swedish reports from Moscow noted that uncertainty remained among Soviet officials as to what exactly was meant by 'cooperation'.[111] In an effort to comprehend the Soviet position, Gunnar Jarring, Sweden's ambassador in Moscow, concluded that the USSR was eager to improve its relations with Bonn and Paris and seemed to be interested in the establishment of subregional security systems.[112]

The Prague Declaration had little impact on NATO, which had anticipated an Eastern initiative but did not want it to influence its own assessments. The declaration was considered not far-reaching enough, as it lacked explicit reference to North American participation.[113] It was, however, received favourably by nonaligned Yugoslavia. Belgrade shifted from scepticism to optimism during this period and began to argue that nonaligned states should participate in the preparatory work for a conference. According to the Yugoslavians, small or medium-sized states such as Romania, Denmark, Bulgaria, Holland and Norway could contribute to creating greater flexibility now that the change of government in Bonn had created a new political climate.[114] This line of argument was shared by Sweden, whose officials at the Foreign Ministry in Stockholm slowly considered opening up to the possibility of a future ESC. Confronted with continual criticism that 'other European states appear more active than Sweden', the Swedes sought ways to take first steps towards the development of a concrete policy.[115]

And, as so often happened during these preparatory years, the Swedes looked to the Brandt administration for orientation. Wilhelm Wachtmeister declared his interest in learning 'how Bonn looks at the European security conference with the background of the Prague meeting'. Wachtmeister wondered what the West Germans thought of 'the ensuring of European security' or the 'renunciation of the use of force or threat of its use', two substantial elements of the Prague Declaration.[116] In the year to come, the responses from Ambassador Nils Montan in Bonn came to serve as guiding points for the Swedish attitude. Montan reported that the Prague Declaration did not come as anything new to the West Germans. Walter Scheel, the new West German foreign minister, viewed the time schedule as proposed in the Prague Declaration as unrealistic and criticized the fact that the Eastern Europeans had not mentioned important matters such as troop reductions.

In Bonn, nobody understood Moscow's 'rush toward a conference that could not solve any acute problems anyways', as Helmut Allardt, West Germany's ambassador to Moscow, put it in a conversation with Gunnar Jarring on 24 November 1969. A conference would certainly not be held during the first half of 1970, Allardt said.[117] As for Berlin and internal German politics, Scheel believed that a solution between the four victorious powers and the two German states was feasible. But the matter had to remain bilateral. The following year, Bonn used the CSCE as a lever in its negotiations with Moscow.[118]

It was against this background that the Swedes concluded that a solution to the German Question was *the* prerequisite for the convocation of the ESC. They would have to wait for the Brandt administration to solve the most acute problems by applying its new policy towards Moscow and Warsaw. Thus, Berlin became a sine qua non in Swedish CSCE policy.[119] The Swedish interest in Willy Brandt's *Ostpolitik* was by no means unique, but the range and weight of its influence on Sweden's European security policy must be considered remarkable.[120] Sweden's nascent role as faithful friend of West Germany owed much to the personal relationship between Olof Palme and Willy Brandt. It was not the result of external influence but rather a natural choice based on the shared ideas and values of two mutually amicable statesmen.[121]

In Paris, this development raised questions. France looked reluctantly at the new West German foreign policy orientation. To the French, Brandt's focus on the East contrasted rather disturbingly with Konrad Adenauer's earlier *Westpolitik*.[122] There were frenzied speculations in diplomatic circles on the motive behind the French perspective. Gunnar Hägglöf, Sweden's ambassador in Paris, stated that many of his colleagues in the French capital believed that the French government saw a need to regain strength after the country's temporary weakness in foreign affairs caused by the transition from de Gaulle to Pompidou in June 1969.[123]

And on the other side of the channel, Michael Stewart, British foreign secretary in Harold Wilson's cabinet, remarked in a speech to the House of Commons that the Prague Declaration had not been a step forward, since it contained no signs of liberalization. Stewart also argued that the neutral states should participate in a future conference, but he made it clear that any substantial agreement depended upon the members of NATO and the Warsaw Pact states. Swedish ambassador Leif Belfrage reported that the British Foreign Office considered the expansion of the agenda from security to economic and other subjects a tactical move aimed at the exclusion of the United States and Canada. In bilateral talks with Swedish diplomats, British officials enquired whether Sweden had experienced pressure from Finland.[124] From the perspective of a peripheral, small state like Sweden, Washington's lack of interest, together with the rather critical stance of France and Britain, was a natural counterweight to the West German position.

At the end of November 1969, the time to summarize had come. A lengthy memorandum of eighteen pages containing information on the Prague meeting, the time schedule, substantial matters such as the declaration on nonuse of force and on economic cooperation, the upcoming NATO summit and the reactions, motives and goals of participating states was drafted. Notably, the introduction of the 'motives and goals' section was basically identical to the statement made by West German ambassador Helmut Allardt to Gunnar Jarring but was not noted as a direct quote.

Allardt's view had been overtaken almost word for word. Accordingly, the Soviet Union's main goals were the de facto recognition of Europe's postwar borders, the recognition of the GDR and the persistence of the status quo in Eastern Europe. This was intended to drive a wedge between the United States and Western Europe. If security in Europe had been accomplished, the argument went, what was the purpose of the continued US military presence in Europe? While smaller countries in Europe could use the multilateralization of security talks to argue for greater participation, the major powers had much to lose and little to win.[125] With this proposal, Sweden assumed the basic position expressed by Bonn regarding the conference. This led to it securing what Holsti would describe as the role of a faithful friend of West Germany.

As mentioned above, these were early signs of a reconsideration of the Swedish role. The political climate in Europe had improved somewhat, Torsten Nilsson acknowledged in a conversation with Soviet ambassador Maltsev[126] – but still not enough in the minds of Swedes. They saw no reason to stick their necks out and develop a proactive line. Naturally, this continued attitude aroused much criticism among Warsaw Pact states but also, more notably, among Western states and the other neutrals. Norway and Finland, for instance, expressed their surprise and dismay over what they called 'Sweden's remarkable passivity in the European security question' in bilateral talks.[127] Such critical voices were met with constant, unflappable composure by the Swedes. This illustrates nicely the limits of influence exerted by prescribed roles. Not convinced that there was anything to gain, the Swedes relied on their own scepticism for several more months.

At the NATO summit held in Brussels between 3 and 5 December 1969, the Western allies, for the first time, responded directly and positively to the idea of a conference on the Warsaw Pact.[128] The NATO declaration stated that the successful development of the negotiations that had been introduced would elevate the chances of a security conference. This included the Berlin talks, Bonn's new policy towards Poland and the Soviet Union, internal German negotiations and a future agreement on negotiations on the so-called mutual and balanced force reductions (MBFR). With this, NATO supported Brandt's *Ostpolitik* by turning it into a bargaining chip in the interbloc communication on the ESC. It maintained that the

Warsaw Pact states had to offer much more before anyone could proceed towards setting up a conference.[129]

US secretary of state William Rogers called the Soviet agenda proposal 'weak' and expressed the unwillingness of his government to participate in a conference that could result in even greater acceptance of the Brezhnev Doctrine. But, despite such declared reservations, Sweden welcomed the outcome of the summit.[130] Eastern media unsurprisingly railed against 'some Western states' who wanted to 'bury' the ESC by 'seeking hindrances'. But to Stockholm, these far-reaching demands were convenient, as they promised a deceleration of the efforts made to set up the conference.[131]

In the aftermath of the Brussels summit, Finland tried to renew the faith of others in its independent motives, leading to the invitation of 5 May. The Finnish government publicly announced that it would continue its bilateral efforts. Widely read articles written by an anonymous columnist that discussed the subject of and condemned NATO's lukewarm response to the calls for a security conference appeared in the *Helsingin Sanomat*. The Swedish embassy believed them to have been written by President Kekkonen himself.[132] Such speculations illustrate that no intimate relationship between Helsinki and Stockholm existed, unlike elsewhere.

West German diplomats assured their Swedish colleagues that the talks between Bonn and Moscow were carried out in a 'highly pleasant' atmosphere. They explained the negative stand taken by NATO as a tactical move designed to force Moscow to make greater concessions.[133] Through such channels, Sweden gained insight into Western positions and strategies, and the acquired information served as reference points in their own positioning. The Eastern bloc, on the other hand, was always regarded from an outsider's perspective. Bonn's strategy would prove correct; by late February 1970 the Kremlin had come to acknowledge that inner-German relations and the Berlin issue had to be solved bilaterally.[134]

The response from NATO had a beneficial effect, as it slowed down the pace of the process, a development long hoped for in Sweden. For the rest of the year and during all of January 1970, general activity was restricted to low-profile bilateral consultations. Belgian diplomats were invited to Stockholm, and views were exchanged with a high-ranking delegation of Yugoslavian diplomats led by Djuro Nincic, the head of the political section at the Foreign Ministry in Belgrade.[135] Therefore, it was natural that Wachtmeister fought off calls for the multilateralization of efforts during a meeting with the deputy foreign minister of Romania, Mircea Malita, arguing that the consultations were themselves valuable.[136]

The course of events at the superpower level was followed thoroughly in Stockholm. Conflicting public statements were made in the East and in the West. Articles in *Pravda* claimed that Swedish diplomats had argued in favour of a conference.[137] The *New York Times,* on the other hand, cited US State Department officials as saying, the 'European members of the North Atlantic Treaty Organization are taking a more sceptical attitude towards the Soviet Union's proposal for a European Security Conference'.[138] In spite of these quarrels, as reiterated by Foreign Minister Ahti Karjalainen to Swedish interlocutors, Finland continued working on the project.

As major states such as Great Britain, the United States, Italy and France had not officially responded to the invitation to attend the conference, the Finnish government considered installing a 'roving ambassador' who would work on the matter.[139] On 30 January 1970, nine months after the invitation had been issued, Martin Hillenbrand of the US State Department's European desk finally handed over Washington's response to the Finnish government. The message from Washington was that the United States was genuinely unenthusiastic due to residual problems of security and disarmament.[140] Trying to make things look better, in a manner quite similar to that used by the Soviets, an official Finnish statement claimed that Washington's response had not been negative.[141]

As mentioned earlier, Eastern European media did try to highlight any perceptions of the Swedish role that were not in line with that of the Swedish government. Eastern European journalists would publicize any domestic criticism of the Swedish government's approach to the security conference. This is nicely illustrated by an *Izvestia* interview with Stellan Arvidsson published on 14 February 1970. A scholar and writer by profession, and a Social Democratic member of the second chamber of the Swedish parliament between 1957 and 1968, Arvidsson was actively involved with organizations favouring the Eastern European regimes.

He had also been one of three hundred representatives, from twenty-three international organizations, originating in twenty-six different countries at the Conférence pour la Sécurité et la Coopération Européennes held in Vienna between 29 November and 1 December 1969.[142] Interviewed by the Soviet paper, Arvidsson argued that the neutral states 'could have been more active'. Sweden, he claimed, supported Finland's initiative to start the practical preparation of the conference. But at the same time', he criticized, 'Stockholm is refusing to normalize relations with the GDR'.[143] Swedish politicians and diplomats generally ignored such criticism of their policy, most likely because it attracted very little public attention.

While Sweden's line remained in harmony with NATO in general and West Germany in particular, its aversion to any early grouping of the neutrals, as proposed and pressed for by the Eastern bloc, eventually created tensions in bilateral relations with other neutral states, such as Austria.

The government in Vienna, led by the conservative chancellor Josef Klaus, agreed that there was no space for the neutral states to act as mediators between the blocs but still wished to shape Austria's strategy in alignment with the other neutrals.[144] Thus, differing perceptions dominated Austro-Swedish relations in 1969–1970.

Vienna started pushing for intensified bilateral consultations between the two countries, as the Austrian policy makers believed that the Warsaw Pact's confidence in Austrian neutrality would be strengthened by close contacts between Austria and the other neutral states. During the seven years prior to that, the only visit that had taken place was private, when Tage Erlander had come to Foreign Minister Kurt Waldheim.[145] More than half a year after the Finnish initiative, the Foreign Ministry still had not given the green light for the meeting at the highest level – of prime or foreign ministers – desired by Austria. Eventually, on 10 December 1969, the Austrians' dissatisfaction culminated in an implicit threat of economic sanctions against Sweden, which was communicated to Stockholm through ambassador Lennart Petri:

> It is, among others, for 'optical reasons', to cite Waldheim, that Austria would gladly see or rather consider itself to be in the need of mutual visits with Sweden on the level of Prime Minister or Minister of Foreign Affairs. The Austrians find it difficult to understand that there would be no time for relations on the mentioned level with neutral Austria while Sweden maintains frequent visits to and from Eastern Europe. According to Austrian understanding, the confidence of the Eastern Powers in Austrian neutrality is strengthened by closest possible and ostentatious relations between Austria and other neutrals. The Swiss government is said to have realized this . . . I would like to add that a higher official, who is closely affiliated with the Socialist Party's leadership, told me that ASEA-Atom's chances to receive the Austrian nuclear power plant contract worth 700 million SEK, [and] regarded important to our nuclear industry, depends on personal interest in this matter to be expressed by the Swedish Prime or Foreign Minister to their Austrian colleagues. This personal interest probably needs to be demonstrated by 1 March.[146]

Two weeks earlier, an internal Swedish report on the general state of ESC discussions and preparations had classified Austria as 'very active'.[147] As in Hungary, the choice of Helsinki as conference venue was seen as a defeat in Vienna. Thus, the new goal of the Austrians was to secure the second stage of the ESC.[148] For this, the Austrians deemed a certain level of activity necessary. Sweden, on the other hand, ignored Vienna's position and expectations and remained keen to maintain what Holsti defined as the role of the 'isolate': a strictly passive line with a minimum of external contacts on all sides.

The Swedish policy makers were thus not willing to soften their stance in favour of cooperation with the other neutral states. In the case of Austria, there were concerns about the capacity of the Austrians to resist increasing pressure from Moscow. Therefore, Sweden chose not to accede to Vienna's wishes as formulated by Walter Wodak, Austria's ambassador to Moscow, in a conversation with his Swedish counterpart, Gunnar Jarring. Wodak had told Jarring that his government hoped that Sweden would work 'hand in hand' with Austria in supporting the ESC.[149] Wachtmeister reacted to this conversation on the very same day in a telegram to the embassy in Vienna:

> The only reason why there is a certain hesitation is the conversation between Wodak and Jarring, which you have been informed about in another telegram today. As you will understand, we do not want to give the Austrians an impression of us being ready to argue the case for Soviet theses regarding the Security conference against the NATO-countries alongside of them.[150]

The major difference between the two neutral countries was Austria's geostrategic position, as the country is located at the heart of Europe and thus was a neighbour of the Warsaw Pact members Czechoslovakia and Hungary. Also, only fourteen years had passed since the ratification of the Austrian State Treaty had re-established the country's sovereignty in 1955. In this region, peace was much more fragile than in the northern part of Europe, as the Prague Spring had proved in 1968. Therefore, anything contributing to an easing of tensions and lasting détente was of great interest to the Austrians. Vienna hoped for a greater balance in continental Europe, a balance that Sweden enjoyed in Scandinavia with NATO members Norway and Denmark in the west and south and with Finland, which had signed a Friendship Treaty with the USSR in 1948, in the east.[151] Ultimately, Austria was ready to act as bridge or mediator, whereas Sweden was not. During this period, therefore, the Swedes made efforts to lower Vienna's expectations for Stockholm's policy.

Despite different starting positions and approaches to the ESC, there were some points of contact as well, such as the question of US and Canadian participation. The Austrian displeasure with the Swedish attitude finally dissipated when Sweden invited representatives of the Bundesministerium für auswärtige Angelegenheiten, the Federal Ministry for Foreign Affairs, to Stockholm for bilateral consultations on the ESC after the turn of the year. During their visit on 9 February 1970, diplomats Wilfried Platzer and Emil Staffelmayr, accompanied by Ambassador Karl Schober and other staff members of the Austrian embassy in Stockholm, elaborated on their country's position to Stellan Bohm, Kaj Falkman, Marc

Giron, Ole Jödahl, Dag Malm and Wilhelm Wachtmeister – the inner circle of the early Swedish ESC diplomats.

The Austrians stated that the Klaus government was of the view that the agenda proposed by the Warsaw Pact foreign ministers' meeting in Prague was 'short' and needed to be 'complemented' but still offered a useful foundation, which, consequently, should not be rejected out of hand. Controversial issues, such as the German Question, the status of Berlin or armed forces reductions and disarmament, were to be left out of the early preparations, the Austrians argued. Therefore, Vienna wanted the neutral states to oppose the widespread scepticism among the NATO members; the idea of a security conference was to be kept alive. The meeting resulted in an agreement between Austria and Sweden to remove from the agenda any proposals and initiatives that were not explicitly approved of within the policies of both blocs. Moreover, bilateral consultations regarding the conference would be intensified.[152]

Back in Vienna, Platzer informed Petri about the successful session in Stockholm but stated that his delegation had gained the impression that Sweden was less positive towards the ESC than was Austria. The difference was, Platzer explained, that 'Austria considers the idea of a conference as good in itself, but Sweden only under particular conditions'.[153] In internal analyses of the meeting in Stockholm, the Austrians described the Swedish position as similar to theirs but more reserved.[154] When Bruno Kreisky entered the chancellor's office three weeks later, Vienna went on the offensive and lobbied even stronger for the conference.

A Strategy of Adjustment

Not until the Prague Declaration of 31 October 1969 had Sweden even considered a re-evaluation of its isolationist role. At their Prague summit, the Eastern ministers had renounced their demand for an exclusively European preparatory meeting. With the Eastern bloc opening up for North American participation, the controversy about US and Canadian participation had been sidelined. As revealed by an internal Swedish evaluation of the Prague Declaration, the assessment of the UD was that the unexpected concessions made by the Kremlin offered new perspectives to other actors, including the smaller states. Consequently, some early content-related preferences were formulated in November 1969. But at the turn of the decade, Sweden's position regarding the ESC discussions was that it would still not take a stand. With this, Stockholm behaved in accordance with the traditional Undénline and upheld *handlingsfrihet*, 'freedom of action', as the most important element in its foreign policy.

Accordingly, a strict form of passive neutrality had to be maintained until substantial changes in East-West relations could be achieved by the greater powers. This made any proactive and constructive contributions during the preparatory stage ultimately impossible. The concept of a more offensive or 'active' foreign policy, later known as *Palmelinjen,* 'the Palmeline', was still in the making. With the superpower détente slowly changing the general framework, a strategic approach was required if Sweden were not to isolate itself completely in the multilateral context of the ESC. The response to this development was a *strategy of adjustment*.[155] The core of the strategy was to remain passive and defensive but at the same time open up to bilateral consultations and discussions of ideas, arguments and concepts. These negotiations would not be launched independently or in cooperation with other neutral states but integrated only bilaterally. In the majority of cases, the explicit notion that any Swedish support must be linked to consensus was added.

A period of intensive bilateral consultations, including meetings between Swedish diplomats and their colleagues from Poland, Yugoslavia, Hungary, Romania and, finally, the Soviet Union, attested to both a new Warsaw Pact offensive and the explicit change of Swedish attitude from *passivity* to *adjustment,* or, in Holsti's terminology, from isolation to independence. Moscow eventually regarded this evolution as an opportunity for making a renewed approach, and on 5 March 1970, the deputy foreign minister of the USSR, Andrei Smirnov, visited Stockholm. During the meeting, Smirnov brought up Ralph Enckell's mission for discussion, pointing out its significance to both Moscow and Stockholm.

The minister expressed the hope of his government that Sweden would offer Finland the 'necessary aid'. In one article published in *Izvestia,* NATO had been accused of implementing an antineutral bloc-to-bloc approach: 'For what reason, one wonders? Why, for instance, must Austria, Sweden and Switzerland, one of the first to support the idea of holding the conference, find themselves overboarded? Is it not because the neutral countries more and more actively play a useful role in the international arena?'[156] Smirnov also proposed a group of three for promoting ESC initiatives, consisting of the USSR, Finland and Sweden. This was in line with the public picture drawn by the Soviet media during the weeks before. 'Enckell is welcome in Stockholm' was all that Jödahl would answer, ignoring Smirnov's proposal.[157] Despite their recent opening up, the Swedes did not want to be defined by what they considered an unjustified role prescription.

Another bloc offensive had been fought off, but it was apparent that the ESC was regaining the momentum it had lost after NATO's Brussels summit in December 1969. Moscow opposed the Western emphasis on bilateralism and claimed that too much emphasis was put on West Germany's ongoing bilateral talks in Warsaw and Moscow. The Soviets argued that it was the other way around and that a security conference would actually improve the conditions for bilateral talks.[158]

The Swedes would not have a quiet minute in March 1970. They rejected rumours claiming that the Nordic countries had decided on a joint coordination group during their consultations in Reykjavik in September 1969.[159] Only a week after Ole Jödahl had turned down Smirnov's proposal, a new approach was presented to Sweden. This time, Romania proposed to convene a preparatory conference at a ministerial or high official level in Bucharest that would be aimed at 'giving support to Finnish ideas'. In Beijing, Hungary's ambassador invited all European colleagues for a lunch, only to surprise his guests by introducing a discussion on the ESC.[160] The Swedes believed the Romanian idea would deflate quickly, as it had not been sponsored by the USSR or Poland; they rejected the offer on 18 March 1970.[161] The following day, Poland sent a request for another visit to Deputy Foreign Minister Willman. The Poles wanted to 'keep the soup warm' and 'talk about their favourite item' now that the atmosphere had dampened down, as Swedish ambassador Wollin remarked ironically in a telegram to Sverker Åström.[162]

An internal Swedish memorandum speculated on whether the rising interest expressed by the smaller Warsaw Pact countries was linked to the Soviet shift towards bilateral consultations with the FRG and an attempt to keep the conference idea alive for its own purposes.[163] This observation was correct, as the Kremlin actively contributed to the development of the Eastern bloc positions during this period.[164] At this early stage, the conference occupied the minds of diplomats but remained only one of many topics addressed at the highest level. When Olof Palme met with Willy Brandt in Bonn, the security conference was overshadowed by Sweden's economic situation between Nordek and the EC and also by West Germany's *Ostpolitik*.[165] This added to the Swedish determination to remain cautious.

As mentioned earlier, prescriptive roles could also originate domestically. This fact persuaded decision makers to portray their role as being in harmony with the expectations of the public. Once the conference had developed into an important subject on the international agenda, by spring 1970 public statements were made on a more regular basis. When Foreign Minister Torsten Nilsson presented the Swedish ESC policy in a speech delivered to the Council of Europe in Strasbourg on 15 April 1970, he clearly emphasized the positive view with which Sweden allegedly regarded the conference.

Nilsson praised the omnipresent desire for improved East-West relations and declared it 'our duty to keep up the momentum of this trend'. A positive atmosphere would certainly not be enough to achieve results on such difficult issues but constituted a necessary precondition for such resolutions. Sweden would welcome the broadening of the conference agenda from security issues, further covering the fields of trade and economic exchange, technology, science and culture. Also, improved opportunities for travel and a freer flow of information between the peoples of Western and Eastern European states should be added to the conference, the Swedish delegation insisted. Thus, Sweden acceded to the broader concept of an 'all-European' conference. Nilsson concluded his speech by stating:

> A conference, if carefully prepared and if conducted in good faith, might well be useful as a means of negotiation between the two big groupings of our continent. But it may also serve as a natural frame for direct co-operation between individual countries in Eastern and Western Europe, outside the context of alliances. The Swedish government has held numerous consultations with other interested governments regarding the conditions for the convening of a Security Conference. These consultations are very useful and will continue on different levels. We believe that the prospects for a European Security Conference will be greater when the negotiations between East and West, which are now in progress and in a preliminary stage, have been going on for some time.[166]

Although the strategy of adjustment implied a declared positive attitude towards the ESC, as manifested in Nilsson's rhetoric, it still did not answer the expectations of West and East European advocates of the ESC. Sweden was still perceived as 'shy and reserved', as the director of the political section of the Belgian Foreign Ministry, Forthomme, characterized its involvement during a meeting between Belgian and Swedish diplomats nine days after Nilsson's Strasbourg speech. Weeks of adjustment had not changed Sweden's image in other capitals as an isolated actor, where role prescriptions were naturally based on Stockholm's otherwise active foreign policy. Wachtmeister responded by claiming, 'So far, there has been a proposal from one military pact to another. In this situation, Sweden does not wish to play a leading role'.[167] During his visit to London between 7 and 9 April 1970, Olof Palme himself stressed the fact that the Soviet goal was to consolidate the status quo through the conference.[168]

The combination of repeated consent without any signs of engagement kept causing problems for Sweden's ambassadors. Poland, for instance, had been pushing for renewed, intensified bilateral consultations on a higher level for months. The delaying tactics brought ambassador Claes Wollin into the same complex situation with his local foreign ministry, just as they had with Lennart Petri in Vienna a few months earlier. Obviously tired of this, Wollin approached 'dear Ole' (Jöhdal), pointing out that the whole issue was getting more and more 'embarrassing, not least for me personally because you are forced to claim repeatedly that we are tremendously interested in these security questions but do not have time to discuss them'. Thus, to grant the Poles a consultation in June or July 1970 would be a 'personal favour', and 'it could be a visit of only one or two days'. The same day, Jödahl replied that the first days in July were the earliest opportunity for the Polish visit.[169]

Wollin's irritation about this matter does not mean that the definition of his role varied significantly from that of his superiors but rather that it became increasingly more difficult to preserve elements of isolation. Apparently, such dramatic appeals had an effect. Other than that, approaches were constantly rejected. The Swedish Riksdag secretly rejected a parliamentary conference, suggested by the Danish *Folketing*, in late May 1970.[170] Finnish efforts were condescendingly thought of as 'signs of them still trying to keep the security conference alive'.[171] By mid-1970, Sweden's attitude could, at best, be described as unresponsive. It could not respond to calls for greater activity, because it had not yet identified its *own* interests. Self-identification is, however, an explicit precondition for adopting an independent role, as demonstrated by Holsti.

A shift occurred when the communiqué from the NATO summit in Rome stated the alliance's certain, though conditional, interest for the first time on 27 May 1970. It acknowledged the growing relaxation of discord in international affairs with reference to the positive development of improved East-West relations, constructive talks on Berlin and discussions on limitations of strategic armaments between Washington and Moscow, among other things.[172] However, NATO expected a clearer response from the East on important subjects, as set out in point 16 of its communiqué:

> Among the subjects to be explored, affecting security and co-operation in Europe, are included in particular:
> (a) the principles which should govern relations between states, including the renunciation of force.
> (b) the development of international relations with a view to contributing to the freer movement of people, ideas and information and to developing co-operation in the cultural, economic, technical and scientific fields as well as in the field of human environment.[173]

Two explanations for this opening up of relations were set out on the Swedish side. According to the analysis of the Swedish embassy in London, the allies now saw opportunities to transform the originally Soviet idea into a tool that would help to 'undermine' the Brezhnev Doctrine. Another memorandum from the Foreign Ministry did not exclude the possibility of NATO making a tactical move to put an end to the Eastern 'monopoly' of the ESC as a political tool.[174] A Swedish working paper drafted shortly after the Rome summit contained information on Norwegian plans to propose a Nordic initiative. For the first time, this was viewed with interest rather than reluctance at the Foreign Ministry in Stockholm.[175]

In the following days, NATO tried to gain neutral support, adopting an attitude towards the neutral states similar to that of the Warsaw Pact. British foreign minister Michael Stewart invited Leif Belfrage, Sweden's ambassador to London, to visit him for a discussion on security and co-operation in Europe.

Stewart informed Belfrage of the British efforts to bring the NATO countries to a course of relaxation through three consecutive stages: bilateral consultations, multilateral consultations or a permanent body and a conference. Belfrage pointed out that questions of military security belonged to the great powers' areas of responsibility and that it was difficult for Sweden to support either side regarding proposals on reductions of armed forces. Belfrage got the impression that Stewart was keen on Sweden's and other neutrals' support of the NATO plan and reported to Stockholm that the British minister 'hopes that we will try to affect the Russians in that direction. He probably has Palme's upcoming visit to Moscow in mind'.[176] Belfrage was correct, as revealed by several reports from Britain's ambassador to Sweden Archibald Ross to the Foreign & Commonwealth Office (FCO) in London.[177] Gradually, even Western calls for Sweden to act as bridge or mediator appeared more regularly.

When Torsten Nilsson spoke to the SSU, the Social Democratic Youth League, in Bommersvik on 10 June 1970, he stressed that Sweden was involved in consultations with numerous governments and welcomed 'the general unity that now seems to prevail regarding the importance of a closer contact of discussion regarding European security problems'. Sweden, he said, would support a conference 'holding prospects of success'.[178] Nilsson's comments attracted a great deal of attention. Officials at the FCO, for instance, generally received them favourably.[179] However, his remarks that a security conference could not overlook disarmament or ignore efforts for 'regional disarmament in our part of the world' did raise questions among British, French and Soviet interlocutors.[180]

Simultaneously, the Swedish Foreign Ministry received Soviet ambassador Maltsev for consultations prior to Palme's visit to Moscow between 16 and 19 June 1970. Again, discussions about procedure and disarmament were central. Jödahl said that he imagined that many would be interested in disarmament issues and that the question of whether or not to include them in the agenda could be left for a later conference, although he emphasized that this was a personal conviction and not a statement of the official Swedish position.[181] The differences between the Swedish-Soviet talks and the Swedish-British consultations were both significant and representative of the relations between the Eastern and Western blocs, respectively. Both were conducted quite cautiously. Swedish diplomats would always say little of substance to Moscow, whereas as soon as NATO signalled receptiveness, Swedish policy opened up. Swedish neutrality was indeed *västorienterad* in security matters.

The Eastern response to NATO's Rome Declaration was not long in coming. On 21 and 22 June, the seven foreign ministers of the Warsaw Pact completed a conference in Budapest by issuing a memorandum comprising three documents relating to the ESC.[182] The memorandum stated that conditions for 'more practicable preparations' were now favourable and counted the United States and Canada as participants.[183] 'Cultural relations' were also added to the agenda. Disarmament, on the other hand, was not addressed as a subject of its own, but the declaration stated that 'security in Europe would be promoted by a discussion of the question concerning the reduction of foreign armed forces on the territories of European states'.

When Poland's deputy foreign minister, Adam Willman, met with Wilhelm Wachtmeister in Stockholm ten days later, he defined in greater detail what the Warsaw Pact states meant by 'practicable'. As talks had progressed rather well, Willman explained, the time for multilateral consultations had now come. One way to do this was a meeting of ambassadors in a neutral country, the so-called tea party solution.[184] Bonn viewed the Budapest Memorandum favourably and deemed it a step in the right direction.[185]

In the Swedish Foreign Ministry's official press release of 8 July 1970, Stockholm, for the first time, took a positive public stand on a substantial Eastern proposal:

> The Foreign Minister welcomed the general unity that now had been achieved on the question of participants to the conference and the closer approach that now had occurred on the essential questions to be discussed regarding security and co-operation in Europe. Considering the unity that is prevailing on a number of basic questions, he expressed the hope that it should now be possible to agree upon the future planning in order to convene an all-European conference holding prospects of success. The Foreign Minister expressed the support of the Swedish Government for the continuing preparatory work in forms upon which interested states can agree.[186]

This had been made possible by the Rome Declaration and the Budapest Memorandum, and it marked the final breach with Sweden's initial ESC policy and the full development of the strategy of adjustment. In 1970, the response from Stockholm to different issues, such as the Danish idea for an interparliamentary conference and a Romanian proposal for a preparatory meeting in Bucharest and the ESC in general, was that Sweden would be supportive in the case of 'general endorsement' (*allmän anslutning*).[187] For the first time, such an endorsement was within reach.

Ostpolitik as Reference Point

The Swedish press release of 8 July 1970 was welcomed by most countries. Hungary's foreign minister, Ferenc Esztergályos, told Sigge Lilliehöök, the Swedish ambassador in Budapest, that the Swedes had come up with the 'first official and unreserved positive' response by any neutral country. The Hungarian minister praised both the wording and the content of the statement as greatly supportive.[188]

During a meeting with Jan De Ranitz, the director of the political section at the Dutch Foreign Ministry, Kaj Falkman argued that both NATO's Rome Declaration *and* the Budapest Memorandum of the Warsaw Pact had been steps in the right direction, claiming that both sides had contributed to a movement closer to each other. At this point, Falkman added, the Swedish government hoped that a procedure allowing a conference to be convened could be agreed on.[189] In his following memorandum, Falkman analysed the relative positions of East and West. He noted that disarmament and military force reductions were the most important issue facing NATO but that there was disagreement on how to discuss them at the ESC and, indeed, whether it was right to do so. The Budapest Memorandum, on the other hand, implied the necessary withdrawal of foreign troops from German soil. This scenario would be nothing short of repudiating the fundamentals of NATO's defence system. But at least, wrote Falkman, the Warsaw Pact seemed to be receptive to discussions.

The most far-reaching Western suggestion was to include 'freer movement of people, ideas and information' before 'cultural, economic, technical and scientific co-operation'. This was considered unrealistic by the Eastern countries, which argued that 'freer movement' would be the natural consequence of 'co-operation'. The 'Harmel Formula', proposing that all participants, including both German states, would meet on the ambassadorial level in a neutral capital to discuss procedural matters, was generally welcomed. The suggestion made by Pierre Harmel, Belgium's foreign minister, was called *salon ouvert*, or Salon des Ambassadeurs.[190]

From a Swedish perspective, a breakthrough in a universal commitment to the conference had been brought about during the summer of 1970. However, the Swedish level of activity still lagged far behind that shown by the other European neutrals: Austria, Finland and Switzerland. The disparity between Stockholm and Vienna was made explicit when Austria published a memorandum on 24 July 1970 that emphasized its positive view on the Finnish initiative and stressed the need for linking MBFR to the security conference.[191]

Immediately after entering office on 21 April 1970, the new *Bundeskanzler*, Bruno Kreisky, started lobbying intensively for a security conference; three months later, the Austrians argued that it would have to deal with substantial troop reductions in Europe. In later speeches – before the Council of Europe on 25 January 1971 and before the Council Conference of the Socialist International in Helsinki fourth months later – Kreisky called for the inclusion of the Middle East in the agenda, and eventually the MBFR became Austria's top priority.[192] By mid-1971, Austria would be one of the most prominent proponents of the project. Sweden remained silent.

The divergence between the neutrals also expressed itself in the Swedish position taken on the Swiss proposal for a system designed for the settlement of disputes. While Finland and Austria were subjected to ever-greater pressure by the Soviet Union due to their geostrategic position, a situation which at times could lessen their credibility among the Western bloc, Switzerland, with its long tradition of neutrality and its less vulnerable location, was more in line with Sweden. Unsurprisingly, internationalism in general and multilateralism in politics were not hailed as important in Switzerland. Its traditional line of neutrality hampered the opening of Swiss politics to multilateralism from 1969 onwards. Switzerland approached the ESC in a way quite similar to that of Sweden: no major issues, such as the German Question, were to be included. The diplomats of the EPD, Switzerland's Foreign Ministry, were constantly monitored by their domestic opponents. Still, Swiss CSCE policy would evolve from scepticism to activism between 1969 and the beginning of multilateral consultations in Dipoli in 1972.[193]

A key role in this evolution was played by an expert group within the Swiss Foreign Ministry headed by Ambassador Rudolf Bindschedler, a renowned professor of international law and the Foreign Ministry's legal advisor. The so-called Bindschedler Report, presented to the EPD on 7 July 1970, recommended Switzerland's active participation, following the rationale that the Eastern bloc would respect Swiss neutrality. With the breakthrough in East-West dialogue following West Germany's Eastern Treaties of 1970, such activism could grow.[194] One year after its establishment, the Bindschedler group contributed to Swiss activity with a proposal on a system of peaceful settlement of disputes. Although rejected by both blocs in the end, it was still of tactical importance, as it forced the Kremlin to take a stance on an uncomfortable question.[195] For Stockholm's part, the Swiss proposal 'did indeed fit with Sweden's view on international matters', as Hans Blix put it to Ambassador Bindschedler when the latter presented the proposal in Stockholm in January 1972.

Sweden refused the idea of publishing the Swiss proposal as a common initiative but did support the proposal nevertheless; in addition, comments on the content of the proposed system were offered by one of the Swedish UD's experts in international law.[196] Switzerland and Sweden were united in the general belief that the superpowers should be responsible for preparing a security conference, and thus they refused to follow up Austrian plans for forming some kind of 'neutral bloc'.[197] But although Switzerland was the neutral country that had most in common with Sweden, Stockholm kept avoiding any direct association between the two countries during the preparatory phase.

Thus, another Swiss proposal on the establishment of close cooperation between the neutral states was refused by the UD, based on the argument of *handlingsfrihet*, 'freedom of action', as the highest principle of Swedish neutrality: 'Wickman explained that Sweden, as is well known, has rejected all proposals from other neutral states on specific groupings. One important element of Swedish neutrality policy was to preserve full freedom of action. Naturally, the Swedish side wanted to discuss the ESC, but this should occur in other forms, bilateral or multilateral'.[198] Despite all of the progress made in the summer of 1970, differing views on the pace of the process remained, rendering a grouping of eventual mediators impossible. An *Atlantic News* article of 14 July pointed out that to the West, it was 'absolutely premature' to think of a meeting of undersecretaries of state.[199] Despite, or probably because of, this, the Finnish Foreign Ministry published a communiqué on a conference at the level of heads of missions as part of the preparations for an ESC only two weeks later.[200]

By inviting the chargés d'affaires rather than ambassadors, both West and East Germany could participate, as only in the Finnish capital did both countries have trade missions. Finland's president, Urho Kekkonen, argued that Bonn's *Ostpolitik* was not a precondition.[201] With this, Finland's position contrasted with that of Sweden. It became increasingly clear that Swedish-Finnish relations in the context of the security conference would remain a story of conflict and misunderstanding. During his visits to Washington and Moscow, Kekkonen had learned that Moscow's belief in the project had been strengthened by the latest development, while Washington was looking at Berlin and SALT as preconditions for real progress. In any case, a preparatory conference of any form was deemed unrealistic before spring 1972.[202]

During the summer break and in the fall, Bonn's bilateral consultations with Moscow and Warsaw dominated the political agenda. Sweden was both clear and adamant that any further steps to be made within the ESC framework depended upon the success or failure of Willy Brandt, its foremost friend. To the Brandt administration, the Treaty of Moscow signed by West Germany and the Soviet Union on 12 August 1970 clearly overshadowed the negotiations on the ESC.[203] The link between the ESC and the Eastern treaties became more apparent and was included in UN General Secretary U Thant's report to the UN General Assembly in September.

During a visit to Stockholm on 24 September, Finland's roving ambassador, Enckell, pointed to the problematic fact that Moscow and Washington had not yet discussed the conference on a bilateral basis. But, Enckell emphasized, since Rome had been a 'positive' step and Budapest a 'realistic' one, the neutral states could now become more active.[204] Also, the many bilateral contacts would have to be summarized first before they could proceed to a series of preparatory meetings.[205] Thus, when Austria asked for Swedish thoughts on the military element of its proposal of 24 July, the diplomats of the UD made it clear that the Swedish government agreed on the need to discuss troop reductions but did not believe the time was ripe.

Wachtmeister told Franz Palla, Austria's chargé d'affaires in Stockholm, that 'we do, for obvious reasons, not wish to actively participate in discussions at this stage'.[206] This was also made clear to the Spanish and Swiss ambassadors in Stockholm, who presented proposals from their governments in October and November.[207] When the negotiations on the Eastern treaties reached their final stages, the Swedes focused on following the development of Bonn's policy and the superpower détente and on analysing the possible prospects they offered.[208] Kaj Falkman also noted that Pompidou and Schumann appeared to look more favourably at the ESC after the conclusion of a French-Soviet communiqué dated 14 October 1970.[209]

The visit of a Swedish delegation under Ole Jödahl to Vienna on 16 and 17 November illustrates the evolution of early Swedish ESC policy. The Swedes had been lagging behind their fellow neutrals only a year earlier. Now, close and explicit consultations were held between the countries. The Austrians stressed the fact that their July memorandum should be understood against the background of their political and military situation, and not as a product of Soviet pressure. The same strategic reasoning was valid for Sweden. Finding themselves in a less-pressured geostrategic position, the Swedes had always appreciated the European status quo more than had the Austrians.

Thus, when Wodak claimed that there was some space for small states to engage in European security, Jödahl replied that mutual armed forces reductions were based on communication between Moscow and Washington and that it was 'not realistic to believe that any side would refrain from the claim for balance maintenance'.[210] As mentioned earlier, disagreement on the extent of cooperation became clear during the meeting since the Swedes rejected Austrian considerations regarding an institutionalization of neutral collaboration at the ESC.[211] Moscow, Vienna and Helsinki all approached Sweden when pushing for renewed efforts to arrange a security conference. But Sweden was waiting for a green light from other directions: the West in general and Bonn in particular. The role of faithful friendship with the latter outweighed any argument presented by the other neutrals, or indeed any Eastern European states.

As negotiations between Bonn and Warsaw progressed promisingly, Finland once again took the initiative in giving impetus to the process. In a second memorandum, dated 24 November 1970, bilateral and multilateral preparations were conflated.[212] And this time, the Swedish response was indeed different from the one to the 5 May initiative. The day after the new Finnish memorandum, Foreign Minister Torsten Nilsson issued a public statement that highlighted Helsinki's contributions and its 'particularly good qualifications for judging the situation in this question'. While the restriction against 'general endorsement' was still valid, Nilsson's statement no longer contained any preconditions regarding the agenda:

> It is therefore encouraging that Finland now makes the appraisal that the bilateral discussions have reached a stage where multilateral contacts might be appropriate. If this should be a generally accepted opinion among the States concerned it should be possible to start unconditional preparatory discussions in Helsinki. Such discussions, in which Sweden would, of course, be prepared to participate, should be able to provide valuable information on the possibilities to convene a conference on security and cooperation holding prospects of success.[213]

The East had accepted US and Canadian participation, bilateral consultations had gone rather well and Brandt's *Ostpolitik* was progressing promisingly. Thus, the most essential conditions requested earlier by Stockholm had been met. Together with the strategy of adjustment, this finally allowed Sweden to shift away from its isolationist role. Support for the Finnish proposal could be issued in time before the signing of the Treaty of Warsaw by West Germany and Poland and before the meetings of NATO in Brussels and the Warsaw Pact in East Berlin in early December 1970, when both blocs would issue new communiqués.[214]

While the Eastern communiqué argued that the preparations made thus far allowed the convocation of a conference, the Western alliance kept linking the future of the CSCE to the resolution of the situation of Berlin. It was a course set by the Americans and the British and forced through against the wishes of smaller states such as Belgium, Denmark and Norway, who had desired a continuation of the positive approach. The initial reaction from Moscow was to accuse Washington and London of undermining the process.[215] But as a matter of fact it was the French who had advocated a tougher line on Berlin at the Brussels convention.[216] From Helsinki, Karjalainen complained that the 'truthful offer has not been rewarded by the NATO countries'; other Finnish officials claimed that 'a country like Finland cannot afford to wait'.[217]

In reality, however, another small step forward had been made, as the latest NATO declaration clearly laid out the preconditions for multilateral contacts for the very first time.[218] Soviet defence minister Andrei Grechko acknowledged this when he visited Stockholm shortly afterwards. Referring to a recent speech of Brezhnev given in Yerevan, Grechko stated that there was reason for optimism regarding Berlin.[219] This optimism was noticeable in a speech delivered by Torsten Nilsson to the Council of Europe in Strasbourg in which he asserted that multilateral consultations, as proposed in the second Finnish memorandum, 'could result in important information for accomplishing a conference on security and cooperation' if all participants agreed that the required conditions were met.[220]

A central working paper, drafted by Ambassador Nils Montan in Bonn, dampened the optimism by voicing the belief that a 'normalization of European affairs cannot be imagined without modus vivendi in the German Question'. The political status of Berlin had been at the heart of negotiations for a while and would remain so. To the West, an inner-German agreement was *the* precondition for further relaxation of tensions between the blocs. By putting the emphasis on 'soft' cooperation, as proposed by Egon Bahr's *Wandel durch Annäherung* (change through rapprochement) strategy, the West had taken steps towards the East, Montan insisted.[221]

The following six months passed without any significant events, as all involved parties were awaiting the results of the Berlin talks. Minor observations were reported to the Foreign Ministry in Stockholm, such as the fact that Finland was cooperating much more closely with an Eastern state like Hungary than with Sweden.[222] In contrast to other international contexts, the Nordic sphere was problematic and did not offer the Swedes the chance to play the role of a regional collaborator. After the initial disagreement following Finland's initiative in May 1969, this was yet another indication of the problematic relationship between Finland and Sweden in the context of the security conference.

France's dismissive policy within NATO and its bilateral contacts with the Soviets caused suspicions among Swedish diplomats about whether Paris was playing a double game.[223] Other than such observations and rumours, the process entered a period of waiting: a 'lull' as Yugoslavian diplomat Djuro Nincic put it during discussions with Lennart Finnmark, Sweden's ambassador in Belgrade.[224] The meeting of the Warsaw Pact foreign ministers in late February 1971 added nothing new to this situation but only paid lip service to earlier declarations by repeating the criticism of the Western position on Berlin.[225]

In the following weeks the Swedes fought off two renewed Soviet inquiries regarding Swedish initiatives. Both times, the Swedes made it clear that one inquiry would now have to wait for the results of the Berlin negotiations before anything further could be done.[226] In consultations with Poland's chargé d'affaires, Wachtmeister claimed that this was not a precondition from a Swedish perspective but rather an acknowledgement of the 'political factum that a large number of countries important to Europe's security have taken this position. This is a political reality which we must live with whether we like it or not'.[227] As demonstrated above, the truth was that solving the issue of Berlin's political status had been a Swedish precondition for several months.

The overall situation remained unchanged throughout the spring of 1971, as Moscow tried to push forward and Washington remained sceptical.[228] To the Swedish Foreign Ministry the standstill was convenient, because important decisions had to be made on economic matters. On 18 March 1971, Olof Palme finally decided against Sweden taking up membership in the EEC. With this, the economic pillar of Sweden's European policy became uncertain, as no one knew what would come out of the negotiations with the EEC and on Nordek. Therefore, the security conference gained further importance to Sweden. Stockholm risked isolating itself completely from European affairs if it did not establish some kind of profile in the process leading up to the security conference.[229] Therefore, the failed EEC membership negotiation precipitated more active participation for Sweden in the lead-up to the security conference.

Between April and August 1971, preparations virtually disappeared from the daily agenda which they had been a part of for almost two years. A number of reports were sent from embassies abroad, but nothing substantial occurred. Reports from Sofia stated that the smaller members of the Warsaw Pact were striving for recognition as independent actors in the ESC process, while René Belding, Sweden's ambassador in Copenhagen, reported rumours that Moscow had tried to use Denmark as its mailman within NATO.[230] After weeks of stagnation, many feared the complete disappearance of the conference idea.

Critical voices were raised against the intractable stand of NATO. At their biannual summit, this time held in Lisbon on 3 and 4 June 1971, the NATO ministers defended their linkage between Berlin and the ESC. But after pressure from France and a number of smaller states, the Americans, Great Britain and the Netherlands agreed to reduce the preconditions to one: Berlin.[231] They also expressed their hope that 'before their next meeting the negotiations on Berlin will have reached a successful conclusion and that multilateral conversations intended to lead to a conference on security and co-operation in Europe may then be undertaken'.[232]

There was no room for manoeuvre, but surely there was for hope. In Stockholm, some important appointments were made during this period. Krister Wickman succeeded Torsten Nilsson as foreign minister on 1 July 1971. Sverker Åström was appointed deputy state secretary of foreign affairs, and Göran Ryding replaced Ingemar Hägglöf as ambassador in Helsinki. Wickman, Åström and Ryding would eventually all play an important role in Swedish CSCE policy.

After months of stagnation in the process leading towards the ESC, Olof Palme gave a press conference on 1 August 1971, concluding his two-day meeting with Social Democrat Party leaders from Austria, Denmark, Finland, Great Britain, Norway and West Germany at his country residence in Harpsund. Palme stated, the 'European security conference proposed by the Eastern bloc is likely to take place in 1972'.[233] Most likely, Palme had received indications about the positive development of the Berlin negotiations from Willy Brandt. Three weeks later, the prime minister explained that Sweden looked favourably on the negotiations for establishing MBFR.

From an early stage, MBFR were a superpower issue, and Sweden could not be expected to seek participation, 'mainly because we have nothing to offer'. On the other hand, MBFR negotiations were perceived as a potential threat to Swedish long-term military planning. Therefore, Stockholm prepared itself for some kind of involvement at a later stage of the negotiations on force reductions.[234] In late August 1971, the Four-Power Agreement on Berlin was finally concluded successfully. Together with the FRG's Eastern treaties, this produced the right conditions for the convocation of a security conference.[235] With this, a new era, manifesting itself in Olof Palme's speech in Landskrona on 28 August, had begun. In his talk, the Swedish prime minister mentioned 'our task', 'duty' and 'responsibility' when speaking of the conference. Palme said:

It is natural for us to support Willy Brandt's *Ostpolitik* and the peace processes it has fuelled. Our responsibility as a European nation does not allow us to distract this political process of historical dimension that has now started in Europe for short-sighted advantages of commercial or other character . . . We cannot stand outside of the reality of Europe. We belong to Europe, for good and for bad.[236]

Conclusion

When Finland responded to renewed Soviet calls for a European security conference and started pushing for support of its own initiative of 5 May 1969, Sweden was in the process of change. After twenty-three years in office, Prime Minister Tage Erlander was succeeded by Olof Palme in fall 1969. Palme, forty-two years old, approached international affairs from a stronger ideological standpoint, but without abolishing the traditional Undén formula of 1956. He quickly established himself as a visible figure in Europe, maintaining close personal ties with other Social Democratic heads of states such as Willy Brandt and Bruno Kreisky.

During Palme's first two years as prime minister, Sweden remained the most passive of all neutral states in the early progress towards the CSCE by adopting a role that corresponded with Holsti's 'isolate'. While the other neutrals – Austria, Finland and Switzerland – driven by varying motives, launched a number of initiatives and pushed for a security and/ or 'all-European' conference, Stockholm remained widely inactive – or, at most, reactive. Finland's initiative in 1969 re-established the idea of a security conference as a whole. Switzerland proposed a system of peaceful settlement of conflicts and put together a group of experts about one and a half years prior to Sweden doing so. Austria declared its positive attitude to the conference from the very beginning and repeatedly mentioned that any obstacles were negotiable. All three countries offered to host preparatory meetings, or even the main conference itself.

Furthermore, on a number of occasions and issues, all of them offered the Foreign Ministry in Stockholm the opportunity to take part in joint initiatives or working groups. Sweden rejected all of these offers and never took any initiative designed to make progress in preparing for a security conference. A later Finnish proposal to appoint Sweden as chair on security matters at the multilateral preparatory talks (MPT) in Dipoli was also turned down.[237] As illustrated by the comparison between Sweden and the other neutrals, noted above, decision makers in Stockholm evaded any effort by Warsaw Pact countries or neutral states to integrate Sweden into some kind of collective activism. Instead, Swedish policy was orientated towards the general state in international affairs, the policy of the superpowers and other actors – primarily Finland and West Germany – and, to a lesser extent, attitudes towards the other neutrals. Indeed, Swedish diplomats tended to refer to forums such as the conference of the Nordic ministers of foreign affairs or NATO ministerial meetings before declaring their own standpoints.[238]

After the Prague Declaration of October 1969, a slight movement towards openness was realized through the implementation of what this author has named a 'strategy of adjustment'. During the year following the Prague meeting, this changed approach met with progress in the general détente. While Richard Nixon and Henry Kissinger remained suspicious of relaxation of tensions in Europe, the West German chancellor, Willy Brandt, launched the *Neue Ostpolitik*. With the help of the 'Change through Rapprochement', as Brandt's chief strategist, Egon Bahr, had defined it in 1963, the Federal Republic of Germany normalized its relations with the nations of Eastern Europe, including the GDR. The Hallstein Doctrine of 1955 – which stated that the FRG would suspend diplomatic relations with any state that recognized the GDR, thereby determining Sweden's postwar relations with the two German states – was finally abolished in 1970.[239] Brandt and Bahr hoped to keep German reunification feasible for future generations with the help of this new strategy.

Acknowledging postwar territorial realities, and despite domestic pressure from the conservative opposition,[240] the Brandt government signed the treaties of Moscow and Warsaw on 12 August and 7 December 1970, respectively. These treaties meant a general breakthrough in Europe and led to a greater belief in future interbloc cooperation. They also paved the way for the Four-Power Agreement, also known as 'Quadripartite Agreement', in Berlin on 3 September 1971, which created the positive climate necessary for continued European security talks. At that point, Swedish policy makers realized that the time was right for evolving from their cautious strategy and adopting an active position that would allow them to contribute to general development in their fields of interest, primarily disarmament. This finally allowed for the definition of its national interests.

It is in the light of this development that we can understand the statements of Torsten Nilsson and Olof Palme as markers of the turning point in the role of Sweden in the early Helsinki Process. The strategy of adjustment offered Sweden greater flexibility to bridge the time gap until the breakthrough in East-West relations in the summer of 1971, when the shift in Swedish policy indicated in Nilsson's statement of July 1970 could finally come into practice. Still, it is not wrong to describe Sweden's role in the two years covered in this chapter as overcautious and isolationist.

The progress of events and the findings presented in this chapter do not fit in with the traditional picture of Sweden's foreign policy during this period. The fact that Sweden gave a wide berth to Europe has earlier been explained by its neutrality policy, which was supposedly in contradiction to the process of European integration per se. Credibility as an essential precondition of a maintainable neutrality policy did not allow membership in the European Community, from a security point of view. Furthermore, the widespread societal and political anti-European Community climate added to the restrictive position.[241] Accordingly, general wariness towards involvement in European matters set limits to any kind of ESC enthusiasm among the political leadership in Stockholm.[242]

At the same time, the evolution from a passive to an active Swedish foreign policy has been defined as marking a shift 'from strategies of adjustment to strategies of change', offering small states the opportunity to ensure their security by contributing to positive change in international affairs.[243] It has also been seen as the necessary response to three implicit lines of conflict that came with the decision to retain neutrality after the emergence of the Cold War.[244] Although participation in a European security conference required no essential commitment comparable to that of taking part in the process of European integration, decision makers in Stockholm did not regard the ESC as a means to allow them to accomplish positive change, as has been shown above. Therefore, this chapter concludes by suggesting further potential reasons for why Sweden remained passive during the earliest stage of the Helsinki Process.

Undoubtedly, the diplomatic staff of the Swedish Ministry for Foreign Affairs paid attention to its country's general framework. Based on this assumption, and in addition to the above-elaborated account, this chapter suggests the significance of the following factors in explaining Sweden's early CSCE policy. First, the idea of a security conference came from 'the wrong side', since Moscow had traditionally been considered the only real 'menace'.[245] The Soviet Union's attempt to use a conference in order to maintain the Brezhnev Doctrine was firmly rejected by Sweden. As phrased by Mikael af Malmborg, 'anyone with the slightest acquaintance with Swedish military planning – and most male citizens had this acquaintance through their military service – knew that there was never talk of more than one enemy'.[246] Stated by diplomat Kaj Falkman, this was also acknowledged by Olof Palme, who considered Sweden a 'vanguard of the U.S. in Europe' in security matters.[247]

Second, Sweden was not exposed to immediate Soviet pressure, as was the case with Finland and to a lesser extent even Austria. Third, the field of greater Swedish interest, disarmament, had yet to be recognized as an integral part of the security conference through a clear link made between the CSCE and the MBFR. Fourth, Stockholm's priority at the time was clearly with global issues treated at the UN, a multilateral forum of much greater interest to Sweden. Finally, Sweden's active foreign policy of the 1970s, the superpower détente and West Germany's New *Ostpolitik* had not reached their apex by 1971.

If we attempt to apply Kalevi Holsti's national role conceptions, Sweden was not willing to take up any role requiring active engagement, such as 'mediator', 'bridge'(-builder) or 'active independent' in the years 1969 to 1971. Such involvement was continuously refused, although it would have corresponded with the role prescriptions of other states. Instead, the role performed by Sweden during this period is best characterized as a blend of what Holsti defined as an 'isolate', a 'faithful friend' and, to a much lesser extent, an 'independent'. The friendly relationship with the West does not indicate some kind of secret membership in NATO, however. It should rather be understood as Sweden's attempt not to oppose policies and goals of governments with which it shared core values. Sweden acted in accordance with its own modest self-conception, argued for the participation of the United States and Canada from the very beginning and remained faithful to Willy Brandt and the West German government throughout the entire period.

In early 1969, prior to Palme's and Brandt's inaugurations, Stockholm could even be labelled as performing only an isolationist role, as the government did not wish to be addressed at all, and was strongly critical of Finland's initiative of 5 May. Although declaring commitment to European security in official doctrine and public statements, both political leadership and the diplomatic staff in Stockholm remained inactive during the emergence of a political process that generated great interest among the vast majority of European states. This fact most probably indicates another important aspect of the antagonism between Sweden's role in European affairs and global politics during the years of détente.

Notes

1. Kurt Almqvist (ed.), *Betydelsen av revolutionsåret 1968: Kårhusockupationen 40 år* (Stockholm: Atlantis, 2008); Sven-Olof Josefsson, 'Året var 1968: universitetskris och studentrevolt i Stockholm och Lund', PhD dissertation (University of Gothenburg, 1996).
2. Ekengren, 'How Ideas Influence Decision-Making', 125–27. For the broader context, see Ulf Bjereld and Marie Demker, *I Vattumannens tid?: en bok om 1968 års auktoritetsuppror och dess betydelse i dag* (Stockholm: Hjalmarson & Högberg, 2005); Kjell Östberg,

1968 när allting var i rörelse: sextiotalsradikaliseringen och de sociala rörelserna (Stockholm: Södertörns högskola, 2002).
3. Engh, 'Conscience', 65–82.
4. See, for example, Per Cramér, *Neutralitetsbegreppet [: den permanenta neutralitetens utveckling]* (Stockholm: Norstedt, 1989).
5. Fischer regards historical roots, domestic context and geostrategic position as the most important factors in this respect; see Fischer, *Neutral Power*, 55.
6. Originally acting as 'the Group of Nine', Austria, Belgium, Bulgaria, Denmark, Finland, Hungary, Romania, Sweden and Yugoslavia had cosponsored Resolution 2129(XX) in 1965. The Netherlands joined this group of small states by parliamentary decision in 1967. Cooperation ceased in the aftermath of the Prague Spring the year after. Resolution 2129 advocated 'actions on the regional level with a view to improving good neighbourly relations among European States having different social and political systems' and welcomed 'the growing interest in the development of good neighbourly relations and co-operation among European States having different social and political systems, in the political, economic, technical, scientific, cultural and other fields'. Available from https://documents-dds-ny.un.org/doc/RESOLUTION/GEN/NR0/218/92/IMG/NR021892.pdf?OpenElement (accessed 25 November 2015). See also Fischer, *Neutral Power*, 76; Leatherman, 'Engaging East and West', 239–41.
7. On the history of détente, see Jussi M. Hanhimäki, 'Détente in Europe, 1962–1975', in Leffler and Westad, *Crises and Détente*, 198–218; Möckli, *European Foreign Policy;* Loth and Soutou, *Making of Détente;* Loth, *Overcoming the Cold War;* Garthoff, *Détente and Confrontation.*
8. Fischer, *Die Grenzen der Neutralität.*
9. For a comprehensive introduction to neutral collaboration in Cold War Europe from the fall of the Iron Curtain to the rise of détente, see Fischer, *Die Grenzen der Neutralität*, 29–80.
10. Csaba Békés, 'The Warsaw Pact, the German Question and the CSCE Process', in Oliver Bange and Gottfried Niedhart (eds.), *Helsinki 1975 and the Transformation of Europe* (New York: Berghahn Books, 2008), 114–24.
11. For the French translation, see 'Message adressé par les États membres du Pacte de Varsovie à tous les pays Européens (Budapest, 17 mars 1969)', available from http://www.cvce.eu/obj/message_adresse_par_les_etats_membres_du_pacte_de_varsovie_a_tous_les_pays_europeens_budapest_17_mars_1969-fr-ad406a56-f121-4d4e-9721-87700f88211e.html (accessed 3 August 2016). For the Russian original, see www.ena.lu/appeal_warsaw_pact_member_states_european_countries_budapest_17_march_1969-020003090.html (accessed 25 November 2015). An unofficial Swedish translation can be found in Falkman, 'Europeisk säkerhetskonferens', 26 March 1969, File 1, Vol. 26, HP 79, UD, RA.
12. Svetlana Savranskaya, 'Unintended Consequences: Soviet Interests, Expectations and Reactions to the Helsinki Final Act', in Oliver Bange and Gottfried Niedhart (eds.), *Helsinki 1975 and the Transformation of Europe* (New York: Berghahn Books, 2008), 176–78.
13. Romano, *Détente*, 56–61.
14. Ibid., 61.
15. Nyström to UD, and Kronvall to Falkman, 21 March 1969, File 1, Vol. 26, HP 79, UD, RA.
16. Interestingly, Austria and Finland were also listed among those Western states expected to react positively to the declaration. See Falkman, 'Bakgrunden till förslaget om en europeisk säkerhetskonferens', 26 March 1969, File 1, Vol. 26, HP 79, UD, RA.
17. Romano, *Détente*, 71–78; Yamamoto, 'Britain, France and West Germany', 65–68.

18. Hakkarainen, *State of Peace*, 23–28.
19. See footnote 16, this chapter.
20. Gilde, *Österreich im KSZE-Prozess*, 59–61; Reimaa, *Helsinki Catch*, 20–21.
21. Rosin, *Die Schweiz im KSZE-Prozeß*, 48.
22. Swedish media put little emphasis on the Budapest Memorandum. See *Dagens Nyheter* of 18 March 1969, Mft 7, R1133, KB [Kungliga Biblioteket].
23. The Soviets approached Finland in a similar fashion; see Thomas Fischer, 'A Mustard Seed Grew into a Bushy Tree': The Finnish CSCE Initiative of 5 May 1969'. *Cold War History* 9(2), 2009, 183 and Reimaa, *Helsinki Catch*, 20.
24. Wachtmeister, 'Samtal med ungerske ambassadören' and Wachtmeister, 'Europeisk säkerhetskonferens', 31 March 1969, File 1, Vol. 26, HP 79, UD, RA.
25. Giron to Heads of Embassies, 14 April 1969, File 1, Vol. 26, HP 79, UD, RA.
26. Hungarian Embassy Stockholm to UD, Note verbale, 31 March 1969, File 1, Vol. 26, HP 79, UD, RA.
27. Wachtmeister, 'Samtal med ungerske ambassadören', 31 March 1969, File 1, Vol. 26, HP 79, UD, RA.
28. Others have defined (elements of) this role as a 'catalyst' (Fischer), 'intermediary' or a 'third party role' (Zielinski). See Thomas Fischer, 'Bridging the Gap between East and West: The N+N as Catalysts of the CSCE Process, 1972–1983', in Poul Villaume and Odd Arne Westad (eds.), *Perforating the Iron Curtain: European Détente, Transatlantic Relations, and the Cold War* (Copenhagen: Museum Tusculanum Press, 2010), 143–78; Leatherman, 'Engaging East and West', 149–52, 437–41, 448–74; Zielinski, *Die neutralen und blockfreien Staaten*, 181–90.
29. These were Washington, London, Paris, Bonn, Rome, The Hague, Brussels and Ottawa. Wachtmeister to Embassies, 'Från polchefen', 31 March 1969, File 1, Vol. 26, HP 79, UD, RA.
30. Belding to Wachtmeister, 'Danska synen på förslaget om europeisk säkerhetskonferens', 31 March 1969; Lagerfelt to UD, 1 April 1969 and Lilliehöök, 'Synpunkter i vissa länder på Budapest-Appellen om europeisk säkerhetskonferens', 10 April 1969, File 1, Vol. 26, HP 79, UD, RA.
31. Montan to Wachtmeister, 3 April 1969, File 1, Vol. 26, HP 79, UD, RA.
32. Hakkarainen, *State of Peace*, 31.
33. Öberg, 'Europeisk säkerhetskonferens', 8 April 1969, File 1, Vol. 26, HP 79, UD, RA.
34. Brilioth to UD, 14 April 1969, File 1, Vol. 26, HP 79, UD, RA. See also Yamamoto, 'Britain, France and West Germany', 66–69.
35. Romano, *Détente*, 71–72.
36. Final Communiqué, 11 April 1969, available from www.nato.int/docu/comm/49-95/c690410a.htm (accessed 25 November 2015).
37. Békés, 'Warsaw Pact', 121.
38. On Romania, see Mihail E. Ionescu, 'Romania, *Ostpolitik* and the CSCE, 1967–1975', in Oliver Bange and Gottfried Niedhart (eds.), *Helsinki 1975 and the Transformation of Europe* (New York: Berghahn Books, 2008), 129–43.
39. Jarring to UD, Cipher telegram, 14 April 1969 and 15 April 1969, File 1, Vol. 26, HP 79, UD, RA. Jarring's telegram of 14 April is cited in a memorandum written by Lilliehöök, 16 April 1969, File 1, Vol. 26, HP 79, UD, RA.
40. 'Offizieller Besuch des schwedischen Ministerpräsidenten Erlander vom 9./10. April 1969', 10 April 1969, 594, 1980/83, E 2001(E), Schweizerisches Bundesarchiv Berne [BAR].
41. Falkman, 'Europeisk säkerhetskonferens', Supplement 5: 'Samtal i Rumänien om en europeisk säkerhetskonferens (Utdrag ur överläggningarna mellan statsministrarna

Erlander och Maurer i Bukarest den 14 april 1969)', 17 April 1969, File 1, Vol. 26, HP 79, UD, RA.
42. Erlander's statements are cited in *Dagens Nyheter;* see Lilliehöök, 'Pressnotiser angående statsministerns och utrikesministerns uttalanden om en europeisk säkerhetskonferens vid de officiella besöken i Schweiz och Rumänien i april 1969', 30 May 1969, File 2, Vol. 26, HP 79, UD, RA
43. Finnish Embassy Stockholm, 'P.M.', 5 May 1969, File 2, Vol. 26, HP 79, UD, RA; Leatherman, 'Engaging East and West', 260–61.
44. Friedman to UD, 'Västtyskland och Budapestappellen', 30 April 1969, File 1, Vol. 26, HP 79, UD, RA.
45. On the intensification of Polish-Soviet relations in this context, see Wanda Jarzabek, 'Preserving the Status Quo or Promoting Change: The Role of the CSCE in the Perception of Polish Authorities', in Oliver Bange and Gottfried Niedhart (eds.), *Helsinki 1975 and the Transformation of Europe* (New York: Berghahn Books, 2008), 147.
46. Jödahl, 'Besök av polske ambassadören', 29 April 1969, File 1, Vol. 26, HP 79, UD, RA.
47. Jödahl, 'Besök av ambassadör Enckell', 5 May 1969, File 2, Vol. 26, HP 79, UD, RA. See also Hans-Adolf Jacobsen (ed.), *Sicherheit und Zusammenarbeit in Europa (KSZE): Analyse und Dokumentation* (Cologne: Verlag Wissenschaft und Politik, 1973), 128; Karl-Friedrich Schramm (ed.), *Sicherheitskonferenz in Europa: Dokumentation 1954–1972: die Bemühungen um Entspannung und Annäherung im politischen, militärischen, wirtschaftlichen, wissenschaftlich-technologischen und kulturellen Bereich* (Frankfurt a.M.: Metzner, 1972), 654.
48. For the background of the initiative and its value to Finnish foreign policy, see Fischer, 'Mustard Seed', 177–201 and Reimaa, *Helsinki Catch*, 21–26.
49. Fischer, 'Mustard Seed', 187.
50. Huldtgren and Erlander received the note on a Saturday, which might explain why many foreign ministry officials still seemed surprised when the Finnish move was made public two days later. Huldtgren to UD, 3 May 1969. Cited in Falkman, 'Europeisk säkerhetskonferens', 5 May 1969, File 2, Vol. 26, HP 79, UD, RA.
51. Huldtgren to Wachtmeister, 6 May 1969, File 2, Vol. 26, HP 79, UD, RA.
52. This rather obscure procedure was kept secret immediately afterwards, and on TV Kekkonen gave wrong information on the number of participants at the Tamminiemi meeting. Fischer, 'A Mustard Seed', 183–87.
53. On Enckell's mission, see Fischer, 'Mustard Seed', 187–91.
54. This view was also expressed to Karjalainen by Sweden's ambassador to Helsinki, Ingemar Hägglöf. See Hägglöf to UD, 6 May 1969, File 2, Vol. 26, HP 79, UD, RA.
55. Jödahl, 'Besök av ambassadör Enckell', 5 May 1969, File 2, Vol. 26, HP 79, UD, RA.
56. Af Sillén to Swedish embassies in Washington and Ottawa, 'Utrikesministerns anförande om östvästförbindelserna i Europarådets ministerkommitté', 8 May 1969, File 2, Vol. 26, HP 79, UD, RA.
57. See Wachtmeister, 'Samtal med Finlands ambassadör om europeisk säkerhetskonferens', 9 May 1969 and Jarring to UD, 6 May 1969, File 2, Vol. 26, HP 79, UD, RA.
58. Petri to Wachtmeister, 14 May 1969; De Besche to UD, 'Ang. Europeiska säkerhetskonferens', 21 May 1969, File 2, Vol. 26, HP 79, UD, RA; 157. 487–4, 14 May 1969, II-Pol/Schweden, Bundesministerium für auswärtige Angelegenheiten [BMfaA], Österreichiches Staatsarchiv/Archiv der Republik, Vienna [ÖStA/AdR].
59. Sundberg, 'Arbetspapper', 23 May 1969, File 2, Vol. 26, HP 79, UD, RA. The conclusion of the Swedes was based on their own assessments as well as on the ambiguous statements made by Finnish officials. While Kekkonen and the Foreign Ministry denied any kind of Soviet pressure, their ambassador in Budapest stated that Finland

had been 'requested' to engage in exploratory bilateral discussions. See Lilliehöök to Wachtmeister, 'Ungern, Budapest-appellen och den finska inbjudan till säkerhetskonferens', 7 May 1969, File 2, Vol. 26, HP 79, UD, RA.
60. 'Protokoll', 10 June 1969, II-Pol/Schweden, BMfaA, ÖStA/AdR.
61. See Lilliehöök in footnote 59 and Wachtmeister, 'Samtal med rumänske ambassadören', 13 May 1969, File 2, Vol. 26, HP 79, UD, RA.
62. Rössel to Nilsson, 'Konferens om europeiska säkerhetsfrågor', 5 May 1969, File 2, Vol. 26, HP 79, UD, RA.
63. Wachtmeister, 'Samtal med rumänske ambassadören', 13 May 1969, File 2, Vol. 26, HP 79, UD, RA.
64. Sten Ottosson, *Sverige mellan öst och väst: Svensk självbild under kalla kriget* (Gothenburg: University of Gothenburg, 2001), 25.
65. Åström to Wachtmeister, 14 May 1969, File 2, Vol. 26, HP 79, UD, RA.
66. Sundberg, 'Arbetspapper', 23 May 1969, File 2, Vol. 26, HP 79, UD, RA.
67. Wachtmeister to Lagerfelt, 'Rumänskt förslag om år 1970 som ett år för 'Fredligt samarbete och säkerhet i Europa', 19 May 1969; Wachtmeister to Leifland/Falkman, 'Europeisk säkerhetskonferens', 20 May 1969; Wachtmeister to Belfrage, Cipher telegram 34, 20 May 1969, File 2, Vol. 26, HP 79, UD, RA.
68. Bagge to Wachtmeister, 23 May 1969, File 2, Vol. 26, HP 79, UD, RA.
69. De Besche to UD, 'Ang. Europeiska säkerhetskonferens', 21 May 1969, File 2, Vol. 26, HP 79, UD, RA.
70. Cf. Yamamoto, 'Britain, France and West Germany', 70–79. Montan to Wachtmeister, 'Europeisk säkerhetskonferens', 22 May 1969; Lagerfelt to Wachtmeister, 'Finsk propå om europeisk säkerhetskonferens', 22 May 1969; Edling to Wachtmeister, 29 May 1969, File 2; Eng to Nilsson, 'Italienarnas reaktion på det finska initiativet till en europeisk säkerhetskonferens', 22 May 1969; Hichens-Bergström to Wachtmeister, 'Europeisk säkerhetskonferens', 2 June 1969; Bergenstråhle to Wachtmeister, 'Europeisk säkerhetskonferens', 11 June 1969; Swedish Embassy London to UD, 'Brittisk syn på förslaget om en europeisk säkerhetskonferens', 24 June 1969, File 3, Vol. 26, HP 79, UD, RA.
71. Hakkarainen, *State of Peace*, 33–39.
72. Wachtmeister to Leifland and Falkman, 'Europeisk säkerhetskonferens', 20 May 1969, File 2, Vol. 26, HP 79, UD, RA.
73. de Besche to UD, 'Ang. Europeiska säkerhetskonferens', 21 May 1969, File 2, Vol. 26, HP 79, UD, RA.
74. Petri to UD, 'Europeisk säkerhetskonferens', 29 May 1969, File 3, Vol. 26, HP 79, UD, RA.
75. Holmquist to Wachtmeister, 'Europeisk säkerhetskonferens', 2 June 1969, File 3, Vol. 26, HP 79, UD, RA. See also Rosin, *Die Schweiz im KSZE-Prozeß*, 49–50.
76. Ingemar Hägglöf to Wachtmeister, 2 June 1969, File 3, Vol. 26, HP 79, UD, RA.
77. Åström to Wachtmeister, 30 May 1969, File 2, Vol. 26, HP 79, UD, RA.
78. Wachtmeister, 'Europeisk säkerhetskonferens', 1 July 1969, File 3, Vol. 26, HP 79, UD, RA.
79. Pressmeddelande UD, 10 July 1969, File 3, Vol. 26, HP 79, UD, RA.
80. Brezhnev's exact statement was 'When forces that are hostile to socialism try to turn the development of some socialist country towards capitalism, it becomes not only a problem of the country concerned, but a common problem and concern of all socialist countries'.
81. Reimaa, *Helsinki Catch*, 15–18.
82. Malm, 'Samtal med tyske chargé d'affaires', 15 July 1969, File 4, Vol. 27, HP 79, UD, RA.

83. Obermayer to AA, 'Das Prinzip der "engagierte Neutralität" und seine Auswirkungen auf die Außenpolitik Schwedens', 18 December 1968, 1473, Bestand [B] 31, Politisches Archiv des Auswärtigen Amtes [PAAA].
84. Von Seth, 'Läget beträffande europeiska säkerhetskonferensen', 20 August 1969, File 4, Vol. 27, HP 79, UD, RA.
85. See, for example, the Polish request for Swedish support in NPT talks with Bonn. Giron, 'Polska synpunkter på frågan om en europeisk säkerhetskonferens och icke-spridningsavtalet', 22 July 1969, File 4, Vol. 27, HP 79, UD, RA.
86. Huldtgren, 'Ytterligare svar på Finlands memorandum om en europeisk säkerhetskonferens', 18 July 1969, File 4, Vol. 27, HP 79, UD, RA.
87. Lagerfelt to Wachtmeister, 'Europeisk säkerhetskonferens', 16 July 1969, File 4, Vol. 27, HP 79, UD, RA.
88. Kronvall to UD, 'Med polsk kommentar om Sverige och säkerhetskonferensen', 19 August 1969; von Seth, 'Läget beträffande europeiska säkerhetskonferensen', 20 August 1969, File 4, Vol. 27, HP 79, UD, RA File 4, Vol. 27, HP 79, UD, RA. See also Jarzabek, 'Hope and Reality', 11–29.
89. Björk, 'Samtal med vice utrikesminister Winiewicz den 1 September 1969', 1 September 1969, File 4, Vol. 27, HP 79, UD, RA.
90. 'Aussprache des Herrn Bundesministers mit dem schwedischen Aussenminister', 18 September 1969, II-Pol/Schweden, BMfaA, ÖStA/AdR.
91. Wachtmeister, 'Samtal med belgiske ambassadören om europeisk säkerhetskonferens', 24 September 1969, File 4, Vol. 27, HP 79, UD, RA.
92. Lagerfelt to Wachtmeister, 'Säkerhetskonferensen', 18 September 1969, File 4, Vol. 27, HP 79, UD, RA.
93. Wachtmeister to Lagerfelt, 'Säkerhetskonferensen', 23 September 1969, File 4, Vol. 27, HP 79, UD, RA.
94. Giron, 'Schweiziske kabinettssekreteraren Micheli om frågan om en europeisk säkerhetskonferens', 22 September 1969; and Wachtmeister, 'Samtal med belgiske ambassadören om europeisk säkerhetskonferens', 24 September 1969, File 4, Vol. 27, HP 79, UD, RA.
95. Micheli to EPD, 'Voyage en Pologne, Finlande et Suède du 8 au 23 septembre 1969', 25 September 1969, 766, 1987/78, E 2001(E), BAR.
96. Hakkarainen, *State of Peace*, 39–53; Yamamoto, 'Britain, France and West Germany', 74–82.
97. A handwritten comment on the report adds that Karjalainen did not believe anything substantial would happen before the NATO summit in December. See Von Seth, 'Läget beträffande europeiska säkerhetskonferensen', 20 August 1969, File 4, Vol. 27, HP 79, UD, RA.
98. Finnish Foreign Ministry to UD, '22 jakande svar', 18 September 1969, File 4, Vol. 27, HP 79, UD, RA; Yamamoto, 'Britain, France and West Germany', 69–71.
99. Åström to UD, 'För polchefen', 2 October 1969, File 4, Vol. 27, HP 79, UD, RA.
100. Ingemar Hägglöf to Leifland, 'President Kekkonen om ett europeiskt fredssystem', 23 September 1969, File 4, Vol. 27, HP 79, UD, RA.
101. Rössel to Nilsson, 9 October 1969; Ingemar Hägglöf to Nilsson, 27 October 1969, File 4, Vol. 27, HP 79, UD, RA.
102. Wollin to Wachtmeister, '53 För chefen av politiska avdelningen. Om det idag påbörjade mötet utanför Prag för utrikesministrarna i Warszawapaktsländerna kan här följande noteras', 30 October 1969, File 4, Vol. 27, HP 79, UD, RA.

103. Declaration of the Consultative Meeting of the Ministers of Foreign Affairs of the Warsaw Treaty Member States; see Czechoslovakian Embassy Stockholm to UD, 31 October 1969, File 4, Vol. 27, HP 79, UD, RA. See also Békés, 'Warsaw Pact', 121–23.
104. Hägglöf to UD, '60 Re europeiska säkerhetskonferensen', 31 October 1969, File 4, Vol. 27, HP 79, UD, RA.
105. Leatherman, 'Engaging East and West', 263–65.
106. On the earlier power struggle between the chancellery and the AA, see Hakkarainen, *State of Peace*, 47–49. For a broader account of West Germany's Eastern policy, see Stefan Creuzberger, *Westintegration und Neue Ostpolitik. Die Außenpolitik der Bonner Republik* (Berlin: be.bra verlag, 2009); Arne Hofmann, *The Emergence of Détente in Europe: Brandt, Kennedy and the Formation of Ostpolitik* (London: Routledge, 2007); Julia Von Dannenberg, *The Foundations of Ostpolitik: The Making of the Moscow Treaty between West Germany and the USSR* (Oxford; New York: Oxford University Press, 2008).
107. Wollin to Jödahl, 'Polen och säkerhetskonferensen', 13 November 1969, File 5, Vol. 27, HP 79, UD, RA. For a broader description of the Soviet-Polish dispute, see Jarzabek, 'Hope and Reality', 17–28.
108. Falkman, 'Pragmötet om europeiska säkerhetskonferensen', 11 November 1969, File 5, Vol. 27, HP 79, UD, RA.
109. Falkman, 'Säkerhetskonferensen', 10 November 1969, File 5, Vol. 27, HP 79, UD, RA, citing a cable of 4 November by ambassador Claes Wollin; Falkman, 'Säkerhetskonferensen', 11 November 1969, File 5, Vol. 27, HP 79, UD, RA, citing a cable of 6 November by ambassador Claes Wollin.
110. Zhukov was a member of *Pravda*'s editorial board and one of the Soviet Union's most renowned political commentators. His comment of 11 November focused on the political aspects of the ESC, while Troyanovsky's article two days later elaborated on its economic aspects. See Jarring to UD, 'Sovjetiska kommentarer beträffande den europeiska säkerhetskonferensen', 14 November 1969, File 5, Vol. 27, HP 79, UD, RA.
111. Jarring to UD, Telegram 332, 14 November 1969, File 5, Vol. 27, HP 79, UD, RA.
112. Jarring to UD, 'President Podgorny uttalar sig om de europeiska säkerhetsfrågorna', 14 November 1969, File 5, Vol. 27, HP 79, UD, RA.
113. Yamamoto, 'Britain, France and West Germany', 83; Romano, *Détente*, 75–76.
114. Finnmark to Wachtmeister, 'Europeiska säkerhetskonferensen', 14 November 1969, File 5, Vol. 27, HP 79, UD, RA.
115. Rappe to Wachtmeister, 'Rumänska ministerkontakter med holländska och belgiska regeringscheferna', 7 November 1969, File 5, Vol. 27, HP 79, UD, RA.
116. Wachtmeister to Swedish Embassy Bonn, 11 November 1969, File 5, Vol. 27, HP 79, UD, RA.
117. Jarring to UD, Cipher telegram 346, 'Från ett samtal med västtyske ambassadören Allardt antecknar jag följande', 24 November 1969, File 5, Vol. 27, HP 79, UD, RA.
118. See Hakkarainen, *State of Peace*, ch. 3; Senoo, *Irrweg*, chs. 4 and 6.
119. Montan to UD, Telegram 893, 12 November 1969 and Cipher telegram 53, 13 November 1969, File 5, Vol. 27, HP 79, UD, RA.
120. Interest in Eastern Europe was reported by several embassies; see, for example, the report from Budapest in Lilliehöök to Wachtmeister, 'Säkerhetskonferensen', 13 November 1969, File 5, Vol. 27, HP 79, UD, RA.
121. This can also be said about Austrian chancellor Bruno Kreisky. Austria was, nevertheless, much less significant to Sweden due to Austria's own problematic relationship with the Soviet Union. The topic of this social democratic triangle remains heavily underresearched, as pointed out by Oliver Rathkolb, 'Brandt, Kreisky and Palme

as Policy Entrepreneurs: Social Democratic Networks in Europe's Policy Towards the Middle East', in Wolfram Kaiser, Brigitte Leucht and Michael Gehler (eds.), *Transnational Networks in Regional Integration: Governing Europe 1945–83* (New York: Palgrave Macmillan, 2010), 152–53.
122. Yamamoto, 'Britain, France and West Germany', 84–89; Senoo, *Irrweg*, 116–23. See also Falkman, 'Läget beträffande europeiska säkerhetskonferensen', 27 November 1969, File 5, Vol. 27, HP 79, UD, RA.
123. Gunnar Hägglöf to Nilsson, 'Frankrike och säkerhetskonferensen', 22 November 1969, File 5, Vol. 27, HP 79, UD, RA.
124. Belfrage to Wachtmeister, 'Brittisk syn på en europeisk säkerhetskonferens', 25 November 1969, File 5, Vol. 27, HP 79, UD, RA. See also, Romano, *Détente*, 74–75; Yamamoto, 'Britain, France and West Germany', 90–92.
125. Falkman, 'Läget beträffande europeiska säkerhetskonferensen', 27 November 1969, File 5, Vol. 27, HP 79, UD, RA.
126. UD to Swedish Embassy Moscow and Swedish UN Delegation New York, 'Sovjetiske ambassadören hos utrikesministern', 2 December 1969, File 5, Vol. 27, HP 79, UD, RA.
127. See, for example, Finnmark to Wachtmeister, 27 November 1969, File 5, Vol. 27, HP 79, UD, RA.
128. Romano, *Détente*, 76.
129. Garthoff, *Détente and Confrontation*, 132; Romano, *Détente*, 175.
130. Falkman, 'Läget beträffande europeiska säkerhetskonferensen', 22 January 1970, File 6, Vol. 27, HP 79, UD, RA.
131. Jarring to UD, 'Artikel om den alleuropeiska säkerhetskonferensen', 8 December 1969 and Bergquist to UD, 'Bryssel-kommunikén i polsk press', 10 December 1969, File 5, Vol. 27, HP 79, UD, RA.
132. Huldtgren to Wachtmeister, 'Artikel om säkerhetskonferensen', 16 December 1969, File 6, Vol. 27, HP 79, UD, RA; Reimaa, *Helsinki Catch*, 28.
133. Jarring to UD, Cipher telegram 368, 12 December 1969, File 5, Vol. 27, HP 79, UD, RA.
134. Grönwall, 'Läget betr. den europeiska säkerhetskonferensen', 26 February 1970, File 6, Vol. 27, HP 79, UD, RA; Békés, 'The Warsaw Pact', 123.
135. Wachtmeister to Göransson, 'Den europeiska säkerhetskonferensen', 19 December 1969 and Grönwall, 'Svensk-jugoslaviska samtal om säkerhetskonferensen', 29 December 1969, File 6, Vol. 27, HP 79, UD, RA.
136. Falkman, 'Samtal med Malita om säkerhetskonferensen', 29 January 1970, File 6, Vol. 27, HP 79, UD, RA.
137. Jarring to UD, 'Deklaration om den alleuropeiska samarbetskonferensen', 13 January 1970, File 6, Vol. 27, HP 79, UD, RA. Moscow continued its efforts to pressure the Nordic states publicly. One article asserted that in Sweden 'many circles among the public, the Swedish government and the political parties argue in favour of an all-European conference to be convened as soon as possible'; see Jarring to UD, 'Pravda-artikel om Norden och den europeiska säkerheten', 23 January 1970, File 6, Vol. 27, HP 79, UD, RA.
138. Swedish Delegation New York to UD, Telegram 49 'För polchefen och pol II', 15 January 1970, File 6, Vol. 27, HP 79, UD, RA.
139. Ingemar Hägglöf to UD, 'Karjalainen om säkerhetskonferensen', 13 January 1970, File 6, Vol. 27, HP 79, UD, RA. See also Reimaa, *Helsinki Catch*, 31–34.
140. Ingemar Hägglöf to UD, Cipher telegram 11 'Den europeiska säkerhetskonferensen. Hbr Hägglöf-Wachtmeister 30 januari 1970', 3 February 1970, File 6, Vol. 27, HP 79, UD, RA.
141. Ingemar Hägglöf to Wachtmeister, 'Den europeiska säkerhetskonferensen', 3 February 1970, File 6, Vol. 27, HP 79, UD, RA.

142. Bergenstråhle to UD, 'Ang. internationell konferens i Wien om europeisk säkerhet och samarbete', 20 March 1970, File 7, Vol. 28, HP 79, UD, RA.
143. Westerberg to UD, Telegram 111 'TASS har den fjortonde dennes distribuerat följande Izvestia-interview med Stellan Arvidsson', 16 February 1970, File 6, Vol. 27, HP 79, UD, RA.
144. Lilliehöök to Leifland, 'Säkerhetskonferensen', 10 December 1969, File 5, Vol. 27, HP 79, UD, RA.
145. Petri to UD, 10 December 1969, File 5, Vol. 27, HP 79, UD, RA.
146. Ibid.
147. Falkman, 'Läget beträffande europeisk säkerhetskonferensen. 'Österrike' in section 'III. Övriga reaktioner', 27 November 1969, File 5, Vol. 27, HP 79, UD, RA.
148. Petri to Wachtmeister, 'Säkerhetskonferensen', 25 November 1969, File 5, Vol. 27, HP 79, UD, RA.
149. Jarring to Jödahl, 8 December 1969, File 5, Vol. 27, HP 79, UD, RA.
150. Wachtmeister to Petri, 8 December 1969, File 5, Vol. 27, HP 79, UD, RA.
151. On the so-called Nordic balance, see, for example, Petersson, *Brödrafolkens väl*, 18–21.
152. Falkman, 'Samtal med Platzer angående europeiska säkerhetskonferensen', 10 February 1970, File 6, Vol. 27, HP 79, UD, RA.
153. Petri to Wachtmeister, 'Österrike och säkerhetskonferensen', 13 February 1970, File 6, Vol. 27, HP 79, UD, RA.
154. Platzer to Waldheim, 'Europäische Sicherheitskonferenz: Arbeitsgespräch des Herrn Generalsekretärs im schwedischen Außenministerium am 9.2.1970; Zusammenfassendes Protokoll', 12 February 1970, II-Pol/Schweden, BMfaA, ÖStA/AdR.
155. Holsti argues that a strategy is roughly equivalent to a role since it 'involves the general orientation of a state toward the external environment and its patterns of commitments and responses over a period of time'. Holsti, 'National Role Conceptions', 252.
156. [Original translation] Jarring to UD, 'Artikel i Izvestia om den all-europeiska säkerhetskonferensen', 27 February 1970, File 7, Vol. 28, HP 79, UD, RA.
157. Leifland to Hägglöf, 'Överläggningar med vice utrikesminister Smirnov', 5 March 1970, File 7, Vol. 28, HP 79, UD, RA.
158. Sandström to UD, 'Samtal med sovjetiska ambassadråd om säkerhetskonferensen och Bonns öst-kontakter', 4 March 1970, File 7, Vol. 28, HP 79, UD, RA.
159. See Rappe to Falkman, Cipher telegram 9, 12 March 1970; Leifland to Swedish Embassy Bucharest, 'Lyngs besök i Bukarest', 13 March 1970; for the Norwegian denial, Bergström to UD, Cipher telegram 3, 16 March 1970, File 7, Vol. 28, HP 79, UD, RA.
160. Björnberg to UD, 'Den europeiska säkerhetskonferensen', 18 March 1970, File 7, Vol. 28, HP 79, UD, RA.
161. Wachtmeister, 'Förberedande konferens för behandling av dagordningen i samband med europeisk säkerhetskonferens', 11 March 1970; Öberg to Swedish Embassy Bucharest, Cipher telegram, 'För information', 13 March 1970, File 7, Vol. 28, HP 79, UD, RA.
162. Wollin to Jödahl, Cipher telegram 9, 'För kab.sekr', 19 March 1970, File 7, Vol. 28, HP 79, UD, RA.
163. Falkman, 'Läget beträffande den europeiska säkerhetskonferensen', 20 March 1970, File 7, Vol. 28, HP 79, UD, RA.
164. Jarzabek, 'Hope and Reality', 30–34.
165. Falkman, 'Europeiska säkerhetskonferensen', 15 April 1970, File 7, Vol. 28, HP 79, UD, RA; 'Besuch des schwedischen Ministerpräsidenten', 10 March 1970, 478, B31, PAAA.

166. Grönwall, 'Säkerhetskonferensen. A. Officiella svenska uttalanden. 3. Inlägg av utrikesministern vid Europarådets ministerkommittes möte i Strasbourg den 15.4.70', 4 June 1970, File 8, Vol. 28, HP 79, UD, RA.
167. Falkman, 'Samtal med M. Forthomme om europeiska säkerhetskonferensen', 24 April 1970, File 7, Vol. 28, HP 79, UD, RA.
168. Belfrage to Nilsson, 'Nato-kommunikén om säkerheten och samarbetet i Europa', 2 June 1970, File 8, Vol. 28, HP 79, UD, RA.
169. Wollin to Jödahl, 15 April 1970; Jödahl to Wollin, 15 April 1970, 'Edert chiffer 11', File 7, Vol. 28, HP 79, UD, RA.
170. Leifland to Swedish Embassies Helsinki and Copenhagen, Cipher telegram, 22 May 1970, File 7, Vol. 28, HP 79, UD, RA; Falkman, 'Parlamentarisk konferens om europeiska säkerhetsfrågor: den svenska riksdagens svar', File 8, Vol. 28, HP 79, UD, RA.
171. Huldtgren to Falkman, 'Europeiska säkerhetskonferensen', 22 May 1970, File 7, Vol. 28, HP 79, UD, RA.
172. 'NATO Ministerial Meeting. Text of Communique issued in Rome on 27 May' in Grönwall, 1 June 1970, File 8, Vol. 28, HP 79, UD, RA. The Rome summit has been called 'the first milestone' on the road to the CSCE; see Yamamoto, 'Britain, France and West Germany', 103. See also Romano, *Détente*, 82; Hakkarainen, *State of Peace*, 97.
173. Grönwall, 'Säkerhetskonferensen. C. Natos inställning till agendan och proceduren såsom de kommit till uttryck i kommunikén och deklarationen från Rom och som därefter utvecklats av utrikesminister Stewart', 4 June 1970, File 8, Vol. 28, HP 79, UD, RA.
174. Belfrage to Nilsson, Nato-kommunikén om säkerheten och samarbetet i Europa', 2 June 1970; Grönwall, 'Säkerhetskonferensen', 10 June 1970, File 8, Vol. 28, HP 79, UD, RA. For a detailed history of the road to the Rome declaration, see Yamamoto, 'Britain, France and West Germany', 109–19.
175. Grönwall, ' Säkerhetskonferensen. D.', 4 June 1970, File 8, Vol. 28, HP 79, UD, RA.
176. Leifland to Palme, Cipher telegram, 'Europeisk säkerhetskonferens', 4 June 1970 and Belfrage to Nilsson, 'Nato-kommunikén om säkerheten och samarbetet i Europa', 2 June 1970, File 8, Vol. 28, HP 79, UD, RA.
177. See, for example, Ross to Foreign & Commonwealth Office (FCO), 22 June 1970, 24 June 1970 and 2 July 1970, FCO 33/1226, The National Archives (TNA).
178. Wachtmeister to Belfrage, 'Säkerhetskonferensen', 9 June 1970, File 8, Vol. 28, HP 79, UD, RA.
179. Belfrage to Wachtmeister, Cipher telegram 44, 10 June 1970, File 8, Vol. 28, HP 79, UD, RA.
180. Jödahl, 'Besök av Sovjets ambassadör' and 'Samtal med brittiske ambassadören om säkerhetskonferensen', 10 June 1970, File 8, Vol. 28, HP 79, UD, RA; Malm, 'Frankrike och den europeiska säkerhetskonferensen', 31 July 1970, File 9, Vol. 28, HP 79, UD, RA.
181. Jödahl, 'Besök av Sovjets ambassadör', 10 June 1970, File 8, Vol. 28, HP 79, UD, RA.
182. Békés, 'The Warsaw Pact', 124–25.
183. See Hungarian Embassy Stockholm to UD, attached to 'Budapestkonferensen om en alleuropeisk konferens', 29 June 1970, File 8, Vol. 28, HP 79, UD, RA.
184. Falkman, 'Vice utrikesminister Willman om alleuropeiska konferensen', 3 July 1970, File 9, Vol. 28, HP 79, UD, RA.
185. Hakkarainen, *State of Peace*, 98. See also Yamamoto, 'Britain, France and West Germany', 122–26.
186. UD, Pressbyrån, Pressmeddelande, 8 July 1970, File 9, Vol. 28, HP 79, UD, RA.

187. Wachtmeister, 'Förberedande konferens för behandling av dagordningen i samband med europeisk säkerhetskonferens', 11 March 1970 and Leifland to Swedish Embassy Copenhagen, 22 May 1970, RA, UD, File 7, Vol. 28, HP 79, UD, RA.
188. Lilliehöök to Wachtmeister, 9 July 1970, 'Alleuropeiska konferensen', 9 July 1970, File 9, Vol. 28, HP 79, UD, RA.
189. Falkman, 'Holländske polchefen om europeiska säkerhetskonferensen', 15 July 1970, File 9, Vol. 28, HP 79, UD, RA.
190. Falkman, 'WP-och NATO-staternas förslag rörande europeiska säkerhetskonferensen', 17 July 1970, File 9, Vol. 28, HP 79, UD, RA.
191. 'Österreichisches Memorandum zur Frage einer Konferenz über die europäische Sicherheit' attached to Falkman, 'Österrikiskt förslag rörande europeiska säkerhetskonferensen', 20 July 1970, File 9, Vol. 28, HP 79, UD, RA. See also Gilde, *Österreich im KSZE-Prozess*, 65–70.
192. Nuenlist, 'Expanding the East-West Dialog', 204.
193. Fischer, Neutral Power, 63–65 and 128–35; Christoph Breitenmoser, *Sicherheit für Europa: Die KSZE-Politik der Schweiz bis zur Unterzeichnung der Helsinki-Schlussakte zwischen Skepsis und aktivem Engagement* (Zürich: CSS, 1996), 131.
194. Fischer, Die Grenzen der Neutralität, chapters 3 and 4.
195. Rosin, *Die Schweiz im KSZE-Prozeß*, 55–62; Nuenlist, 'Expanding the East-West Dialog', 205.
196. Falkman /Blix, 'Schweiziskt förslag om ett europeiskt system för fredlig lösning av tvister', File 16, Vol. 31, HP 79, UD, RA.
197. Schober to Kirchschläger, 'Engere Zusammenarbeit der neutralen Staaten Europas; schwedische Haltung', 17 November 1970, II-Pol/Schweden, BMfaA, ÖStA/AdR; Nuenlist, 'Expanding the East-West Dialog', 207.
198. MemCon Wickman-Mattila, 29 November 1971, File 1, Vol. 26, HP 1:200, UD, RA.
199. Falkman to Bergenstråhle, 'Europeiska säkerhetskonferensen', 20 July 1970, File 9, Vol. 28, HP 79, UD, RA.
200. Huldtgren to Falkman, '273', 30 July 1970 and Falkman, 'Säkerhetskonferens', 31 July 1970, File 9, Vol. 28, HP 79, UD, RA.
201. Huldtgren to UD, Cipher telegram 68, 5 August 1970, File 9, Vol. 28, HP 79, UD, RA.
202. Ingemar Hägglöf to UD, '75. Samtal här med deltagare i president Kekkonens besök i Moskva respektive Washington ger följande bild av den finska inställningen till säkerhetskonferensprojektet', 20 August 1970, File 9, Vol. 28, HP 79, UD, RA.
203. Falkman, 'Läget beträffande europeiska säkerhetskonferensen', 20 August 1970, File 9, Vol. 28, HP 79, UD, RA. See also Hakkarainen, *State of Peace*, 120–26.
204. Falkman, 'Läget beträffande europeiska säkerhets- och samarbetskonferensen', 11 November 1970, File 10, Vol. 29, HP 79, UD, RA.
205. Grönwall, 'Europeiska säkerhets- och samarbetskonferensen', 24 September 1970 and Wachtmeister to Ingemar Hägglöf, 28 September 1970, File 10, Vol. 29, HP 79, UD, RA.
206. Wachtmeister, 'Den österrikiska promemorian rörande säkerhetskonferensen', 4 September 1970, File 10, Vol. 29, HP 79, UD, RA.
207. Grönwall, 'Spanien och säkerhetskonferensen', 23 October 1970, File 10, Vol. 29; Wachtmeister, 'Schweiziske ambassadören angående europeiska säkerhetskonferensen', File 14, Vol. 30, HP 79, UD, RA.
208. See, for example, Lilliehöök to Wachtmeister, 'Ungern, Moskvafördraget och säkerhetskonferensen', 29 October 1970 and Löfberg to Falkman, 'Brittisk-tjeckoslovakiska diskussioner om säkerhetskonferensen, 19 November 1970, File 10, Vol. 29, HP 79, UD, RA.

209. Falkman, 'Läget beträffande europeiska säkerhets- och samarbetskonferensen', 11 November 1970, File 10, Vol. 29, HP 79, UD, RA.
210. Falkman, 'Samtal i Wien om europeiska säkerhetskonferensen', 23 November 1970, Falkman, 'Läget beträffande europeiska säkerhets- och samarbetskonferensen', 11 November 1970, File 10, Vol. 29, HP 79, UD, RA.
211. Schober to Kirchschläger, 'Engere Zusammenarbeit der neutralen Staaten Europas; schwedische Haltung', 17 November 1970, II-Pol/Schweden, BMfaA, ÖStA/AdR.
212. Fischer, *Neutral Power*, 111–16.
213. UD, Press Release, 'Foreign Minister Torsten Nilsson has made the following observations in connection with the Finnish statement today on the question of the conference on European security', 25 November 1970, Falkman, 'Läget beträffande europeiska säkerhets- och samarbetskonferensen', 11 November 1970, File 10, Vol. 29, HP 79, UD, RA.
214. Yamamoto, 'Britain, France and West Germany', 133–44; Hakkarainen, *State of Peace*, 126.
215. Yamamoto, 'Britain, France and West Germany', 145–50.
216. Falkman, 'Läget beträffande europeiska säkerhets- och samarbetskonferensen', 26 January 1971, File 11, Vol. 29, HP 79, UD, RA.
217. Ingemar Hägglöf to UD, Telegram 437, 'Finske utrikesministern om säkerhetskonferensen' and Ingemar Hägglöf to Wachtmeister, 'Finland, säkerhetskonferensen och Sovjetunionen', 17 December 1970, File 10, Vol. 29, HP 79, UD, RA.
218. Falkman, 'Läget beträffande europeiska säkerhets- och samarbetskonferensen', 8 December 1970, File 10, Vol. 29, HP 79, UD, RA.
219. 'b. Warszawapakten' in Falkman, 'Läget beträffande europeiska säkerhets- och samarbetskonferensen', 26 January 1971, File 11, Vol. 29, HP 79, UD, RA.
220. 'Svenskt inlägg om öst-västrelationerna vid Europarådets ministerkommittés möte den 11 december 1970', in Falkman, 'Läget beträffande europeiska säkerhets- och samarbetskonferensen', 8 December 1970, File 10, Vol. 29, HP 79, UD, RA.
221. Montan to UD, 'Berlinfrågan och säkerhetskonferensen', 22 December 1970, File 10, Vol. 29, HP 79, UD, RA. For a thorough analysis of Bahr's contribution, see Senoo, *Irrweg*, ch. 2.
222. Ingemar Hägglöf to Nyström, 'Ungerns premiärminister Jenö Focks besök i Finland januari 1971', 25 January 1971 and Ingemar Hägglöf to Wachtmeister 'Finland och säkerhetskonferensen', 26 January 1971, File 11, Vol. 29, HP 79, UD, RA.
223. Wachtmeister to Hamilton, 'Frankrike och europeiska säkerhetskonferensen', 28 January 1971, File 11, Vol. 29, HP 79, UD, RA.
224. Finnmark to Wachtmeister, 'Jugoslavien och europeiska säkerhetskonferensen', 8 February 1971, File 11, Vol. 29, HP 79, UD, RA.
225. Johan Lilliehöök, 'Konferens mellan utrikesministrarna i Warszawafördragsstaterna; den europeiska säkerhetskonferensen', 25 February 1971, File 11, Vol. 29, HP 79, UD, RA.
226. Nyström, 'Samtal mellan Utrikesministern och Sovjetunionens ambassadör: frågan om en europeisk säkerhetskonferens', 26 February 1971, File 11; Jödahl, 'Besök av sovjetiske chargé d'affaires Streltsov angående säkerhetskonferensen', 19 March 1971, File 12, Vol. 29, HP 79, UD, RA.
227. Wachtmeister, 'Samtal med Polens chargé d'affaires rörande säkerhetskonferensen', 11 March 1971, File 11, Vol. 29, HP 79, UD, RA.
228. Falkman, 'Läget beträffande europeiska säkerhets- och samarbetskonferens', 26 March 1971, File 12, Vol. 29, HP 79, UD, RA.
229. See Palme's reflections during a speech at the Austrian Association for Foreign Policy and International Relations, 15 April 1971, Länderbox Schweden, Bestand VII.1, BKAF.

230. Lagerfelt to UD, 'Bulgarisk delegation besöker Haag för samtal rörande huvudsakligen den europeiska säkerhetskonferensen', 13 May 1971; Belding to Wachtmeister, 'Kring Tserapins besök', 4 June 1971, File 12, Vol. 29, HP 79, UD, RA.
231. Belfrage to Wachtmeister, 'Öst-västförbindelserna i Europa', 11 June 1971, File 12, Vol. 29, HP 79, UD, RA; Yamamoto, 'Britain, France and West Germany', 180–84.
232. For the Lisbon communiqué, see www.nato.int/docu/comm/49-95/c710603a.htm (accessed 25 November 2015).
233. Berg, 'Europeiska säkerhetskonferensen', 25 August 1971, File 13, Vol. 30, HP 79, UD, RA.
234. Berg, 'Läget beträffande planerna på ömsesidiga och balanserande styrkereduktioner i Europa ('MBFR')', 27 August 1971, File 13, Vol. 30, HP 79, UD, RA.
235. Hakkarainen, *State of Peace*, 143–44. See also Mary E. Sarotte, *Dealing with the Devil: East Germany, Détente, and Ostpolitik, 1969–1973* (Chapel Hill: University of North Carolina Press, 2001), 113–23.
236. 'Utdrag ur statsministerns anförande i Landskrona den 28 augusti 1971', in Berg, 'Läget beträffande planerna på en europeisk säkerhets- och samarbetskonferens', 31 August 1971, File 13, Vol. 30, HP 79, UD, RA.
237. Nyström, 'Svenskt ordförandeskap i arbetsgrupp vid det multilaterala förberedande ESK-mötet i Helsingfors?' 28 April 1972, File 19, Vol. 32, HP 79, UD, RA. and Nyström, 'Förslag till föredragning av utrikesministern om ESK inför utrikesnämnden den 24 maj 1972', 23 May 1972, File 20, Vol. 32, HP 79, UD, RA.
238. For reference to the Nordic Conference of the Ministers of Foreign in Affairs in Copenhagen on 24 April 1969, see Wachtmeister, 'Europeisk säkerhetskonferens', 1 July 1969, RA, UD, HP 79, Vol. 26: 2. For reference to NATO, see Wachtmeister, 'Samtal med belgiske ambassadören om europeisk säkerhetskonferens', 24 September 1969, RA, UD, HP 79, Vol. 27: 4.
239. Alexander Muschik, *Die beiden deutschen Staaten und das neutrale Schweden: eine Dreiecksbeziehung im Schatten der offenen Deutschlandfrage 1949–1972* (Münster: Lit, 2005), 179–229.
240. The opposition comprised the Christian Democratic Union of Germany (Christlich Demokratische Union Deutschlands; CDU) and the Christian Social Union in Bavaria (Christlich-Soziale Union in Bayern; CSU).
241. af Malmborg, *Neutrality and State-Building*, 160–169; Bjereld et al., *Sveriges säkerhet*, 261–65.
242. Bjereld et al., *Sveriges säkerhet*, 274.
243. Lodén, *För säkerhets skull*.
244. As mentioned earlier, these lines of conflict ran between national sovereignty (independence) and international interdependence, between ideological identification with the West and nonalignment, and between democratic openness and military preparedness.
245. For a broader historical background, see Gunnar Åselius, *The Russian 'Menace' to Sweden: The Belief System of a Small Power Security Elite in the Age of Imperialism* (Stockholm: Almqvist & Wiksell International, 1994).
246. af Malmborg, *Neutrality and State-Building*, 152.
247. Cf. Fischer, *Neutral Power*, 106, n298.

CHAPTER THREE

1971–1972: Assuming the Role of the Realist

> *Sweden actively supports the proposal of the Warsaw Treaty Member States to convene an all-European Conference on Questions of Security and Cooperation.*
>
> —Olof Palme, 12 February 1972

> *It is natural that Sweden as a small nation takes up a flexible position and above all seeks to work towards agreement among the decisive powers.*
>
> —Kaj Falkman, 6 April 1972

Following the breakthrough in the Berlin Question, Olof Palme publicly invoked 'Sweden's responsibility as a European nation'. These words are a useful expression of Sweden's slow opening towards the CSCE between September 1971 and November 1972. During this time, Palme's active foreign policy gathered pace. How did it express itself in the European sphere? It is important to recognize the hierarchy of priorities established by the Swedish government and the Ministry for Foreign Affairs during the final phase of multiple bilateral preparations before we can understand the search for balance between national security interests and solidarity in Sweden's approach to Europe.

After Berlin

The Four Power Agreement on Berlin and the successful negotiations of the Brandt administration on the Eastern relations of West Germany resulted in a shift in Sweden's way of looking at Europe. The Berlin Agreement confirmed the rights and responsibilities of the victorious powers and laid the groundwork for improved conditions of travel and communication between the sectors west and east of the Berlin Wall. More importantly, in terms of security, it laid the foundations for the redefinition of inner-German relations, which would be formalized in the so-called Basic Treaty (*Grundlagenvertrag*) between Bonn and East Berlin a year later.[1]

With this, the Swedish requirements for the convocation of the CSCE, which had been based on NATO's 1970 Brussels summit, were met. The status of Berlin had been the central obstacle on the road to the conference and had left smaller countries impotent, as Yamamoto correctly puts it.[2] The success in negotiations was thus considered important in many European capitals, including the neutral ones.[3] Although the treaties had yet to be ratified, arrangements leading towards the establishment of the CSCE were made in Stockholm. Willy Brandt's *Ostpolitik*, which was vigorously supported by Olof Palme and his government, had paved the road to the conference. Developments on the superpower level were also favourable, as the United States, the Soviet Union and France actively contributed to rapprochement between the blocs during this phase.[4] Encouraged by the continuation of European and superpower détente, the Swedish Foreign Ministry launched practical arrangements for the conference in late 1971.

Early Preparations

Throughout September 1971, the constructive spirit hanging in the air led the Swedes to develop an interest in a more active engagement in discussions on European security. The meeting of the Nordic foreign ministers in Copenhagen on 7 September 1971 was concluded with the statement that a conference on security in Europe was 'a natural step on the road towards further relaxation in Europe'.[5] *TASS* proudly cited an interview given by Olof Palme to the Finnish magazine *Forum* in which the Swedish prime minister declared that international détente was a 'keystone of Sweden's policy'.

Palme said he believed that the security conference would improve the political climate further and that, consequently, it was natural for his government to support it actively.[6] Palme's words were more than mere lip service. During a visit of the deputy prime minister of the Soviet Union, Vladimir Novikov, to Stockholm, Palme was confronted with Moscow's desire to begin multilateral consultations in the near future. The Soviets seemed satisfied with a sympathetic statement in this regard made by Foreign Minister Krister Wickman shortly beforehand.[7] Palme responded by supporting Wickman's position:

The Prime Minister [Palme] for his part confirmed that the Soviet Union can count on Swedish support for its proposal on multilateral preparations. The Prime Minister added that preparations bringing together all states that will participate in the conference were a constructive step. What the Swedish side refuses, according to the Prime Minister, are gatherings of some groups of future conference participants, simply because this could have a detrimental effect on the ambitions to arrange a conference.[8]

With the earlier requirements met and the West satisfied, Sweden could now express some support for the Soviet Union. From the point of view of the Warsaw Pact states, Swedish willingness to consider a more active role was a move in the right direction – one which they had been hoping for since the Budapest Appeal in spring 1969. Naturally, they welcomed this early transition, as it fit with their expectations.

Although this might be viewed as 'a specific commitment to support the policies of *another* government' and evidence of acting as a faithful friend, one of the roles defined by Holsti, it would be incorrect to identify the Swedish behaviour in this way. There was neither much substance to it, nor a repetitive pattern, beyond such friendly declarations as had been made in support of the Soviet Union's CSCE policy. With the benefit of recent historical hindsight, there is little to suggest that the Soviets expected Sweden to appear as a friend. Rather, they were happy with them developing an independent role. The latter included the definition of its own goals and, in consequence, taking a stance in favour of the conference's convocation. Therefore, Stockholm's position at that point was congruent with Moscow's objectives. It is very unlikely that the Soviets would have expected Sweden to go further than functioning as bridge or mediator after the failed attempts in 1969 and 1970.

During this time, the Swedish Foreign Ministry closely monitored the positions of key countries. It was aware of the existence of opponents of détente in both the Eastern and Western camps but viewed détente as stable and believed it to have good chances of improving further. This belief was based upon the closer relationship growing between the United States and China, resulting in Richard Nixon's visit to Beijing in February 1972, which was seen as a reason for Leonid Brezhnev's interest in ensuring that the conference would grow.[9]

Therefore, efforts to prepare the Foreign Ministry in Stockholm for the task were intensified. A standing conference with a wide range of subjects, including those with immediate security implications and with more than thirty participating states, was a new experience, different from efforts made at the UN or the Conference of the Committee on Disarmament (CCD);[10] it therefore required extraordinary efforts. The Swedes looked beyond their own borders to take inspiration from the way other countries prepared themselves. UD officials reported with interest how comparable states prepared for matters expected to be treated at the conference. They also analysed the composition of specific CSCE expert groups.[11]

Impressions from the other neutrals and Sweden's Nordic neighbours were of the greatest interest in this respect, but ultimately it was Switzerland which served as a role model. In Berne, a working group under the chairmanship of Ambassador Rudolf Bindschedler had been preparing for the CSCE for about a year and a half. Bindschedler, an acknowledged scholar in international law, had worked intensively on a proposal on the establishment of a System of Peaceful Settlement of Disputes.[12] Swiss documents were handed over to Swedish officials, and in talks with Finnish interlocutors, the prospects of future cooperation between the neutrals were deemed positive.[13] Sweden expected itself to take up a role comparable to that of similar actors, which shared their small-state approach to international negotiations. There were no Swedish ambitions to play a role that would vary significantly from that of other comparable actors, as was the case in the UN and global affairs. In contrast to the isolation outlined in the previous chapter, considerations of future involvement now included more active roles.

In addition to looking at the formation of CSCE working structures abroad, the political department, led by Wilhelm Wachtmeister, collected information on developments related to the conference. Other departments at the Foreign Ministry in Stockholm began developing positions on issues that were likely to become part of the agenda. By mid-October 1971, Sweden acknowledged that the CSCE was likely to start, 'in one form or another', as early as 1972 and that it would not only treat security matters but also discuss cooperation in other areas.[14] The ESC had evolved into the CSCE.

The optimism regarding the timetable was shared by other Nordic countries and made public in an interview of the Swedish tabloid *Aftonbladet* with the prime ministers of Denmark, Finland, Norway and Sweden. This was the second positive statement in six months used by Eastern media to change the public perception of Sweden. *Pravda* and *TASS* both highlighted the statements made by the Nordic heads of states.[15] Policymakers in Stockholm did not reject such Eastern propaganda, because it concealed the Swedish *Berührungsangst* towards European security matters. Therefore, it was actually congruent with the desired image of Sweden as active. The image was upheld successfully, in line with the fact that the Swedish government received little domestic criticism.

Based on responses to an enquiry sent out to a larger number of Swedish embassies in Western and neutral countries, it was concluded that the sheer number of important subjects on the agenda required 'consistent leadership'. In order to provide such leadership, it was decided that Swedish negotiations would be led by the director of the political department rather than by higher-ranking officials, such as Foreign Minister Krister Wickman or State Secretary for Foreign Affairs Ole Jödahl. In charge of the matter since 1968, Wilhelm Wachtmeister was the foremost expert on the CSCE among the diplomats of the UD.

The Swedish embassy in Helsinki was assigned a significant role in terms of administrating materials related to the CSCE. Representatives from the Ministry of Defence and the defence staff were invited to participate in the work on security matters. On other issues, heads of relevant departments at the Foreign Ministry, as well as officials from other ministries, would be included in the CSCE group. The political department was assigned the task of overall coordination. Additional staff for diplomatic and administrative tasks was assigned to positions in Stockholm and Helsinki.[16]

These were important measures, which shaped Sweden's policy making in the long term. Self-evidently, the government defined the broader framework in which diplomats acted. But within the government's wider agenda, positions on factual issues were often developed following a bottom-up approach, as they required the expertise of lower-ranking diplomats or ministerial experts. As a result, Sweden's role conceptions were not exclusively shaped by the highest rank of decision makers. In contrast, the Swedes remained dismissive regarding MBFR. Due to a negative statement from Olof Palme in this respect, efforts from NATO to establish immediate contact and have its secretary-general Manlio Brosio visit Stockholm in October 1971 were postponed.[17]F

After Palme and Wickman had publicly stated their support, the Ministry for Foreign Affairs started briefing all involved officials and departments on the substantial matters of the CSCE. NATO was expected to adopt a common position at its June 1972 summit, after the ratification of West Germany's treaties and Richard Nixon's visit to Moscow in May. The road to the conference consequently became of greater interest. Like most other states, Sweden favoured multilateral preparations led by the heads of missions and supported by experts rather than other procedures, such as groups of states representing other participants, multilateral preparations on a representative basis or a multiplication of bilateral consultations (the last suggested by Finland).

Different designs of the multilateral preparations were discussed: first, a Salon des Ambassadeurs; second, a meeting of deputy foreign ministers or heads of departments; third, a meeting of lower-ranking experts. Stockholm thought that multilateral preparations they favoured would allow thorough preparations and the establishment of Helsinki as a future venue.¹⁸ It was clearly important to Sweden that its policy should not conflict with Finland and the West, in particular West Germany.

The form and agenda of the conference itself were also discussed intensively. Both the original Soviet proposal to hold one concise conference and establish an organ that would deal with the outcome in the aftermath and the alternative idea for a series of shorter conferences, proposed by some Eastern European states, were out of the question as far as Sweden and the NATO member states were concerned. Instead, they preferred one single conference to treat all substantive issues at once. There was also agreement on the most important goals to be accomplished, namely a declaration on principles defining the relations between states and stipulating the nonuse of force. The great powers dismissed a link between the CSCE and MBFR, whereas minor states, among them Yugoslavia and Austria, argued that it should be included in the agenda of the CSCE.¹⁹

Differences also emerged regarding human contacts. At its Rome summit in May 1970 NATO had defined 'cooperation' as a way of 'contributing to the freer movement of people, ideas and information and to developing co-operation in the cultural, economic, technical and scientific fields, as well as in the field of human environment'. The Warsaw Pact states had responded a month later by stating that they sought 'expansion of commercial, economic, scientific, technical and cultural relations on a footing of equality for the purpose of developing political co-operation between European States'.²⁰ As part of its intensified efforts, Sweden started defining preferences and goals in each of these areas.

The Foreign Ministry favoured the establishment of three committees (1) on *security*, (2) on *economic, industrial* and *technical cooperation* and (3) on *cultural cooperation*. Sweden hoped for the first committee to address the realization of principles on collective responsibility for security and the end of the Brezhnev Doctrine through concrete and binding principles on relations between states, regardless of bloc constellations. Here, a future organ could 'interpret, monitor and settle disputes regarding the principles'. Swedish expertise would be offered to explore opportunities of regional disarmament, which had been under consideration since mid-1970. Three aims were formulated for the second committee: the establishment of a permanent organ for cooperation that would strengthen the Economic Commission for Europe (ECE), the definition of concrete and practical measures and the representation of specific Swedish interests, such as the multilateralization of credits. In the third committee, on cultural cooperation, Swedish focus was expected to be on the exchange of students and researchers, on TV programmes and newspapers and on tourism.²¹

It is notable that human contacts and a freer flow of information were not defined as Swedish goals at the CSCE. On this historically most essential subject, Sweden differed from the Western states, with which it otherwise agreed in large part.[22] These early preferences persisted and marked Sweden's realist approach to the CSCE, which excluded the option of defending values strongly attached to its regularly cited humanitarian tradition. To this decision, the role expectations of the Swedish public were irrelevant.

In order to tackle these objectives, a group of experts was appointed on 6 December 1971. At this stage, it comprised officials of the Foreign Ministry's political department only. Wilhelm Wachtmeister and his deputy director Axel Edelstam led the group; the other members were the heads of the first and second political bureau along with Kaj Falkman, a ministerial secretary. Its composition and tasks were quite similar to the Swiss workgroup in Berne created two years earlier.[23] Starting in January 1972, the Swedish CSCE working group was to meet every Friday at 3 p.m. in Wachtmeister's office, where gatherings would be introduced with reports from Falkman.[24] Since the conclusion of the Four Power Agreement on Berlin, the Swedish Foreign Ministry put efforts into the establishment of work routines that allowed it to develop a more positive approach to the CSCE.

Exploring the Limits: 'Certain Cautiousness and Realism'

NATO and the Warsaw Pact states held their semiannual summits in Brussels and Warsaw, respectively, in early December 1971. After more than two months of bilateral negotiations, the Soviet Union had forced West Germany to accept a linkage between the ratification of the Berlin Agreement, the CSCE and the Treaty of Moscow.[25] This delayed the preparations for a conference further. The United States and Britain supported West Germany, whereas France, Denmark and Norway argued that a solution for Berlin had been accomplished and that it should no longer stand in the way. At Brussels, the West Germans succeeded in gaining NATO's support for their demand to delay the CSCE until the ratification of the Berlin Agreement.[26]

While the two blocs continued to increasingly converge on economic issues, the differences over security and human issues remained considerable. The Eastern Europeans took up a stronger position on the renunciation of the use or the threat of force, while the NATO allies pointed out that a conference would have to address the basic principles of relations between states, 'irrespective of political and social systems'. The communiqué of the Eastern bloc did not mention human contacts or MBFR, whereas the Western allies reiterated their positions on these matters.[27] In particular, the Western allies criticized the absence of an Eastern response on MBFR.[28] Quoting 'well-informed NATO circles', the Swedish embassy in Brussels reported to Stockholm that the Soviet hesitation about inviting NATO's secretary-general Manlio Brosio for discussions on the subject created further delay to the preparation talks for the CSCE until May or June 1972.[29] Sweden did not criticize these delays but welcomed them as part of the thorough preparations on which it had insisted from the beginning.

During this period, Austria and Finland made careful attempts to introduce talks on neutral collaboration at the CSCE. Western countries wondered why the neutrals were so reluctant to make common statements on the CSCE. Italian officials told Swedish ambassador Brynolf Eng in Rome that the neutral countries 'would certainly make an impact'.[30] Press reports about the formation of a "league of neutrals" or a "club of neutrals" appeared. With the background that the CSCE was an essential element of Finnish foreign policy, Helsinki naturally welcomed such remarks. Switzerland and Sweden, on the other hand, had always been reluctant to support such grouping efforts and saw no reason for a change of mind.[31] Göran Berg, a diplomat who eventually became a member of the delegation to the CSCE, criticized as 'very vague' a first Swiss proposal in this respect. Berne argued that consultations between the neutral states would actually avoid other states perceiving them as a bloc.

Wachtmeister responded to the Swiss ambassador in Stockholm that Sweden was not interested in such initiatives. He added that the situation could change at the conference proper but that, for the time being, the Swedish government dismissed neutral cooperation. Foreign Minister Wickman publicly confirmed this position.[32] Sweden rejected group efforts since they would have contributed to the country being pushed towards the role of mediator, or even more. At that stage, Stockholm had rather more modest ambitions.

Nevertheless, this did not prohibit its support for neutral endeavours. The most important idea in this respect was Switzerland's concept of a System for the Peaceful Settlement of Disputes (SRPD), which was presented to Sweden on 15 January 1972.[33] The matter was discussed primarily between Rudolf Bindschedler, a scholar in international law and arguably the most influential diplomat at Berne, and Hans Blix, his Swedish counterpart in terms of expertise and influence. Bindschedler elaborated on the idea, which the Swiss had first introduced in July 1970, and argued that it was not enough to forbid the use of force but was also necessary to have a mechanism that would actually *solve* disputes. According to the

Swiss proposal, legal disputes would be solved through the mandatory judgements of a court composed of five judges: three from neutral countries and one each from both involved parties.

Disputes on existing international law were considered to be of a political nature and would, therefore, be passed on to a supranational authority: a commission of five members composed in the same manner as the court that would reach a decision to be respected by all involved parties. Although the Swiss themselves held no illusions regarding occurring political realities, the proposal was regarded 'as a test case' by the Swedish side. Blix stated that 'third party determination' was in line with Sweden's policy at the UN and, therefore, supported the idea, adding his suggestion to consult both blocs before presenting the proposal officially. It would harm the reputation of the neutral states if the proposal were to be pulled to pieces by the East, Blix argued.[34]

The close working relationship with the Auswärtiges Amt in Bonn continued throughout the period preceding the multilateral talks at Dipoli. Just prior to Christmas 1971, Götz von Groll, the head of the West German working group on the CSCE, suggested an exchange of views between the two ministries. The Swedes were very interested in the views of von Groll and his superior, Jürgen Diesel, the deputy head of the political department, as they considered the West Germans as highly interesting peers. The ensuing consultations between the two sides in January 1972 were held in an intimate and friendly atmosphere. The Swedes received comprehensive West German memoranda on the CSCE as part of the preparations for the talks between experts from the two ministries.[35] The excellent relationship between Bonn and Stockholm was expressed in various ways. When an unwelcome Finnish idea on inner-German relationships worsened West German–Finnish relations, for instance, it was the Swedes whom Bonn asked for mediation.[36]

In general, Sweden was well informed about the state of discussions within NATO, since bilateral consultations with West Germany and the Nordic NATO members, Denmark and Norway, secured a certain flow of information. In some cases, information was handed over by the Norwegians under the explicit condition that the source would not be revealed.[37] In this context, Norway and Sweden would meet in their respective capacity of NATO member and neutral state, rather than as part of any form of Nordic cooperation. The Nordic dimension was discussed from time to time but never materialized to a relevant extent.[38]

Regional-subsystem collaboration, as Holsti called it, remained a rather peripheral matter. Instead, it was the Western orientation that was important to Sweden. In a report about the first meeting of the CSCE working group, held on 7 January 1972, Kaj Falkman stated that Sweden 'basically support[s] Western proposals on freer movements of ideas, etc.'.³⁹ At the same time, Sweden did not share the Western interest in the subject and would, therefore, refrain from making sacrifices in this respect, despite its otherwise unconditional support of the West.

Sweden's intensification of preparations did not pass unnoticed. In consultations shortly after the installation of the CSCE working group, the Romanian ambassador to Stockholm, Gantcho Gantchev, stated that Sweden seemed to be more positive about a conference.⁴⁰ But Sweden's openness did not mean that the insecurity over Moscow's motives was put aside from one day to the next. Internal assessments linked Soviet policy with Willy Brandt's *Ostpolitik*, as the Swedes believed that the Soviets were eager to make use of West Germany's reorientation. This was considered reason for concern since Brandt had 'achieved his position through elections and can be forced to resign . . . He could also [have] a heart attack'.⁴¹

Swedish relations with the members of the Warsaw Pact were friendly but far more distant than those with the West and neutral Switzerland. To the West, Sweden was a faithful friend; with the East, Sweden kept a friendly tone. When Ole Jödahl travelled to Warsaw to meet with Poland's deputy foreign minister Adam Willman, the discussion of the CSCE contained little more than an exchange of niceties and a general review of the state of affairs, such as Brandt's policy towards securing the end of the Hallstein Doctrine and the strong opposition he had met in the *Bundestag*.⁴² The talks with the Romanians and Poles illustrated that the Swedish officials played their cards close to their chest. No exchange of documents or sensitive information occurred. Thus, the Eastern bloc did not exert any immediate influence on the way Sweden looked at the CSCE.

The level of preparations remained a contested theme, and not only on an internal diplomatic level. The idea of an interparliamentary conference to be held in November 1972, brought up by Denmark and Finland, was discussed in the Riksdag in Stockholm between Parliamentary Speaker Henry Allard and the leaders of the parliamentary parties. The conclusion was that there was nothing in favour of including parliaments in the preparation process and that the CSCE should be left in the hands of the respective governments.⁴³ An international meeting of activists from twenty-seven countries was convened in Brussels between 11 and 13 January 1972 at the invitation of Sécurité et Coopération Européennes, a Belgian organization that had been monitoring the negotiations on setting up a conference since 1969. At the meeting it was decided to prepare a congress in early June 1972 in Brussels, with the aim of expressing the 'opinion of the people' on matters of European security and cooperation.

In this case, 'the people' meant activists from the far left. National committees were given the task of appointing officials who would cooperate with the newly established Secretary Office. Sweden's representatives at these meetings were prominent socialists, such as Stellan Arvidsson and Bertil Svanström, the latter being one of the founders of the anti–Vietnam War movement (Svenska Vietnamkommittén).[44] In a press interview, prominent authors Ivar Lo-Johansson, Torsten Bergmark and Göran Palm offered their views on the role that Sweden could play at the conference. Referring to statements made by Foreign Minister Wickman, they argued that Sweden belonged to the European continent and therefore should contribute to the creation of a new Europe.[45] Approaching the CSCE from the declaratory foreign policy level, left-wing activists perceived it as natural that Sweden would play a role similar to the one they played in the UN. This did not, however, accord with the security policy carried out by the Foreign Ministry.

In early February 1972, two extensive memoranda summarized Sweden's position in the ongoing détente, maintaining that the multilateral preparations should be held in Finland or that, if one of the stages of the conference were to be moved, they should be held in Austria or Switzerland. These preferences were a natural consequence of the well-established relationships between and similarities with these countries. Soviet attempts to sustain the Brezhnev Doctrine by arguing that peaceful coexistence applied only to the relations between capitalistic and socialistic states, and not within the blocs, were rejected. From the Swedish perspective, principles guiding relations between states had to be in accordance with the UN Charter and applicable regardless of the social system of a country.

A link between the CSCE and the UN was highly valued, as it would strengthen the UN and Europe and fit with the charter's eighth chapter on regional arrangements. Notably, the actual diplomatic approach to the CSCE was outlined for the first time. It was acknowledged that a certain degree of flexibility would be necessary in case of deadlocks, although the goal for the CSCE was to establish concrete and binding principles. Therefore, the memorandum emphasized, principles on relations between states and human contacts, considered to be the most sensitive questions, should be approached with 'certain cautiousness and realism'.[46] This was considered the safest way to complete the transition from an isolate to an independent actor.

Sweden's support for a neutral venue, its preference for regional arrangements through a linkage between the CSCE and the UN and its acknowledgement of political realities were the elements of the realist view it had maintained since 1969. In early 1972, the Swedes followed the general development, particularly the attitude of the West Germans, who tried to control the pace of the process, Switzerland and their Nordic neighbours. They reacted calmly to repeated postponements caused by the connections between the Eastern treaties and the Berlin Agreement and used the delays to refine their role as somewhere between independent neutral and faithful friend of the West.[47]

Taking Stock

In the following weeks, ministerial experts joined the staff of the political department in the CSCE working group. A first general gathering of this enlarged working group took place on 15 March 1972. Under the chairmanship of Wilhelm Wachtmeister, a total of eighteen officials discussed which course to set. Among them were representatives from the ministries of industry, education, trade and defence, along with nondiplomats such as Nils Andrén, at the time Sweden's most prominent political scientist.[48] At the meeting, members conducted a broad analysis of Swedish goals at the CSCE. There was general agreement on the vital Swedish interest in disarmament.

Jan Prawitz of the Ministry of Defence stated that the CSCE would affect national defence planning and require greater manpower and expertise than had the CCD. He recommended that Sweden actively contribute to negotiations on force reduction and disarmament and pointed to the drafting of concrete proposals based on Swedish expertise and analysis of non-Swedish proposals and studies related to Northern Europe as possible activities. He added that the Swedish military needed to prepare itself for participation in future operations, possibly as observer, as a consequence of the CSCE and MBFR. Thus, force reductions and MBFR were also considered to be important, since they could eventually affect Swedish security. Nevertheless, as stated by Prime Minister Palme in August 1971, there was no belief in a realistic possibility of engaging in the early talks between NATO and the Warsaw Pact states.[49]

Since Sweden had rejected membership in the EEC, discussions on economic and commercial cooperation at the CSCE, as well as exchanges on science and technology, were also very appealing. Ole Jödahl emphasized that it was important to make sure that the CSCE would stimulate cooperation between states in the East and the West, rather than between military blocs. He also argued that the Geneva-based United Nations ECE was an existing forum for discussion of related issues. As part of the Swedish desire for a strong link between the CSCE and the UN, the Swedish delegation to the CSCE would lobby for use of the ECE. Kaj Falkman added that small states, such as Sweden, should strive for the multilateralization of the granting of credits in order to strengthen their position, and Axel

Edelstam pointed out that while the Soviet Union had no sympathy with the ECE, it could eventually be forced to cooperate with it.[50]

Wachtmeister then introduced NATO's proposal on the freer movement of people, information and ideas, maintaining that the subject was 'sensitive to the Warsaw Pact' and arguing that Sweden's goals in this area should be limited to what was 'politically feasible'. Therefore, Swedish focus should be on exchanges of students, journalists, scientists, artists and TV programmes, along with the intensification of tourism and a link of these ideas to UNESCO (United Nations Educational, Scientific and Cultural Organization). This approach, defined as one of 'cautiousness and realism' in an earlier memorandum, undercut earlier statements on Sweden sharing the Western view on the subject.[51]

Requests to sponsor proposals had been received from both blocs but were turned down altogether because Sweden did not wish to declare 'a more concrete position'. This allowed the Swedes to conceal essential differences between publicly declared policy and reality. It is of interest that solidarity was not invoked as motive and that controversial subjects such as the reunification of families were excluded from the list of priorities. In response to a younger diplomat who wondered about concrete preferences, Wachtmeister stated that the Swedish government did not want to risk being identified as standing on any side and that the overall goal was for all states to attend the multilateral preparatory talks (MPT) with good intent; his conviction was that the consultations would be useful to everyone.

According to Wachtmeister, this was the only way for the CSCE to succeed.[52] If we attempt to analyse this first comprehensive discussion on Sweden's role using Holsti's typology, it is clear that the priorities presented by Wachtmeister and Falkman's statement both represent self-identification as a small state with limited influence. The natural conclusion, to the decision makers, was to remain pragmatic and seek an independent role, allowing them to focus on national interests first. Thus, in early 1972, the Swedish self-perception continued to match Switzerland but distinguished itself from Austria and Finland. The Swedes and the Swiss felt they had little to gain from such a conference, whereas the Austrians and the Finns hoped to use it to improve their political situation, in particular with regard to their relations with the Soviet Union.[53]

After this important first meeting, UD officials followed up their earlier contact with the West German Foreign Ministry with two rounds of renewed consultations. Again, the West Germans shared extensive internal memoranda and asked for Swedish comments on them.[54] West German diplomats explained that the Brandt administration viewed the CSCE as one of several instruments for European détente but considered it inferior to European integration. Generally, the Swedes complied with the wishes of the West Germans. They affirmed their support for German as a conference language and did not even disagree when Germans questioned Helsinki as the venue for the main conference – an objection made for rather trivial reasons, such as availability of hotels, range of spare time activities, the general climate and the winter darkness.[55]

These talks were rather one sided, as it was the West Germans who explained, argued and demanded most of the time and the Swedes who listened and agreed. To Sweden, these consultations were 'an important part in the Swedish preparations'.[56] Wachtmeister himself travelled to Bonn on 21 April 1972 to meet with Berndt von Staden, the head of Foreign Relations and Security at the Federal Chancellery.[57] With clear goals of their own, and with close Nordic cooperation still absent, the friendly ties with the FRG remained an important reference point.

The West Germans were aware of this and also observed that Sweden still preferred refraining from discussions about specific question, as pointed out in internal reports of the AA.[58] Knut Thyberg, councillor at the Swedish embassy in Bonn, learned that the West Germans and the Americans were in agreement concerning the central role of the 'human factor'. He expected the FRG to apply a cautious, 'step-by-step' style to negotiations with the Soviets, and he suggested to the Foreign Ministry in Stockholm that Sweden propose interbloc cooperation on development aid:

> We need to avoid the CSCE from appearing to be directed against the developing countries. Something positive must therefore be said on development aid. The big question is to what extent East and West can cooperate in developing countries. On at least one occasion, the Russians have offered cooperation in a developing country to the Federal Republic [of Germany] in order to get to the Chinese. Ultimately, it is necessary to stop competing and fight each other in the Third World, which is hard for the power-seeking politicians. Would it not be a good idea for a Swedish initiative [on this subject] at the CSCE? This was also one of Dag Hammarskjöld's ideas.[59]

Thyberg's proposal was a natural call for Sweden to consolidate the position of *developer* it held in global affairs. The idea did not, however, correspond with those of high-ranking decision makers in Stockholm, whose pragmatic approach focused almost exclusively on power and ways to maintain the status quo in Europe. East German officials, such as Ambassador Kurt Nier and Peter Steglich of the GDR trade mission in Stockholm, complained about the obvious Swedish loyalty to the FRG.[60] The East Germans were not wrong, as Sweden also was very mindful of the Hallstein Doctrine. This is illustrated by the fact that the West

Germans were notified before Swedish diplomats met with officials of the GDR.⁶¹ East Germany was generally on the defensive at that time, having failed to use the CSCE as a means towards de jure recognition by Bonn.⁶²

The other important peers, besides the West Germans, were the Americans and the Finns. Leif Leifland and Jan Eliasson met with State Department officials from the Europe Desk and a working force on CSCE and MBFR. Their American interlocutors expressed scepticism about the intentions of the Soviet Union but acknowledged that there were '35–40 items' to be discussed at Helsinki. They explained that Washington was interested in an exchange of thoughts and ideas with neutral countries like Sweden, because these would eventually come to play an interesting role at the conference, where NATO would coordinate their actions but would want to avoid a rigid bloc-to-bloc constellation.⁶³ Simultaneously, ambassador Göran Ryding proposed consultations at the ambassadorial level with Finland in order to deepen and improve Swedish-Finnish relations, since many other countries, including Norway, Switzerland, Denmark, Poland, France, Italy, the Netherlands and the Soviet Union, had already been in touch with Helsinki.⁶⁴

In subsequent consultations with the Finnish Foreign Ministry, the Swedish delegation, led by ambassador Ryding, declared its readiness to proceed to the multilateral preparation stage. This caused internal criticism from some diplomats, who still found that the preparations made were inadequate and asserted that discussions had only touched upon general political and procedural questions and had failed to embrace security issues and industrial cooperation. When asked by the Finns if Sweden would take the role of chair of a working group at the multilateral preparations, no answer was given.

On the one hand, Sweden sought ways to 'actively contribute' to the CSCE, but on the other hand, it looked unfavourably on adopting a special role as arbitrator.⁶⁵ The political department therefore recommended the compilation of 'a concrete survey of established questions, a stock-taking of Swedish questions and ... the development of preliminary statements from related ministries'.⁶⁶ Hence, existing irritation about the relations it had with the two countries—over Vietnam with the United States and over the right approach to the security conference with Finland—did not influence the basic Swedish position on these matters. Finland and the United States remained important partners of Swedish foreign policy. This, in consequence, is indicative of the Swedish pragmatism we have already seen.

Foreign Minister Krister Wickman presented parts of the Foreign Ministry's deliberations in a government declaration to the Swedish parliament on 23 March 1972. His explanation of the Swedish standpoint was based completely on the CSCE meeting eight days earlier. Wickman praised the contribution of West German *Ostpolitik* to détente, emphasizing that Sweden had supported it from the beginning and adding that bilateral consultations progressed well and were expected to allow small states to actively participate at the CSCE.[67] The congruence between the CSCE working group meeting and Wickman's parliamentary statement illustrates the combination of top-down and bottom-up elements present in the development of political positions.

A number of telegrams from this period indicate that the role played by non-state actors was not completely irrelevant. Gunnar Jarring, Sweden's ambassador in Moscow, reported that Western European ambassadors and high-ranking Soviet officials considered the alternative leftist conferences mentioned in the previous chapter essential.[68] The Soviets argued that their participation could provide a 'decisive acceleration' of the process towards the actual CSCE. This belief also received support from Britain, when Baron Gerald Gardiner, former lord chancellor and influential Labour politician, sent a message of support to the organizers of the Brussels conference.

In Sweden, domestic activities took place during a meeting of communist parties in Stockholm.[69] The role ascribed to leftist activities by Soviet propaganda was nevertheless a gross exaggeration, as the Soviets tried to compensate for lost momentum by exploiting public opinion. Such activities were attempts to raise expectations that Sweden would play a more idealistic role outside of the Swedish Foreign Ministry, in the hopes that Sweden would become a defender of values originating in its humanitarian tradition and current altruism. They never had any real impact on the country's policy, however.

What mattered most to the government and the UD was that the official policy enjoyed the support of the opposition parties, as illustrated by a *Pravda* interview in which Olle Dahlén, a longstanding member of parliament for the Liberal Party, stated, 'Basically, we do little ourselves to speed the convocation for this conference, because we think that this is a matter for the government. But in debates that are held in this country on the theme, we express our point of view and actively support the idea of the conference'.[70] In contrast to the Wedén affair, or maybe as a consequence of it, the cautious approach to the CSCE and lack of solidarity with it did not cause criticism from the opposition parties.

Multiplying Efforts

After the spring of 1972, the pieces started falling into place. Negotiations in Helsinki and bilateral talks between the United States and the Soviet Union created good prospects for the signing of the first SALT agreement during Richard Nixon's visit to Moscow in late May 1972. From Washington, Leif Leifland reported in detail how disarmament authorities, the State Department and the Pentagon had worked on MBFR but needed more time to coordinate their results with the White House and NATO. His analysis pointed out that CBM, such as the observation of military manoeuvres and prenotification of troop movements, were likely to become an integral part of future agreements.[71] Due to more substantial disarmament discussions left to MBFR, CBM soon became the foremost subject of interest in Swedish CSCE policy.[72]

In May 1972 the Swedish Foreign Ministry initiated a new phase of preparations, which were described as 'very active' in internal correspondence.[73] Preparations were now scheduled for the MPT to start after the summer of 1972 and the conference proper in 1973. It was also suggested that one high-ranking official would be assigned the specific task of preparing the Swedish delegation.[74] Finally, the earlier 'wait-and-see attitude', still viewed critically by the other neutrals,[75] was abandoned for good. Sweden was isolated no more. Consultations on the CSCE were intensified with diplomats and politicians from Belgium, the United Kingdom, Italy and Switzerland, and the contact between the UD and its embassies on the matter multiplied.

Press reports and published studies from numerous countries were sent to the Foreign Ministry's political department in Stockholm for evaluation and analysis.[76] Thenceforth, Sweden began to advocate its 'cautiousness and realism' approach more actively. In a meeting with Britain's ambassador in Stockholm, Wachtmeister emphasized the sensitive nature of facilitating freer movement of ideas to Eastern European regimes and stressed the importance of avoiding the issue so as not to risk leading the CSCE to failure.[77] Other countries quickly observed this shift in Swedish policy. The British ambassador in Stockholm reported to London:

> Hitherto the Swedish Government's comments in public about the Conference on Security and Co-operation have been restricted to the well-known view that it should be well-prepared, open to all interested countries and take place in the early or very early future. Now that the Swedish Ministry of Foreign Affairs has a clearer picture of the views and positions of countries in both Eastern and Western Europe on the Conference, they consider that the time has come to place Swedish views on record in more detail.[78]

The Foreign Ministry in Stockholm took to heart earlier criticism about the lack of preparations and, as a consequence, concretized its position on a number of questions. Unsurprisingly, the role of mediator was still not in reach. Stockholm agreed to turn down the Finnish offer to chair the working group on the conference agenda at the MPT, with Wachtmeister explaining to Göran Ryding that 'we are eager to avoid giving special responsibility to the neutral countries during the conference', a view shared by Switzerland at the time.[79] Instead, the Swedes thought that participants should elect the chairs following common UN practice.[80] On 23 May 1972, Foreign Minister Wickman presented a report on Sweden's approach to the CSCE to the Advisory Council on Foreign Affairs. This was the first time that the opposition parties were briefed in greater detail.

The document contained a historical overview, a summary of Eastern, Western and Swedish positions and a detailed description of technical details. Once again, the general framework was based on Western positions, as this memorandum resembled a Belgian document in terms of structure and with regard to the assessment of the situation agreed on by early 1972. The single individual actor who stood out in the report in terms of references was West Germany's chancellor Willy Brandt. Sweden's general Western and West German orientation left a clear mark on the report; NATO's positions were elaborated in detail, whereas the Eastern bloc was only mentioned in passive terms. It also explained the reservations about human contact and the freer flow of information, which 'touch upon very sensitive nerves in the societal structure of the Communist countries'.[81] With this single exception, the role of Stockholm as Bonn's faithful friend ran like a red thread through the Swedish positioning process.

By mid-1972, Western faith in military advantages from MBFR had dwindled, as many understood that the Soviet Union would not agree to symmetrical force reductions. Therefore, even the most enthusiastic proponents of a linkage between the CSCE and MBFR abandoned their hopes and accepted the position of the United States and France, which had always maintained their separation. As a result, binding the Warsaw Pact states to force reductions became a political rather than a military interest, and the military content of the CSCE was reduced to CBM.[82] NATO wanted to achieve this through a parallelism between the two negotiations, as was proposed by US Secretary of State William Rogers at the NATO summit in Bonn on 30 and 31 May 1972.[83]

The Bonn communiqué stated, 'In the interest of security, the examination at a CSCE of appropriate measures including certain military measures, aimed at strengthening confidence and increasing stability would contribute to the process of reducing the dangers of military confrontation'.[84] With the West German ratification of the Moscow and Warsaw treaties, the agreement on the Anti–Ballistic Missile Treaty and SALT I between 12 and 29 May 1972 and the NATO communiqué two days later, the West was almost ready to enter multilateral preparations and hoped that the last hurdle—the parallelism between the CSCE and MBFR—could be overcome after the following summit in Paris.[85]

Thus, after more than three years of negotiations, final discussions on preconditions were introduced on various occasions; Canadian foreign minister Mitchell Sharp, who called the Bonn summit the 'most pleasant' of his time in office, told this to Åke Malmaeus, Sweden's ambassador in Ottawa. Sharp claimed that the road to beginning the multilateral preparations in November 1972 was now clear, emphasizing that freer movement of people and ideas was the most essential subject to Canada and refusing Malmaeus's objection that a hard-line Western position on this might turn out to be counterproductive.[86]

In Washington, Leif Leifland received a different, and more correct, picture from the State Department's NATO office, which stated that there had been disagreements regarding the role of the Europeans and further delays.[87] Renewed discussions on the venue marked the beginning of a new stage, nevertheless. West German foreign minister Walter Scheel declared his government's readiness to accept Helsinki as a venue, on the understanding that Finland would restrict itself to accommodating technical questions.[88] With this, Bonn gave up Egon Bahr's idea to establish Berlin as a CSCE location.[89] The progress was noted with interest in Stockholm, where an essential meeting of the CSCE working group took place a few days after the NATO summit. Again, representatives from five ministries met at the UD.

This time, four study groups, which would cooperate with the Swedish delegation at Helsinki and contribute to the development of Swedish proposals and positions, were formed. The study group on disarmament, chaired by Axel Edelstam, comprised Captain Torgil Wulff and Jan Prawitz of the Defence Ministry and Per Olof Forshell and Ulf Ericsson of the UD. Together with Rune Nyström (UD), Wulff and Prawitz also belonged to the second study group on general principles of relations between states chaired by Hans Blix. The third study group, on economic, industrial, commercial and technical-scientific cooperation, consisted of its chairman, Hans Ewerlöf (UD), Nils Börje Leuf (Ministry of Trade), Sten Niklasson (Ministry of Industry), Kaj Falkman (UD) and Marianne Thorén (Ministry of Education). The fourth study group dealt with cultural relations and freer communications and was chaired by Manfred Nilsson (UD); its other members were Cai Melin (UD), Ilmar Bekeris (Ministry of Education) and Göran Berg (UD).

One member of each group served as a contact person between a ministry and the CSCE working group. These contact persons were Prawitz, a researcher at the Swedish Defence Research Agency (Försvarets forskningsanstalt), Bekeris, Leuf, Niklasson and Nyström.[90] The study groups' chairs were supplied with the necessary documents by the Foreign Ministry's political department and maintained close ties with the Foreign Ministry's CSCE working group, which comprised Wachtmeister, Giron, Edelstam, Nyström and Falkman. The task of the study groups was to present the results of their deliberations by the end of August 1972.[91] With this, the foundation of Sweden's CSCE policy was laid. The widely branched hierarchy allowed positions to be concluded bottom up when necessary.

Encouraged by the momentum the CSCE had gained from Richard Nixon's visit to Moscow and Soviet foreign minister Andrei Gromyko's consultations in Paris, the Soviet Union pushed even harder for convocation by June 1972.[92] At the UN, the Soviet delegation presented a resolution 'in support of the earliest convocation of a European Conference on Security and Cooperation'. Moscow wanted at least one Nordic country to support the proposal. Since Finland refrained because of its status as conference host, the Swedes were approached.

When the Swedish delegation in New York asked the Foreign Ministry in Stockholm for 'immediate instructions' on the voting, Stockholm ordered it to consult with the other Nordics, 'but without discussing details on the CSCE'.[93] Evidently, the regional collaborator role remained problematic in the eyes of the Swedes. Eventually, an alternative formulation, avoiding direct support of the Soviet resolution, was presented on behalf of Sweden, Denmark, Norway and Iceland.[94] But in contrast to May 1969, when the Soviets were rebuffed on successive occasions, Sweden now consented to certain activities that paved the way to the conference.

The alternative leftist conference in support of the CSCE, held between 2 and 5 June 1972 in Brussels, added to the rising public interest, although it did not influence the role conceptions of state representatives. Several hundred participants from labour unions, youth and women's movements and churches and other religious bodies, as well as diverse groups of intellectuals and artists, participated in and debated on different committees about how to support European détente.

They adopted, among other things, concrete proposals on the renunciation of the use of force and the convocation of the CSCE.[95] The official attendees from Sweden were Stellan Arvidsson, Nils Bengtsson, Bernt Carlsson, Tord Ekström, author Per Olov Enquist and Gunvor Ryding, the last a member of parliament from the Swedish communist party. The meeting was observed by the Swedish Foreign Ministry, which received reports from the embassy in Brussels and added the brochure published by the Brussels conference to its official CSCE folders. Once again, Soviet propaganda vociferously promoted the meeting as proof of public support for a quick convocation of the CSCE.[96] And, once again, the Swedes, like many other Western and neutral states, remained completely ignorant of it. After all, the CSCE lacked the potential to spark off public controversy, due to its complex and abstract nature. Therefore, decision makers in foreign ministries could afford to ignore alternative conceptions of the role their countries should play. In this respect, Sweden was no exception to the rule.

With the preparations carried out over spring of 1972, the Swedish Foreign Ministry extended its infrastructure in order to tackle the upcoming conference. In comparison with similar states, the Swedish CSCE machinery was widely ramified, leaving the country well prepared for the conference.[97]

Entering the Home Straight

During the summer, the CSCE was overshadowed by a number of major political events. The Inner-German Transit Agreement and the Eastern treaties came into force when the Four Power Agreement was ratified on 3 June 1972. Shortly afterwards, the Basic Treaty on inner-German relations, ratified on 11 May, also became effective.[98] With this, the most important problems regarding Germany—*the* precondition for a conference from Sweden's perspective, as shown in the previous chapter—had been solved. Now, the only thing that was due was a superpower agreement on the linkage between CSCE and MBFR.

In West Germany, terrorists Andreas Baader and Ulrike Meinhof of the left-wing Red Army Faction were arrested on 1 and 15 June, respectively. In the United States, the arrest of five men for the attempted burglary of the Democratic National Committee's office in Washington, DC, marked the beginning of the Watergate affair. On 22 July, the EEC and EFTA reached a free trade agreement, and nine days later, Northern Ireland's Bloody Sunday shook Britain. In September, eleven Israeli athletes attending the twentieth Summer Olympics and five Palestinian terrorists were killed in the so-called Munich massacre near Fürstenfeldbruck, following a hostage taking in the athletes' village.

These events, together with the escalation of the war in Vietnam, engaged decision makers and dominated the headlines of the international press; relatively little space was left for diplomacy on a high level. In the case of the Swedes, the United Nations Conference on the Human Environment, held in Stockholm between 5 and 16 June 1972, added to the eventful summer, as it tied up considerable resources at the Swedish Foreign Ministry.[99]

In Sweden, very few meetings on the CSCE were held during the summer. In early July, the UD agreed with the Foreign Office in London on the visit of a delegation to London for a meeting on 24 August with Crispin Tickell and the staff in charge of British CSCE preparations.[100] Other than that, only one additional talk occurred, when Rune Nyström travelled to East Berlin for an exchange of views with the East German Foreign Ministry.[101] Although nothing new came out of this meeting itself, it was reason enough to cause a West German reaction. The West German ambassador in Stockholm complained to Ole Jödahl about Nyström's trip, arguing that it should have been 'arranged' with Bonn. While the criticism was excused with reference to the 'narrowness of the meeting', this illustrates quite well the intimate Swedish–West German relationship at the time.[102]

When Axel Edelstam presented early results of the study group on disarmament that he was heading, he argued that it was uncertain how much space the topic would be given at the CSCE. The reason was that the term 'disarmament' itself implied the reduction of weapons and troops, an issue dealt with as MBFR elsewhere. Despite some remaining resistance against its inclusion in the conference agenda, it was expected that most of the participating countries would take a positive stance on disarmament. Therefore, the Swedish experts believed that certain results could be achieved; they started compiling official statements and available materials from both blocs together with earlier plans and ideas on disarmament in Europe, such as the Rapacki[103] and Undén Plans[104] of 1957 and 1961, respectively. Most importantly, the group would formulate recommendations for Sweden's general CSCE policy.[105]

In the following years, the disarmament study group became the most important for Swedish policy, and Axel Edelstam quickly became one of the most influential actors in Sweden's policy towards the CSCE. The fact that one of its valued foreign policy issues might turn out promising added to the attraction of Sweden taking a more active role in the context of the CSCE. As an isolate or exclusively faithful friend of the West, Sweden would not have been able to defend its own interests. Therefore, it continued moving towards an attitude which Holsti's typology defines as independent.

Stagnation occurred when the NATO states failed to accomplish convergence between their differing positions. Disagreement also prevailed on the organization of the conference and on how to approach some of the most vital points of its agenda, such as principles guiding relations between states and freer movements. To US state secretary Rogers, achievements related to freer movements in Eastern Europe were a requirement for the CSCE to be 'truly useful'. The Netherlands disagreed with a French proposal to organize the CSCE in three stages, and its connections with MBFR and SALT were yet to be defined. Within the EC, a common foreign policy was still in the making by the Davignon Committee, which discussed how to reach the commonality of the Inner Six.[106] The Soviets, on the other hand, were very clear on their position. When Foreign Minister Andrei Gromyko visited Brussels in early July 1972, he announced a policy change towards the conference and stated that Moscow wanted the MPT to reach consensus on the agenda of the conference proper.[107]

Such developments were noted with great interest in Stockholm and circulated in lengthy memoranda to all ministries as well as to Olof Palme and King Gustaf VI Adolf.[108] But the most substantial hurdle remaining was the linkage between the CSCE and MBFR, on which Americans and Soviets negotiated behind closed doors. While waiting for the green light from Washington and Moscow, the Swedes observed the situation closely and tried to include any details of interest in their early definitions of their own aims.

The CSCE also engaged a prominent voice outside of the Foreign Ministry. Professor Gunnar Myrdal of the Stockholm International Peace Research Institute (SIPRI), an eminent Swedish economist and 1974 Nobel laureate, sent a letter to the Soviet government regarding the relation between the CSCE and ECE. Myrdal had served as executive secretary of the ECE between 1947 and 1957, and he shared the Swedish Foreign Ministry's interest in strengthening the commission through the CSCE. In a written note to Foreign Minister Krister Wickman, to which he attached his letter to the Soviets, Myrdal argued that the Soviets could not be trusted. He stressed his lack of faith in the CSCE, with reference to the Soviet Union's sole interest, which he believed was to make manifest European division. Myrdal concluded that the Soviet silence following calls for the conference to make use of ECE was grounded in Moscow's general unwillingness to establish a general link between the CSCE and the UN:

> There are two reasons for their utter silence. Partly, they are not interested in engaging the UN. They've had a majority against them from the beginning and the rise of the many underdeveloped countries has not helped the Russians much other than in special questions such as decolonization. The other reason is that the Russians have a very different view of a secretariat than us. They are still thinking in terms of Troika. They want a secretariat consisting of delegates of the two power blocs, which then will negotiate. They don't like the idea of an independent secretariat of experts. I hardly need to add that our interest is the complete opposite. We do not want to be bystanders in such a confrontation.[109]

To his surprise, Myrdal received a note verbale on his letter, which was handed over by Georgij Motjalov of the Soviet embassy in Stockholm. The fact that the note ignored the factual issue raised by Myrdal only confirmed his earlier conclusions.[110] This anecdote illustrates the rising interest in the CSCE within Swedish political circles and the appearance of role expectations on different levels, in contrast to earlier years, when the Foreign Ministry had worked in almost complete anonymity on the matter. With the notable, and still uncontroversial, exception of a few leftist activists, few voices were raised for Sweden to pursue a more vociferous and idealistic policy.[111]

Bilateral consultations with the Foreign Office in London offered Swedish CSCE diplomats useful ground-level reports on Western standpoints. Great Britain was just as worried about the motives of the Soviet CSCE policy as Sweden. During the talks, the Swedes once again held that freer movement touched on essential points in the socialist system and that they hoped for the West to be flexible and open to compensation in other areas, in case the goals of achieving the freer movement complex were not accomplishable. The British response was similar to that of the Americans, and Crispin Tickell, in charge of Britain's CSCE policy, made clear that there would be no Western concessions on freer movement.

The British were ready for a 'squabble', whereas the Swedes wanted to align with the Soviets. One of Tickell's staff members, colleague General RE Lloyd of the Arms Control and Disarmament Research Unit, reacted harshly to Sweden's willingness to discuss nuclear weapon–free zones. Lloyd wondered how 'anyone but an Eastern state could even think about proposing nuclear weapon–free zones' and whether the Swedes had thoroughly considered the possible consequences of proposals such as those the Rapacki Plan might have for Swedish security.[112] His criticism was rejected immediately and left the Swedish position unchanged.

In early September 1972, the US State Department finally confirmed its approval of many of the essential preconditions necessary for the convocation of the MPT. The United States accepted Finnish ambassador Richard Tötterman as chairman and agreed with the Soviets that 22 November 1972 should be the commencement date if Moscow agreed to parallel MBFR talks.[113] In Stockholm, the four study groups presented their first conclusions and recommendations for a Swedish policy at the CSCE. The disarmament study group based its assessment on a memorandum drafted by Ulf Reinius, which contained accounts of the Rapacki, Gomulka, Undén and Kekkonen plans as well as alternative discussions on nuclear weapon–free zones in Scandinavia and the Baltic Sea.[114] Reinius argued that the Soviets could not be expected to agree to plans on free zones in the foreseeable future.[115] Axel Edelstam added that the final memorandum of the disarmament study group would offer the Swedish government different options for drafting proposals or reacting to those of other states.

Edelstam asserted that it was natural for Sweden to conduct an active disarmament policy at the CSCE. This activeness would have to be manifested early on, which could be done by proposing disarmament as a stand-alone agenda point by giving it substantial space in the opening speech at the MPT and presenting it as a formal initiative, in the same way that Switzerland had proposed a system for the settlement of disputes.[116] The working group addressed Edelstam's comments and offered new conclusions some two weeks later, stating that a distinction between nuclear, biological and chemical weapons would be useful. A biological weapon–free zone would be uncontroversial for the Swedish delegation to demand. In contrast, chemical weapons, prohibited by the Geneva Protocol of 1925, were part of the weapons stockpile of many European countries, which made it harder to prohibit their use.

The overall conclusion of the study group was that Sweden should present a proposal at the CSCE on a biological weapons–free zone in a way similar to how Undén had presented his idea at the UN in 1961.[117] Ulf Ericsson, who drafted the final version of the disarmament memorandum, argued that a similar tactic allowed Sweden to 'reap the general political merits of an initiative on nuclear weapons' without getting involved in 'delicate factual statements on nuclear weapons which are so important to the security policy of so many European states'.

Nuclear weapons were essential to the strategy of key actors, and this was unlikely to change, wrote Ericsson. Also, a nuclear-free zone was not very like to prohibit the outbreak of nuclear war. Therefore, the rationale, and the goal of related proposals, should be to minimize the risk of regional conflicts escalating into nuclear wars. Terror balance could be considered a positive factor, reducing the risk of escalation and diminishing the role of minor nuclear weapons, and as a consequence Sweden should try to link regional disarmament with SALT.[118] Regardless of its prospect of real influence, the disarmament study group contributed to establishing a more active role for Sweden.

The Swedish embassy in Bonn learned through the Auswärtiges Amt that Kissinger and Brezhnev had reached an agreement on the timetable in Bonn on 19 September 1972. After renewed consultations in Moscow, the superpowers had agreed on conditions for separate but parallel negotiations at the CSCE in Finland and on MBFR in Vienna. The commencement date for the multilateral preparatory talks was set to 22 November 1973 and for the CSCE in late June 1973. Henry Kissinger was pleased, as he had reached his two main goals: parallelism between the CSCE and MBFR and postponement of the conference until the summer of

1973. Leonid Brezhnev, for his part, succeeded in getting the Americans to accept Helsinki as the venue for the CSCE and to agree to participate without preconditions related to the results of the MPT. This deal was presented to the NATO council on 20 September 1972 as a Soviet proposal but was considered a Soviet-American agreement by insiders, as West German sources explained to Swedish ambassador Sven Backlund.[119]

With the separation of CSCE and MBFR, one of the three pillars of European détente was placed outside the CSCE. Whereas status quo détente and economic and cultural détente were integral to the conference, disarmament détente, the most important to Sweden, was treated separately.[120] This contributed further to the very pragmatic way in which Stockholm viewed the CSCE. With the agreement between Washington and Moscow accomplished, the preparations for the conference entered the home straight. The following weeks were spent finalizing the position Sweden would take at the MPT. Developments in other countries were observed more closely again, and the Swedes kept making their case for Western caution about freer movements in bilateral talks.[121]

Determining Swedish Positions

The US-Soviet agreement opened up the opportunity for a last round of diplomatic dealmaking all over Europe. During a meeting between Ole Jödahl and Austrian diplomat Walter Wodak in Stockholm, it was brought to Swedish attention that Austria would offer Vienna as a venue and lobby for the CSCE to be concluded with a treaty.[122] Sweden, on the other hand, traditionally preferred declarations. The only voice to be raised against it at the Swedish Foreign Ministry in Stockholm was that of Ambassador Tore Tallroth, who pointed out that the difference between treaty and declaration, in particular with regard to cultural issues, was marginal but that a treaty would actually deter states from neglecting their duties.[123]

West Germany remained a major channel of information, as internal papers on different subjects, such as the aims and goals of the Soviet Union, were circulated and discussed between the Auswärtiges Amt and the Utrikesdepartementet.[124] At the Quai d'Orsay, Embassy Councillor Gustaf Hamilton af Hageby was told that the French 'would like to see closer consultations' with Sweden once Stockholm's position had been consolidated.[125] In contrast, Warsaw Pact member states had abandoned attempts to establish similar ties with Sweden.

As the MPT, soon known as the Salon des Ambassadeurs, loomed, the four study groups at the UD sped up their work and finalized their conclusions. As mentioned earlier, disarmament was the main area of

Swedish interest. The Soviet Union had become more flexible towards discussing disarmament at the CSCE but remained strictly against treating it as a separate agenda point. Only the Americans shared this view, whereas the majority of the member states of both the Warsaw Pact and NATO were generally open to negotiations. Many small and midsized countries shared the concern that the conference could degenerate into a playground for the superpowers; Poland and Belgium even suggested putting disarmament on the agenda.

Disarmament was also important to Sweden's neighbours. Norway feared a swelling in the number of Soviet troops in the north, and Finland considered relaunching a renewed version of the Kekkonen Plan. The CSCE grew more attractive in the eyes of the Swedes in this respect, since they did not expect that the CCD or other future global disarmament conferences would allow developments in *regional* disarmament.[126] With this background, and with very little to gain, it made even less sense to Sweden to engage on a regional level.

However, as Axel Edelstam summarized in a working paper, overall interest in disarmament was rather weak. Edelstam recalled the 1972 government declaration and a speech given by Olof Palme at the UN on 20 October 1970, in which the Swedish prime minister had called disarmament 'the decisive and most pressuring question of our time' and claimed that his country's foreign policy, which 'contributed heavily to our goodwill and prestige in the world', was grounded in Sweden's firm interest in disarmament. Edelstam pointed out that 'it would appear strange if we remained passive in this area at the CSCE'. He concluded:

> Regional disarmament measures in Europe, our neighbourhood, would doubtless be of importance to Sweden from a national security perspective. This is true for both weapons of mass destruction, which we do not possess ourselves, as well as for large standing troops equipped with 'conventional' weapons, which exist against each other in Central Europe. A precondition for our national security to profit from regional disarmament measures is certainly that the current approximate balance between East and West is not disturbed seriously.[127]

For these reasons, the study group on disarmament recommended that Sweden lobby for the subject to be established as a separate agenda point, despite the obvious opposition it would meet. This gives empirical support to the widespread assumption that the expectations of others have considerably less influence on decisions and actions—the 'role performance'—than do the NRCs of the ego. In the aftermath, the Swedes decided to try to relaunch an upgraded version of the Undén Plan modified by the inclusion of all weapons of mass destruction.

The goal would be the establishment of free zones of weapons of mass destruction in Europe, in which the production and the storing of A, B and C weapons would be prohibited. Despite such ambitious considerations, the Swedes always maintained their realism. Edelstam himself did not expect that any of his proposals would actually result in the destruction of weapons, but he hoped that the threshold for their usage could be raised.[128] Edelstam's ideas did not pass without criticism. Leif Leifland emphasized that the superpowers were determined not to allow discussions on free zones of weapons of mass destruction, or even on tactical weapons, at the CSCE. With this background in mind, he ruled out Edelstam's proposal completely, maintaining, 'I believe that a formal initiative of the type you are sketching would meet with massive resistance and thus would be deemed to be buried quickly'. Instead, Leifland argued, Sweden could bring up these issues during a speech at the UN General Assembly.[129]

Now even the other CSCE study groups of the Swedish Foreign Ministry intensified their efforts. The Ministry of Industry presented a memorandum on 27 September 1972 which reiterated positions taken earlier rather than offering salient proposals on industrial and technical cooperation. The Ministry of Trade, for its part, recommended that Sweden support the West more openly by emphasizing a stronger role for the ECE, which was in the interests of many states.[130] As economic and scientific cooperation were not strongly ideologized, and thus not expected to become a battleground like disarmament or human rights, preparations in these areas were less extensive. At that time, there was little talk about their role in the overall strategy of Sweden.

Dealing with a more delicate subject, the study group on cultural relations and freer communications recommended that Sweden not take part in ambitious joint ventures on cultural issues. Instead, the group argued, the Swedish delegation should work on improving existing cultural relations 'bottom up', rather than contributing to the 'top-down' approach of the CSCE. It further recommended that existing cooperation between the Organisation for Economic Co-operation and Development (OECD) and UNESCO be revisited before considering new forms of collaboration. The Foreign Ministry wished to work as comprehensively as possible and sent out an inquiry telegram to the Swedish embassies in Europe in an attempt to collect information on the policies of other governments. The Western proposals on freer communications were praised as 'interesting and realistic'; in their memorandum, the group held that

> Sweden should try to promote greater freedom regarding contacts over borders both for institutions and individuals. This attitude is quite close to the one championed by Western states. At the same time, it is important to move

within the boundaries of what is politically feasible towards the Eastern bloc. The Swedish strategy should consist of an active move during the early discussions, consisting of proposals which can be discussed in the following. All too modest proposals ought to result in vague and hollow declarations.[131]

With its analysis and recommendations, the study group on cultural relations and freer communications opposed the policy that Sweden had maintained so far. Its view was not specifically focused on the role Sweden should play per se but rather on the definition of what was realistic and feasible. It did not, nevertheless, leave a mark on the role perception of the decision makers in Stockholm, who continued to favour a minimalist approach to human rights at the CSCE. As a result, the human dimension of the conference would not become an integral part of the Swedish role.

The study group on the principles guiding relations between states consisted of four members but was very much dominated by Hans Blix, who authored three influential memoranda: on principles for European security, on methods to strengthen the security of European states and on institutions for European security. In these papers, Blix tried to link the theoretical foundations of the subject matter to practical measures that could be taken at the CSCE. He reiterated the importance of compatibility between any CSCE outcome and the UN Charter and pointed to the fact that articles two[132] and four[133] of the North Atlantic Treaty did not allow a Brezhnev Doctrine–like attitude, in case Western states drifted towards communism, but acknowledged that what the real behaviour should be in such a scenario remained vague.

Blix put much emphasis on the importance of the principle that states should refrain from the threat or use of force and noninterference, but he remarked critically that principles on human rights implied problems for Eastern and other European governments alike.[134] With this, he supported the Swedish government's early role performance and defended the Swedish attitude against internal criticism and contrasting views.

Blix also reviewed numerous methods which had the potential to strengthen European security, such as collective security, great power responsibility, regional organizations, military alliances, arms control, demilitarization and policies of neutrality. He argued that despite the large number of methods invented over the course of centuries, history had shown that 'all methods for the strengthening of security . . . have proven infirm'. Blix did not regard them as completely meaningless, however: military alliances could deter attacks, and armed neutrality could contribute to necessary balance.

Mechanisms of consultations could contribute to the solution of potentially dangerous situations.[135] And so, in his memorandum on institutions,

Blix discussed the necessity of the CSCE creating a permanent organ, as requested by the Eastern bloc. He defended the rather sceptical position taken by Sweden, arguing that any meaningful discussion on a permanent organ would have to be defined by the outcome of the conference itself. Thus, states that wanted to await the outcome had the right to do so. He pointed out that there was no pan-European organ that could ease tensions or solve disputes. The UN machinery had intervened in a number of questions, but the Quadripartite Agreement on Berlin had shown that the most essential questions were dealt with outside the UN. It was obvious to Blix that both the East and the West disliked foreign interference in internal issues, and, as a consequence, an organ would have to deal with tensions and friction *between* the East and the West.[136]

He also believed that the multilateralization of European diplomacy regarding security and cooperation could potentially offer neutral countries like Sweden greater opportunities for participation. Such multilateralization, Blix explained, could be set up through an annual meeting of ambassadors in Helsinki or Vienna or in a permanent court, in accordance with the Swiss proposal, which it was natural for Sweden to support due to Sweden's own 'firm tradition of third-party-participation in conflict resolution'.[137] These extensive elaborations stamped Blix's authority on matters of international law—authority he used with the cooperation of his Swiss counterpart, Rudolf Bindschedler. It has been pointed out that Sweden was the only neutral country not to produce a prominent CSCE diplomat.[138] Had it not been for Sweden's lack of clear goals at the CSCE, Hans Blix would most likely have been the one to close that gap.

The Blix papers were the final nails in the coffin of a more altruistic and idealistic Swedish line towards human contacts. When Wachtmeister, Leifland and Jan Eliasson met with leading US State Department officials, including George S. Springsteen, on 17 October 1972, the Swedes argued that the subject of freer movements was 'problematic' and that only 'very marginal' results, such as reduction of travel restrictions, could be achieved. Overall, a careful, realistic approach was required to avoid a deadlock. Springsteen assured the Swedes that the American delegation would avoid polemics but made it clear that it regarded the subject itself as substantial. It was a core issue of détente and the State Departments' policy; thus, 'some rough going' would be inevitable.[139] Interestingly, it was American diplomats who argued for the value of greater individual rights, not officials representing the government of Olof Palme. Here, in contrast to Sweden's general foreign policy profile at the time, visions of greater freedom and justice were not part of the country's role in international affairs.

At a meeting between the CSCE working group and the four study groups on 20 October 1972, the reports of the latter were subjected to closing discussions and went through final editing. In the Western camp, different opinions prevailed on how extensive and profound discussions at the MPT should be. France argued in favour of the MPT establishing a detailed agenda and defining the mandates of three committees on security, economic issues and cultural cooperation. Great Britain, on the other hand, feared an early deadlock on sensitive issues. The position of the United States was somewhat unclear, not least because the British spread rumours about Washington's declining interest in thorough preparatory talks. These rumours were dismissed by Sweden's ambassador in Washington, Hubert de Besche, who confirmed that despite 'problems of coordination' the Americans were decided on thorough preparations.[140] The Warsaw Pact member states wanted to proceed as soon as possible and called on the West to stop complicating the MPT.[141]

In late October 1972, all remaining issues were settled between Washington and Moscow. Geneva was decided upon as the venue for the second and main stage of the negotiations.[142] No immediate linkage was established between CSCE and MBFR. Discussions in Helsinki and Geneva were limited to notifications on militarily manoeuvres, while collateral constraints were negotiated between the superpowers.[143] With only weeks left until the start of multilateral preparations at Dipoli, many thought it was obvious that the CSCE was of low priority to Kissinger and that the Soviets were still trying to diminish its security element.[144]

Between Sweden and the Soviet Union, disagreement existed on the procedure and content of the MPT, disagreement that characterized consultations between Sverker Åström and Soviet ambassador Valerian Zorin.[145] Some Western states, such as Canada, France and West Germany, were eager to avoid an early atmosphere of confrontation and therefore considered mitigating their standpoint on human rights–related issues by proposing a discussion of 'improved communications' instead of 'freer movements'. This was only opposed by Britain and the United States, the latter of which, as stated earlier, was willing to accept 'some rough going'.[146]

A meeting between Sweden and Finland took place on 26 October 1972; four days later, Foreign Minister Wickman was briefed comprehensively before presenting the Swedish approach to the CSCE to the Swedish government.[147] The question of Nordic cooperation came up again when Norway presented its position to the Swedes and expressed hopes that the Nordic countries would keep in close contact at the conference. But real cooperation was not in the interest of any Nordic country, and it was consequently acknowledged that formalization or institutionalization of cooperation of any kind would be rejected and that contacts would remain as informal as possible.[148] Thus, Sweden was not unique, because the role of regional collaborator was not an option for any of these countries.

The Swedish interests at the MPT were finally defined in a memorandum drafted by Hans Blix and Axel Edelstam, which stated that any measures fostering security in Europe were of general interest. It maintained that Sweden would leave the door open for mediation efforts on the principles of relations between states—matters which it had no interest in itself. Formulations on nonuse or threat of force, nonintervention and the peaceful settlement of disputes would have to be reconciled with the Brezhnev Doctrine, and Sweden hoped for a formula on the contribution of nonaligned states to stability. Regarding the creation of institutions, Sweden would remain flexible. Security questions were not supposed to profit from a large apparatus but rather from a regularly recurring meeting of ambassadors and a small secretariat for administrative purposes. Finally, any outcome of the CSCE would have to allow the inclusion of future disarmament discussions.[149]

The memorandum confirmed that Sweden considered making a transition to active independence, which was defined by Holsti as a simultaneous emphasis on 'independence, self-determination, possible mediation functions, and active programs' (see Figure 3.1). While it was decided that the delegation would struggle to ensure that ECE would not be undermined and that the Swiss proposal would be supported as much as possible, it remained unclear whether Sweden would make proposals on confidence-building measures. Blix and Edelstam held that Sweden's major area of contribution could be on increasing mutual interdependence, which would prevent quarrels and destructive tactics in future negotiations. As bureaucratic structures in Eastern Europe hindered cultural and technological cooperation, they stated, 'Maybe one should highlight that really *close* cooperation can hardly be realized as long as the views on human rights differ from each other so much in East and West'.[150]

Blix and Edelstam had a genuine understanding of the potential of human rights but did not believe in the ability of the CSCE to bring about change. This was also communicated in bilateral talks. In high-level talks between Wickman and Austrian foreign minister Kirchschläger, it became clear to the Austrians that the Swedes 'do not have high expectations with regard to "freer movement of persons and ideas"', wished for a confirmation of the status quo and hoped to avoid conflicts at the CSCE.[151]

On 9 November 1972 the Finnish Foreign Ministry finally issued an invitation to thirty-four ambassadors in Helsinki from 'countries that are in charge of European security'. In accordance with general procedure, Ambassador Göran Ryding of the Swedish embassy in Helsinki was charged with the chairmanship of the Swedish delegation. Diplomats Kerstin Asp and Göran Berg and Press Attaché Jan Olsson were permanently at his service, while other members of the delegation would alternate with each other. These were Wachtmeister, Edelstam and Nyström from the Foreign Ministry and Wulff and Prawitz from the Defence Ministry. Among the experts who travelled to Finland on demand were Blix, Nilsson, Ewerlöf, Leuf, Niklasson and Bekeris.[152]

Conclusion

When Willy Brandt's *Ostpolitik* reached its climax with the agreement on Berlin in September 1971, Sweden was arguably the most criticized of all European states with regard to the CSCE. Largely due to its self-proclaimed role as active critic, mediator and bridge builder in international affairs, the expectations that other governments, and Swedish activists, had for Sweden's success were high. Sweden's declared 'active foreign policy' shaped domestic and foreign role expectations, as did the belief that an idealistic approach to European détente was natural to decision makers in Stockholm.

Roughly two years later, most of these critical voices had been silenced. Sweden left its strategy of adjustment, explained in the previous chapter, behind it and opened itself up to adopt a more flexible role. Acknowledging the CSCE as a political reality, the Swedes introduced internal preparations for constructive efforts on their part and defined their own interests. Most instrumental in this respect was the appointment of a group of experts in December 1971. Some of Sweden's most eminent diplomats and experts were engaged in the work of this group, among them Wilhelm Wachtmeister, Axel Edelstam and Hans Blix. Well-known scholars such as Nils Andrén, Gunnar Myrdal and Karl Birnbaum were adjunct to the Ministry for Foreign Affairs (see Figure 3.1 below). Compared to those of similar small states, such as Austria and Switzerland, Swedish preparations were thorough, widespread and far reaching.

Disarmament quickly became the single most important issue to the Swedes, clearly overshadowing less controversial topics, including economic cooperation and the rather feared question of freer movements. This was an obvious, yet surprisingly uncontested, policy. While Olof Palme publicly reiterated Swedish solidarity with the weak and vulnerable in the Third World, his government took the strongest possible realist approach to the CSCE. No one involved in the making of this foreign policy appears to have developed significant faith in the opportunities that Western politicians and diplomats believed in, namely that the CSCE could bring about substantial improvements to the life conditions of people in Eastern Europe. Instead, it was believed that any attacks on the essence of the socialist system should be avoided and that focus should be on what was realistic and feasible. Wilhelm Wachtmeister, Axel Edelstam and Hans Blix were the three key actors who played a decisive role in the formation of the Swedish attitude.

To all of them, history had taught enough lessons about the limits of international cooperation. During the transition from passive adjustment, the Swedish role performance developed, retaining a focus on realism and political calculation. It comprised a blend of features, including the role of faithful friend to Finland and West Germany (and the West more generally) and its own status as an independent actor. This was possible since being the '[one that] support[s] the policies of another government', as Holsti defined a faithful ally, did not conflict with Swedish interests.

As earlier isolationism was abandoned after September 1971, the commitment to support, or at least not to impede, Finland's striving for credible neutrality and West Germany's *Ostpolitik* was firm. At the same time, leading figures stated explicitly that Sweden did not wish to play the role of mediator or bridge. Interest in regional disarmament, in combination with the support of Finland, also demonstrated a certain interest at the regional level. Due to the differing national interests and loyalties of the Nordic countries, however, Sweden's modest self-perception as a regional leader or regional collaborator was never integrated into the actual NRC of Sweden's policymakers.

Not all Swedes shared this perception of the country's role in relation to the CSCE. A small number of diplomats and experts, as well as leftist activists and prominent intellectuals who engaged in international activist meetings, suggested that Sweden should be more active and consider solidarity as part of its policy. This was due to the general perception of Swedish foreign policy as based on its profile in relation to global matters. To activists and observers, Sweden appeared to be a natural bridge builder. Due to the paradox between change orientation in global affairs and status quo orientation in European matters, decision makers considered no such activism, however.

In order to present a harmonious picture, public speeches and official interviews were delivered by Palme, Wickman and leading diplomats alike in a way that gave a prettified picture of the role Sweden was really playing on the road to the CSCE. The 'cautious and realist' approach eventually chosen was the general premise for Sweden's CSCE policy until the start of the multilateral preparatory talks at the Dipoli conference centre in Otaniemi, a suburb of Helsinki, on 22 November 1972. Until then, Sweden did not come up with any initiative or other kind of active contribution to the ongoing process, neither of its own nor as cosponsor with other states.

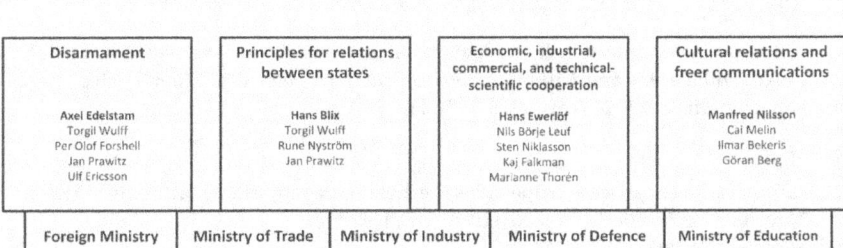

Figure 3.1. CSCE working structure at the Swedish Ministry for Foreign Affairs after December 1971

Notes

1. The West Germans did not attempt to create a linkage between the CSCE and the inner-German treaty, however, as pointed out in Hakkarainen, *State of Peace*, 142–49. See also Senoo, *Irrweg*, 91–94.
2. See Yamamoto, 'Britain, France and West Germany', 148, 266.
3. Gilde, *Österreich im KSZE-Prozess*, 56; Rosin, *Die Schweiz im KSZE-Prozeß*, 38, 58; Reimaa, *Helsinki Catch*, 39.
4. Hanhimäki, *Rise and Fall of Détente*, chs. 3 and 4.
5. Jarring to UD, Telegram 716, 14 September 1971, File 13, Vol. 30, HP 79, UD, RA.
6. Westerberg to UD, Telegram 756 'Statsminister Palmes uttalande för den finländska tidskriften Forum', 27 September 1971, File 13, Vol. 30, HP 79, UD, RA.
7. Nyström to Jarring, Cipher telegram, 'Novikovs besök hos utrikesministern', 14 October 1971, File 13, Vol. 30, HP 79, UD, RA.
8. Nyström, 'Besök hos statsministern den 13.10.71 av sovjetiske vice ministerrådsordföranden Novikov och sovjetambassadören', 13 October 1971, File 13, Vol. 30, HP 79, UD, RA.
9. Bohm, 'Några reflexioner över de aktuella avspänningssträvandena', 19 October 1971, File 14, Vol. 30, HP 79, UD, RA.
10. The CCD existed as a UN committee authorized by the General Assembly between 1969 and 1979 and was the predecessor of the 'Conference on Disarmament' (CD).
11. Nyström to Petri, Cipher telegram, 4 October 1971 and Nyström to Böök, Cipher telegram, 12 October 1971, File 13, Vol. 30, HP 79, UD, RA.
12. Bindschedler to Blix, 'Europäische Sicherheitskonferenz – Vorschlag für ein System der friedlichen Streiterledigung', 22 October 1971, File 14, Vol. 30, HP 79, UD, RA. See also Rosin, *Die Schweiz im KSZE-Prozeß*, 55–65; Fischer, *Neutral Power*, 120–41.
13. Ryding to Wachtmeister, 'Europeiska säkerhetskonferensen', 18 November 1971, File 14, Vol. 30, HP 79, UD, RA.

14. Sverige Utrikesdepartementet (ed.), *Utrikesfrågor: offentliga dokument m m rörande viktigare svenska utrikesfrågor 1971* (Stockholm: Utrikesdepartementet, 1972), 96.
15. Westerberg to UD, Telegram 972, 'Pravda återger idag under rubriken "stöder konferensen" följande TASS-Notiz', 1 December 1971, File 15, Vol. 30, HP 79, UD, RA.
16. Nyström, 'Svenska organisatoriska förberedelser för den europeiska säkerhets- och samarbetskonferensen', 18 October 1971, File 14, Vol. 30, HP 79, UD, RA.
17. Wachtmeister, 'Belgiske ambassadören angående MBFR', 14 October 1971, File 13, Vol. 30, HP 79, UD, RA.
18. Falkman, 'Läget beträffande europeiska säkerhets- och samarbetskonferensen (ESK)', 19 November 1971 and Falkman, 'Sverige och europeiska säkerhets- och samarbetskonferensen (ESK)', 24 November 1971, File 14, Vol. 30, HP 79, UD, RA.
19. Ibid.
20. Ibid.
21. Falkman, 'Sverige och europeiska säkerhets- och samarbetskonferensen (ESK)', 24 November 1971, File 14, Vol. 30, HP 79, UD, RA.
22. Romano, *Détente*, 103–21.
23. Rosin, *Die Schweiz im KSZE-Prozeß*, 51–62.
24. Wachtmeister, 'Förberedelsearbetet för en konferens om Europas säkerhet', 6 December 1971, File 15, Vol. 30, HP 79, UD, RA.
25. Hakkarainen, *A State of Peace*, 144–49.
26. For the broader context of the discussion of these linkages, see Yamamoto, 'Britain, France and West Germany', 190–97 and Hakkarainen, *A State of Peace*, 149–53. See also Falkman, 'Samtal i Köpenhamn om ESK', 17 December 1971, File 15, Vol. 30, HP 79, UD, RA.
27. NATO Summit, 9–10 December 1971, Final Communiqué available from www.nato.int/cps/en/natolive/official_texts_26812.htm (accessed 29 November 2015).
28. Falkman, 'ESK: WP- och Nato-staternas möten i december 1971', 13 December 1971, File 15, Vol. 30, HP 79, UD, RA.
29. Göransson to Wachtmeister, 'Samtal angående europeisk säkerhetskonferens och MBFR', 8 December 1971; Thyberg to UD, 'Natos ministerråd diskuterar säkerhetskonferensen', 23 December 1971; De Besche to UD, Cipher telegram 262, 17 December 1971, File 15, Vol. 30, HP 79, UD, RA.
30. Eng to Wachtmeister, 'Den europeiska säkerhetskonferensen', 21 January 1972, File 16, Vol. 31, HP 79, UD, RA.
31. Fischer, *Neutral Power*, 145–50.
32. Falkman, 'Läget beträffande europeiska säkerhetskonferensen (ESK)', 7 December 1971, File 15, Vol. 30; Berg, 'Konsultationer mellan de neutrala staterna angående ESK', 5 January 1972, File 16, Vol. 31, HP 79, UD, RA. See also Fischer, *Neutral Power*, 141–50.
33. On the background of the SRPD, see Fischer, *Neutral Power*, 128–35 and Rosin, *Die Schweiz im KSZE-Prozeß*, 54–59.
34. Falkman/Blix, 'Schweiziskt förslag om ett europeiskt system för fredlig lösning av tvister', 25 January 1972, File 16, Vol. 31, HP 79, UD, RA.
35. Thyberg to Wachtmeister, 'Utbyte av synpunkter på säkerhetskonferensen', 23 December 1971, File 15; Thyber to Wachtmeister, 'Bonn och säkerhetskonferensen'; Thyberg to Wachtmeister, 'Konsultation om ESK', 12 January 1972, File 16, Vol. 31, HP 79, UD, RA.
36. Thyberg to Wachtmeister, 'Säkerhetskonferensen och Kekkonens förslag', 21 December 1971, File 15, Vol. 30, HP 79, UD, RA and Thyberg to Jödahl, 'Bonn och Kekkonens tyska initiativ', 25 February 1972, File 16, Vol. 31, HP 79, UD, RA.

37. Larsson to UD, 'Säkerhetskonferensen', 9 December 1971, File 15, Vol. 30, HP 79, UD, RA.
38. See, for example, Falkman, 'Samtal i Oslo om ESK', 20 December 1971, File 15, Vol. 30, HP 79, UD, RA.
39. Falkman to Leifland, Cipher telegram 9, 11 January 1972, File 16, Vol. 31, HP 79, UD, RA.
40. Jödahl, 'WP-staternas diskussion om säkerhetskonferensen', 9 December 1971, File 15, Vol. 30, HP 79, UD, RA.
41. Ericsson, 'Säkerhetskonferensen: Ryssarnas avsikt med säkerhetskonferensen', 27 December 1971, File 15, Vol. 30, HP 79, UD, RA.
42. Wollin to Jödahl, 26 January 1972, File 16, Vol. 31, HP 79, UD, RA.
43. Ryding to Nyström, 'Parlamentarisk säkerhetskonferens i Helsingfors', 26 January 1972, File 16, Vol. 31, HP 79, UD, RA.
44. Falkman, 'Den belgiska organisationen "Securité et Coopération Européennes"', 22 December 1971, File 15, Vol. 30; Duhs to UD, 'Förberedande möte för en internationell kongress om den europeiska säkerhetskonferensen', 20 January 1972, File 16, Vol. 31, HP 79, UD, RA.
45. Westerberg to UD, 23 February 1972, File 17, Vol. 31, HP 79, UD, RA.
46. Falkman, 'Europeiska säkerhets- och samarbetskonferensen (ESK)', 1 February 1972; Falkman, 'Sverige och ESK (Europeiska säkerhets- och samarbetskonferensen)', 3 February 1972, File 17, Vol. 31; Falkman, 'Sverige och ESK', 6 April 1972, File 19, Vol. 32, HP 79, UD, RA. HP 79, UD, RA.
47. Huldtgren to Nyström, 'Den europeiska säkerhetskonferensen', 9 February 1972; Belding to Nyström, 'Danska samtal i Helsingfors om förberedande av säkerhetskonferens', 17 February 1972; Hichens-Bergström to UD, 'ESK och MBFR under polskt besök i Oslo', 17 February 1972; Nyström, 'Kekkonnen-planerna', 28 February 1972; Ryding to UD, Cipher telegram 6, 3 March 1972, File 17, Vol. 31, HP 79, UD, RA. See also Hakkarainen, *State of Peace*, 154 and Fischer, *Neutral Power*, 130–31.
48. Andrén (1918–2004) was considered the 'grand old man' of Swedish security policy. See Bo Hugemark, 'Säkerhetspolitikens Grand Old Man—Still Going Strong', *Vårt försvar*, 112(2), 2001.
49. Falkman, 'Expertmöte om europeiska säkerhets- och samarbetskonferensen (ESK),' 15 March 1972, File 18, Vol. 31, HP 79, UD, RA.
50. Ibid.
51. Ibid.
52. Ibid.
53. Rosin, *Die Schweiz im KSZE-Prozeß*, 61–62; Gilde, *Österreich im KSZE-Prozess*, 72–77.
54. See, for example, Thyberg to Nyström, 'Säkerhetskonferensen', 23 March 1972, File 18, Vol. 31; Nyström, 'Svensk-tyska ESK-samtal', 3 May 1972, File 19, Vol. 32, HP 79, UD, RA. There was no comparable exchange of documents with other states.
55. Falkman, 'Samtal i Bonn om europeiska samarbets- och säkerhetskonferensen (ESK)', 22 March 1972, File 19, Vol. 32, HP 79, UD, RA.
56. Wachtmeister to Falkman, 'Besök i Bonn för samtal om den europeiska säkerhets- och samarbetskonferensen (ESK)', 17 March 1972, File 18, Vol. 31, HP 79, UD, RA.
57. Wachtmeister to Jödahl, 'Västtyskt ESK-dokument', 7 April 1972, File 19, Vol. 32, HP 79, UD, RA; Von Groll to NATO germa and embassies, 'KSZE als Thema der deutsch-schwedischen Direktorkonsultationen am 21.4.72 in Bonn', 26 April 1972, IA5, 429, B 31, PAAA.
58. 'Schwedische Haltung zur KSE', 13 April 1972, IIA3, B 32, PAAA.

59. This suggestion was addressed to Andrén and Jödahl, amongst others. Thyberg to Nyström, 'Bonn och säkerhetskonferensen', 14 March 1972, File 18, Vol. 31, HP 79, UD, RA. It cannot be stated with certainty whether this report was considered at the gathering of the Swedish CSCE working group the day after.
60. Nyström, 'Samtal med östtysk diplomat', 2 June 1972, File 20, Vol. 32, HP 79, UD, RA.
61. Sjölin to Nyström, 11/12 August 1972, File 21, Vol. 32, HP 79, UD, RA. On the relation between Sweden and the two German states, see also Muschik, *Die beiden deutschen Staaten*, 245–56 and Ann-Marie Ekengren, *Av hänsyn till folkrätten? Svensk erkännandepolitik 1945–1995* (Stockholm: Nerenius & Santérus, 1999), 273–89.
62. Hanisch, *Die DDR im KSZE-Prozess*, 36.
63. Leifland to Wachtmeister, 'ESK och MBFR', 28 March 1972, File 19, Vol. 32, HP 79, UD, RA.
64. Wachtmeister, 'Europeisk säkerhetskonferens', 20 March 1972; Eng to Wachtmeister, 'Finland och den europeiska säkerhetskonferensen', 22 March 1972; Petri to UD, 'Säkerhetskonferensen', 28 March 1972, File 18, Vol. 31, HP 79, UD, RA.
65. Nyström, 'Hbr Wachtmeister-Ryding, H-fors', 'Svenskt ordförandeskap i arbetsgrupp vid det multilaterala förberedande ESK-mötet i Helsingfors?', 28 April 1972, File 19, Vol. 32, HP 79, UD, RA.
66. Nyström, 'Svensk-finska samtal om ESK', 28 April 1972, File 19, and 'Säkerhetskonferensen', 10 May 1972, File 20, Vol. 32, HP 79, UD, RA.
67. DSFP 1972, 22–32. See also Kaj Falkman, 'Sverige och ESK', Promemoria, 6 April 1972, File 19, Vol. 32, HP, HP79, UD, RA.
68. Jarring to UD, Cipher telegram 137, 18 April 1972, File 19, Vol. 32, HP 79, UD, RA.
69. Jarring to UD, 19 April 1972; Enclair telegram 348, 20 April 1972; Cipher telegram 148, 25 April 1972, File 19, Vol. 32, HP 79, UD, RA.
70. The only notable difference to official statements was the request for East Germany's participation; see Jarring to UD, 'Pravdaartikel om svenska inställningen till en alleuropeisk säkerhetskonferens', 22 May 1972, File 20, Vol. 32, HP 79, UD, RA.
71. Leifland to Wachtmeister, 'SALT och MBFR', 5 May 1972, File 19, Vol. 32, HP 79, UD, RA.
72. On the latter role of CBM in Swedish policy, see Makko, 'Das schwedische Interesse', 191–202.
73. Wachtmeister, 'Svenska organisatoriska förberedelser till konferensen om säkerhet och samarbete i Europa (ESK)', 26 May 1972, File 20, Vol. 32, HP 79, UD, RA.
74. Ibid.
75. See, for example, the Austrian remarks on the Swedish position, 'Offizieller Besuch des Herrn Bundeskanzlers in Schweden vom 31. Mai bis 3. Juni 1972', 3 June 1972, Länderbox Schweden, Bestand VII.1., BKAF.
76. See, for example, Jarring to UD, 'Professor Galtung om europeiska säkerhetskonferensen', 22 May 1972, File 20, Vol. 32, HP 79, UD, RA.
77. Nyström, 'Samtal med brittiske ambassadören om ESK', 17 May 1972, File 20, Vol. 32, HP 79, UD, RA.
78. Millard to Douglas-Home, 'Swedish Foreign Policy', 4 April 1972, FCO 33/1884, TNA.
79. Rosin, *Die Schweiz im KSZE-Prozeß*, 61–62.
80. Wachtmeister to Ryding, 'Säkerhetskonferensen', 5 May 1972; 'Säkerhetskonferensen', 25 May 1972, File 20, Vol. 32, HP 79, UD, RA. See also, Fischer, *Neutral Power*, 149–50.
81. See Nyström, 'Förslag till föredragning av utrikesministern om ESK inför utrikesnämnden den 24 maj 1972', 23 May 1972, File 20, Vol. 32, HP 79, UD, RA. For the role of Bonn in Swedish preparations for the CSCE, see also Berg, 'ESK-Dokument', 31 May 1972, File 20, Vol. 32, HP 79, UD, RA.

82. Yamamoto, 'Britain, France and West Germany', 229–43. See also Haftendorn, 'Link between CSCE and MBFR', 237–58; Romano, *Détente*, 106–7; Hakkarainen, *State of Peace*, 180–82, 198.
83. Kieninger, 'Transformation or Status Quo', 74–78. See also Morgan, 'United States', 171–73.
84. 'Collateral constraints', in Berg, 'Europeiska säkerhets- och samarbetskonferensen (ESK)', 12 July 1972, File 21, Vol. 32, HP 79, UD, RA. For the Bonn communiqué, see www.nato.int/cps/en/natolive/official_texts_26844.htm (accessed 30 November 2015).
85. Ingemar Hägglöf to UD, Cipher telegram, 16 June 1972; Göransson to Wachtmeister, 'Samtal i utrikesministeriet ang. säkerhetskonferensen m.m.', 17 June 1972, File 20, Vol. 32, HP 79, UD, RA.
86. Yamamoto, 'Britain, France and West Germany', 237–38; Malmaeus to Wachtmeister, 'Samtal med utrikesminister Sharp', 8 June 1972, File 20, Vol. 32, HP 79, UD, RA.
87. Leifland to Wachtmeister, 'Samtal om ESK och MBFR', 9 June 1972, File 20, Vol. 32, HP 79, UD, RA. See also Hakkarainen, *State of Peace*, 181.
88. Earlier Finnish remarks and proposals on inner-German relations had caused irritation in Bonn, which called on Finland to stop 'exceeding its competences' as envisaged host. See also Backlund to UD, Telegram 370, 'Enligt uppgifter i tysk press förekom bl.a. följande vid NATOs ministerråds behandling av säkerhetskonferensen', 31 May 1972; 'Inhämtat följande i Auswärtiges Amt om NATO-mötets behandling säkerhetskonferensen', 2 June 1972, File 20, Vol. 32, HP 79, UD, RA.
89. Hakkarainen, *State of Peace*, 190–93.
90. Nyström, 'Svenska förberedelser för ESK; deltagare i studiegrupper', 31 May 1972 and 'Svenska förberedelser till konferens om säkerhet och samarbete i Europa (ESK)', 12 June 1972, File 20, Vol. 32, HP 79, UD, RA.
91. Ibid.
92. Garthoff, *Détente and Confrontation*, 11–14, 139, 325–62; Van Oudenaren, *Détente in Europe*, 320–21. For a background of the Soviet position, see Rey, 'USSR, and the Helsinki process', 65–82.
93. Huldtgren to UD, Telegram 201, 19 June 1972, File 20, Vol. 32, HP 79, UD, RA.
94. Lidström to Falkman and Bekeris, Telegram 214, 27 June 1972, File 20, Vol. 32, HP 79, UD, RA.
95. Göransson to UD, 'Internationellt möte i Bryssel till stöd för en alleuropeisk säkerhetskonferens', 15 June 1972, File 20, Vol. 32, HP 79, UD, RA.
96. Göransson to UD, 'Dokument från opinionsmöte i Bryssel 2–5 juni 1972 rörande säkerhet och samarbete i Europa', 26 July 1972 and Westerberg to UD, 'Brysselmötet om alleuropeisk konferens m.m.', 27 July 1972, File 21, Vol. 32, HP 79, UD, RA.
97. Fischer, *Die Grenzen der Neutralität*.
98. Senoo, *Irrweg*, 201–12.
99. It has also been asserted that the Environment Conference was one important reason Stockholm was never offered as a venue. There is, however, little evidence to support the assumption that Sweden would have made such an offer to the CSCE if it had not hosted another conference in the early 1970s.
100. Nyström to Belfrage, 'Svenskt-brittiskt informationsutbyte rörande ESK', 11 July 1972, File 21, Vol. 32, HP 79, UD, RA.
101. Nyström, 'Samtal i östtyska utrikesministeriet den 15 augusti 1972: allmänt', 21 August 1972 and 'Samtal om ESK i det östtyska utrikesministeriet den 15 augusti 1972', 23 August 1972, File 21, Vol. 32, HP 79, UD, RA.
102. Jödahl, 'Västtysk demarché', 24 August 1972, File 22, Vol. 32, HP 79, UD, RA.

103. Maruzsa, 'Denuclearization in Central Europe?', 225–64. Available from http://www.coldwar.hu/html/en/publications/Online%20PublicationMar.pdf (accessed 29 November 2015).
104. Annika Norlin, *Undénplanen: Ett lyckat misslyckande* (Gothenburg: Department of Political Science, University of Gothenburg, 1998).
105. Edelstam, 'Nedrustningsfrågorna i samband med konferensen om säkerhet och samarbete i Europa (ESK)', 17 July 1972, File 21, Vol. 32, HP 79, UD, RA.
106. Möckli, *European Foreign Policy*, 311–15; Romano, *Détente*, 157–67.
107. See supplement to Berg, 'Europeiska säkerhets- och samarbetskonferensen (ESK)', 16 August 1972, File 21, Vol. 32, HP 79, UD, RA. On the French proposal, see Berg, 'ESK: det franska förslaget om en "trestegskonferens"', 30 August 1972, File 22, Vol. 32, HP 79, UD, RA.
108. See, for example, Falkman, 'Sammanfattning av läget beträffande europeiska säkerhets – och samarbetskonferensen (ESK)', 22 August 1972, File 21, Vol. 32, HP 79, UD, RA.
109. Gunnar Myrdal to Wickman, 23 August 1972, File 22, Vol. 32, HP 79, UD, RA.
110. Myrdal to Wickman, 27 September 1972, File 23, Vol. 33, HP 79, UD, RA.
111. Interviews with Karl Edvard Birnbaum, head of the Swedish Institute for International Affairs and expert on the CSCE, between 1960 and 1970 (Stockholm, 18 May 2010), and Kaj Björk (Stockholm, 12 May 2010).
112. Ekholm to UD, 'Svenskt-brittiskt samtal rörande den föreslagna konferensen om säkerhet och samarbete i Europa (ESK)', 30 August 1972, File 22, Vol. 33, HP 79, UD, RA.
113. Yamamoto, 'Britain, France and West Germany', 238–43; De Besche to Swedish Embassies Moscow and Helsinki, Cipher telegram 164, 7 September 1972, File 22, Vol. 33, HP 79, UD, RA.
114. On the Kekkonen Plan, see Osmo Apunen, 'Three "Waves" of the Kekkonen Plan and Nordic Security in the 1980s', *Security Dialogue*, 11(1), 1980, 16–32.
115. See attachment, 'Planer och idéer om europeiska nedrustningsåtgärder, som framförts och diskuterats under efterkrigstiden, av särskilt intresse för Sverige' in Edelstam, 'Nedrustningsfrågorna i samband med konferensen om säkerhet och samarbete i Europa (ESK)', 8 September 1972, File 22, Vol. 33, HP 79, UD, RA.
116. Edelstam, 'Skiss till slutpromemoria från studiegruppen rörande nedrustningsfrågorna i samband med konferensen om säkerhet och samarbete i Europa (ESK)', 8 September 1972, File 22, Vol. 33, HP 79, UD, RA.
117. Ericsson, 'Synpunkter på svenska initiativ i ESK om B- och C-vapen-fria zoner', 20 September 1972, File 23, Vol. 33, HP 79, UD, RA.
118. Ericsson, 'Synpunkter på svenskt initiativ i ESK om A-vapenfri zon', 20 September 1972, File 23, Vol. 33, HP 79, UD, RA.
119. Backlund to UD, Cipher telegram 49, 'Har för strängt förtroligt kännedom erfarit följande i Auswärtiges Amt om Kissingers samtal med Brezjnev om säkerhetskonferensen', 19 September 1972, File 22, Vol. 33, HP 79, UD, RA. See also, Yamamoto, 'Britain, France and West Germany', 243–44; Romano, *Détente*, 173–80.
120. The concept of a European détente based on three pillars is taken from Yamamoto, 'Britain, France and West Germany', 227.
121. Nyström/Wilkens, 'Samtal om ESK mellan polchefen, utrikesrådet Wachtmeister, och chefen för det italienska utrikesministeriets politiska avdelningen, herr Ducci', 19 September 1972, File 22, Vol. 33, HP 79, UD, RA.
122. Nyström/Wilkens, 'Samtal om ESK mellan kabinettssekreterare Jödahl och generalsekreterare Wodak i det österrikiska utrikesministeriet', 26 September 1972, File 23, Vol. 33, HP 79, UD, RA. See also Austrian embassy Stockholm to Kirchschläger, 'Besuch in

Schweden 26.–30.10.1972 – Besprechungsunterlagen', 3 October 1972, II-Pol/Schweden, BMfaA, ÖStA/AdR.
123. Tallroth, 'ESK-kulturellt samarbete och friare kommunikationer', 19 October 1972, File 24, Vol. 33, HP 79, UD, RA.
124. Nyström, 'Den sovjetiska inställningen till ESK', 25 September 1972, File 23, Vol. 33, HP 79, UD, RA.
125. Nyström, 'ESK-samtal', 22 September 1972 and Ingemar Hägglöf to Wachtmeister, 'Frankrike och ESK', 30 September 1972, File 23, Vol. 33, HP 79, UD, RA.
126. Edelstam, 'Utkast till slutpromemoria från studiegruppen rörande nedrustningsfrågorna i samband med konferensen om säkerhet och samarbete i Europa (ESK)', 28 September 1972, File 23, Vol. 33, HP 79, UD, RA.
127. Ibid.
128. Edelstam to Ryding, 'Nedrustningsfrågorna vid den europeiska säkerhetskonferensen', 6 October 1972, File 23, Vol. 33, HP 79, UD, RA.
129. De Besche to Edelstam, Cipher telegram 198, 19 October 1972, File 24, Vol. 33, HP 79, UD, RA.
130. Asp/Eriksson, 'Förslag till kompletteringar av industridepartementets promemoria 1972-09-27 angående industriellt och tekniskt samarbete inför ESK', 6 October 1972, File 23 and Lundberg, 'Ekonomiskt, kommersiellt, och tekniskt-vetenskapligt samarbete inom ESK', 24 October 1972, File 24, Vol. 33, HP 79, UD, RA.
131. Berg, 'ESK – kulturellt samarbete och friare kommunikationer. Diskussioner inom den svenska arbetsgruppen', 6 October 1972, File 23, Vol. 33, HP 79, UD, RA.
132. 'The Parties will contribute toward the further development of peaceful and friendly international relations by strengthening their free institutions, by bringing about a better understanding of the principles upon which these institutions are founded, and by promoting conditions of stability and well-being. They will seek to eliminate conflict in their international economic policies and will encourage economic collaboration between any or all of them'. Available from www.nato.int/cps/en/natolive/official_texts_17120.htm (accessed 30 November 2015).
133. 'The parties will consult together whenever, in the opinion of any of them, the territorial integrity, political independence or security of any of the Parties is threatened'. Ibid.
134. Blix, 'Principer för europeisk säkerhet', 20 October 1972, File 24, Vol. 33, HP79, UD, RA.
135. Blix, 'Metoder för att stärka staters säkerhet', 20 October 1972, File 24, Vol. 33, HP79, UD, RA.
136. Ibid.
137. Blix, 'Institutioner för europeisk säkerhet', 20 October 1972, File 24, Vol. 33, HP79, UD, RA.
138. Fischer, *Neutral Power*, 337.
139. Eliasson, 'Samtal om ESK i Department of State den 17 oktober 1972,' 24 October 1972, File 25, Vol. 34, HP 79, UD, RA.
140. De Besche to UD, Cipher telegram 196, 19 October 1972, File 24, Vol. 33, HP79, UD, RA. See also Yamamoto, 'Britain, France and West Germany', 243–44 and Sarah B. Snyder, 'The Helsinki Process, American Foreign Policy, and the End of the Cold War', PhD dissertation (Georgetown University, 2006) 43–46.
141. Berg, 'Läget beträffande den europeiska säkerhets- och samarbetskonferensen', 17 October 1972, File 24, Vol. 33, HP79, UD, RA.
142. Leifland to Wachtmeister, Cipher telegram 200, 24 October 1972, File 24, Vol. 32, HP 79, UD, RA. See also Romano, *Détente*, 175–80.

143. Berg, 'ESK och MBFR', 2 October 1972, File 23, Vol. 33, HP 79, UD, RA. For a summary of opinions abroad, see Prawitz, 'Vissa synpunkter på MBFR', 20 September 1972, File 23, Vol. 33, HP 79, UD, RA.
144. Eliasson to Wachtmeister, 'Säkerhetsfrågor vid ESK resp. MBFR', 24 October 1972 and Jarring to UD, 'Sovjetunionens och Europas säkerhetsproblem SALT, MBRF och ESK', 30 October 1972, File 25, Vol. 34, HP 79, UD, RA.
145. Berg, 'Samtal om ESK med sovjetiske ambassadören med särskilt uppdrag, Zorin den 31 oktober 1972', 8 November 1972, File 25, Vol. 34, HP 79, UD, RA.
146. Berg, 'ESK–kulturellt samarbete och friare kommunikationer', 27 October 1972, File 25, Vol. 34, HP 79, UD, RA. See also Hakkarainen, *State of Peace*, 195–99.
147. Åström to Ryding, Enclair telegram 286, 13 October 1972, File 23, Vol. 33, HP 79, UD, RA.
148. Hichens-Bergström to Wachtmeister, 'Norska synpunkter på ESK och MBFR', 14 October 1972, File 24, Vol. 32, HP 79, UD, RA.
149. Blix, Edelstam, 'Svenska intressen vid ESK', 1 November 1972, File 25, Vol. 34, HP 79, UD, RA.
150. Ibid.; emphasis in the original.
151. 'Resuméprotokoll über das Arbeitsgespräch zwischen Bundesminister Dr. Kirchschläger und Aussenminister Wickman am 27.10.1972 im Schwedischen Aussenministerium', II-Pol/Schweden, BMfaA, ÖStA/AdR.
152. Ryding to Berg, Telegram 390, 31 October 1972; Ryding to UD, 'Finskt memorandum rörande den europeiska säkerhetskonferensen', 9 November 1972, File 25; Berg to Swedish Embassy Helsinki, Enclair telegram 324, 20 November 1972, File 26, Vol. 34, HP 79, UD, RA.

CHAPTER FOUR

1972–1973: Engaging in the Dipoli Tea Party

Therefore, we look forward to the day when Europe will no longer be divided. The United States believe that understanding among peoples is fundamental to this end. We seek a more open world—open to closer cooperation and to greater contacts among people, as well as to a free interchange of ideas and information.

—US ambassador Val Peterson, 4 December 1972

Another pre-requisite, just as fundamental, is that deliberations should be based on the actual differences in social systems of various participating states. Should efforts towards cooperation be combined with an attempt to change the social systems of the opposite party, the result will undoubtedly be entirely negative. This means that possibilities of cooperation have definite limits.

—Ambassador Göran Ryding, 30 November 1972

Two and a half years after the Budapest Appeal, the delegations of thirty-four states gathered in Finland for final preparations. How did the transition from bilateral to multilateral preparations change the role conceptions of the diplomats and the reactions from activists and the public? Only weeks after the introduction of the talks, Palme launched his famous 1972 Christmas Speech (*Jultal*), a fierce criticism of the US war in Vietnam. What did this mean to Swedish relations with the United States and NATO in the context of the CSCE? Answering these questions requires exploring the evolution of the Swedish role during the multilateral preparatory talks in 1972–1973.

Coping with Early Quarrels

The Swedish delegation entered negotiations at Dipoli with cautious optimism and growing interest in the possibilities that the CSCE eventually would offer. After years of relaxation following the events of 1968, the Swedish Foreign Ministry believed in continuing détente, as affirmed by recommendations for future government budgeting.[1] The key question of concern to Swedish policy makers and diplomats was still what the Soviets really wanted and what offers they were willing to make at Helsinki.

A few days before the start of the MPT, the Swedish embassy in Moscow reported that the Kremlin opposed further West European integration and intended to try to diminish the role of the United States in Europe. According to the embassy's source, Moscow saw the CSCE as merely a symbolic forum, which would eventually result in shallow declarations without substantive content.[2] The Swedes were told by other interlocutors that Washington feared wide-ranging discussions on disarmament in Finland could disturb the upcoming MBFR negotiations in Vienna.[3] The disparities between the superpowers were matters that worried the Swedes and added to their existing reluctance to play the role of a mediator at the upcoming conference.

Foreign Minister Krister Wickman actively engaged in the preparations for Dipoli. On the very first day of the MPT he palpably irritated Axel Edelstam by advising him to prepare statements on various subjects. In response, Edelstam held that existing elements of uncertainty made it necessary to await the course of events before preparing concrete positions.[4] Most likely, Edelstam thought that Wickman had little substantial knowledge on the issues. It was experts such as Edelstam, who had gained the deep knowledge of the CSCE which members of the government lacked, who designed the policy framework. This was not a Swedish phenomenon but rather a general trend. Petri Hakkarainen writes:

> The true heroes of the CSCE process were, without doubt, the mid-level civil servants doing the invisible legwork in the committees and subcommittees in Geneva. For most of the time, the CSCE specialists were able to operate with a fairly high degree of independence, often even writing their own instructions. Yet there were also moments when decisive turning points in the CSCE required interventions from high politics.[5]

Over the course of the following days, Wickman and Kaj Björk engaged in developing the strategy for the Swedish delegation, commenting upon scheduling and content of speeches.[6] The growing interference from high-ranking officials stemmed from the increasingly important role that the CSCE played. It did not result in abrupt policy changes, because the role conceptions of diplomats had been developed within the boundaries defined by the government in Stockholm.

At Dipoli, drafts and completed proposals were registered by a secretariat. The first agreed upon document on procedural arrangements set the course for the conduct of the MPT. It affirmed that all states participated on the basis of sovereign equality and outside of military alliances. All decisions would have to be taken by consensus, which was defined as 'the absence of any objection expressed by a representative and put forward by him as constituting an obstacle to the taking of the decision in question'.

The working groups that would deal with the different subjects were also to be appointed by consensus, and their chairmanship would be performed by rotation. It was decided that no minutes of meetings would be kept and that all meetings would be closed. Only in exceptional cases would the public be informed about the progress of the conference.[7] These were important decisions reflecting the very nature of the CSCE. The consensus rule heavily influenced the character of the talks, most significantly by allowing minor states to participate as equals. Secrecy diminished the threshold of inhibition and allowed the delegations to disregard public opinion.[8]

As head of the Helsinki mission, Ambassador Göran Ryding was to present the opening speech on behalf of the Swedish government. The manuscript for his speech had originally been drafted by Kaj Björk but went through various stages of drafting, as it was subjected to the views of a number of higher officials at the Foreign Ministry in Stockholm. Björk had originally argued that Ryding needed to stress that consensus rule in response to procedural questions and the later work on the agenda issues was a prerequisite. Björk argued that the main task of the CSCE was to agree on a lowest common denominator between states with different social systems, rather than to produce expressions of majority opinion. Therefore, Sweden should not oppose a common declaration as an outcome of the conference, even if it served Soviet more than Western goals. As a result of the exchange of opinions, numerous original text passages pointing to the antagonism between the two alliances were deleted in an attempt to give the speech a constructive undertone.[9]

At Dipoli, intensive debate on procedure broke out immediately upon the arrival of the delegations. The Romanians challenged the election of Jaakko Iloniemi as vice-chairman, as proposed by Richard Tötterman, the Finnish undersecretary of state and chairman of the MPT. In their view, the appointment should take place only after consulting the general meeting. Willing to establish itself as independent from the Soviets, the Romanian delegation requested a rotating chairmanship and vice-chairmanship. It was Switzerland's ambassador Samuel Campiche – actively assisted by

Göran Ryding, with whom he had excellent personal relations – who finally convinced the Romanians to agree to a compromise; according to this compromise, the vice-chairman and the chairmen of the working groups would be chosen on the basis of a daily rotation principle.[10]

Discussion arose on another aspect of the Romanian objection: their request for a written acknowledgement that all states participate 'on the basis of complete equality and independence'.[11] The Soviets, and some of their allies, immediately opposed the idea. The EC countries, for their part, disliked the notion of 'blocs' put forward in a Polish compromise proposal.[12] Further difficulties came from the West German insistence on being placed next to the GDR, which almost resulted in a 'diplomatic incident' that could only be overcome after a shift to a French language seating order.[13] These quarrels in the first week gave a taste of what was ahead of the diplomats.

The first week of the 'Dipoli Tea Party', as some called the talks, was dominated by the attempt of the Romanian delegation to establish an independent profile in international politics and overcome the status as a satellite of the USSR by using economic and other opportunities offered by the CSCE.[14] This was celebrated by Sweden and many other small states, who believed that the Romanian attitude would help avoid the dominance of the great powers which, according to the Swedish perception, had been 'remarkably passive'.[15] Initially, all sides showed readiness to compromise, and the overall atmosphere remained good, despite a drawn-out procedural debate.

The Finnish chairmanship was under critical observation, with many delegates using the slightest opportunity to voice harsh criticism in cases in which the Finns were seemingly violating objectivity.[16] Although the aforementioned cooperation with the Swiss had led to the successful solution of an early obstacle, and despite reports on growing consensus between the EC Nine, Sweden remained critical of becoming part of a neutral group.[17] Years of passivity and cautiousness loomed too large for minor excursions to cause immediate change to the Swedish attitude.

Therefore, the Swedes strictly rejected renewed proposals on including non-European observers such as Algeria and Israel.[18] The Swedes wanted the conference to remain focused on key issues relating to the situation in Europe. Consequently, Sweden rejected supporting Austria's and Chancellor Bruno Kreisky's repeated calls for treating Middle Eastern problems at the CSCE. Even when the conflict between Israel and its Arab neighbours intensified, and despite Swedish-Austrian relations growing closer over the course of the conference, this attitude remained unchanged.[19] Never considering the CSCE to be a forum where peace and war outside of Europe could be discussed was one part of the realpolitik policy carried out by Sweden.[20] The ties with Vienna were not as strong as those with Bonn or Helsinki and were too weak to force a change of view on the Middle East.

After a week of lengthy discussion on procedural matters, the general debate was introduced on 29 November 1972, and on the following day Swedish ambassador Göran Ryding entered the stage. The opening statements generally held few surprises and bored many of those present. Reportedly, Soviet delegate Viktor Maltsev killed time by folding paper hats during the Swedish statement.[21]

Ryding, addressing the audience in French, started off by stressing the important role played by the Finnish host. He also pointed to the positive effects of détente, resulting in West Germany's Eastern treaties and the upcoming negotiations on MBFR. With this opening statement, Sweden reaffirmed the support of its two closest partners, Finland and West Germany. To Sweden, said Ryding, the balance between the blocs was a safeguard of peace and stability, even if a Europe without the presence of military alliances was the desirable long-term goal. The ambassador stated that his government appreciated the growing understanding of Sweden's neutrality policy but, nevertheless, chose to reiterate that 'it should be realized everywhere that this policy will not be changed'. The explicit statement on the Swedish neutrality policy and nonalignment was a response to constant criticism that Sweden had earlier faced in the context of the CSCE.

Rejecting this criticism was a clear signal of Sweden's role as an independent actor and its will to decide its own destiny. A central feature of Ryding's speech was the connection between the CSCE and MBFR. Despite the centrality to Sweden's general approach to the conference of this linkage, and the country's expressed hopes that it would be dealt with in conjunction with its independent stance, he acknowledged that Sweden could not make any contributions at this early stage. It would remain an ultimate goal to achieve results in this respect, which required 'continuity in organized efforts to develop cooperation between the states of Europe'.[22] Ryding described human contacts as 'appropriate to give useful, mutual impulses and complement the rising trust between governments with a rising trust between the peoples'.[23] It was important, he argued, that the peoples would benefit from the CSCE. At first glance, this gives the impression that Sweden might finally have considered the role of what Holsti defines as defender of the faith. But this was by no means the case, as becomes clear from the following statement:

> One fundamental prerequisite for a productive conference is, thus, that all participating states should mutually respect one another's choice of security policy.

Another prerequisite, just as fundamental, is an acceptance of the actual differences in social systems of various participating states. Should efforts towards cooperation be combined with an attempt to change the social systems of the opposite party, the result will undoubtedly be entirely negative. This means that possibilities of cooperation have definite limits. A group of states with similar social systems has much greater scope for promoting close cooperation than a group of states with quite different social systems. This limitation should be borne in mind when we are considering the areas of cooperation, which offer prospects of constructive results. The purpose of a conference on security and cooperation in Europe cannot be to bring about a confrontation between representatives of differing social systems.[24]

Also, the appellation 'freer movements', as invoked by the West, did go unmentioned in Ryding's speech.

The Swedish opening statement was a follow-up to earlier appeals to Western states to remain realistic and refrain from controversial projects, but it was very much in conflict with the Swedish policy on Vietnam, on which Palme would give his famous Christmas speech just three weeks later. Historians have described the Swedish position on the subject as 'disinterest,' and there is no indication that Sweden paid lip service to realism and followed any kind of hidden, more idealistic, agenda.[25] Instead, Ryding pointed out that differing social systems were not to be seen as barriers to the development of trade and economic cooperation.[26] With this, he stated that the Swedish delegation intended to maintain its pragmatism.

Due to its technical character, the CSCE was overshadowed in the public's perception by matters which attracted greater attention, such as international terrorism in the aftermath of the Munich massacre, the Vietnam War and the second stage of the SALT negotiations, which commenced the day before the MPT at Dipoli. The fact that the CSCE was unlikely to attract public attention and have a domestic effect allowed the Swedes to maintain their ambivalent, even contradictory approach: pragmatic regarding human rights in Europe but confrontational about the same issues in Vietnam.[27]

In the following days, Sweden's opening speech was praised in the Eastern European press. Ambassador Agda Rössel reported that major Czechoslovakian newspapers, such as *Rudé Právo* and *Prace,* praised Sweden for its insistence on taking a realistic approach and emphasizing the democratization of economic relations between European states.[28] The Soviets and their allies were pleased with Sweden's critical stance towards the Western approach to human contacts. Despite the Swedish effort to prevent gaining an image of being a mediator or bridge builder at the CSCE, their general reputation at the time was continuously instrumentalized as such in Eastern Europe.

The Swedish delegates, for their part, listened carefully during the opening session and put much effort into assessing the early positions taken by other participants and understanding existing role expectations. In their view, Poland's statement was 'strikingly close' to the Soviet one, and the Western Europeans took a 'fairly similar' stand, with the exception of the French, who were being 'more general than the others', and suggesting that West Germany's ambassador remained 'unexpectedly vague'.[29] The Swedes also looked favourably upon Yugoslavia's call to address the issue of disarmament and many other states bringing up military aspects of security at this early stage of the MPT.

With the exception of Romania, the Warsaw Pact states were speaking with one voice.[30] The approach of the two blocs to the MPT differed substantively. The West favoured a comprehensive round of negotiations, further stimulating détente, while the Eastern bloc wanted to keep the preparatory talks concise and on a declaratory level.[31] Sweden positioned itself in the middle between these two approaches, agreeing with the Western demand for thorough treatment of all issues and rejecting putting a strong emphasis on individual freedoms and a freer flow of peoples, ideas and information. Against their own will, this predestined them further for a later role as bridge and mediator.

Settling at Dipoli and First Evaluations

At the conclusion of the opening session, numerous proposals on the agenda and modus operandi were presented to the secretariat. Yugoslavia received Eastern support for its proposal to start off with an exchange of views on the procedure, whereas the French delegation proposed immediately establishing a provisional agenda and then deciding on procedure and structure. Great Britain was eager to make sure that the agenda setting would not forestall final decisions and that agreement on topics and mandates for committees was provisional. The West Germans agreed to the latter and added that agendas, committees and mandates should be discussed together.

The complexity of the situation created an opening for parties interested in hammering out compromises. Early on, relations between Sweden and the Alpine neutrals developed well, and views were exchanged between them before they circulated official documents. Trying to bring together the many approaches mentioned above, the Swiss informed the Swedish delegation that they were planning to propose a provisional agenda to which all states could add the issues that they wished to address. The Swiss delegation expected this to result in an initial list consisting of 150 points, which then could be distributed to all participants for a consensual grouping of subjects under the four major headings.[32]

The lively participation of smaller states did not go unnoticed. Flora Lewis, foreign relations columnist at the *New York Times*, observed that they had not formed a neutral bloc but had used the talks actively:

> The smaller countries that had watched the exclusive rites of power-balance performed far over their heads all year are speaking up. They have not formed a neutralist non-bloc bloc, as new countries sought to do when they entered the United Nations and tried to counter the weight of power blocs. Rather, they seem to sense that that weight may be coming to matter less in the problems of transformation shared by Europe and the honorary Europeans of North America. Helsinki has not changed anything yet. Nobody expects drama. The old diplomats have not displayed any dazzling new tricks. But change is in the air.[33]

Such early, if modest, observations presaged the later roles performed by states such as Sweden.

In a first reaction to the ongoing negotiations in Finland, Axel Edelstam instructed the Swedish delegation to secure an agreement that disarmament would be treated at the conference proper. Edelstam asked for closer cooperation with the Yugoslavians, who had presented a similar position during the opening session. He argued that a joint proposal should place the subject in the section on security, as 'questions referring to arms control and confidence-building measures in the military field' could be prepared. This materialized when Risto Dzunov, Yugoslavia's ambassador in Stockholm, approached Wilhelm Wachtmeister five days before the return of the delegations to Helsinki. After an exchange of niceties on Swedish-Yugoslavian collaboration at Dipoli, the two diplomats agreed on joint efforts, with the goal of establishing disarmament on the agenda of the CSCE.[34]

As no immediate consensus could be reached on the agenda, focus at Dipoli shifted towards the upcoming Christmas break and the mandates, or 'terms of reference', to be awarded to the working committees of the conference proper. The Soviets strictly opposed the term 'mandate' and wished for more imprecise terminology. In the Swedish perception, this was about more than semantics. They viewed it as a reflection of the Soviet approach to the conference, how it should be planned and what tasks it would take up.

To minimize the impact of definitions agreed on at the MPT was part of Soviet strategy, with the goal of moving on to the conference proper without substantial debate. On this, Sweden sided with the West, arguing that the mandates had to be settled on at Dipoli in order to guarantee thorough preparation of the conference proper. This would make it easier for the foreign ministries to prepare themselves for the first stage of the CSCE. The Swedes noted with interest that the Soviets fought hard to keep their allies together. Most notably, Romanian attempts at establishing an independent line were targeted. Debate also broke out about the length of the Christmas break.[35] The controversy was fuelled by the fact that the Soviets had failed to force a decision on the date and venue of the CSCE during the first weeks of the MPT. Despite the request of the Warsaw Pact states to restrict the Christmas break to eleven days, it was decided to adjourn the talks between 15 December 1972 and 15 January 1973.[36]

An evaluation of the first three weeks was provided to the Ministry for Foreign Affairs in Stockholm shortly after the adjournment. Göran Ryding reported that the Western delegations were satisfied with the role that he had played along with the Swiss delegate, Samuel Campiche, in controversial moments such as the Christmas break debate. Ryding described in detail the special dynamics of the negotiations, which had created political anomalies, such as Spain siding with the Soviets rather than with the West during the first weeks. Norway and Finland, the ambassador added, had 'not said a word' after their opening speeches and had been remarkably quiet.[37] Swiss documents confirm Ryding's reports, pointing out that the collaboration with the neutrals had taken a surprising turn:

> Austria, which with the exception of Finland has been the most active among the neutrals in favour of the conference, has made a rather modest contribution in Helsinki. Sweden, on the other hand, not very active before the consultations, has come to the forefront through numerous distinctive interventions. In ambassador Ryding, Sweden has an experienced and able diplomat with great charisma.[38]

The absence of Nordic cooperation in the context of the CSCE continued at Dipoli. Although this had been a fact for several years, the Swedes reacted with surprise when a member of the Norwegian CSCE delegation told the press explicitly that there had been consultations with the other members of NATO and the EC Nine but not with the other Nordic neighbours.[39] Nordic cooperation was a well-known and often-stated key feature of Swedish foreign policy, and the Swedes did not want the absence of regional collaboration to be highlighted. But the Nordic sphere proved problematic, nevertheless. Max Jakobson, Finland's ambassador to Stockholm, communicated a critical note on behalf of his government to Sverker Åström.

The Finns were displeased with the fact that Sweden's opening statement had portrayed Finland's CSCE policy as a selfless effort for peace, rather than for Finnish neutrality. The Finnish government criticized the fact that the Swedes had ignored the reference to Finnish neutrality made by President Kekkonen and Ambassador Matti Tuovinen at the opening banquet and during the first session of the MPT. Although Åström assured the Finns that Sweden regarded the speech as a polite address, and had not been aware of the Finnish position, he was asked to forward the message to Foreign Minister Wickman and was requested to hint to the Swedish delegation that it should make such a reference to neutrality in the near future.[40]

In contrast to that of Sweden, Finland's foreign policy centred heavily on Europe. Kekkonen and his diplomats hoped that the CSCE would stabilize European détente and, consequently, Finland's position in the international arena.[41] Against this background, and with an awareness of continuing Swedish affinity with their point of view, it was natural for the Finns to expect far-reaching Swedish support. In other foreign policy areas, the often-cited Nordic balance helped avoid tension. With this concept absent from the CSCE, and with every Nordic country focusing on its own objectives, Finland's tense relationship with the Soviet Union began to spread to influence Finnish-Swedish relations. This elucidates the nature of the relationship between the two Nordic countries euphemistically described as 'differing points of departure' by Leatherman.[42]

Shortly before Christmas Eve, Göran Ryding received the Soviet CSCE delegates Lev Mendelevich and Valerian Zorin, accompanied by Ambassador Viktor Maltsev, at the Swedish embassy in Helsinki. The 'Soviet troika', as the Swedish ambassador labelled his guests, expressed concerns related to the question of mandates and to the fact that a number of Western delegations had pushed for concessions unacceptable to the Kremlin. The Soviets believed that this confrontational attitude originated in the simple fact that the conference had been proposed by Moscow.

Over the course of the conversation, conducted in an 'informal and relaxed atmosphere' according to the Swedish minutes, Mendelevich's mistrust of the Swedish attitude became evident.[43] Suspicion was a constant, and mutual, feature in Swedish-Soviet relations during the Cold War, and the CSCE was no exception to the rule. Soviet worries did not come as a surprise to the Swedes, who had maintained close bonds with the West since preparations for the conference intensified in 1969, and continued to do so. The head of the Belgian delegation to the CSCE visited Stockholm shortly before the resumption of talks.[44] In London, the British delegation reported that the Swedes, alongside Switzerland and Malta, were particularly helpful to the West.[45]

Negotiations recommenced in January 1973 on the basis of the Yugoslavian proposal, registered as document CSCE/HC/16/Rev.1 on 8 December 1972, complemented by several additions. The Swedish delegation travelled back to Finland, believing that the MPT would continue for another month or two. It expected the Warsaw Pact states to continue seeking recognition of postwar borders, an agreement in principle on the relations between states in Europe, and the need for greater economic cooperation in order to acquire Western know-how.[46]

As mentioned earlier, Romania was the major exception to this otherwise homogenous alliance, as President Nicolae Ceausescu was eager to weaken the Brezhnev Doctrine. For this reason, his delegation emphasized at length the need to issue a guarantee that states would not use, or threaten to use, violence under any conditions. The main concern of NATO and the United States, on the other hand, remained with the MBFR talks, which were introduced in Vienna at the end of that month. In Dipoli, the Western allies shared Romania's goal of achieving an erosion of the Brezhnev Doctrine through the application of the principles to states regardless of their social systems. Other Western goals were the imbuing of greater confidence in the military field and support for greater freedom in Eastern Europe.[47]

Upon return to Finland, Ryding and his staff tried to put Sweden on the map. The Swedish delegation contributed to the general progress of the MPT and sought to participate in discussions other than those on the agenda. During the first week after the break, the Swedes expressed their support for a Swiss proposal to complement existing formulations on the settlement of disagreements in the UN Charter by introducing further principles. Kaj Björk participated actively in drafting speeches and defining positions and exerted considerable influence during this time. Björk proposed to add 'questions relating to the control of armaments' to the conference agenda, arguing that this would allow broader discussions on disarmament than had the cautious formulation presented earlier by the Netherlands.[48] The development of concrete positions on economic cooperation and protection of the environment was also fostered, but, most notably, the Swedes suggested the establishment of a committee that would work exclusively on disarmament.[49] The exact proposal read as follows:

> The Swedish delegation considers that the CSCE must examine questions relating to the control of armaments in Europe. Accordingly, the Swedish delegation proposes
> I.   That the following item be included in the agenda under the heading relating to security questions: 'Questions relating to the control of armaments'.
> II. That the terms of reference of a committee on security questions shall contain the following item: 'The Committee shall examine questions relating to the control of armaments'.
> III. That a sub-committee on the subject be established. Its terms of reference will be drawn up later.[50]

Sweden's proposal was neither propaganda nor tactics but rather an expression of its firm belief in advancing high-level disarmament negotiations through the CSCE. It was supported by the Norwegians and complemented by an Italian proposal to found a subcommittee on CBM, to which the Dutch added a supplement linking it with MBFR. To the Swedes, these amendments were highly welcome, as they supported Stockholm's main goal, namely, the establishment of disarmament as an integral part of the CSCE. Ambassador Ryding applauded the Western contributions and suggested to the Foreign Ministry in Stockholm that Sweden accept the Dutch amendment.[51]

The first rounds of negotiations after the break signalled clearly that things had not gone the way that Moscow had hoped. The Western states, together with the neutral and nonaligned states, dominated the negotiations. The Austrians made renewed attempts to establish the Middle East on the agenda, while Switzerland, Cyprus and Yugoslavia brought attention to the Mediterranean area. Belgium presented proposals on the general agenda and on economic and environmental cooperation, Denmark on cultural exchange and human contacts and Italy on security, while the Warsaw Pact states made hardly any statements at all.

Kaj Björk's aforementioned formulation on disarmament was registered as document CSCE/HC/21 and enjoyed the support of a number of smaller states, although the reaction of the major powers was more reserved. It was anticipated that the plenary assembly would carry out an extensive review of the many proposals after the Eastern states had presented their comments and proposals in response.[52] During this period, Sweden and the other nonaligned states were far from acting as a third bloc or functioning as bridge or mediator.

The Soviets realized that their original approach had driven the neutral and nonaligned states into the arms of the West.[53] Therefore, they tried to adopt a more flexible approach and, despite their concerns regarding Western propaganda, they were ready to accept 'cultural cooperation' as a separate agenda point by late January 1973. Moscow also agreed to invite all interested European states, including the group of neutral and nonaligned states, to the MBFR talks in Vienna.[54] Declarations on these revised positions were released by the Soviet Union and Poland. Soviet negotiator Viktor Maltsev, who had earlier been ambassador in Stockholm, revealed the inclusion of 'certain measures to strengthen stability and confidence', albeit without specifying what such measures actually were or making any explicit reference to the term 'military'.

The Eastern Europeans also widened the definition of 'cultural cooperation' by adding a phrase on 'contacts among organizations and people and of dissemination of information'. Furthermore, they acknowledged that the CSCE could result in a consultative committee. A Polish delegate added that MBFR and the CSCE needed to remain separate, as the latter could not be burdened with disarmament 'in the strict sense of the word'. Despite the Soviet insistence that these statements represented substantial signs of goodwill, Sweden reacted critically, particularly to the fact that nothing had been said on the question of mandates for the committees.[55]

Once more, the West German Auswärtiges Amt shared its analysis of the first two months in Dipoli with the Swedish Ministry for Foreign Affairs. According to Bonn, it became more and more obvious that the Soviets had never grasped the full range of effects and consequences of their own initiative. Instead of allowing them to accomplish their general declarations and prosecute their economic advantages, the conference was turning into a catalyst for a West European common foreign policy. Accordingly, those considering any Eastern proposal as perfidious and wily had been disabused. During the earlier bilateral preparations, it had been the Soviets who acted and the West who reacted; now the situation had turned upside down. Therefore, the West Germans predicted, the Soviet Union would not escape the question of mandates either.[56]

The favourable position of the West was taken into account in internal considerations between Swedish officials. Ryding recommended that Sweden maintain its position on arms control until (the unlikely case of) being granted access to the MBFR talks. The adherence to its adopted position would also allow further specification and elaboration on the Swedish train of thought once the general review of the oncoming registered proposals began.[57] During this time, the communication between the delegation in Dipoli and the working groups in Stockholm functioned well. The latter were provided with advice on the wording and content of working papers, speeches and written proposals.

Slowing Down: A Taste of Cold War Dynamics

In the last days of January 1973, the hard part of the negotiations finally began. A decision on whether the subcommittees would be awarded 'mandates' or 'tasks' – or nothing at all – had to be made. The Soviet delegation maintained its position and presented formulas on the subcommittee on security and on principles governing the relations between states to the plenary assembly. In both cases, activities were labelled 'tasks' instead of 'mandates'. Switzerland presented a proposal which grouped the many topics into four categories, soon known as the 'baskets'. The four baskets were (i) *security*, (ii) *economic cooperation*, (iii) *cultural exchange and human contacts* and (iv) *follow-up procedures*. It was agreed that the plenary would work through chapter by chapter, with the possibility of cross-referencing – a method the French defined as *horizontalo-perpendiculaire*.[58]

On the Swedish side, Foreign Minister Wickman intervened personally. He agreed to an amendment regarding the proposed arms control subcommittee, which differed from a similar Dutch idea in that it omitted any reference to MBFR. Wickman claimed that the Swedish delegation could refrain from its demand for a separate arms control subcommittee in favour of a single subcommittee on CBM at a later stage if forced to.[59] Although there was consensus on the issue at the Foreign Ministry in Stockholm, Wickman asked for Alva Myrdal to be consulted.[60]

In his speech to the assembly on 30 January 1973, Ryding explained that the proposal of his delegation suggested that the subcommittee would be placed in the first basket. This would allow the conference to deal with disarmament-related issues in a general and broad way, instead of conducting narrow negotiations on disarmament and arms control.[61] The Swedish document in which this was presented shared the fate of a number of other proposals that did not concur with the Soviet position. The day after Ryding's speech, Mendelevich targeted it during one of the longest talks ever given at the MPT until then.[62] The leader of the Soviet delegation, in what the Swedish perceived as a 'sharp attack', argued that his country had never accepted the term 'arms control' but only 'disarmament'. Mendelevich accused Sweden of creating unnecessary confusion by introducing a term that had never been included in any treaty ratified by the Swedes themselves.

The Soviets argued that there were other ways of discussing disarmament in Europe and completely dashed the Swedish proposal on regional measures, calling it 'entirely artificial'. It would be strange, closed Mendelevich, if the CSCE were to end up giving instructions to another conference.[63] The Soviets were not the only ones to be confused by what the Swedes meant by 'regional negotiations'. Ryding himself had to consult the Foreign Ministry in Stockholm before being able to provide a satisfactory response to the criticism. In a cable, he asked whether 'regional' did in fact cover negotiations between all European states, the MBFR talks, negotiations among Balkan countries and negotiations on nuclear-free zones. If that was the case, Ryding pointed out, the delegation would have to be briefed about Sweden's priorities in these areas, with consideration to ongoing negotiations on a number of matters such as SALT, CCD and MBFR.[64]

The problem of disarmament formulations originated in their making, since the inclusion of Alva Myrdal had resulted in confusion about semantics. Despite the need for further clarification, there was little understanding among the Swedes of the motive behind the Soviet 'attack'. The

Swedish delegation at Dipoli had privately circulated its readiness to change the term 'arms control' if necessary but did not receive a response from the Soviets. Therefore, the Swedish delegates felt caught off guard by the Soviet 'outburst'.[65] Axel Edelstam believed the Swedish wording to be 'fairly modest', as he put it in his follow-up correspondence with Alva Myrdal.

Among the officials responsible, speculations circulated as to whether altering the tone was not in fact a means for the Soviets to accuse those members of the Warsaw Pact that signalled interest in the Swedish proposal. Another explanation for the Soviet attitude discussed by the Swedes was that Moscow wanted to enforce early Swedish involvement in MBFR by preventing discussion on disarmament at the CSCE.[66] As we can see from this example, the multilateral stage created a greater number of more subtle role expectations. This affected the role conceptions of decision makers and delegates and complicated the maintenance of a consistent role performance.

Göran Ryding, who responded soberly to the Soviet criticism, believed in neither of the abovementioned theories, viewing the Soviet attack as a tactical mistake instead. In his view, it had been 'biased' and 'dishonest'. Ryding believed that the Russians were simply surprised at and displeased with the outspoken attitude of the neutral countries. Younger members of the Soviet delegation had insinuated that certain circles in the Kremlin wondered whether the neutrals were actually 'NATO's instrument' for delaying the MPT. Ryding warned Stockholm that such 'nonsense' could reappear and suggested that the ministry draft 'position papers' in the second and third baskets, as well, and become 'a bit active in areas other than disarmament'.[67] It seems as if Ryding's suggestions did not go completely overlooked. Karl Anders Wollter, acting Swedish consul general at Leningrad, was sent to Finland in early February 1973 to support the delegation on economic matters.[68] The Mendelevich incident certainly gave Sweden a first real taste of Cold War dynamics in the course of the MPT.

In contrast to the tense relationship with the Soviets, Swedish-US relations progressed well. Washington expressed sympathy with Sweden's interest in MBFR and briefed Swedish diplomats Jan Eliasson and Leif Leifland properly. Officials also discussed the motives for the Soviet move to invite interested countries to MBFR. The Swedes were relatively well informed about MBFR and found themselves in a good position for developing an appropriate strategy. According to their sources, the US State Department expected the Vienna talks to last between eight and twelve weeks.

The Americans were very pleased with the situation at Dipoli, since the Soviets had been forced to make concessions on human contacts and security matters and seemed to be considering alternatives to Helsinki as the venue for the conference proper. Another welcome effect of the way the MPT developed was that the flexible attitude of the Eastern states had fostered greater readiness to compromise among NATO states. One US official was cited saying that one could already 'see the [Western] handwriting on the wall'.[69] As became obvious from Sweden's contact with US officials in January and February 1973, Palme's famous comparison between the US bombings in Vietnam and Nazi crimes during World War II did not do any damage to diplomatic relations at the operational diplomatic level.[70] In Washington, few viewed Sweden as a problem, and the Americans seemed confident about Sweden expanding its role as a faithful friend of West Germany to the entire West.

Many Western observers shared the positive evaluation of the Americans, which garnered the CSCE more and more attention from the highest levels. During a visit by Wickman to Ottawa, Canadian foreign minister Mitchell Sharp, who wished to discuss human contacts, brought up the CSCE. At Dipoli, the Swedes had told the officials of the Canadian delegation that they looked favourably on Western efforts but did not believe that the whole conference should be jeopardized by pressuring the East too much on one subject. The Warsaw Pact states had not yet taken a decisive stand. Therefore, the Swedes believed it would be tactically smart to await the compromises the East would offer before proceeding.

Aware of Sweden's role as defender of human rights–related values in global affairs, the Canadians were surprised by the heavily one-sided focus on disarmament expressed in Ottawa.[71] In contrast to earlier years, the Swedes were no longer perceived exclusively in terms of a passive-active dichotomy. Instead, they were viewed critically because of their very specific preferences. Evidently, other states recognized this inconsistency, just as Göran Ryding had done.

By mid-February 1973, the different positions on security principles and conflicting interests became clearer.[72] It was obvious that it would not be an easy task to analyse the massive amount of information and finish creating an agenda acceptable to all parties. In order to allow more time for thorough preparation of the undertaking, the MPT were adjourned for another two weeks. This allowed the Swedish delegation to consult their experts in Stockholm on a number of issues, such as how to correctly translate the term *rustningskontroll* ('arms limitation', 'regulation of armaments' or 'arms control') or how to define and motivate 'regional negotiations'.

These were not easy problems to solve, and it took several days before the delegation in Finland received clarification on the latter. Only then did Axel Edelstam telegraph a response from the Foreign Ministry in

Stockholm to Dipoli explaining to the Swedish delegation that 'arms limitation' simply meant the same thing as 'arms control' and 'regulation of armaments' in §11.1 of the UN Charter: an international rule of limitation and regulation which also was the subject of the other negotiations mentioned in Ryding's enquiry.[73]

Alva Myrdal rejected this definition, maintaining that 'arms control' was not mentioned in the charter and that Sweden had always avoided the term due to its ambiguity. She regretted that it had found its way into the official language used by the Swedish delegation at the MPT. Myrdal argued that it was highly important to overcome obstacles and find a formula that would allow keeping disarmament on the conference agenda, as substantial small-state and neutral-state interests were at stake.[74] Edelstam, for his part, admitted that it was problematic to further specify the term 'regional negotiations' at such an early stage, as this would require 'considerable spadework'.[75] 'It is not an easy task to seek support if we can not specify what we mean', Ryding responded, baffled.[76]

The break was also used to do a lot of persuading, since the Swedish proposal for a subcommittee on the limitation of armaments had been supported only by Norway and Denmark. There had, on the other hand, been considerable opposition, with France siding with the Eastern bloc on the subject.[77] In this pressured situation, the Foreign Ministry in Stockholm asked Sweden's permanent delegation to the CCD for assistance.[78] Trying to avoid a further loss of credibility, the Swedish delegation at the MPT finally asked for 'arms control' to be replaced with 'regulation of armament'.[79]

Shortly before the February break commenced, numerous telegrams on the matter were sent between Stockholm, Helsinki, Delhi, Ottawa and Geneva. Disarmament was of outstanding importance to Sweden. In contrast, there was little interest in the second basket, on economic cooperation, as the working groups and departments at home had few or no views at all on its content at that time.[80] Questions of human contacts were also left to other actors, such as Denmark, which launched a proposal on the reunification of families, for which it received harsh criticism from Poland.[81] Critical voices had been raised against this one-sided Swedish policy, and the question remained of whether there would be a change of attitude in the following period. The additional adjournment was very welcome in Stockholm. At Dipoli, specifying and maintaining the independent role, together with the faithful friend role still at the core of the Swedish NRC, proved a major challenge.

Facing Disarmament Realities

During the break, and due to the consent of the Swedes to change their disarmament terminology, the Soviets shifted towards a carrot rather than a stick approach. On 9 February 1973, Mendelevich invited Göran Ryding, Axel Edelstam and Hans Blix for a lunch meeting and took the opportunity to praise the Swedish acknowledgement of the Soviet criticism as a 'very constructive' step, which 'avoided any kind of ambiguity'.[82] Afterwards, Ryding stated that he still believed that the disarmament struggle could be successful if all six sponsors – Austria, the Netherlands, Sweden, Switzerland, Spain and Yugoslavia – pooled their strengths.[83] For the first time, a leading Swedish figure considered the potential synergizing effect of grouping and joining efforts in a more planned and formal way.[84] At this point, the general problem was that still no one knew how to structure this work and proceed with the MPT.

The delegates had the choice between participating in 'open-ended working groups' and letting delegations work separately on their earlier proposals with the goal of reaching compromise formulas. The Swedes now believed that the MPT would last until late April 1973, regardless of the procedure chosen. Their hope for this troubled period was for continuity to be maintained. They decided to closely monitor developments in the area of disarmament and support the Swiss proposal on the settlement of disputes. Both subjects required further specification of means and goals, as pointed out by members of the Swedish delegation.

While the Mediterranean and Middle Eastern questions remained peripheral, a growing awareness of the need to develop a profile in the second and third baskets became noticeable. The follow-up debate in the fourth basket, however, was considered a subject to be saved for later. Göran Ryding, the head of the Swedish delegation, again pointed out that, in order to be able to cope with the upcoming challenges, the delegation at Dipoli needed to be equipped with an additional two to three experts.[85]

Following his request, efforts were made to sort out a broader Swedish approach after the resumption of talks. The Foreign Ministry in Stockholm ordered the departmental study groups to draft eventual proposals for a discussion at a general CSCE meeting on 23 February 1973. In the second basket, a draft proposal on science and technology maintained that cooperation could be established on four levels: between individual researchers, between research groups or institutes, between organizations and academies and on the government level.[86]

Inga Thorsson, Sweden's delegate to the 1974 United Nations World Population Conference in Bucharest (which later developed into the ICPD) and a previous ambassador to Israel, advocated active Swedish support for inclusion of the environment as an agenda point.[87] The commitment should not result in a new organ or concrete projects, Thorsson explained, but rather in guidelines which could be followed by the ECE. Such a position would be in conformity with tabled proposals of the Belgian and Finnish delegations. Erik Kronvall and Ulf Lönnqvist of the Ministry of Agriculture rejected Thorsson's ideas, arguing that, although Sweden should not oppose other countries if they brought up the matter, there was no objective reason to include environmental matters at the CSCE. They believed that there was no need for a reference to the ECE either, since other European organs had dealt with the subject already.[88]

A full analysis of the CSCE working group on the role of ECE in relation to economic issues was completed in early March 1973. It concluded that many states were critical of the ECE's earlier record. Regardless of this, Sweden went on to stress the fact that there was no indication that a new political body created by the CSCE would be more successful than the ECE. Also, decisions made in the second basket would assign the ECE 'concrete, defining and active tasks'. On this matter, the Swedish position remained at the same level, with the Swedes arguing that the experience of the ECE should be used. The memorandum also suggested that the environment would merge with issues in the second basket.

With regard to the controversy on the mandates, the Swedes prepared themselves by working on a conflation of proposals made by the Soviet Union and Belgium. The study group on economic matters suggested two alternative wordings to the working group, both of broader design, allowing compromise formulas at an early stage and concrete proposals in the subcommittees. Focus was directed at the improvement of business contacts and exchange of information relating to trade opportunities, the simplification of administrative procedures and the introduction of measures for the improvement of transport and communications in Europe.[89] These were early signs of the sort of efforts described by Holsti as mediating and bridging, which Sweden had earlier rejected. As the MPT progressed, it became obvious that the neutral states were predestined for certain tasks.

There existed no ambiguity in the third basket, although the Swedish Foreign Ministry's CSCE working group and the Ministry of Education provided separate proposals. The study group on cultural relations and freer communication presented drafts to set out the point of the agenda, provide mandate proposals for the relevant subcommittee at the conference, define the areas to be explored and specify which measures could promote cultural exchange through contact between institutions in areas such as education, research, humanitarian aid, youth, tourism and sports. It recommended that the MPT treat both questions of copyright and the work conditions of journalists and correspondents.[90] The language used in the document was consciously attuned to Danish (CSCE/HC/19) and Soviet (CSCE/HC/32) proposals.

The aim was to force the Soviets to further specify their position regarding 'ties', 'exchanges' and 'contacts'.[91] This meant no radicalization or Westernization of the Swedish attitude on freer movements, however, but was part of subtle tactics. For the same reason, another internal Swedish paper proposed that cultural and scientific contacts could be transferred to the second basket, which opposed the Western idea of creating four subcommittees in the third basket on human contacts, cultural exchange, education and freer information. In the fourth basket, Sweden was more reserved than Austria or Switzerland and opposed permanent institutionalization of the CSCE.[92] Slowly but steadily, Sweden placed itself into a middle position which made its capacity to take up the role of bridge or mediator more and more plausible.

The first basket, on security, remained a top priority; nevertheless, Axel Edelstam and Ambassador Lennart Eckerberg of the Swedish delegation to the CCD developed the Swedish position further. Eckerberg, a skilled diplomat who served as ambassador in Bonn and London in the 1980s and 1990s, drafted a rather ambitious proposal, which used the McCloy-Zorin Accords of 1961 as the point of departure.[93] Certain formulations were changed or abstracted in order to take the edges off. 'Peace and' was deleted from the beginning of a sentence in the first paragraph, which continued with 'the strengthening of confidence in Europe is closely related to disarmament'. 'Reduction in military expenditures coupled with an increase of assistance to developing countries' was limited to 'balanced reductions in overall military expenditures'.

Another two paragraphs were deleted: one which stated that 'all disarmament measures should be implemented under effective international control', the other that the 'widest possible agreements at the earliest possible date shall be sought on the provisions mentioned above. Efforts should continue without interruption until agreement has been reached upon all provisions'. The three following measures recommended by Eckerberg were also completely deleted: 'g) undertakings not to be the first to use nuclear weapons and not to use or threaten to use nuclear weapons against non-nuclear weapon states. h) a freeze on the deployment and stock-piling of weapons of mass destruction. i) agreement on a European zone free of weapons of mass destruction'.[94]

After a week of work on these changes, Edelstam hoped to meet the demands of the other delegations: first and foremost those of the Danes, Norwegians, Irish and Yugoslavians.[95] This revised version was approved by Alva Myrdal, who applauded the effort and asked for only one slight modification.[96] With the cuts listed above, Sweden gave in to calls for greater realism in relation to disarmament, which was most vociferously uttered by the Soviets.

The break in February 1973 served to allow not only for internal planning but also for renewed bilateral consultations. In Ottawa, Foreign Minister Krister Wickman had learned that 'control of armaments' was also considered problematic with reference to SALT and CCD. When Wickman once more highlighted the limited possibilities for freer movements, his Canadian counterpart responded that the CSCE had not been convened to simply confirm the status quo.[97] The Yugoslavian and British foreign ministries shared internal papers on the future of the MPT; the latter ministry was firmly decided that Ryding had to ask Rune Nyström to keep it 'within a small circle even in the [Foreign Ministry] department'.[98]

Czechoslovakia's ambassador in Stockholm asked interlocutors at the UD whether Sweden wanted a specific CSCE subcommittee on disarmament at any cost.[99] Finally, Finland's Max Jakobson approached his Swedish counterpart, Sverker Åström, asking him to publicly praise Finnish objectivity at the CSCE, as it had been doubted in a number of European newspapers. But as a matter of fact, the Swedes were sympathetic to the criticism that some Western states and the neutral Austrians had levelled against Finland. Many minor flaws had accumulated, building up an impression of the Finns as being under Soviet influence, and it was believed that it would be rather counterproductive if this was publicly denied.[100] The role of the faithful friend had limits.

Despite the many reservations about the Swedish disarmament proposal, and the fact that the time schedule and venue for the conference proper remained uncertain, Edelstam telegraphed the delegation that Stockholm was satisfied with how the MPT was progressing. If the 'warm atmosphere' and the evident will to compromise could be preserved, the CSCE, which Sweden had been supporting 'since it was discussed seriously', would become a reality in the near future.[101] Despite the positive signals from the Swedish capital, however, Göran Ryding seemed baffled. He was himself the dominant Swedish figure at the MPT, leading a delegation that often lacked manpower, and was without a well-conceived and flexible strategy.

The early reluctance to embrace disarmament had hampered proper preparations and the construction of a multifaceted approach needed in order to deal with the matter at a complex conference such as the CSCE. Another problem was that dominant figures such as Åström and Blix, or Foreign Minister Wickman himself, intervened regularly in important matters, despite their distance from and consequent lack of understanding of the specific dynamics at Dipoli, where changes could occur over a lunch or a coffee break.

Swedish ambassador Tord Hagen at The Hague reported to Stockholm that Dutch diplomats had informed him of the West's satisfaction with the role that the neutral states had played so far. The members of NATO held the view that three-quarters of the content produced during the first months of the MPT was in line with Western objectives. The Warsaw Pact states were conscious of this fact, and so the remaining negotiations, in the controversial first and third baskets, were expected to be difficult. In what was to come, the West would also have to take into account the balance between MBFR and the CSCE.[102] Rushing too fast into areas sensitive to the Soviets and their allies was likely to cause 'sabotage' from Moscow's side at Vienna, said the Dutch and many of their Western colleagues.[103]

During the first day after the February break, on 26 February 1973, the parties agreed on France's proposal to appoint a group that would focus solely on the agenda.[104] The following day, NATO briefed the Swedes about the tactical approach of the West for the coming weeks, 'under strict confidentiality'. The allies would not abandon the key principles in the first basket (i.e. *respect for territorial integrity, respect for human rights and fundamental freedoms, equal rights and self-determination of peoples, fulfilment of obligations under international law* and *peaceful settlement of disputes*). Also, France remained in strict opposition to any notion of CBM and regional disarmament measures.[105]

Italy's ambassador enquired into Wilhelm Wachtmeister's opinion on an EC Nine proposal for a steering committee, which would lead and coordinate the second stage of the CSCE. Wachtmeister was also asked not to mention this information to anyone outside of the EC Nine and the neutral states.[106] Comparable briefings, allowing relatively good insight into internal tactics, never took place with the Eastern bloc. This marked the continuity of Sweden coming to an accommodation with the West.

Bitter End Instead of Breakthrough

Shortly upon returning to Finland, bad news reached the Swedish delegation from Vienna. The MBFR talks had deadlocked completely, due to a dispute between Moscow and Washington over the participation of Hungary and Italy.[107] Since both the Americans and the Western Europeans wanted to profit from their good position in the MPT, they slowed down the pace of negotiations for tactical reasons in the following days.[108]

Meanwhile, at Dipoli, three working groups were established in order to deal with the large amount of information on the catalogue of principles, on the peaceful settlement of disputes and on questions related to the Mediterranean. These so-called minigroups were chaired by Austria,

Switzerland and Yugoslavia, respectively. Despite their initial refusal, the neutral and nonaligned states were eventually assigned special duties – another step towards occupying a middle role between East and West. As this method quickly turned out to be an effective one, several other minigroups followed within a short time, and on 9 March 1973 Swiss delegate Edouard Brunner was named chairman of the minigroup on political security.[109]

Two days earlier, Axel Edelstam had presented the specifications of the Swedish proposal on principles guiding relations between states. Sweden was of the opinion that some progress had been made and that 'the positions may not be as far from each other as a study only of the documents presented would indicate'. As all principles proposed by then were in accordance with the UN Charter and the UN Declaration concerning friendly relations among states, the Swedes had no objections. What remained important from their perspective was that the principles adopted by the CSCE at a later point in time must meet the same standards and be applied 'in the same manner between all participating states and under all circumstances' – a hint at the Brezhnev Doctrine. Edelstam summarized the view, arguing:

> The principles of non-recourse to the use of force or the threat of use of force and the non-intervention and non-interference in internal affairs are, in our opinion, the basic ones and should be sufficient really to guarantee the security of all participants. If states abstain from direct acts of violence against each other across frontiers and from subversive activities within each other's territory, it should be possible for each and every state to shape its political system according to the needs and wishes of its own people ... Out of the principle of non-use of force follows that frontiers may not be violated.[110]

A few days later, the Swedish delegation agreed that CBM would be treated in a minigroup other than the one on political security. Therefore, a CBM minigroup was established, with Axel Edelstam as its chairman.

Positions in the military field had hardly changed since late 1972, and the fact that the big question as to whether a linkage to MBFR and armaments would be discussed in addition to CBM during the main conference loomed large.[111] Edelstam's leadership in the new group would quickly be highly appreciated, and his performance was praised as 'quiet, coherent and efficient'.[112] His efforts proved that Sweden could offer its services for resolving disagreements, contributing further to a growing role expectation of Sweden as bridge or mediator. Yet at the same time it became increasingly obvious that the Swedes would not be able to establish their formula on regional disarmament, as more and more countries took a stand against it. Swedish officials in Stockholm and at Dipoli were well aware of this but pursued their strategy to present highly ambitious proposals, which would be defended in subsequent meetings.[113]

The goal was to preserve as many of these propositions as possible. But the resistance of the superpowers made the task almost impossible, despite support from Norway, Denmark, Switzerland, Ireland and Yugoslavia. At this point, the Swedes merely hoped that Washington and Moscow would 'gradually' accept 'a general and very vaguely formulated statement on disarmament'.[114]

Analyses of the general state of affairs by late March 1973 noted that the bloc-to-bloc constellation, expected by many, never fully materialized. This allowed the neutral states to establish themselves as well-regarded presenters in procedural matters and in situations in which members of blocs were at their wits' end. This added to expectations of the neutral states' growingly obvious suitability as bridges and mediators. In the second basket, Sweden made the case that there should be flexibility from all sides and preferred general formulas that allowed a quick end of the MPT so that substantial matters could be treated in depth at the main conference instead. Human contacts remained problematic, as did security and the catalogue of principles. Sweden considered the Danish proposal too detailed and criticized its confused goals and means. The Soviet counterproposal generally overlapped with Sweden's interests but suffered from unspecific wording. More problematic was its exception clause, which threatened to make future revisions and renegotiations meaningless.[115]

Ultimately, instead of the long-desired breakthrough, the situation worsened as the days passed. When the Danish delegation presented a Western concession in the form of a trimmed revision of its proposal on the subcommittee mandates, the Soviets responded by moving in the opposite direction on freer movements and presented an amendment that argued that cooperation would have to respect the sovereignty, law and practice of the signing state.[116] This made further progress before Easter impossible, and when the third stage of the talks ended on 6 April 1973, Göran Ryding summarized on the behalf of the Swedes the belief that, 'unfortunately, the naked truth is that the visible result of six weeks of toil in the first three baskets is quite poor'.[117]

An extensive memorandum, prepared shortly afterwards, described the atmosphere during the last day of the negotiations as 'gloomy'.[118] Yet, although signs of fatigue and irritation became obvious towards the end of the MPT, it was only with the Soviet foray in the third basket that the good atmosphere was completely ruined. The Soviet move proved counterproductive; even they considered it as purely tactical, since it gave further impetus to the so-called maximalists in the Western camp. In the view of Swedish officials, however, this was not necessarily negative. At least, the MPT had proved that the major challenge was to reconcile the Soviet position on the inviolability of frontiers with the concessions on human contacts sought by the West. This polarization of standpoints was considered to foster positive developments, as it forced everybody to accept that compromises could not be reached in isolation. The linkage between the first and third baskets had been manifested, and Göran Ryding believed that this made barter deals inevitable, which created further room for diplomatic manoeuvres.[119]

While Sweden had cooperated well with neutral Switzerland and non-aligned Yugoslavia during most of the MPT, there was basically no cooperation with the Nordic states. Although Sweden met with the Nordics on a weekly basis, the disparities in their interests and allegiances proved irreconcilable. Göran Berg noted, on human contacts, that 'the fact that Denmark presented the most controversial subject of the security conference, freer movements of people and ideas, and human contacts (i.e., reunification of families) ought to make Nordic cooperation impossible in this area'.[120]

Despite Norwegian and Danish support for Sweden's proposals in Basket I, cooperation was limited to the exchange of information and selective support. Finland was a special case. As host of the talks, the Finns were in constant fear of losing their credibility. Sustaining a traditional Cold War attitude, Sweden, for the most part, supported and defended Finland.[121] When rumours were circulated that Stockholm might be a base for one or several minigroups, or even a venue for the conference proper, rejections were issued immediately.[122] Sweden's almost unconditional support of Finland resulted in considerable frustration for fellow neutral Austria, which held ambitions of organizing the CSCE itself.[123] By the time the negotiations at Dipoli moved towards their end, the Swedish government had fully grasped the importance of the CSCE to the country's foreign policy. This expressed itself when yet another internal working group was established in April 1973.

A lengthy memorandum issued by Jan Prawitz from the Ministry of Defence elaborated on CBM and 'collateral constraints', a term that covered the prohibition of manoeuvres in certain border areas. Two opinions existed in the Western camp. The 'American school' defined collateral constraints as an element supporting force reductions, while the 'English school' argued that their value was completely separate from force reductions. The latter definition could bring CSCE and MBFR closer together and result in bilateralization and subregionalization. The possibility of such scenarios taking place made it necessary for Sweden to prepare for reinterpretations of its defence interests. In consequence, Defence Minister Sven Andersson, who would become foreign minister later that year, decided to establish an informal group to study defence goals resulting from CSCE negotiations.[124] The group operated directly under the under-secretary of state and consisted of Commander-in-Chief General Stig Synnergren and two experts, Torgil Wulff and Jan Prawitz.[125]

Final Breakthrough and Drafting the Blue Book

When the Salon des Ambassadeurs was nearing the end, Sweden found itself in the role of a bridge and heading towards that of a mediator, although it had strictly rejected any such notional activity in the previous years. By Easter 1973, the Swedes had accepted the fact that the reality of the neutrals being considered well-suited mediators had caught up with them. Internal documents also witnessed to this development, starting to list specific efforts under the subheading 'Sweden's possibilities of mediating'. One important area in this respect was the catalogue of principles in the first basket. Hans Blix drafted a compromise drawing a connection between the different principles in order to bring together Soviet and Italian positions on the inviolability of frontiers. While drafting his paper Blix maintained close contact with Lev Mendelevich and Edouard Brunner and succeeded in pleasing all sides, resulting in a formula that was acceptable to all delegations.

The role of minigroup coordinator, as the chairmanship was called, was viewed with ambiguity in Stockholm. It allowed the Swedish delegation to direct discussions to a certain extent but also compelled it to show a constant will to compromise. This could potentially force upon the Swedes unwelcome positions in security matters. In the second and third baskets the Swedish delegation had always maintained a rather pragmatic approach, aiming at the removal of obstacles by creating and making use of contact areas and by exchanging information.[126] These shifts, caused by the dynamics of multilateralism, forged 'active' diplomacy at last.

This version of active foreign policy differed from the established notion of Sweden's active foreign policy of that era in that it did not claim the moral high ground with reference to the advocacy of values and defence of the weak. Despite the narrow outlook, the Swedes decided to undertake one last attempt on disarmament. On 17 April 1973, the embassies in Moscow, Washington, London, Paris, Warsaw, Prague, Sofia, Budapest and East Berlin were ordered to brief the foreign ministries of their host countries and lobby for the Swedish position.[127] Shortly afterwards, French diplomats informed Stockholm that the appeal on disarmament had been discussed at the highest level, but this had not changed the strict *non* from Paris.[128]

When the last round of talks was introduced on 25 April 1973, the general mood improved quickly, as the Soviets opened up and showed more flexibility.[129] Moscow was willing to conclude the talks as soon as possible and had to take into account NATO's determination not to give consent to final texts in the first two baskets unless the Soviets themselves would make concessions in the third. Therefore, the deadlock in the first and third baskets persisted for a little longer. Eventually, the Blix papers boosted progress on the catalogue of principles.

Blix's proposal to define the linkage to existing international law as being 'in conformity with the purposes and principles of the United Nations' was acceptable to everyone. On the application of the principles, he suggested that the wording be applied 'regardless of their geographic location, economic, political or social system' and that 'it shall express the determination of the participating states to respect and apply the principles equally and unreservedly and lay down the corresponding right of every participating state to benefit fully from their application'.[130] These formulations were skilful enough to allow the Soviet Union to accept them without losing face in relation to the Brezhnev Doctrine.

During the second week of May, Blix's formulas were used in the drafting of the preamble of the first basket. The only obstacle left was the maximalist link to MBFR, whereas drafting progressed quickly in the second basket, which remained uncontroversial. The solution to the remaining obstacle came in the form of a proposal originally drafted by the delegation of the Holy See and reintroduced by Yugoslavia, which stated that there was no need to repeat principles. During the discussion on the third basket on 10 May, Sweden expressed its support of the paper.[131] This paved the way for the long-awaited breakthrough, which finally came with a Soviet proposal on the preamble for the third basket on 17 May 1973. In Stockholm, the final Soviet move was viewed as 'a retreat from the initial positions' held by Moscow, according to Swedish ambassador Ryding; shortly afterwards, the Western states officially accepted it.[132]

Due to persistent resistance from a group of states, most notably France, Sweden had to retreat from the maximalist stance on disarmament it had held for months. Originally a firm conviction, the position had by now become rather more tactical and symbolic. After the turn of the year, the question was now only how much of the original ambition would be left by the end of the MPT. Security and the first basket remained the only real preference held by the Swedes throughout the whole period. When Chairman Axel Edelstam brought together positions for the final compromise, not much was left of either the originally envisaged regional dimension or the measures additional to CBM. Arguing that there was nothing that could be done in the subcommittee, nor hope for changes to occur during the meeting of ministers, Göran Ryding recommended that Sweden accept reality.[133]

Six days later, on 28 May, West German foreign minister Walter Scheel met with Wickman in Stockholm for a lengthy discussion of the MPT.[134] At the FCO in London, British diplomats analysed Sweden's position on disarmament. The British had never been as close to the Swedes as the West Germans. They accepted Sweden's interest in the topic but were decided on avoiding lengthy discussions and did not view it as a suitable area in a possible future follow-up process. Crispin Tickell, who was in charge of London's CSCE policy, remarked with slight irritation that 'the Swedes have got broadly what they want, and we must merely make sure that this is not allowed to distort the main Conference'.[135]

Against expectations, however, this was not the end of the Dipoli story, as France's strict stand against the maximalists provoked yet another (minor) turn, written down in the so-called Blue Book, which delayed the presentation of the recommendations for another two weeks. It was on 8 June 1973 that France finally presented a paper acceptable to the maximalists, which formally ended the MPT after more than seven months.[136] The very same day, Sverker Åström, Wilhelm Wachtmeister and Krister Wickman discussed the first stage of the CSCE at the Foreign Ministry in Stockholm.

They concluded that it required timely and thorough preparation and hoped for Sweden to be allowed to speak 'relatively early and preferably before the other Nordic appearances'. Furthermore, they planned for Wickman to issue a lunch invitation to those 'colleagues who are of special interest in the context of the CSCE'. These were the Netherlands, Belgium, Italy, Yugoslavia, Switzerland and Austria.[137] The friendship with the West persisted, the relationship of the other neutral and nonaligned states gained weight and, most notably, neither the Nordic neighbours nor the West Germans were on the list.

Conclusion

Over the course of the multilateral preparatory talks at Dipoli, Sweden's policy metamorphosed. After several years of cautiousness, and an initial refusal to play a significant role on the road to a conference on European security, the Nordic country found itself in the role of bridge and on the brink of becoming what Holsti calls mediator-integrator, when the Blue Book was drafted in June 1973. This development was the result of the configuration of the MPT, with Switzerland and Sweden eventually proving to be brokers of value to both blocs. Based on the excellent personal relationship between Sweden's ambassador to Helsinki Göran Ryding and Swiss ambassador Samuel Campiche, the two neutral countries became the nucleus of the later group of neutral and nonaligned states, often abbreviated as N+N.

A further step to the eventual institutionalization of N+N cooperation was taken through the special invitation issued to Yugoslavian ambassador Djuro Nincic in early June 1973. Sweden's declared policy of neutrality further made it a natural candidate for these roles. The role of the N+N as chairs of the minigroups was also instrumental, as it had helped Sweden to overcome its earlier reluctance and allowed it to grow into the role of mediator-integrator.

The internal working structure at the Ministry for Foreign Affairs in Stockholm, consisting of a steering working group and four study groups supported by officials and experts from five ministries, played an important part during the MPT. Working efficiently and invisibly in the background, lesser-known officials such as Hans Ewerlöf, Jan Prawitz and Per Olof Forshell helped the Swedish delegation in Finland, headed by Göran Ryding, to analyse the overwhelming amount of information and shape positions of their own. The efforts of diplomats like Ryding, Hans Blix and Axel Edelstam ultimately earned Sweden a good reputation. All three made welcome contributions to the catalogue of principles on matters of military security and disarmament and to the compromise formula on human contacts. Thus, little of the criticism that Sweden had received from all sides still prevailed by the summer of 1973.

With its own interests finally defined, Sweden also came to complement the role of faithful friend with that of independent actor. On the other hand, Sweden assumed none of the altruistic roles offered in Holsti's typology of NRC, such as defender of the faith, liberation supporter or developer. To the Swedish delegation at the MPT, defending values to support the peoples of Eastern Europe was never an option, let alone a priority. Their mission was about disarmament and securing strategic advantages, about stabilizing and maintaining détente and strategic balance in Northern Europe, all with the prospect in mind of eventually exporting features of the latter to the European continent as a whole.

As mentioned by Ryding during the opening session of the MPT in November 1972, and as reiterated by Foreign Minister Krister Wickman in talks with Canadian foreign minister Mitchell three months later, Sweden did not regard the possibilities of freer movements central to its aims but was, rather, concerned with the limitations of the subject. The main struggle of the Swedish delegation regarded the inclusion of an additional level of disarmament in the recommendations for the CSCE as important, not the promotion of long-standing visions aimed at transforming Socialist societies. Pragmatism, grounded in the general realpolitik approach, remained a guiding principle.

Sweden's formulation of its own interests, its adoption of the roles of bridge and independent actor and its rejection of the West's far-reaching demands on human contacts also had an effect on its relations with the West. In contrast to earlier years, it now made 'policy decisions according to [its] own interests rather than in support of the objectives of other states'. First-hand information from Western circles was still regularly received, but discomfort with the Western standpoint on human contacts prevailed throughout – although it was not expressed as harsh criticism. Sweden remained a faithful friend to NATO and the West but, in the sense of Holsti's definition, a friend *with reservations*. As Sweden's general loyalty was to the West as a whole, traditional relations with Norway and Denmark were less significant than one perhaps might expect, although both countries helped gather information about positions within NATO and the EC Nine.

Foreign Minister Krister Wickman and Kaj Björk were actively involved in the strategy applied by the delegation on the ground. Ultimately, however, Swedish policy at Dipoli was the responsibility of Olof Palme, and it was based on the country's declared neutrality policy, its limitations and its implications. After all, it was at the highest level that the general premises governing the approach to the CSCE were set. In the context of the CSCE, Palme was a pragmatic politician: solidarity was excluded from Sweden's approach to the MPT. His severe criticism of the bombing of Hanoi, too, did not have any noticeable effect on the diplomatic relations with the delegation of the United States. At Dipoli, relations with Washington and the rest of the West were stable and highly valued during a time otherwise known in the literature as the 'Year of the Frost' in Swedish-US relations.

Notes

1. Ericsson, 'Förslag till avsnitt om säkerhetspolitiska överväganden, att tas in i prop 1973:1 (bilaga 6), för offentliggörande i januari 1973', 15 November 1972, File 26, Vol. 34, HP 79, UD, RA.
2. Berg, 'Läget beträffande ESK', 17 November 1972, File 26, Vol. 34, HP 79, UD, RA.
3. Nyström, 'ESK och MBFR', 21 November 1972, File 26, Vol. 34, HP 79, UD, RA.
4. Edelstam to Wachtmeister, Enclair telegram 331, 22 November 1972, File 26, Vol. 34, HP 79, UD, RA.

5. Hakkarainen, *State of Peace*, 215.
6. Nyström, 'Tidpunkten för svenskt inlägg i generaldebatten vid FMÖ', 25 November 1972, File 26, Vol. 34, HP 79, UD, RA.
7. Swedish Embassy Helsinki to UD, 'Procedurordningen för FMÖ', 5 December 1972, File 27, Vol. 34, HP 79, UD, RA.
8. A very detailed explanation of the rules of procedure is offered in Fischer, *Neutral Power*, 155–62.
9. Ferraris, *Report*, 9–10; Kaj Björk, 'Synpunkter på svenskt anförande vid Helsingforssamtalen', 20 November 1972, File 26, Vol. 34, HP 79, UD, RA.
10. Rosin, *Die Schweiz im KSZE-Prozeß*, 68–71.
11. The Romanian protest has been described as 'dropping a little bomb'; see Fischer, *Neutral Power*, 157.
12. Ryding to UD, Telegram 436, 'Ang Helsingfors-Konsultationerna', 28 November 1972, File 27, Vol. 34, HP 79, UD, RA; Ferraris, *Report*, 11; Fischer, *Neutral Power*, 158–62. See also Reimaa, *Helsinki Catch*, 56–60.
13. Hakkarainen, *State of Peace*, 215–18.
14. Ionescu, 'Romania, *Ostpolitik* and the CSCE', 134–35.
15. Ryding to Wachtmeister, Cipher telegram 51, 29 November 1972, File 27, Vol. 34, HP 79, UD, RA.
16. Ibid.
17. Kling to Wachtmeister, 'Utrikesministermötet i Haag', 24 November 1972, File 27, Vol. 34, HP 79, UD, RA.
18. Nyström to Swedish Embassy Algier, Cipher telegram 28, 21 November 1972, File 26, Vol. 34, HP 79, UD, RA.
19. Gilde, *Österreich im KSZE-Prozess*, 80–87, 97, 128.
20. For a broader discussion on the relevance of the CSCE to those regions, see Nicolas Badalassi, 'The Mediterranean Stake of the CSCE, 1972–1975', in Elena Calandri, Daniele Caviglia and Antonio Varsori (eds.), *Détente in Cold War Europe: Politics and Diplomacy in the Mediterranean and the Middle East* (London: IB Tauris, 2012), 61–73.
21. Fischer, *Neutral Power*, 163.
22. DSFP 1972, 129–34.
23. Ibid.
24. Ibid.
25. Gilde, *Österreich im KSZE-Prozess*, 131.
26. Ibid. See also Nyström to Ryding, 'Svenskt anförande vid FMÖ', 27 November 1972, File 27, Vol. 34, HP 79, UD, RA.
27. This remained a fact throughout the MPT and the first two stages of the CSCE and was also observed abroad. British reports pointed out, 'In Sweden, public and political interest in the CSCE negotiations has subsided. The current negotiations are too complicated and too technical to be followed by any but a small group of experts, mainly in the Swedish Ministry for Foreign Affairs'; see Mallet to McLaren, 18 October 1974, FCO 41/1549, TNA.
28. Rössel to UD, Telegram 244, 1 December 1972, File 27, Vol. 34, HP 79, UD, RA.
29. Swedish Embassy Helsinki to UD, Telegram 441, 'FMÖ', 29 November 1972, File 27, Vol. 34, HP 79, UD, RA. The Poles defined their interest as 'emerging from the national interest of Poland as a member of the socialist community'; cf. Jarzabek, 'Hope and Reality', 37.
30. Ryding to UD, Telegram 442, 30 November 1972 and Ryding to UD, Telegram 444, 1 December 1972, File 27, Vol. 34, HP 79, UD, RA.

31. It was part of Western strategy to frustrate the Soviets without giving the impression of undermining détente. See Romano, *Détente*, 122–24; Jarzabek, 'Hope and Reality', 37–41.
32. Ryding to UD, Telegram 456, 'Ang FMÖ' and Swedish Embassy Helsinki to UD, 8 December 1972, 'Översänder förslag framlagda vid FMÖ', 8 December 1972, File 28, Vol. 35, HP 79, UD, RA. See also Fischer, *Neutral Power*, 165–67; Gilde, *Österreich im KSZE-Prozess*, 80–87, 97, 128; Peter, *Die Bundesrepublik im KSZE-Prozess*, 88–92; Rosin, *Die Schweiz im KSZE-Prozeß*, 67–68; Senoo, *Irrweg*, 227–42.
33. Flora Lewis, 'Helsinki Talks Redefine "Europe": Geography, Rather Than Boundaries, Coming to Fore', *New York Times*, 4 December 1972.
34. Edelstam to Swedish Embassy Helsinki, Cipher telegram, 11 December 1972, File 28 and Wachtmeister, 'Samtal med jugoslaviske ambassadören', 10 January 1973, File 29, Vol. 35, HP 79, UD, RA.
35. Fischer, *Neutral Power*, 164–65.
36. Ryding to UD, Cipher telegram 56, 8 December 1972 and Telegram 467, 'FMÖ. Veckosammandrag 11–15 December 1972', File 28; Berg, 'De förberedande multilaterala överläggningarna i Helsingfors rörande sammankallandet av en konferens om säkerhet och samarbete i Europa (FMÖ)', File 29, Vol. 35, HP 79, UD, RA.
37. Ryding to Wachtmeister, Cipher telegram 58, 18 December 1972, File 28, Vol. 35, HP 79, UD, RA.
38. Swiss embassy Vienna to Thalmann, 'Zusammenarbeit mit Österreich und Schweden in Helsinki', 13 Dezember 1972, Cable Nr. 176, 36, 1997/83, E 2200.53(-), BAR.
39. Hammarskjöld to Nyström, 'Mevik om FMÖ', 22 December 1972, File 29, Vol. 35, HP 79, UD, RA.
40. Åström, 20 December 1972, File 28, Vol. 35, HP 79, UD, RA.
41. Leatherman, 'Engaging East and West', 230–36.
42. Ibid., 428–29.
43. Ryding to Wachtmeister, Cipher telegram 60, 20 December 1972, File 28, Vol. 35, HP 79, UD, RA.
44. Swedish Embassy Brussels to UD, 'Samråd med Belgien om FMÖ', 22 December 1972, File 28 and Edelstam to Swedish Embassies Helsinki and Brussels, 27 December 1972, File 29, Vol. 35, HP 79, UD, RA. See also, Romano, *Détente*, 133.
45. Elliott to FCO, 18 December 1972, FCO 28/1709 and 10 February 1973, FCO 41/1288, The National Archives (TNA).
46. Ryding to Berg, 'FMÖ', 21 December 1972 and Berg, 'FMÖ i Helsingfors, 22.11–15.12.1972', 10 January 1973, File 29, Vol. 35, HP 79, UD, RA.
47. Ibid. See also Yamamoto, 'Britain, France and West Germany', 246–47.
48. Kaj Björk, 'Utkast till anförande vid FMÖ i anslutning till dagordningspunkten om säkerhetsproblem', in Wachtmeister to Ryding, Enclair telegram 9, 15 January 1973, File 29, Vol. 35, HP 79, UD, RA.
49. Ewerlöf to Ryding, Enclair telegram 12, 16 January 1973 and Ryding to UD, telegram 39, and UD, Pressbyrån, Pressmeddelande, 17 January 1973, File 30, Vol. 35, HP 79, UD, RA.
50. UD, 'FMÖ 29.1–30.1973', 31 January 1973, File 32, Vol. 36, HP 79, UD, RA.
51. Ryding to UD, 18 January 1973, Second in Lundvik, 19 January 1973, File 30, Vol. 35, HP 79, UD, RA.
52. Ryding to Wachtmeister, Cipher telegram 52, 19 January 1973, File 30, Vol. 35, HP 79, UD, RA.
53. Snyder, *Human Rights Activism*, 21–23.

54. Ryding to Wachtmeister, Cipher telegram 3, 19 January 1973 and Leifland to UD, telegram 140, 19 January 1973, File 30, Vol. 35, HP 79, UD, RA.
55. Ryding to UD, Telegram 54, 22 January 1973, File 30, Vol. 35, HP 79, UD, RA. See Fischer, *Neutral Power*, 173–85; Romano, *Détente*, 136–39; Senoo, *Irrweg*, 227–51.
56. Backlund to UD, Cipher telegram 6, 24 January 1973, File 30, Vol. 35, HP 79, UD, RA.
57. Ryding to UD, Cipher telegram 5, 24 January 1973, File 30, Vol. 35, HP 79, UD, RA.
58. Swedish Embassy Helsinki to UD, Telegram 85, File 32, Vol. 36, HP 79, UD, RA
59. Edelstam to Swedish Embassy Helsinki, Cipher telegram 11, 29 January 1973, File 32, Vol. 36, HP 79, UD, RA.
60. Myrdal was head of the Swedish delegation to the CCD in Geneva at the time. See Edelstam to Alva Myrdal, Enclair telegram 28, 29 January 1973, File 32, Vol. 36, HP 79, UD, RA.
61. Swedish Embassy Helsinki to UD, Telegram 85, and Ryding to UD, Telegram 86, 30 January 1973, File 32, Vol. 36, HP 79, UD, RA.
62. Ryding to UD, Telegram 88, 31 January 1973, File 32, Vol. 36, HP 79, UD, RA.
63. Ryding to UD, Telegram 89, 31 January 1973, File 32, Vol. 36, HP 79, UD, RA.
64. Ryding to UD, Telegram 97, 5 February 1973, File 33, Vol. 36, HP 79, UD, RA.
65. See also Jarring to UD, Cipher telegram 69, 2 February 1973 and Edelstam to Swedish Embassy Moscow, Cipher telegram 37, 2 February 1973, File 32, Vol. 36, HP 79, UD, RA.
66. Edelstam to Alva Myrdal, Cipher telegram, 1 February 1973, File 32, Vol. 36, HP 79, UD, RA.
67. Ryding to Edelstam, Cipher telegram 7, 2 February 1973, File 32, Vol. 36, HP 79, UD, RA.
68. Wollter to Swedish Embassy Helsinki, Enclair telegram 46, 2 February 1973, File 32, Vol. 36, HP 79, UD, RA. See also, Johannes Krohn, 'Karl-Anders Wollters samling på filmarkivet i Grängesberg', MA thesis (Uppsala University, 2010), 10.
69. Wilkens, 'MBFR-ESK', 2 February 1973, File 32, Vol. 36, HP 79, UD, RA.
70. For the diplomatic crisis between the United States and Sweden resulting from Palme's statement, see Leif Leifland, *Frostens år: om USA:s diplomatiska utfrysning av Sverige* (Stockholm: Nerenius & Santérus, 1997); Staffan Thorsell, *Sverige i vita huset* (Stockholm: Bonnier fakta, 2004), 118–64.
71. Ryding to Lundvik, Cipher telegram 8, 5 February 1973, File 33, Vol. 36, HP 79, UD, RA.
72. Ryding to UD, Telegram 94, 5 February 1973, File 33, Vol. 36, HP 79, UD, RA.
73. Edelstam to Swedish Embassy Helsinki, Enclair telegram 50, 5 February 1973, File 33, Vol. 36, HP 79, UD, RA.
74. Lewenhaupt to Lundvik, Cipher telegram 10, 6 February 1973, File 33, Vol. 36, HP 79, UD, RA.
75. Edelstam to Swedish Embassy Helsinki, Enclair telegram 51, 6 February 1973.
76. Ryding to UD, Telegram 101, 7 February 1973, File 33, Vol. 36, HP 79, UD, RA.
77. Ryding to UD, Telegram 99, 6 February 1973, File 33, Vol. 36, HP 79, UD, RA.
78. Edelstam to Eckerberg, 'FMÖ; nedrustningssporsmål', 6 February 1973, File 33, Vol. 36, HP 79, UD, RA.
79. Nyström to Swedish Embassy Ottawa, Enclair telegram, 10 February 1973, File 33, Vol. 36, HP 79, UD, RA.
80. Forshell to Nyström, Enclair telegram 52, 6 February 1973, File 33, Vol. 36, HP 79, UD, RA.
81. Ryding to UD, Telegram 107, 7 February 1973, File 33, Vol. 36, HP 79, UD, RA.
82. Ryding to Blix and Edelstam, Telegram 109, 9 February 1973, File 33, Vol. 36, HP 79, UD, RA.
83. Ryding to Wachtmeister, Cipher telegram 11, 12 February 1973, File 33, Vol. 36, HP 79, UD, RA.

84. There was no Austrian or Swiss interest in the issue, however. Switzerland was busy with its own proposals and the question of the venue of the conference proper; see Fischer, *Neutral Power,* 201–16; Gilde, *Österreich im KSZE-Prozess,* 115–18; Rosin, *Die Schweiz im KSZE-Prozeß,* 61, 73–79.
85. Ryding to Wachtmeister, Telegram 111, 12 February 1973, File 33, Vol. 36, HP 79, UD, RA.
86. Ericsson, 'FMOE – Förslag om vetenskap och teknologi', 20 February 1973, File 35, Vol. 37, HP 79, UD, RA.
87. Thorsson had been Sweden's ambassador in Israel between 1967 and 1970. She succeeded Alva Myrdal as head of the Swedish delegation to the CCD in 1974; see Petri, *Sverige i stora världen,* 455.
88. Nauckhoff, 'Dagordningsförslag i miljöfrågor inför ESK ('korg 2')', 21 February 1973, File 35, Vol. 37, HP 79, UD, RA.
89. See attachments of Wollter, 'Inför den europeiska säkerhetskonferensen – svenska synpunkter avseende "Korg II"-samarbete på det ekonomiska området', 9 March 1973, File 36, Vol. 37, HP 79, UD, RA.
90. Arbetsgruppen för Kultursamarbetsfrågor, 'FMÖ, svenskt förslag beträffande dagordningspunkt III vid ESK och kommitté för denna punkt', 21 February 1973, File 35, Vol. 37, HP 79, UD, RA.
91. Arbetsgruppen för Kultursamarbetsfrågor, 'Kommentarer till det svenska förslaget till dagordningspunkt III vid ESK', 21 February 1973, File 35, Vol. 37, HP 79, UD, RA.
92. Utbildningsdepartementet, 'FMÖ, Synpunkter beträffande förslag till dagordningspunkt vid ESK för kulturellt samarbete och friare kommunikationer', 21 February 1973, File 35, Vol. 37, HP 79, UD, RA; Fischer, *Neutral Power,* 173–77; Gilde, *Österreich im KSZE-Prozess,* 121–24.
93. The McCloy-Zorin Accords were a path-setting treaty between the United States and the Soviet Union on future negotiations and treaties in relation to nuclear and general disarmament under international control.
94. Eckerberg to Edelstam, 'FMÖ; nedrustningsspörsmål', 16 February 1973, File 35, Vol. 37, HP 79, UD, RA.
95. Edelstam to Eckerberg, 'FMÖ, nedrustningsspörsmål', 23 February 1973, File 35, Vol. 37, HP 79, UD, RA.
96. Björnberg to Edelstam, Cipher telegram 38, 1 March 1973, File 35, Vol. 37, HP 79, UD, RA.
97. Identical to 'regulation of armaments', Malmaeus to UD, 'Utrikesminister Wickmans överläggningar i Ottawa', 14 February 1973, File 35, Vol. 37, HP 79, UD, RA.
98. Ryding to Nyström, 'FMÖ, jugoslaviskt förslag till procedurregler', 12 February 1973 and 'Organisationen av FMÖ:s fortsättning', 13 February 1973, File 34, Vol. 37, HP 79, UD, RA.
99. Åström to Swedish Embassies Prague, Helsinki, Paris, London, Vienna, 'För information', 16 February 1973, File 35, Vol. 37, HP 79, UD, RA.
100. Åström to Swedish Embassy Helsinki, Cipher telegram, 12 February 1973 and Ryding to Åström, Cipher telegram 12, 13 February 1973, File 33, Vol. 36, HP 79, UD, RA.
101. Edelstam, 'Förberedande arbetet i Helsingfors inför konfernsen för säkerhet och samarbete i Europa', 27 February 1973, File 35, Vol. 37, HP 79, UD, RA.
102. Yamamoto, 'Britain, France and West Germany', 249–56.
103. Hagen to UD, 'ESK och MBFR', 23 February 1973, File 35, Vol. 37, HP 79, UD, RA.
104. Bundy to UD and Ryding, Telegram 135, 27 February 1973, File 35, Vol. 37, HP 79, UD, RA. See also Fischer, *Neutral Power,* 185.

105. Ryding to UD, Cipher telegram 15, 28 February 1973 and Ingemar Hägglöf to UD, Cipher telegram 38, 4 March 1973, File 35, Vol. 37, HP 79, UD, RA.
106. Wachtmeister, 'ESK', 6 March 1973, File 36, Vol. 37, HP 79, UD, RA.
107. Leifland to UD, Cipher telegram 68, 9 March 1973, File 36, Vol. 37, HP 79, UD, RA.
108. Ryding to Wachtmeister, Cipher telegram 17, 9 March 1973, File 36, Vol. 37, HP 79, UD, RA.
109. Fischer, *Neutral Power*, 185–87.
110. Ryding to UD, 'FMÖ; svenskt inlägg i arbetsgruppen om principerna för förbindelserna mellan de deltagande staterna', 7 March 1973, File 36, Vol. 37, HP 79, UD, RA.
111. Ryding to UD, Telegram 175, 16 March 1973, File 36, Vol. 37, HP 79, UD, RA.
112. Hagen to Wachtmeister, Cipher telegram 25, 22 March 1973, File 37, Vol. 38, HP 79, UD, RA.
113. Ryding to UD, Cipher telegram 25, 22 March 1973, File 37, Vol. 38, HP 79, UD, RA.
114. Ibid.
115. Ryding to UD, Telegram 200, 28 March 1973 and Nyström to Swedish Embassy Helsinki, Cipher telegram 30, 29 March 1973, File 37, Vol. 38, HP 79, UD, RA.
116. Bundy to UD, Telegram 209, 30 March 1973, File 37, Vol. 38, HP 79, UD, RA.
117. Ryding to Åström, Cipher telegram 32, 6 April 1973, File 37, Vol. 38, HP 79, UD, RA.
118. Berg, 'Läget i FMÖ vid den tredje etappens slut den 6 April 1973', 6 April 1973, File 37, Vol. 38, HP 79, UD, RA.
119. Ryding to Wachtmeister, Cipher telegram 34, 6 April 1973, File 37, Vol. 38, HP 79, UD, RA.
120. Berg, 'Förberedande multilaterala överläggningar i Helsingfors (FMÖ) i frågan om sammankallande av en konferens om säkerhet och samarbete i Europa (ESK)', 20 March 1973, File 37, Vol. 38, HP 79, UD, RA.
121. For a comprehensive background of the so-called Finland Argument, see Krister Wahlbäck, *Jättens andedräkt: Finlandsfrågan i svensk politik 1809–2009* (Stockholm: Atlantis, 2011); Olof Kronvall, 'Den bräckliga barriären: Finland i svensk säkerhetspolitik 1948–1962', PhD dissertation (Swedish National Defence College, 2003); Widén, *Väktare, ombud, kritiker*.
122. Wachtmeister to Eng, Cipher telegram, 'Vill göra följande två kommentarer till din depesch nr 283 ang. FMÖ', 14 March 1973 and Ryding to UD, Cipher telegram 21, 16 March 1973, File 36, Vol. 37, HP 79, UD, RA.
123. Örn, 'Österrike och ESK', 4 April 1973, File 37, Vol. 38, HP 79, UD, RA.
124. Prawitz, 'Sveriges intressen i förtroendeskapande åtgärder and 'collateral constraints' vid ESK- och MBFR-förhandlingarna. Behov av mindre utredning', 26 March 1973, File 37, Vol. 38, HP 79, UD, RA. The paper was based on information partly drawn from talks between Swedish and Norwegian military experts. On the military cooperation between the two countries in the early Cold War, see Petersson, *Brödrafolken*.
125. *Försvarsdepartementet* (FD) to Åström, 6 April 1973, File 37, Vol. 38, HP 79, UD, RA.
126. Berg, 'Synpunkter på Sveriges agerande vid FMÖ', 16 April 1973, File 38, Vol. 38, HP 79, UD, RA. See also, Blix, 'ESK-FMÖ-principerna', 23 May 1973, File 39, Vol. 38, HP 79, UD, RA.
127. Edelstam to Swedish Embassies, 17 April 1973, File 38, Vol. 38, HP 79, UD, RA.
128. Bundy to UD, Telegram 241, 27 April 1973, File 38, Vol. 38, HP 79, UD, RA.
129. Malmaeus to Nyström, Cipher telegram 14, 3 May 1973, File 38, Vol. 38, HP 79, UD, RA.
130. Ryding to UD, Telegram 253, 7 May 1973, File 39, Vol. 38, HP 79, UD, RA.
131. Ryding to UD, Telegram 262, 11 May 1973, File 39, Vol. 38, HP 79, UD, RA.

132. Ryding to UD, Telegram 28, 21 May 1973, File 39, Vol. 38, HP 79, UD, RA and Ryding to UD, Telegram 301, 28 May 1973, File 40, Vol. 39, HP 79, UD, RA.
133. Ryding to UD, Telegram 290, 22 May 1973, File 39, Vol. 38, HP 79, UD, RA.
134. Von Groll to Referat 204, 'Besuch des Herrn Bundesministers in Stockholm am 28. Mai 1973', 23 May 1973, 111518, ZA, PAAA.
135. Tickell to Elliott, 'CSCE: The Swedish Case for Disarmament', 4 June 1973, FCO 41/1343, TNA.
136. Ryding to Edelstam, Telegram 319, 8 June 1973, File 40, Vol. 39, HP 79, UD, RA.
137. Wachtmeister to Edelstam, Cipher telegram 236, 8 June 1973, File 40, Vol. 39, HP 79, UD, RA.

CHAPTER FIVE

1973–1975: Making the Helsinki Final Act

> *Decisions on human contacts and increased information across national borders have not yet been finally approved by all participants. Sweden will be continuing its efforts to ensure that their content is in harmony with our democratic and humanitarian traditions. When judging the results possible in this field it must be borne in mind that the Conference cannot eliminate differences due to political, economic or social systems.*
>
> —Sven Andersson, foreign minister of Sweden, 19 March 1975

> *Agreements have been reached on improved human contacts across frontiers and better access to information from each other . . . We are all aware that the peace and stability in Europe which the Final Act is intended to protect does not imply that political and social developments on our continent will come to a standstill. The demands for change will not cease. Social and economic security for our citizens, increased influence for the people on their daily life, on conditions of work and in the political field, are essential factors for building solidarity and social cohesion within each individual nation . . . It is my hope that the future of Europe will be built on ideas of democracy, solidarity and social justice.*
>
> —Olof Palme, prime minister of Sweden, 31 July 1975

The previous chapter illustrated and explained Sweden's adoption of a pragmatic role during the multilateral preparatory phase, which laid the foundation for the CSCE proper. Between the summers of 1973 and 1975, thirty-five European and North American states negotiated issues relating to security, economy, technology and science and human rights in Europe. What was Sweden's contribution to these negotiations? In turn, what was the importance of the CSCE in Sweden and to the foreign policy of the

Swedish government? It is time to return to this interrelationship, which can be understood with the help of Holsti's NRC typology.

Reviewing Dipoli, Preparing for Helsinki

Once the Dipoli talks had been concluded successfully, the participating states had less than four weeks to evaluate and prepare for the first stage of the CSCE, a five-day-long meeting of the thirty-five foreign ministers in Helsinki. In his report on the MPT, Swedish ambassador Göran Ryding emphasized that both the smaller and the neutral states had played a 'balancing and mediatory' role and that this had been possible because their efforts often served the interests of the two blocs. Conversely, neutral efforts were short-lived once they did not serve the interests of the greater powers.

At Dipoli, neither side had given up on its basic positions. Therefore, Swedish diplomats thought that 'there is all reason to believe that the CSCE will not result in concrete solutions of various political problems in Europe'.[1] As we have seen, the Swedish pessimism of the late 1960s persisted well into the conference proper. This lack of belief in the value of the CSCE and the core objectives of the West stood in sharp contrast to the general Swedish approach to international affairs and kept prohibiting the country from taking up a more prominent role in the negotiations. With Olof Palme's moralism, as Bo Stråth calls it, conspicuous by its absence, the role of a defender of the faith was not considered an option.[2]

The Ministry for Foreign Affairs in Stockholm was positive that the delay of the Dipoli talks had been caused by procedural discontinuity due to the rotating chairmanship, rather than by propaganda. It was noted that, with the exception of France, the EC Nine had acted homogenously, while on the Eastern side, the Soviets had dominated, despite Romania's independent standpoint on procedural matters.[3] In the eyes of the Swedes, the first round of extensive multilateral negotiations had confirmed their concerns about the ability of the CSCE to bring about constructive change. Meanwhile, their colleagues in Berne, Bonn or Vienna looked much more favourably at the recently concluded negotiations.[4]

At the MPT, the Swedish delegation had managed to maintain a certain level of participation in all four baskets after the initial imbalance, particularly during the third and fourth rounds of the talks. It had been struggling with a lack of expertise on the spot, which had hampered the establishment of grassroots contacts with other delegations. In his review of the many months of intense negotiations, Ryding viewed such contacts as necessary if the Swedish government wanted its diplomats to be able to push through proposals of their own. He mentioned Sweden's relations with its Nordic neighbours explicitly, as these relationships differed greatly from standard procedure:

> A few words on Nordic cooperation. It is clear that at an international conference like this, Nordic cooperation can have utterly limited substance only, regular exchange of information and impressions for the most part. There simply have not been realistic possibilities to put forward Nordic proposals ... Denmark has been following action patters agreed upon by the Nine. This effected Norway's position, which already has to regard NATO. For political reasons and in an effort to secure Helsinki as a venue of the CSCE, Finland has chosen to follow a passive and cautious line.[5]

Clearly, and as mentioned earlier, there was no congruence between the Nordic states that could facilitate their traditional cooperation. This made it impossible for Sweden to take up the role of a regional collaborator.

In the days following the end of the MPT, Foreign Minister Krister Wickman's opening speech for the first stage of the CSCE was prepared at the Foreign Ministry in Stockholm.[6] A first draft was delivered to all members of government; the state secretaries in the ministries of defence, trade, industry and education and all officials belonging to the CSCE working and study groups. Wickman himself approached Alva Myrdal, Sweden's delegate to the UN disarmament conference in Geneva, on the matter. On the other hand, the Advisory Council on Foreign Affairs, the organ of communication between the government and the Parliament, in which the opposition parties were represented, was excluded from this communication.[7] Kaj Björk made substantial changes to the first draft of Wickman's upcoming speech in the last days of June 1973. He dampened down the euphoria over the accomplishments of the MPT, the overall development of détente and its effects on the Cold War and the rising role of morality in international affairs – elements which had characterized the first draft.

The structure and style of the speech that Foreign Minister Wickman gave on 4 July 1973 at the first stage in Helsinki was mainly shaped by Björk,[8] who decided to state that Sweden would strive for the establishment of a 'contact forum' rather than a 'permanent organ' in the fourth basket, as the latter was considered politically charged. The phrase 'differences in political ideologies and social systems' was reduced to 'differences'.[9] The making of Wickman's speech illustrates the Swedish working routine in this context and reveals how positions were shaped as a mixture of top-down and bottom-up approaches.

The Swedish delegation to the first stage of the CSCE, held in Helsinki's brand new Finlandia Hall between 3 and 7 July 1973, was composed of fifteen members. Foreign Minister Krister Wickman was accompanied by Sverker Åström, Göran Ryding, Kaj Björk, Wilhelm Wachtmeister, Tore Tallroth and Axel Edelstam. They were joined by an administrative staff consisting of Rolf Ekéus, Göran Berg, Kerstin Asp and Jan Olsson.[10] Among the accredited experts who did not travel to Finland were Hans Blix, Lennart Rydfors, Torgil Wulff, Jan Prawitz and Désirée Edmar.[11] The fact that there were so many prominent members in the delegation clearly indicates the weight of the CSCE in relation to other foreign policy issues.

As delegates arrived in Finland, preparations stretched out before them, from final changes to speeches to organized lunch meetings and dinners – meals which were not only acts of courtesy but also a reflection of the relationships established during the MPT and of state priorities. Wickman invited his Belgian, Canadian, Yugoslavian, Finnish, Swiss and Dutch counterparts for a luncheon on 4 July and accepted a Danish invitation to a dinner of the Nordic foreign ministers on the same day.[12] The day after, all delegations that had actively engaged in military questions at the MPT met for lunch, at the invitation of the Dutch delegation. Western contacts were also maintained during a dinner at the French embassy, and there was a bilateral exchange of views between Wickman and British foreign secretary Alec Douglas-Home.[13] On the eve of the conference proper, it was obvious how much closer Sweden had positioned itself to the West than to the East. The question was whether and how that would affect the country's role performance.

Entering the Public Stage: Wickman at Finlandia Hall

The first of three stages of the CSCE was the meeting of foreign ministers, where Krister Wickman was the tenth speaker to take the stage.[14] In the introduction to his speech, Wickman praised Finland and West Germany for their earlier efforts and the Soviet Union and the United States for the constructive roles both had played so far. As it had done in the first statement at Dipoli, Sweden underscored its close ties with the countries to which it had been a faithful friend; the additional reference to the superpowers can be seen as an expression of the evolution of the Swedish role towards that of a bridge and even mediator-integrator. Wickman stressed that conformity with UN principles and international law was indispensable in times of military parity between the blocs, before warning his surprised audience that closer cooperation between Washington and Moscow should not 'prejudice the legitimate interests of other states'.

Wickman argued that the economic and military dominance of the United States and the Soviet Union could force dependence upon the rest of the world and, therefore, had become a threat to the national self-determination of other states.¹⁵ The Swedish foreign minister stated that because any attempt to change postwar frontiers had become too risky negotiations were crucial. With reference to rising tensions in the Middle East, he called for multilateral détente on a global level, rather than leaving essential issues completely to Washington and Moscow.¹⁶

Notably, this rare case of explicit superpower criticism was linked exclusively to strategic thinking. With regard to European security, Sweden advocated realpolitik first and foremost, and in this particular case such a statement offered the additional benefit of (partially) supporting Austrian chancellor Kreisky, who lobbied for a discussion on Middle Eastern conflicts at the CSCE. In late 1972 the Swedes rejected Austria's suggestion for concentrated efforts on adding the Middle East to the agenda of the CSCE. Now, Wickman offered some support by emphasizing the relevance of global détente in relation to the conflicts raging in the Middle East.

Sweden, Wickman stated, was eager to support measures aimed at the settlement of international disputes and arms limitation. He linked the reunification of families directly with détente and stressed the importance of increased cultural contacts to stable and trustful relations between states. In clear contrast to the actual attitude of Sweden during the years preceding the CSCE, he then emphasized that his government was of the opinion that a freer flow of information was an 'essential value itself' and that it aimed to 'safeguard by legal means freedom of speech and freedom of information but also to improve the material conditions for a free flow of opinion and information' on an international level. The value of the CSCE would diminish if it failed to bring about 'a broader exchange of information and improved human contacts'. Wickman closed his speech with a solemn appeal:

> For too long, mutual mistrust and fear have prevented our governments from exploring thoroughly the possibilities for a peace which is something more than the mere absence of war. However much may divide us, it is essential to identify and build upon what unites us. By gradually developing real cooperation, increasing mutual trust, and reducing armaments, we could create a climate where war between our countries becomes inconceivable and where every chance for a better future for our peoples is grasped and pursued through common endeavour.¹⁷

Wickman also stated that 'increased cooperation between our countries ... should not be allowed to counteract the liberation of peoples in other parts of the world from various forms of political and economic dependence'.¹⁸

What he said did not convey much of the real role that Sweden had played in the quadrennial process leading up to the conference, including the MPT. Freer movements had never been a Swedish priority. The importance assigned to them in Wickman's speech must, therefore, be seen as a gross exaggeration. The divergence between Sweden's actual policy and the characterization of it in the public speech can be explained by the fact that the latter served three purposes. It was in line with the popular image of Sweden's strong humanitarian tradition; it supported West Germany's position; and it portrayed Sweden as a vociferous critic of superpowers and as a defender of values, in harmony with its general active foreign policy of the time. But this was done at the cost of concealing the real nature of Sweden's pro-Western and status quo–oriented approach to the CSCE. Behind closed doors, in consultations on a bilateral level and at the MPT, the Swedes had disregarded human contacts and focused almost exclusively on security.

Wickman's remarks on human contacts and identification of superpower dominance as a threat attracted specific attention. Shortly afterwards, Poland's chargé d'affaires in Stockholm, Czulinski, paid two visits to the Swedish Foreign Ministry. Czulinski wondered whether the far-reaching implications of Wickman's speech could not be considered a violation of the compromise on human contacts, as coded in the Blue Book. He also wondered whether the Swedish government really considered US-Soviet collaboration a danger for small states, a question on which the Swedish National Radio followed up after Wickman's appearance.[19] The Swedes rejected this interpretation, arguing that their government only wished to emphasize the right of smaller countries to have a say on important issues. Wilhelm Wachtmeister explained that his country's view on human contacts was 'principally identical' with that of the West but assured his Polish interlocutor that Sweden had consideration for the fact that this implied problems for 'certain participating states'.[20]

It was, in fact, this consideration for Eastern regimes that distinguished Sweden's approach to the third basket from that of the West. Sweden was not convinced of its own ability to protect the rights of Eastern European citizens, and was, therefore, not willing to pay any political price in order to protect them. This was quite similar to Sweden's position in the late 1940s, when it succumbed to pressure from Stalin and expelled some 2500 Wehrmacht soldiers, along with 167 Balts who had served in the Germany army, to the Soviet Union,.[21]

The public effect of Wickman's speech soon became clear when a statement of socialist parliamentarians from ten European countries, among them Swedish Social Democrat Evert Svensson, was handed over to Foreign Minister Wickman by Lord Peter Archer, a Labour Party member of the British House of Lords. In their letter, the signatories strongly emphasized the significance of human contacts in the third basket. Based on Wickman's portrayal of Sweden as a defender of the faith, but unaware of Sweden's actual approach, the signatories were certain that the Swedish government would 'take note of this initiative of ours'.[22]

The Swedes were not the only ones to draw a picture of their policy that differed from reality. At the first stage, many states seemingly defaulted to their traditional pre-Dipoli positions. With his pre-eminent understanding of both the dynamics of the negotiations and the interrelationship between secret negotiations and public statements, however, Göran Ryding did not consider this a cause for anxiety. To the experienced ambassador, these were essentially tactical moves caused by the imminent round of negotiations.[23]

The focus quickly shifted from the ministerial meeting to preparations for the crucial second stage, which would be introduced in Geneva in September 1973. To the Swedish government, the CSCE had become 'an important component' of its foreign policy. Referring to Sweden's neutral stand, and the country's interest in extensive European cooperation and normalization of the relationship between Western and Eastern Europe, Foreign Minister Wickman stated that it was important to make an 'active effort' to participate during the second stage.[24] The government's interest in taking up a more active role can be understood against the background of the failure of renewed EEC/EC membership negotiations in 1971 in combination with the development of the MPT.

In an internal paper dated 9 July 1973, Sverker Åström suggested that the Swedish delegation in Geneva should exchange information with Switzerland, Austria and the Nordic countries.[25] The role of West Germany, on the other hand, which had been essential during the bilateral preparatory phase between 1969 and 1972, lost some momentum due to the multilateralization of the CSCE. Sweden continued to draw on its earlier subjects of interest and developed them further in collaboration with its neutral and nonaligned partners. General priorities remained unchanged.

A new working group, based at the Ministry of Defence, was appointed to study how to create a linkage between détente and disarmament and include it in the final declaration. This further indicates the persistent significance of disarmament to Sweden. In the second basket, Swedish interest revolved around energy supply and rail and road transport, while uncertainty prevailed about the possibilities of environmental and industrial cooperation. On human contacts the line was clear and clearly different from what had been suggested publicly shortly before. Regardless of its public statements, Sweden did not intend to enter the forefront of charged debates on human rights concessions:

> There is reason to consider presenting a Swedish paper on guidelines for cultural exchange aiming to oppose the centralistic thinking, which characterizes

France and the Eastern bloc in this area. Regarding the politically charged matter of freer flow of information et cetera, the foreign minister has clearly stated what we think. At CSCE I [the first stage of the CSCE], we mainly restricted ourselves to mediating. A large number of proposals have been put forward or announced from the West. Eventual Swedish proposals would hardly offer any news and would most likely risk to doubling Western proposals.[26]

In consultations with Soviet ambassador Mikhail Yakovlev, and in his dealings with the press, Wickman stated that he believed the CSCE negotiations would be 'protracted' and 'difficult'.[27] To experts at the UD this meant 'at least six months' of further negotiations at Geneva.[28] This estimate reflected the optimism that followed the positive experience of Dipoli. But it proved still too optimistic. 'None of the participants ... can have foreseen how long a road they had just embarked on', as Finnish historian Petri Hakkarainen puts it, and in the end, Geneva would last four times as long as expected.[29]

Setting the Agenda for Geneva

A first result of internal preparations for the second stage was a strategic paper presented by Axel Edelstam, the head of the study group on disarmament. The paper argued that Sweden should support the British working paper CSCE/I/18, which included an approach to CBM and sought a way to reintroduce a number of other military questions. Yugoslavia and Turkey had already backed the British idea: the former suggested the 'early cessation of the armaments race', and the latter stressed 'a need for a multilateral reaffirmation of the principle of undiminished security for all European countries'.

These formulations were all considered important points of departure by the Swedes, who were eager to secure the survival of security issues and a certain say for the small states. Drawing on the basic thoughts of Kaj Björk, who did not believe that the CSCE would come to affect European security on short notice and who, therefore, argued that the focus should be on creating a wider framework for future measures, the study group proposed that a common maximalist paper be presented immediately after the commencement of the second stage in Geneva.[30]

Relations with the West continued on an intimate level. In early August, halfway through the summer preparations, Belgium's ambassador to Stockholm handed over to the Swedish Foreign Ministry copies of all third basket documents drafted by the EC Nine. He added that the Western states were open to receiving neutral comments and criticism.[31] Sweden and the Western bloc continued to trust each other. Sweden's role as a faithful friend of the West relied on such trust and goodwill, while there were no equivalent relations with members of the Warsaw Pact states.

At the gathering of the CSCE working and study groups on 17 August 1973, Richard Hichens-Bergström was appointed head of the Swedish delegation to the CSCE. Despite Ryding's and Edelstam's past complaints about the lack of personnel and Hichens-Bergström's expertise, Hichens-Bergström, sixty years old at the time, retained his post as ambassador in Rome and commuted to Geneva on demand. Lennart Eckerberg, a Geneva-based disarmament expert who would serve as Swedish ambassador in Bonn and London in the 1980s and 1990s, was assigned responsibility for military matters, supported by experts such as Hans Blix, Ulf Reinius and Torgil Wulff.[32] Bertil Arvidson, who had been ambassador in Lagos until 1972, and Magnus Vahlquist, a young diplomat and later ambassador in Oslo and Tokyo, were assigned the responsibility for the second basket, supported by Karl-Anders Wollter, Stanislaw Patek, Mats Ringborg and Lennart Watz.

Ambassador Tore Tallroth, an experienced cultural attaché and the oldest member of the delegation, and Kaj Falkman took charge of human contacts, supported by Ilmar Bekeris and Désirée Edmar.[33] In each basket, one senior official would lead the negotiations together with a younger colleague, supported by amanuenses and experts based in related ministries in Stockholm. In total, twenty-five accredited diplomats and experts participated in the work of the delegation during the second stage.[34] With this, the Swedes had a larger number of officials at their disposal than did most comparable states. But, as most experts remained in Stockholm, excluded from the conference environment, the workload for those diplomats actually present remained considerable and was therefore subject to consistent criticism from members of the delegation.

All involved officials were introduced to their task at the above-mentioned meeting, which was crucial to Swedish policy at the second stage of the CSCE, as it also dealt with the full range of topics that would be treated in Geneva. Officials and experts from six ministries and the Swedish military participated in setting the course for the role Sweden would eventually play. As was the case with the drafting of speeches, many positions that would be adopted for the meetings were defined following a bottom-up approach, as they required very specific expertise from a range of individuals.

At the meeting, Sverker Åström recommended that a discussion paper on Swedish views on disarmament be presented on the first day of the Geneva negotiations. The idea was to put out a few feelers to see whether the time was ripe for concrete discussions. Regarding the catalogue of principles, Blix explained that Sweden had to join a majority compromise, as there was nothing in favour of a move of its own. The support for the Swiss SRPD project, that is, the peaceful settlement of disputes, continued, but it was hoped that Berne would soon wind down from its high level of ambition. The creation of a distinctive Swedish profile in the second basket was considered problematic, as the Ministry of Industry, represented by Mats Ringborg, who later became ambassador to the OECD and UNESCO, refused to bring up energy, the only area highlighted by the Foreign Ministry.

In response to the objections of Björk and Åström, who pointed out that nuclear power and uranium supply were interesting topics in the field of energy that could be highlighted at the CSCE, Ringborg explained that adequate bilateral agreements already existed with the United States and the Soviet Union but acknowledged that certain improvements in rail and road traffic with the Soviet Union could be within reach. Lennart Rydfors, a trade expert who had earlier worked on GATT, argued that Sweden should be 'cautious' and refrain from making proposals in the second basket.

Rydfors maintained that monetary questions offered nothing to Sweden, while business contacts and industrial cooperation were significant areas in which the Swedes would have to safeguard their interests. There was consensus on maintaining distance from 'freer movements' and on a Swedish paper on environmental problems proposed by Åström.[35] Thus, there was agreement on how to approach disarmament and freer movements, the two most critical aspects. Flexibility was greater on more technical questions relating to economic and scientific cooperation. No calls for a role change occurred, as the Swedish role conceptions remained coherent prior to the second stage of the CSCE.

In the weeks afterwards, the study groups followed up on the meeting of 17 August. The disarmament study group presented the findings of four meetings in a substantial memorandum that explored the differences between 'confidence-building measures' and 'collateral constraints'. It explained that CBM were only 'political gestures expressing the goodwill of states', while collateral constraints were factual restrictions on military activity which would have military effects. The difference between them was that they aimed at greater *confidence* and greater *stability*, respectively. Ultimately, the realization of these goals relied on the success of linking CSCE and MBFR, and this was something that the Swedish delegation would have to bring up for discussion. The memorandum focused heavily on defining Swedish interests and emphasized that earlier, comprehensive notices of military manoeuvres were substantial, as they would diminish the risk of surprise attacks against Swedish territory.

The memo also pointed to the necessity of drafting specific clauses in order to counterbalance potentially negative effects of arms control agreements on Central Europe, stress the importance of preserving Sweden's military freedom of action and affirm its right to invoke neutrality.[36] Thus the Swedes were aware of the limited influence of the CSCE and negotiations on CBM, which raised hopes for greater political confidence, whereas greater military stability was dealt with between the Soviet Union and the United States at the MBFR talks in Vienna.

By mid-September 1973, the Swedish course for Geneva was set. On a number of occasions, officials reiterated that Sweden had no reason to support attempts to undermine the Brezhnev Doctrine. The catalogue of principles was viewed as a 'sensitive matter' in which Sweden had 'no primary interest' from 'a national security perspective'. No goal was specified in the third basket, either, and only in cases of deadlock would the Swedish delegation try to contribute with compromise formulas.[37] The Swedes did not intend to defend human rights–related values in Geneva, as they maintained their realist approach to the CSCE. In contrast to the early bilateral preparatory phase in 1969 and 1970, there were no such (role) expectations from other state representatives, either. A belief in values as a priority of Swedish CSCE policy was only present in domestic public opinion, largely due to the recurrent references to Sweden's 'humanitarian traditions' in the public statements of Prime Minister Olof Palme and Foreign Minister Krister Wickman.

Early external consultations had been introduced with the other three neutrals in late August at the invitation of Berne. Initially, Finland had been left out, allegedly 'because Sverker Åström had not asked for their participation'. Only after the Swiss Foreign Ministry had conferred with Stockholm did the Finns receive an invitation.[38] As illustrated earlier, Sweden and Switzerland were the pivotal participants in the group of neutral and nonaligned states. At the same time, Sweden was eager to support the Finns and had no interest in Finland having its neutrality and objectivity questioned.

The Swedish delegation was well prepared following the extensive briefings from the coordination committee of the CSCE, which laid down the procedural rules for the second stage. Three committees were set up for each basket, dealing with security, economic cooperation and human contacts, respectively. Subcommittees on principles guiding the relations between states (Subcommittee A) and on military questions (C) were pooled in the first basket, together with a special working group on the application of the principles (B). In the second basket, five subcommittees treated commercial exchange (D), industrial cooperation (E), science and technology (F), environment (G) and cooperation in other areas, such as transport or tourism (H). Finally, in the third basket, four subcommittees dealing with human contacts (I), information (J), culture (K) and education (L) were established.[39]

Shortly before the commencement of the second stage, dark clouds were visible on the horizon on the question of human contacts. In a confidential talk with Wachtmeister, Czechoslovakian ambassador Dzunda signalled Eastern irritation at the Western approach, as the NATO states had already affirmed that only improvement in that particular area would allow for results in the other baskets. This, Dzunda argued, was nothing less than an attempt to disturb the socialist system in Eastern Europe. Responding to Dzunda's question as to where Sweden stood on this, Wachtmeister replied that his country was in favour of the best possible relations between states and peoples. These ambitions were natural to countries with liberal ideals and held no subversive element; they did not 'strive to disturb existing systems' per se, the Swedish host argued.[40]

Internal Dissent

Two days before the diplomats gathered for the second stage of the CSCE, important political changes occurred in Sweden. Weakened by the so-called IB affair, a scandal surrounding the activities of the Information Bureau (Informationsbyrån, a formerly unknown intelligence service), and the Centre Party's stand against nuclear power, the ruling Social Democrats returned their worst result since 1932 at the general election of 16 September 1973. Despite calls for resignation following a stalemate, with 175 seats for both the leftist parties and the centre-right wing opposition, Olof Palme and his government remained in power.[41] Shortly after the election, Palme announced that Sven Andersson would change office after sixteen years as defence minister to replace Krister Wickman as foreign minister. Yet, while revelations over the extent to which the IB had operated in Finland created greater space for Helsinki to apply pressure for Swedish support at the CSCE, the shift from Wickman to Andersson had little impact on Swedish CSCE policy.

When the second stage of the CSCE opened in Geneva on 18 September 1973, it was generally hoped that the conference would create lasting détente. The only exception was the United States, whose new foreign minister Henry Kissinger regarded the conference as 'an exercise, at best significant for public opinion.'[42] According to the government in Stockholm, Sweden's contribution to the controversial third basket would be as follows:

According to the assessment of the Swedish government, participation in the CSCE is currently an important element of Swedish foreign policy. With the background of our neutral position and on basis of our interest in an extensive European cooperation, Sweden is preparing itself for an interested and active effort at the second stage of the CSCE in Geneva and its follow-up . . . Sweden wants to take a pragmatic approach, among other ways by seeking a better understanding of the obstacles and difficulties that impose themselves on many of the areas of such exchange, and pointing at ways for improvement of the practical conditions for a greater exchange which can be achieved by discussing experiences and viewpoints.[43]

This statement of intent corresponded with the growing importance of the roles of bridge and mediator-integrator in the role conception of the Swedes, whilst simultaneously allowing them to retain their pragmatism, as portrayed in the previous chapter.

Upon the opening of the second stage in Geneva, the Swedes highlighted their prominent role in the military subcommittee using a well-known method, namely falling back to a more conservative position. In a first address, given on 28 September 1973, Lennart Eckerberg renewed the Swedish stance on military security, arguing that the CSCE was obligated to deal with military questions that could contribute to lasting relaxation. Eckerberg introduced opportunities beyond CBM, such as a more open information policy regarding military spending, and reintroduced proposals which had been rejected at Dipoli, such as regional disarmament measures.[44] The idea of allowing greater insight into military budgets quickly gained the support of the other neutrals.[45] Eager to highlight signs of growing Swedish activity, the Foreign Ministry in Stockholm issued a press release on the initiative.[46] In Geneva, however, Western diplomats reacted rather cautiously.

The British delegation informed the FCO in London that it intended to signal its consent only because it preferred 'leaving it to the Russians and their allies to shoot down this proposal'.[47] At this early phase of the second stage, Sweden welcomed the role of mediator as 'useful and promising'. The suggestion that bilateral consultations be compulsory, as proposed by the Eastern European countries, was rejected, as this could limit Sweden's freedom of action and was therefore considered incompatible with its neutrality policy.

During the first weeks at Geneva, Swedish diplomats perceived the situation in quite different ways. Based on the intensive internal considerations of the summer, it seemed unlikely to Axel Edelstam that the real and concrete problems of East-West trade could be solved by the discussions in the second basket. What could be done, 'at best', Edelstam argued, was to identify problems and address them in the final document, which might help 'nudge' subjects 'treated for years only to end up in the thicket of international organizations' in the right direction. Regarding the third basket, the earlier position seemed immovable:

> At the same time, we are conscious that the Soviet bloc views far-reaching demands in this area as unwarranted interference in internal affairs. Essentially, they aim at an erosion of the Communist system. Where such intentions exist behind Western demands, they are not shared by us. We believe that current relaxation needs to be based on realities and that one should avoid a confrontational policy, which is an echo of the Cold War.[48]

To Edelstam, realism was indispensable. Other influential actors, such as Åström, Blix and Wachtmeister, shared this position, and there is no evidence to suggest that it was not shared, and even determined, by Olof Palme himself. This rejection of the Western intent to achieve change through rapprochement marked the absence of solidarity and moralism as guiding principles in Sweden's approach to Europe. In the Western camp there was awareness of the Swedish attitude and of the fact that the Nordic country did not consider adopting any altruistic role:

> My impression from this discussion is that the Swedes have certainly decided to present a lower profile in this stage of the CSCE, especially on Basket III, and will concentrate on their own ideas on disarmament. They hope that this line and their status as neutrals will in due course give them the opportunity of playing a rewarding role as honest brokers.[49]

Analysing the course of events during the first two months, Edelstam felt vindicated, as he viewed the situation at Geneva as 'rather confusing'. Large delegations had to deal with diverse subjects in numerous working groups, and many of the involved diplomats were wondering whether they 'had bitten off more than they could chew', he wrote in a report. For this, Edelstam blamed the fragmentary development in the three baskets. In the first basket, and with regard to military questions, the French and the Americans remained passive, while the Soviets adopted a completely dismissive attitude.

In the third basket, meanwhile, the Western delegations refused to adopt a preamble on the sovereignty of states and noninterference proposed by the Soviets. The Swedes made early mediatory efforts by arguing that a compromise between 'permissible influence and impermissible coercion' could be accomplished if all sides acknowledged that growing interdependence modified traditional concepts. Governments had the right to make positive or negative statements, which could not be labelled 'interference' as long as they were not linked to coercive pressure, the Swedes argued.

During this time, progress was only made in the five subcommittees of Basket II.[50] Edelstam believed that in a number of areas the time was simply not ripe for definite multilateral measures. This belief was triggered by a speech of Leonid Brezhnev in Moscow on 26 October 1973, in which the Soviet leader emphasized the principle of noninterference in internal affairs and condemned the demands of the West at the CSCE. The quarrel over the first and third baskets narrowed the room for negotiation and threatened the feeling of mutual will to cooperate that still prevailed among the diplomats: the so-called spirit of Dipoli.[51]

Edelstam's critical reflections quickly became the official Swedish line, as Åström and Wachtmeister shared his general views. Against this background, the most influential Swedish actors distanced themselves more and more from the West German 'change through rapprochement' approach. Despite the maintenance of mutual consideration and exchange of information, this contributed to the faithful friend role losing further momentum. As a consequence of the continued intricate situation at the CSCE, and due to its generally careful approach to European affairs, Sweden favoured the improvement of existing conditions over seeking change.

Not all Swedes shared this scepticism. Richard Hichens-Bergström, the head of the delegation, agreed that the first weeks at Geneva had been disappointing and that the outcome of the negotiations was unpredictable. But he also noticed that Soviet-US relations were improving, which he believed could balance out negative factors. Based on his personal observations from the conference, Hichens-Bergström argued that the Foreign Ministry's pronounced pessimism seemed unjustified. He described the spirit at the conference venue in Geneva as 'constructive' and stressed that all involved parties sought compromise. In his view, progress was achieved slowly but steadily, despite the slow pace of the working bodies and external disruptions such as the escalation of the Middle East crisis into the Yom Kippur War in October 1973. This was a 'conference of mutual restraint', Sweden's head of delegation argued, asking for his differing opinion to be presented to Prime Minister Olof Palme personally.[52]

Edelstam's pessimism was also refuted in another Swedish report from Geneva, which held that the Eastern delegations remained moderate in their approach despite the tough attitude of the West on human contacts. Cautious diplomatic overtures to secure a possible exchange of concessions in the first and third baskets were made and, in his overall judgement, Swedish diplomat Lars Bergquist deemed them successful enough to praise them as evidence of a general 'desire for détente'.[53]

The debate about the start of the second stage reveals the difference in views between influential position holders of the realist camp, comprising Åström, Wachtmeister and Edelstam, and the softer and more positive approach of the likes of Hichens-Bergström and Tore Tallroth, the main negotiators in the third basket. This split between realists and idealists would eventually result in serious discontent and lead to the replacement of Tallroth.

As these early signs of internal dissent emerged, the Swedish government simultaneously pledged itself more openly to the CSCE. At the UN general debate in New York on 11 October 1973, Krister Wickman defined the conference as 'a complement to the efforts of the UN to safeguard international peace' and argued that important steps had already been made.[54] The growing commitment also expressed itself in the appointment of an additional administrator. Furthermore, another four external experts were placed at the disposal of the Swedish delegation to the CSCE. With this, the Foreign Ministry was acknowledging and responding to renewed complaints from Tore Tallroth, who argued that there was a need for even more personnel if Sweden was to present proposals in the subcommittees.[55]

In Geneva, the Swedish delegates followed up on the departmental meetings of the summer, where it had been decided that they would try to evade controversies and focus on mediating between the two camps.[56] When disagreement regarding human contacts occurred between the blocs once again, it was the neutral countries that tried to soften the respective positions and mediate between them. The neutrals were also in charge of the working schedules, which were laid down every fourth week and contained thirty-six meetings per week. With this, they provided an important administrative service to the progress of the negotiations. With increasing speed it became clear that mediatory efforts helped them achieve their own interests and serve those of other states to a significant extent.[57] Here, role expectations corresponded with role conceptions, resulting in a growingly coherent role performance for Sweden as mediator-integrator.

Swedish-Swiss ties remained strong and were considered valuable by both countries. Therefore, Sweden did not refrain from its support of Berne's SRPD project.[58] The delegation also attempted to develop a more heterogeneous profile and engaged actively in discussions on tourism and scholarly exchange; in the subcommittee on human contacts it also brought up the role of less-privileged individuals being excluded from the opportunities enjoyed by political, diplomatic or social elites.[59]

Nothing changed in Sweden's relation with its Nordic neighbours. Finland was supported in its role as quiet host, while ties with Denmark and Norway were limited to the exchange of information. Danish diplomats often supplied their Swedish colleagues with reports on developments within the EC Nine, while Norway, generally one of the most sympathetic NATO states towards the neutrals, was a preferred discussion partner on the alliance.[60] Before leaving Geneva for the Christmas break, Jaakko Iloniemi, the head of the Finnish delegation to the CSCE, invited the directors of political sections of the Nordic foreign ministries to a meeting in January 1974 in order to 'compare notes'.[61] In general, the Nordic states maintained insubstantial but polite relations. Even on questions of regional character, the Nordic dimension remained insignificant because of the general setting at the conference.

In contrast, the friendship of the three Social Democratic prime ministers – Willy Brandt, Bruno Kreisky and Olof Palme – was viewed with interest. Brandt and Kreisky had both spent several years in Stockholm during World War II, where they had belonged to a circle of exiled socialists who discussed concepts for the postwar era.[62] Over the course of the following decades, they had included Olof Palme in their intense friendship and often discussed the role of socialism in international politics.[63] After their meeting in the small West German town of Schlangenbad, near Frankfurt, on 2 December 1973, many delegates in Geneva wondered whether there had been a decision on introducing the oil crisis to the CSCE.[64] Willy Brandt had taken the initiative to use this meeting with his Austrian and Swedish friends to discuss the consequences of the Yom Kippur War. In light of the oil crisis that the aftermath of the war had caused, Brandt argued in favour of bringing up the issue of energy at the CSCE.

The West German chancellor convinced Palme and Kreisky, and eventually the Swedish Foreign Ministry ordered its delegation to sound out the possibility of bringing up the issue with the West Germans, Austrians, Swiss and possibly the Nordics. Discussions between Sverker Åström and his West German colleague Götz von Groll concluded that the subject could be placed in the second basket.[65] Western media viewed it as a necessary step, if the conference were to achieve genuine results.[66] In the following weeks, Bonn moved on with the issue on two separate tracks: bilaterally and at the CSCE. A working paper suggested that West Germany, Austria and Sweden would deal with the issue trilaterally and Bonn would then present it to NATO at the upcoming summit in Copenhagen and to the EC Nine in January 1974.[67]

This endeavour, remarkably forged by transnational social democracy, quickly encountered resistance, however. When the Swedes and Austrians introduced the subject in the subcommittee on industrial cooperation, they were asked by the Soviet ambassador to the United States, Anatoly

Dobrynin, whether they had lost their sense of reality. Eventually, however, Dobrynin agreed that questions of energy in Europe would be of interest to the CSCE. The West Germans completely avoided this debate in Geneva due to a veto from the other EC states, which caused considerable irritation among the Swedes and the Austrians.[68] The situation had changed, and the neutral states had taken the place of West Germany as Sweden's most important partners or, to speak in terms of role analysis, most faithful friends. Sweden opened up for active independence, a role that according to Holsti includes 'self-determination, possible mediation functions and active programs'.

When the second stage of the CSCE adjourned for a one-month Christmas break on 14 December 1973, most Swedish delegates were left with the feeling that the previous round of negotiations had been a 'valuable survey' but had failed to create substantial results. On the one hand, at least the conference had not degenerated to mere propaganda, as many in the West had feared before its convocation. On the other hand, many were already combating fatigue, as the mills of the CSCE ground very slowly. The Swedes were particularly critical of the idle state that befell the maximalists and minimalists in the military subcommittee after a productive and promising start in September. Thus, the Christmas break was welcome.[69] A report addressed to Sven Andersson, the newly appointed foreign minister, dampened expectations on disarmament. Equally problematic, from a Swedish perspective, were the far-reaching and detailed Western proposals on the freer flow of information and the liberation of human contacts.

Although the Swedes were generally supportive of them, the Western demands seemed out of reach in the eyes of Swedish diplomats, who thought that the Western attitude also could be considered illusory and cynical. Hichens-Bergström remarked that it actually was the Eastern Europeans who had been realistic. The work in the second basket was singled out as the only one progressing. Nordic cooperation remained limited but was nevertheless appreciated. With Norway, the Swedish head of delegation pointed out, relations had almost been 'brotherly'. In general, however, not much was expected from the conference, which was described as a 'conference *sui generis* [of its own kind]' that 'bears the heavy legacy of the Cold War'.[70]

At the turn of 1973–1974, general scepticism still prevailed in Stockholm. The first round of negotiations strengthened the position of Sweden within the neutral group, while excellent relations with NATO and the West were maintained. Information on strategy and the positions of the EC Nine, and especially West Germany, were continuously supplied and taken into consideration.[71] As mentioned earlier, the diplomatic tension between Stockholm and Washington following Palme's criticism of the US war in Vietnam did not affect security relations, as stated explicitly in a confidential Swedish memorandum dated 21 December 1973. Quarrels between the 'détente seeking superpower' and a 'small state eager for peace', as it was put in one report, did not change the fact that Sweden and the United States shared core values, basic convictions and certain interests.[72] The faithful friendship between the two countries was clearly too strong to allow serious effects on the negotiations at the CSCE. In fact, as Leifland mentions in his account, Washington was thankful for Sweden's 'assistance' in Geneva.[73]

Deadlock and the Formation of the N+N

Shortly after the resumption of talks in mid-January 1974, it became apparent that the second stage would take more time than expected. It was recognized that at least four to five additional months would be necessary in order to bring the negotiations to a fruitful end. The Swedish delegation believed that East and West would eventually realize that time was pressing, as long, drawn-out negotiations were likely to create a permanent loss in the confidence necessary for a positive conclusion of the CSCE. Therefore, the delegation dissuaded Foreign Minister Sven Andersson from publicly criticizing the slow progress of the conference.[74] The risk of complete failure did need to be borne in mind, but it was not believed to be immediate, according to departmental experts. Due to this attitude, the Swedes also refused to introduce discussions on a follow-up conference in the fourth basket.[75]

When the general debate on the preambles of the principles was concluded in late January, it left numerous far-reaching proposals unresolved, postponing the actual drafting process further. The Western bloc refused any mention of World War II, as it did not want the CSCE to become a substitute for a postwar peace conference, and a Yugoslavian proposal on anticolonialism attracted general criticism, as most participants were tired of additional distractions. Austria proposed a clause that would protect neutral states from the negative effects of decisions made by political, military or economic alliances, with the support of the Swedes, who argued that neutral states had the right to be heard.[76] Harsh criticism of the CSCE also came from the Council of Europe; many members of the assembly asked for the abandonment of the conference if substantial results in the third basket were not possible.[77]

All of this intensified Swedish cooperation with the other neutral and nonaligned states, as well as with its Nordic neighbours. With Sweden's

Nordic neighbours, a specific meeting was held in Oslo on 28 January 1974, at which Richard Hichens-Bergström and Axel Edelstam proposed that the Nordics actively mediate on human contacts, as they were regarded as 'honest brokers' by the Soviets. It was argued that the external criticism was due to the CSCE remaining rather anonymous, with little information reaching the public and national parliaments.[78]

But, as with earlier meetings between the Nordic states, no concrete long-term measures were decided. Therefore, the Oslo meeting remained at the level of stocktaking. Again, the Nordic path proved a dead end, and the lesson was that Sweden would have to apply to the N+N if it wanted its goals to be realized. Against this background, and although the tone remained friendly throughout, Sweden's relationship with Norway and Denmark in particular cannot be described as a faithful friendship, simply because their differences were too great to allow these countries to support a sufficient number of each others' policies.

In February 1974, the first basket on military subjects finally came to a complete standstill. On numerous occasions, dispute broke out over a single term or even a comma. The negotiations on the first principle, sovereign equality, were a typical example. After three weeks of negotiations a compromise was only achieved with reservations, marked by several parentheses, and with Western demands for the possibility of a peaceful change of frontiers completely rejected by the Soviets.[79] Since the Western bloc insisted on parallelism between all baskets, the problematic situation in the first basket overshadowed positive achievements that were made elsewhere, such as in the second basket, or in the subcommittees on culture and education, or in the third basket, where the first formulas had been agreed on. In order to make the working procedure more effective, and to overcome the deadlock, the Swedes, together with the Swiss, proposed additional consultations between subcommittee chairs and delegations that engaged in the controversy.

This was yet another mediatory effort; nevertheless, it was rejected by a number of delegations, such as those of the Netherlands, Italy and Romania, which insisted on their maximalist positions.[80] The mood worsened further due to the growing number of rumours that circulated through the corridors of the conference centre in Geneva. Reportedly, the Central Committee of the CPSU was assailed by doubts over letting Soviet citizens read Western newspapers and listen to Western radio in exchange for receiving Western acknowledgement for what had been political realities for three decades already.[81] In a meeting with his Italian counterpart, Aldo Moro, Soviet Foreign Minister Andrei Gromyko described the Western attitude as an attempt to 'erode the social system of the USSR'.[82] Human contacts had long been the most important Western objective. It was also the only substantial matter not fully supported by the Swedes, who started to look with growing frustration at the Western course in the third basket.

From Washington, Sweden's chargé d'affaires Leif Leifland reported that the State Department dismissed rumours of declining Soviet interest and maintained its belief in the good progress of the CSCE.[83] With the notable exception of US secretary of state Henry Kissinger, the Americans seemed to grow more amenable to the conference the more the Soviets became frustrated. This was illustrated by the increasing activity of the American delegation, which had been rather anonymous since the early days of Dipoli.[84] Despite the deadlock in the first basket, Sweden rejected any considerations of ending the CSCE abruptly with a shortened declaration.[85]

The standstill in early 1974 triggered what has been dubbed 'the birth of the N+N' – the de facto formalization of neutral and nonaligned cooperation at the CSCE. Smaller countries outside of alliances and groups realized that they could not achieve their goals on their own. Their cooperation was also fuelled by the growing significance of the EC Nine and the continuing resistance from the Eastern Europeans. Initially, the N+N comprised Austria, Cyprus, Finland, Sweden, Switzerland and Yugoslavia. A first expression of this 'quasi-institutionalisation'[86] was a common proposal on the military aspects of security in the military subcommittee dated 19 February 1974 and registered as CSCE/II/C/13.[87] As the N+N quickly proved useful in satisfying Swedish ambitions, the Nordic track was ruled out completely. Finland's part in the final decision for the N+N and against the Nordics was considerable.

Swedish irritation over the Finnish attitude increased, as the Swedes felt that Urho Kekkonen and his staff relied constantly on Stockholm's support while withholding information from their own consultations with the Soviet Union. A second meeting of the political directors of the Nordic foreign ministries, held in Copenhagen on 5 April 1974, proved insubstantial once more. Therefore, the idea of renewed meetings in Stockholm in May 1974 was put aside, allegedly because the delegations were 'too busy negotiating'.[88] In reality, however, the prospect was simply not worth the effort.

The deadlock in Geneva persisted until the start of the Easter break five weeks later, and a growing number of delegation leaders expressed their dissatisfaction. In March 1974 negotiations stalled in the third basket as well, both on the preamble and in the subcommittees on human contacts and information.[89] Shortly before the departure from Geneva for the Easter break in early April, the West proposed a compromise on the inviolability of frontiers acceptable to the Soviet Union. In Western circles it was generally expected that an offer at this point would allow the Soviets to return the favour after the break by offering concessions in the third basket. In this way, Western strategists thought, a breakthrough would allow a quick conclusion of the CSCE in 1974, a belief shared by the Swedes.[90]

After the sojourn, however, the anticipated breakthrough remained conspicuous by its absence, as the Soviets did not respond to the Western move in the first basket. This was a heavy disappointment to Western advocates of a more cooperative line towards the Warsaw Pact states. It also surprised the Swedes, who had been assured shortly before by the Soviet ambassador to Stockholm that a successful conclusion of the CSCE at the highest possible political level was central to the Kremlin's aims.[91] In a speech to the Council of Europe on 6 May 1974, Foreign Minister Sven Andersson, therefore summarized the Swedish perception of the conference in an admonition:

> The Conference on Security and Co-operation can be regarded as an expression of the process of détente, and also as an instrument to promote this process . . . I think we have reason for optimism in the fact that an acceptable solution has been found to the problems connected with the principle of the inviolability of frontiers. Let us hope that this compromise indicates that a constructive spirit will prevail . . . We are also anxious to reach practical results in the field of information and human contacts. But I want to stress the necessity of being realistic about what can be achieved . . . The conference reflects today's political situation in Europe and there is no reason to believe that a few months of international discussion will radically change this situation. At the same time we are anxious that the Conference should be viewed in its proper historical perspective. We wish to see it as part of a continuous process, which will gradually lead to a more stable foundation for the preservation of peace on our continent and for the future cooperation between the states concerned.[92]

For the first time, and as a response to the continuing stalemate, a high-ranking Swedish decision maker used the term 'realist' publicly. With this, Sweden sharpened its profile, or set of roles, as an active independent and more outspoken mediator-integrator: both slightly more active variants of the roles of independent and bridge, respectively.

Nevertheless, Andersson's hopes were quickly disappointed. The drafting of the fourth principle on the territorial integrity of states came to a standstill as a consequence of the Soviet refusal to make concessions in the third basket.[93] In the military subcommittee, the best possible result during this period was removing parentheses. At the Swedish Foreign Ministry in Stockholm, numerous possible explanations were considered for the uncooperative attitude of the Soviet Union. It was speculated that Moscow had fallen back on traditional tactics, maintaining a restrictive position so that a concession from them would seem more substantial than it actually was. Another scenario was that the Kremlin had imposed restrictions on its delegation in Geneva until domestic developments in West Germany, France, Great Britain and the United States became clearer.[94] In the aftermath of an espionage scandal, West German chancellor Willy Brandt resigned the same day that Sven Andersson gave his speech in Strasbourg.

French president George Pompidou had died the month before, seemingly opening up the possibility of a policy change, depending upon the outcome of the election between the socialist candidate, François Mitterrand, and his conservative opponent, Valéry Giscard d'Estaing. In the United States, Richard Nixon struggled with the release of the Watergate tape transcripts, and in Britain, the February election had produced a hung Parliament, forcing a second election later that year.[95] Under these circumstances, the only thing certain was a further delay of the CSCE until the end of 1974, as 'deception and anger' prevailed within NATO. The members of the Western alliance had decided not to follow the example of the Soviets and instead awaited an acceptable solution in the third basket.[96] The second week of May 1974 was considered the worst time since the beginning of the second stage in Swedish reports, which stated that a 'mood of crisis' prevailed in Geneva.[97]

Soviet negotiator Anatoly Kovalev retreated from earlier statements of the Soviet embassy in Stockholm and confirmed to Richard Hichens-Bergström that no concessions would be made in the third basket.[98] Also, the Polish ambassador in Stockholm told Sverker Åström that the negotiations were unlikely to be concluded before October or November 1974.[99] Many delegations, among them the Nordics and especially the Finns, equated another summer break with the quasifailure of the CSCE. During this period, the US and French delegations were extremely quiet, causing observers to 'wonder whether they are participating in the conference'. Therefore, Edelstam was asked to direct Foreign Minister Andersson's full attention to the dilemma in Geneva.[100]

In the context of this negative situation, Hichens-Bergström issued a press release on 17 May 1974 expressing regret at the absence of a clear linkage between military and political security, the lack of advancement in the military subcommittee and the lack of concessions on human contacts. The statement expressed recognition of the ongoing struggle between East and West over crucial political issues and appealed to the good will of all present delegations.[101] For the second time in only eleven days, Sweden publicly stated its disappointment at the CSCE.

In Washington, where interest had been growing over the course of the spring, officials from the State Department's Europe Desk told Wilhelm Wachtmeister that the conference was of 'marginal interest' to American foreign policy.[102] After further consultation with members of the British,

Danish, American and neutral delegations, Richard Hichens-Bergström reaffirmed on 22 May 1974 to Stockholm that the situation was 'worryingly stagnating'.[103]

Leaning Out of the Window: Detours to the 'Package Deal'

The fact that the negotiations had hit a dead end on the most essential questions had a negative impact on the CSCE as a whole. In the third basket, subcommittees earlier spared from the general quarrel now suffered the same fate. Negotiations in the education subcommittee, for instance, stalled when the Soviets refused a Swedish compromise formula on the exchange of information as part of scientific cooperation.[104] With the situation becoming unbearable, ways were sought to get rid of the destructive spirit that had dominated for weeks. Against the background of Richard Nixon's upcoming visit to Moscow in late June 1974, leading diplomats in Stockholm hoped to attract the interest of the two superpowers to solve the situation in Geneva. Wachtmeister believed that Nixon would use the CSCE as a bargaining chip.[105] It was also speculated that the upcoming meetings of the EC and the summits of NATO in late May and June would give new impetus to the negotiations in Geneva.

The deadlock also paved the way for the most ambitious Swedish initiative during all of the CSCE. It was Foreign Minister Andersson who proposed an additional Swedish move at the highest level. Despite criticism from some officials, Andersson proposed to push for a meeting of deputy foreign ministers and undersecretaries for an overall evaluation of the situation. Hichens-Bergström, the head of the Swedish delegation, acknowledged that such an initiative might reassure the Swedish public and other participating states about the importance assigned to the CSCE by the Swedish government, but he argued that it would not make any real impact.

If anything made sense, claimed Hichens-Bergström, it was only a proposed meeting between higher officials and the CSCE coordination committee. Regardless of the exact wording of documents drafted in Geneva, the underlying realities were too substantial and complex to leave space for the smaller states to bring about change. After all, Hichens-Bergström argued in his statement to the foreign minister, SALT, MBFR and other Soviet-American negotiations that influenced the overall situation were out of the reach of minor actors.[106]

Taking this suggestion into account, the Swedes moved on with the proposal for a special meeting between the coordination committee and secretaries general of the foreign ministries. Prime Minister Olof Palme himself was 'worried about the international political repercussions for his government of a failure to end Stage II reasonably soon'.[107] Based on their continuous development into the more active roles of mediator-integrator and active independent roughly six months after their adoption, the Swedes felt able to launch their first major proactive effort at the CSCE.

The first step was to approach the other neutrals and gain their support at the highest possible level. The response from Finland was outright negative. President Kekkonen claimed to be sympathetic to the Swedish plan but believed that it had little or no chance of success. Still, Sverker Åström travelled to Berne on 28 May 1974 to discuss the matter further with Swiss foreign minister Pierre Graber and then proceeded to introduce the matter to Austrian chancellor Bruno Kreisky.[108] When the idea of a statement *extraordinem* was introduced to the other neutral delegations in Geneva, all three reacted by expressing respect for Swedish efforts to overcome the crisis but viewed their chances of success negatively.[109]

The same day, the Swedes learned that the EC Nine stood by their position and considered discussions on the third stage as premature and meaningless as long as there was no progress on essential points.[110] In Moscow, Kreisky told Swedish interlocutors that he was rather pessimistic but would support the Swedish plan nevertheless. He would, however, cosponsor it only if Switzerland did so too, explaining that he did not want to give the impression of being used by Brezhnev.[111] Sverker Åström faced a similar reaction in Berne. Swiss diplomats acknowledged the concessions made by the West, considered the negotiations deadlocked, and did not really believe that a neutral initiative could solve the problem.[112] After four hours of discussion at the Swiss Foreign Ministry, Åström concluded that the time might not be ripe for the Swedish idea after all.[113] Sweden's first high-profile action was on a clear course to failure.

In the middle of consultations, a Finnish diplomat revealed the Swedish activities at Geneva, claiming that Stockholm's initiative was doomed to fail. Åström immediately intervened by approaching ambassador Max Jakobson, saying that he was 'surprised and shocked' over the egregious violation of secrecy and lack of support from Finland.[114] After the plan was leaked, Soviet negotiator Lev Mendelevich approached Lennart Eckerberg in Geneva, acknowledging that the idea would be a good one if invited high-ranking diplomats were to stay in Geneva for a longer period. Mendelevich stated that Swedish pragmatism was welcome, not least since the USSR 'could not haggle' in the military subcommittee. To Eckerberg's disappointment, Mendelevich also added that prior notifications of military movements would have to be moved to the fourth basket and postponed. The Swedes replied that the lowest common denominator should not be allowed to be diminished to the point where it became meaningless.[115]

On the afternoon of 31 May 1974, alarmed by rumours that the West was considering adjourning the CSCE for six months, or even for an indefinite period of time, the seven neutral and nonaligned states gathered at the invitation of Yugoslavia, Cyprus and Malta. Following the analysis of the recent hearings of the coordination committee, there was consensus that the N+N could 'not wait for the superpowers to do their global exam'. Instead, they agreed to work vigorously on questions vital to themselves to avoid having these items swept under the rug.[116]

After the meeting, the Swedish initiative gained some momentum, despite renewed negative notices. This time, Canada and Great Britain communicated their disbelief at the move. From Paris, Ambassador Ingemar Hägglöf reported general frustration over the CSCE.[117] Norway shared the assessment of the Swedes but, nevertheless, refrained from offering support. The Yugoslavians went even further and told ambassador Lennart Finnmark in Belgrade that the time of 'détente romance' was over.[118] For the first time, Sweden was accused of actually lacking realism.

With the Swedish proposal having little prospect of success, Finland sought alternative ways out of the stalemate. After receiving specific indications from the Soviets and the Americans, the Finns suggested transferring the problematic clauses from the first to the third basket – the so-called package deal.[119] Göran Ryding did not believe it to be of Finnish origin when he learned about it from Finland's foreign minister Ahti Karjalainen in Helsinki and noted in a telegram to the UD in Stockholm:

> During today's meeting between Karjalainen, the Norwegian and Danish ambassadors, and me, the [Finnish] foreign minister spent much time on a proposal recently presented at the CSCE... Karjalainen repeated several times that one 'believed to know' that the Russians were open to further concessions in the third basket and that the Finnish proposal was suited for a softening of the Soviet position. Karjalainen also said that they [the Finns] had mentioned the neutrals in advance and briefed the Americans. He 'believed' that the latter would eventually consider the Finnish initiative but was not certain in this regard.[120]

Thus, by the first week of June 1974, two concurrent neutral proposals existed.[121] On 7 June 1974, Lennart Petri informed Sverker Åström that he had been approached by the Dutch ambassador regarding circulating rumours about a Swedish CSCE initiative potentially endangering Western goals. Petri denied knowledge of the plan and referred to consultations between the neutrals as 'routine'.[122] Encouragement to move on with the idea came only from the Soviets, whose representatives claimed that Sweden could argue that smaller states had a certain responsibility in such situations. Accordingly, a meeting of the directors of the political departments, as proposed by the Swedes, would certainly give new impetus to the negotiations, and 'Sweden with its good reputation in all camps and whose voice is listened to' would inevitably step in at this point.[123] With the Soviets welcoming a Swedish move that the West seemed to repudiate, the Swedes found themselves in an uncomfortable situation. Yet no immediate decision to call it off was taken.

Instead, Sverker Åström consulted the delegation in Geneva, asking whether a move could be made at the forthcoming meeting of the coordination committee. Then, a first draft was presented to the N+N, but, after further consultations between the delegation and the Foreign Ministry, the Swedes finally accepted the continued criticism of the West and abandoned the initiative at the last minute.[124] Edelstam had to make hasty changes to the speech manuscript of Hichens-Bergström and added that Sweden would 'continue to sound out the situation'.[125] Åström acknowledged to the Soviet ambassador in Stockholm that his efforts of the past weeks had failed and that a compromise was out of reach, blaming the general tactical considerations of the conference participants. Therefore, he explained to his interlocutor, Sweden had decided to await the 1974 NATO summit and Richard Nixon's visit to Moscow in late June before reconsidering significant engagement.[126]

The N+N states welcomed this change of course and shifted their full attention to the Finnish package deal. The Yugoslav and Swiss delegates stressed that the N+N states had to keep their own interests in mind, which should not be abandoned in an overhasty deal that would benefit the superpowers. Both Switzerland and Austria also emphasized the value of securing concrete results in the third basket.[127] The situation was different for Sweden, which had just suffered a severe blow and never had held ambitions with regard to human contacts.

During this period, Sweden also stood in the spotlight for reasons other than its failed initiative. When Foreign Minister Sven Andersson criticized Soviet policy in a discussion with Mikhail Yakovlev, the Soviet ambassador in Stockholm, the response included countercriticism of the proposal that Alexander Solzhenitsyn should receive his 1970 Nobel Prize in Literature in person at the upcoming ceremony. Andersson explained that he had no influence over the actions of the Nobel committee and would be dismayed by any diplomatic tension resulting from its decisions.[128] Evidently the CSCE did not exist in a vacuum. At certain points in time, involved parties tried to drag in issues from outside into the ongoing horse trading.

In an attempt to explain the confusing atmosphere at Geneva to his superiors at the Foreign Ministry, Hichens-Bergström described in detail how the many working groups, informal meetings, lunch breaks, dinners and coffee breaks had gradually created a special atmosphere which often fostered rumours and insecurity. In many cases, the interplay between national and group interests was fluid rather than well defined and constant.[129]

After Åström's abovementioned detour, the Swedes fell back to their earlier wait-and-see attitude, which was favoured by most parties at the time of the deadlock. Evidently, their shifting between different roles depended on both the general climate of negotiations and the role expectations of other states. Thus, moving from independent to active independent, or between bridge and mediator-integrator, were not options available at all times. From Copenhagen, Ambassador Hubert de Besche confirmed that 'the Swedish activity regarding the CSCE has attracted large attention all over Europe. Taking into account the latest Russian démarche, the Danish side considers a neutral initiative to be no longer current'.[130]

With the Swedish initiative failing, Finland assumed further control and presented its package deal to the rest of the N+N on 24 June 1974.[131] A new, more pro-Western preamble for the third basket was agreed upon, and, despite different approaches to certain formulations in the first principle on sovereignty or the general meaning of the term 'deal', the N+N countries agreed to present it as a common proposal. Finland's proposal for the preamble of the first principle stated that the 'participating states respect each other's right to choose its political, economic and cultural system, as well as its right to determine its laws and regulations'. On the initiative of Hans Blix, the Swedes asked for changes and proposed two alternative wordings which avoided 'laws and regulations'.[132] Both alternatives were eventually rejected, due to the growing pressure from the other N+N states, and in the end the Swedes were again forced to accept a Finnish position.[133]

In their first reactions, the NATO member states announced that any kind of package deal between baskets I and III was premature.[134] This contributed further to Sweden's aversion to it. In addition to alternative wordings, another Swedish idea – of a cautious, two-step approach which would have allowed the group of N+N states to retreat from the package deal themselves and save face if necessary – was rejected. Therefore, Sweden withdrew its support for the package deal proposal on 5 July 1974, leaving it to the other N+N states, which now even included Liechtenstein. Interestingly, the Swedes assured their partners that their criticism of the content of the package deal would not be made public:

> On Sweden's part, the problem has been whether we can take part as cosponsor to formulations with which we cannot identify for a number of objective reasons and, even less, bind ourselves to defend. We have, however,

promised not to go against the text in case they are presented officially but remain silent, out of consideration to the neutral group. If another state than the neutrals should have presented the same text, we would have been compelled to argue against them.[135]

To Finland, always counting on the unconditional support of their neighbour, the Swedish retreat was not acceptable, and the very same day, a reaction occurred at the highest level when Prime Minister Kalevi Sorsa made a telephone call to Olof Palme and urged him to intervene.

Palme stated to his staff that he supported the Swedish delegation to the CSCE but pointed out that Sorsa's intervention was 'a political fact' that could not be overlooked. During his four years in office, he had never been approached in such a manner, the Swedish prime minister said.[136] Hichens-Bergström was very disturbed by the Finnish approach, which the Swedes 'have never really understood' and which was designed and carried out without 'putting the cards on the table'.

Generally, the Swedes disliked the fact that the Finns forced them to play the role of the faithful friend whenever it was considered convenient but kept their distance when they believed it wasn't. As regarded the package deal, the Finns had not consulted Sweden ex ante, which was why their 'poorly balanced' proposal could not be cosponsored. After all, 'We shall not over-interpret the episode, but it elucidates how constrained, or rather little, the common denominator really is in the neutral and non-aligned group. Unfortunately, the same can often be said about the Nordic group in which only the Swedish-Norwegian cooperation is without discord and works faithfully. Grateful [if you provide] briefing [to] Prime Minister Palme'.[137]

Eventually, Sweden did cosponsor the package deal proposal after another several days of intensive negotiations, which resulted in slight modifications to the aforementioned formulation and the adoption of the expression 'comply in good faith with their international obligation' to the tenth principle.[138] The revised deal was presented at the 12 July session of the coordination committee. The Swedes quoted Soviet sources that Moscow's ideologists were 'kicking their heads in despair' over the fact that their own delegation had allowed the West to bring up the issues of the third basket; the sources went on to say that most of them just wanted to 'put an end to it all'.[139] In the end, the package deal was agreed upon after two weeks of extensive debate.[140]

Although it had not been developed in the way Sweden had originally preferred, its aftermath proved propitiatory. Ambassador Michael Shenstone of the Canadian delegation commended the Swedes for introducing a reference to obligations under international law, which had 'made it possible for us to accept the whole deal as such'.[141] Other Western delegations, such as the British, were more critical of the Swedish performance, claiming that, while Switzerland and Finland had been the most active among neutral and nonaligned delegations, 'the Swedish delegation is of low calibre and has had little to contribute'.[142]

The way to the package deal illustrates well the many twists and turns that the Swedish delegation faced during the two years of the second stage. Lacking the dogmatic position of the military alliances, the Swedes were often caught in the middle of foreign interests and tactics. As a consequence of their failed initiative in the summer of 1974, the decision makers at Stockholm abandoned even their faintest ambitions of playing a prominent role at the CSCE. This ultimately resulted in Swedish disillusionment with the conference.

The report of the Swedish delegation blamed the 'Western obsession' with the third basket for the constant delays and claimed that Henry Kissinger's resentment regarding the CSCE had been justified. It also pointed to Denmark's strong involvement with the EC Nine and Finland's special role, which had hindered Nordic cooperation from flourishing. In contrast, the 'trustful' relationship or 'advanced neutral camaraderie' with Switzerland and Austria were praised to the skies. As for its own goals, Sweden, a maximalist on disarmament and CBM ever since, would soon have to prepare for lower ambitions if the conference was to be concluded in due time.[143]

A more general fear was caused by the escalation of the Cyprus dispute. The Turco-Greek conflict and Turkey's invasion on 20 July 1974 further complicated the situation for the diplomats in Geneva, as war threatened to break out between two participants of a conference on European security and cooperation.[144] Despite the compromise that had just been achieved, Swedish delegates, therefore, left Geneva for the summer recess with bad feelings.

Cautiousness and Controversy: Retreating to a Lower Profile

During the summer of 1974, events in the United States dominated the headlines. US secretary of state Henry Kissinger advised the Western Europeans of the EC Nine to compile a 'shopping list' comprising their goals and move towards ending the CSCE. His attitude caused notable irritation in Western European capitals.[145] On 9 August, and after months of rising pressure relating to the Watergate scandal, President Nixon finally gave in to the continuing criticism and resigned.[146] These turbulences added to the uncertainty that had taken over the negotiations in Geneva. Thus, little new was added to the Swedish assessment presented at the Foreign Ministry's CSCE meeting in Stockholm at the end of the summer break. There, Sverker Åström, Tore Tallroth, Kerstin Asp, Ilmar Bekeris, Richard Hichens-Bergström, Axel Edelstam and Kaj Björk all participated actively in a lively discussion. It was decided that Sweden would avoid statements on typical East-West issues, such as the German Question, the inviolability of frontiers, human rights, the Brezhnev Doctrine and references to the third basket.

The focus would be exclusively on framing and drafting compromise formulas with the rest of the N+N. Björk emphasized that it was not a Swedish goal to erode the socialist system with the help of the third basket. A change of attitude was also decided for the military subcommittee, where a lower profile was envisaged 'without abandoning the course of our cooperation with the other neutrals in any spectacular manner'. This rather surprising decision was justified with the deterioration of détente, which meant that 'it is in our interest both to at least achieve some results in the CSCE and the possibility to return to military questions in an eventual follow up'. On the third basket there was

> [general] agreement that we should be extraordinarily cautious and reserved on these especially sensitive questions. We do not have a national interest in actively designing a compromise policy and we do not necessarily participate in all discussions. As regards the reunification of families, it is in Sweden's interest to mark our humanitarian tradition. It is, however, not in Sweden's national interest to demand concessions from the East in the area of information, even if we acknowledge the value of freedom of information in principle. We should, however, keep a low profile.[147]

The only objection to this opinion was raised by Hichens-Bergström, who referred to former Foreign Minister Wickman's order to maintain an active role at the CSCE. Kaj Björk responded in no uncertain terms, claiming that the period of activity was over. Obviously, the Swedes had taken a lesson in the summer with their failed initiative, and their delegation was now prepared for 'a certain reticence and passivity' when it returned to Geneva in early September 1974.[148] The renewed Swedish pessimism on the third basket was not hidden from the other neutrals. Edelstam, for example, called Swiss hopes for a more significant role in this respect 'illusory'.[149] With this, Sweden responded to its disillusionment by retreating from its short-lived role as active independent and, furthermore, by restricting its commitment to functioning as mediator-integrator. The latter role prevailed mostly due to Sweden being part of the group performance of the N+N states.

During the first weeks of the new round of negotiations, the Cyprus crisis was the focus of discussions in the subcommittee on principles. In the military subcommittee the Soviets maintained their position on pre-registration of texts regarding the notification of manoeuvres; in the third basket France presented a proposal aiming to increase the effectiveness of the working procedure, suggesting an increase in the number of informal meetings, parallel treatment of questions and an immediate presentation of all remaining questions. Informal meetings, over coffee, lunch or dinner, gained further importance, as did forums for discussions on problematic areas such as reunification of families, access to culture and printed information or the circulation of filmed and broadcasted information. Preambles were being drafted in the subcommittee for education only, whereas positions remained locked regarding human contacts and freer information.[150]

At a meeting of the N+N states on 17 September 1974, the Swiss informed the rest of the group that the Soviet Union expected further compromise proposals from them. During his recent visit to Berne, Soviet negotiator Anatoly Kovalev had called the Western demands regarding CBM 'completely unrealistic', which validated the Swedish feeling of hopelessness on the issue that was the most vital of all to them. At the meeting, Malta was assigned the task of drafting a statement on the Cyprus crisis after consulting both Turkey and Greece; Switzerland and Yugoslavia urged further activation of the N+N group. Sweden, in conformity with the orders from Stockholm, remained reserved and did not actively seek a part in this mediation.[151]

The West Germans, now under the leadership of the new chancellor Helmut Schmidt, kept briefing ambassador Sven Backlund, who reported to Stockholm that Soviet foreign minister Gromyko had pointed to 'untapped potentials' in Geneva during talks in Bonn.[152] At the Quai d'Orsay, Swedish diplomats met with Emmanuel de Margerie, the director of the French Department of European Affairs. The Frenchman argued that the second stage of the CSCE could not be finished before February 1975, as several important sections had not been treated at all. In Rome, Swedish diplomats learned details of the position adopted by the EC Nine at their latest summit on 20 September 1974.

Most importantly, the Western Europeans agreed to adopt an American text on the peaceful change of borders and decided to intensify the work on the seventh principle respecting human rights and fundamental freedoms. They also re-emphasized that the catalogue of principles and the rest of a future declaration would be of equal value. With this, the Western Europeans took an expectant attitude on CBM and focused on the most substantial elements of the third basket in order to conclude the negotiations.¹⁵³ Such exchanges confirmed and strengthened the faithful friendship between Sweden and the West, with the exception of the dissent on human contacts and despite the general disillusionment in the Swedish camp.

The general atmosphere was described as 'observant', as Cyprus continued to dominate the conference and with marginal progress being made. The Swedish embassy in Moscow believed that the slowdown was part of the Soviet strategy to avoid the impression of being in a hurry and so weakening their bargaining position.¹⁵⁴ In Geneva, the Swedish delegates were further unsettled by a proposed declaration on the Mediterranean. From the early stages, any special treatment of developing countries had been viewed as unacceptable. It became known among CSCE circles that Stockholm was far more pessimistic with regard to the third basket than Switzerland and now simply hoped for a quick conclusion of the conference.¹⁵⁵ The Swedish delegates were eager not to appear too negative, however, and therefore couched their criticism in a cautious manner.¹⁵⁶ The reason was that they had to keep their recently acquired good reputation. But their frustration was almost total.

One month after the resumption of negotiations, the package deal had still not brought any improvement to the general situation in Geneva. The Western concession on safeguard clauses regarding internal laws and regulations did not result in Eastern concessions on human contacts. Instead, they were misused by the Warsaw Pact states, which reintroduced other safeguard clauses, such as 'mutual acceptable conditions', as preconditions for rules on family reunifications. This damaged Soviet credibility further, causing the N+N states to refrain from further mediation efforts involving elements from different baskets, despite rumours that the West was hoping for renewed activity from them.¹⁵⁷

The situation was gloomy, and the Swedes, who had hoped for the talks to conclude in early 1974, veered away from controversial items for the remainder of the conference. But, with the other N+N states forced to refrain from activity as well, the Swedish attitude did not stand out as it had prior to the Four Power Agreement on Berlin in 1971. This time, few politicians and diplomats from neutral states expected a different performance from the Swedes than the one they were conceiving for themselves.

During this period of depression in the fall of 1974, the spirit within the Swedish delegation worsened considerably. Long-standing tensions between younger members of the delegation, who strictly followed orders from Stockholm, and Ambassador Tore Tallroth, responsible for the third basket and considered too soft on the Soviets in the eyes of many, culminated in open conflict and the replacement of the latter. In essence, the conflict was over the right approach in the third basket. Tallroth, with a background in cultural diplomacy, took an idealistic stand on human contacts and tried to compromise, whereas others wanted to pursue a tough line on the Soviets. This resulted in rising irritation in the other neutral delegations, in particular Finland. Axel Edelstam, one of the most determined Swedish realists, naturally took the side of the younger faction, which described the situation as 'intolerable'. Referring to the complaints, Edelstam told Hichens-Bergström that Tallroth could not stay in Geneva.[158]

He also reported to Åström that Austria and Norway had issued several complaints over Tallroth's soft line during the past week.[159] Hichens-Bergström, the head of the delegation, generally preferred cooperation over conflict, but all attempts to defend Tallroth were in vain. Hichens-Bergström had to acknowledge that Tallroth seemed to be refusing to follow the decisions taken at the Foreign Ministry in the summer, but he explained that the internal tensions were due to the narrow and lengthy conference environment. He assured Edelstam that he would be very clear on the matter upon his next trip from Rome to Geneva.[160] When the fronts became further entrenched, Edelstam became even more decided and moved on with the matter, as he believed it would soon cause serious complications in Sweden's foreign relations. He proposed replacing Tallroth with Håkan Wilkens from the Swedish delegation to the EC in Brussels and had Sverker Åström inform Foreign Minister Sven Andersson on the matter.[161]

Åström ordered Tallroth to restrict himself to the third basket and remain passive until the issue could be solved.[162] Sven Andersson did not immediately agree with the tough approach proposed by Edelstam and Åström but changed his mind after learning that Sweden had been excluded from an informal meeting on third basket preambles because of Tallroth's attitude.[163] Further consultations with the heads of the Austrian, Finnish and Norwegian delegations confirmed that there had been 'temporary irritation at the most'.[164]

Finland's head of delegation, Jaako Iloniemi, for instance, said that Tallroth had 'often been a little imprecise'.[165] Therefore, Hichens-Bergström finally agreed that 'it would probably be good if this results in you, maybe rather quickly, appointing a new head for the Basket III'.[166] Sverker Åström finally informed the delegation in Geneva of the decision on 7 October 1974: 'We have discussed the conditions of the delegation at the CSCE on the basis of a presentation by Edelstam. We have been compelled to conclude that they are not satisfactory. We do not want to blame anyone in particular, but we do consider that certain measures must be taken, not least with regard to the upcoming final negotiations'.[167]

This implied important personnel decisions. With Tallroth being put in the second row, focus shifted towards repairing relations with Austria and Finland. In order to do so, responsibility in the third basket would have to go to someone who 'does not know culture or human rights at all, but instead has a tough political nose so he can help us with the very hard bailiwick that is the third basket', as Hichens-Bergström put it.[168] The head of delegation himself was ordered to stay put in Geneva for the time being and limit his travels to Rome to cases of emergency.

Gustaf Hamilton af Hageby was appointed to take his place in Geneva in such cases. Also, additional officials were appointed to the third basket. At the same time, the Stockholm-based experts were released from their assignment as reference groups, since the Foreign Ministry felt that the CSCE had moved on from the technical to the political stage of negotiations. Clearly, the essential facts had been negotiated in detail already, which left the remaining work to the purely political will of the involved parties.[169] The complete abandonment of ambitions was a natural result of the series of disappointments suffered since the failed initiative in the early summer.

Tallroth himself, naturally, reacted sceptically to the Foreign Ministry's orders. In his view, even taking a passive stand for the rest of the conference required experience, a certain standing and authority based on earlier work and personal contacts in the subcommittees. It was there, he argued, that the real work was done, and not at the head of delegation level. He added that in the third basket questions were politically entangled to a degree that often forced active participation from the heads of delegations, and so it would be a mistake to further dilute responsibilities, as this would ultimately diminish Sweden's ability to exercise any influence.[170]

In essence, Tallroth's problem was his alternative interpretation of the role Sweden should play in negotiations of this kind. As he had fully embraced the official rhetoric of active foreign policy, he perceived his task as correspondingly more active and idealistic than did his superiors (and others of his rank). Given this belief, he did not embrace Sweden's retreat from the roles of active independent and mediator-integrator. His criticisms suggest that he also considered a more friendly relationship with the Soviet Union necessary to bring the negotiations forwards. This was not a unique case of varying role conceptions. A similar, if much more controversial, case had occurred the year earlier in Chile, when Swedish ambassador Harald Edelstam, the brother of Axel Edelstam, ignored orders from Stockholm and carried out attempts to save the political opponents of Augusto Pinochet.[171] In the perception of Harald Edelstam, similar to that of Tallroth in that it emphasized soft power and values, it was natural for Sweden to offer refuge to the vulnerable.

By early October 1974, the only states believing the CSCE to be on the right track were the Soviet Union and West Germany.[172] Most other countries, among them the United States, France and the Netherlands, were in complete disagreement. As impatience started spreading through the corridors of the conference centre in Geneva, Norwegian diplomat Leif Mevik acknowledged to Hamilton af Hageby and Hichens-Bergström that the Swedish initiative for gaining impetus from a higher political level earlier that year had perhaps not been such a bad idea after all.[173] Sven Andersson brought up the deadlocked situation in Geneva during talks with Soviet foreign minister Gromyko. While Gromyko expressed his general satisfaction, claiming that most of the remaining controversy was 'artificial', he wondered why countries like France wanted to establish a library in the Soviet Union when existing libraries in fact held hundreds of thousands, 'if not millions', of French volumes.

In Moscow, Gromyko maintained, nobody was against human contacts or cultural exchange if they were in conformity with existing principles on noninterference and domestic laws. The Soviet minister finally praised Swedish efforts for compromise but made clear that the CBM remained 'very doubtful'. If adopted in the proposed form, the Soviets would have to notify others of the natural movements of their troops from winter to summer quarters, which he viewed as an administrative burden and a source of unnecessary turmoil.

Andersson replied that his country was ready to take on a reasonable position on all subjects but stressed that some substantial results had to be achieved.[174] This discussion reflects the growing discomfort over the many trouble spots that were putting an end to détente. Without Brandt, who had been a guide for the Swedes down the road to European détente (or a commitment of the strongest kind to any group or set of particular aims at the CSCE), the Swedes lacked the motivation necessary to maintain a position beyond their pre-1971 reservation towards the CSCE. Therefore, they returned to a behaviour which matches the definition of an isolate in Holsti's typology.

The Swedish retreat to a position of reservation and passivity went hand in hand with the second stage turning into a diplomatic roller-coaster. In October 1974, signs of renewed movement in the deadlocked subjects were recognized. By applying the so-called French method – preliminary, simultaneous discussions on five questions – minor progress could be achieved in the subcommittee on human contacts. In the military subcommittee, the approach helped register some first sentences on the prenotification of manoeuvres. This became possible mostly due to growing Western unity on the most essential issues. Whereas the Europeans had been urged by Kissinger to lower their ambitions earlier, now the American delegation adjusted to the position of the EC Nine, particularly on the relation between the first and third baskets.[175]

However, according to the Swedish delegation, this did not bring about an improvement: 'During the [past] week, the work in the different baskets progressed unexpectedly slow after the positive signs noticed earlier. A serene atmosphere still rules in Basket III thanks to the more flexible attitude on procedural questions shown by all parties but there have not been any results on factual issues nonetheless'.[176] Instead, the crisis became all the harder to grasp.[177] On the one hand, there was no complete stagnation, but at the same time, there was a considerable lack of hope for progress among the delegates. Neither of the two blocs showed significant zeal, and few believed the CSCE could be concluded before early 1975. Interest in neutral and nonaligned activity reoccurred on a number of occasions in late 1974, often from Norway and Denmark, whose representatives acknowledged, nevertheless, that not all Western states agreed with them on this matter.

The Warsaw Pact states showed ambivalent behaviour towards the N+N states, believing that they 'encourage . . . such attempts but turn highly critical when they take place', as one Swedish report criticized. On one specific occasion, when the N+N presented a compromise proposal for the minipreamble in the education subcommittee, the Eastern European reaction had been 'scathing'.[178] The general situation was further complicated by the attempts of both blocs to bring the neutrals to their side with regard to the minipreambles in the third basket. All in all, the Swedes felt vindicated and strictly maintained their passive position during most of the fall of 1974. Their approach was mimicked by Austria, while Finland and Switzerland remained more proactive.[179] Under such conditions, a Swedish return to activity was unthinkable, as any further political faux pas were to be avoided. Nothing suggested that the Swedish decision to abandon active independence was wrong.

Attracting Finnish Anger and the Search for an Exit Strategy

Although the controversy around Tallroth was settled in early October 1974, the Swedish delegations' working conditions remained troublesome for the rest of the year. Continuous stalemates caused rising frustration among delegates, which eventually created renewed frictions. Only a few weeks after changes had been made to the delegation, another remarkable episode took place.

At a cocktail dinner on the evening of 25 October 1974, Jaako Iloniemi, the Finnish head of delegation, had an outburst of rage, an 'explosion' as it was called in Swedish reports, at young Swedish delegates Kerstin Asp and Göran Berg. Iloniemi told the surprised Swedes that their countries had similar social systems and should, therefore, share a natural interest in good results in the third basket. But instead, Iloniemi claimed, Sweden showed no vital interest in the subject at all and even tried to 'sabotage' the work towards a solution on human contacts.

Iloniemi added that he was aware of this position being the responsibility of Sven Andersson, Sverker Åström and Axel Edelstam. Asp and Berg were rebuked when they responded that it was natural to leave activism on human contacts to the Austrians, who chaired the subcommittee. Iloniemi also rejected any arguments defending Sweden's timing and any assessment of the chances for success of the compromise proposals. The matter would be brought up during the upcoming visit of King Carl Gustaf, said Iloniemi, before walking away from the conversation.[180] Once again, Finnish-Swedish relations had turned out to be complicated. A faithful friendship between the two countries seemed natural to both sides, but differing perceptions of how to build and maintain it kept colliding.

To Swedish officials in charge, such as Gustaf Hamilton, Iloniemi's outburst was 'unexplainable'. Had the Eastern Europeans not declared that they were not interested in any kind of package involving human contacts?[181] Eventually, the story came to nothing, except to a rather informal exchange between Sverker Åström and Finland's ambassador in Stockholm, Max Jakobson, following Sweden's official complaint to Helsinki about Iloniemi's behaviour.[182] Based on his long experience of diplomatic service in the Finnish capital, Göran Ryding explained to Swedish diplomats in Stockholm that Iloniemi was well known for his temper, and shortly thereafter the Swedes put an end to the story by claiming that Iloniemi's 'nonsense' did not represent the Finnish position.[183]

This occurrence was indeed a diplomatic curiosity.[184] But it was, nevertheless, deeply rooted in the politics of the involved countries. To Finland, whose neutrality policy centred on Europe, the CSCE was a unique opportunity to strengthen the country's neutral status by advancing multilateralism on a continental level. Sweden, on the other hand, was less interested in Europe. It had been rather reluctant about European integration in the 1960s and preferred the status quo in matters of European security.[185] Focusing on global politics as its natural foreign policy forum, Stockholm disregarded systemic modifications, especially if they carried the political cost of dissent between the blocs.

By early November 1974, Swedish delegates considered the results of two months of intensive negotiations after the summer break 'utterly marginal'. They saw no signs of improvement in the near future, as several subcommittees remained completely deadlocked. In the first basket, discussions on the seventh principle, on respect for human rights and fundamental freedoms, had been going on since July. No progress was made in either the special working group on the catalogue of principles or in the military subcommittee. The situation remained the same in the third basket, where signs that earlier had suggested improvement proved a figment of the imagination. Neither East nor West seemed interested in compromise, which made further delays unavoidable. Even in the second basket, where there had been substantial progress throughout the first and second stages, discussions on the most problematic questions came to a standstill. 'Patience' became the major slogan of the CSCE.[186]

An evaluation of the Swedish Foreign Ministry in Stockholm elaborated that only half of the mandates of the Dipoli Blue Book had been processed after fourteen months of negotiations. It maintained that future development depended heavily on upcoming high-level summits and consultations. The report also addressed the recent Swedish attitude and confirmed that it was the right response to the stalemate at Geneva. It concluded that the Swedish delegation would remain passive and only participate in neutral efforts towards new compromise formulas if both blocs assured their support for such mediation. This meant that mediatory efforts would be limited to what Holsti calls a bridge, a 'communication function', in a few isolated instances. The earliest possible conclusion of the CSCE was now Sweden's top priority.

The only exception to this minimalist stance was the standpoint on CBM, where Sweden maintained its maximalist position despite clear indications from the Soviets that compromises and scanty results were very likely.[187] During the fall of 1974, Sweden took only one minor initiative at the CSCE, when it suggested the deletion of controversial passages regarding military budgets which it had proposed itself a year before.[188] The country's ambitions, which had never reached the level suggested by its official rhetoric after all, were lowered to the level of the time before the breakthrough of the West German *Ostpolitik* in 1970: 'So far, I assess our low profile as correct. This is not a heroic attitude, of course, but considering the exhausting consensus rule and the heavy weight of the East and the [EC] Nine in comparison to the Neutrals, our role can never be more than marginal anyways'.[189]

The Soviet Union eventually accepted this retreat after a number of failed calls for renewed Swedish activism and started to show sympathy for the more anonymous role taken by the N+N states. In talks with Swedish delegates, Ambassador Anatoly Dobrynin stated that the influence of prominent active actors, such as Swiss ambassador Edouard Brunner, was rather harmful. The Soviet negotiator also informed his interlocutors that the Kremlin had reconsidered concessions on human contacts. Dobrynin promised to keep the Swedes informed on the matter upon returning from Moscow.

When Finland suggested that the neutrals could propose an informal meeting between the heads of delegations, it was disregarded by Sweden and Austria on the basis of Dobrynin's statement.[190] With increasing frequency, the cooperation among the N+N states was characterized by uncertainty. According to Richard Hichens-Bergström, there was agreement among his fellow delegation leaders that the N+N states were a constrained group whose views corresponded only sporadically.[191] Ultimately, the many twists and turns had taught most neutral diplomats that one swallow did not make a summer and, therefore, with increasing regularity, they decided to wait and see.

During the royal Swedish visit to Finland in late November 1974, the CSCE was discussed between foreign ministers Ahti Karjalainen and Sven Andersson. The host brought up the subject first touted by Iloniemi, and it was agreed that the prospects of renewed neutral efforts would be explored.[192] Yet again, Finland tried to force a change in the Swedish attitude by intervention at the highest political level. The Finns would also forge discussions on the third stage of the CSCE at a meeting between the neutrals in Kloten near Zürich on 18 December 1974.[193] There, they held that this move was necessary because of statements made by Bruno Kreisky. On several occasions, the Austrian chancellor had indicated that the third and conclusive stage should not be reduced to a ratification procedure in which politicians simply executed the will of their diplomats. For obvious reasons, Finnish president Urho Kekkonen feared that Kreisky's approach could jeopardize the whole conference.[194]

Just prior to the Kloten meeting, Hichens-Bergström and the influential Swiss ambassador Rudolf Bindschedler met for a bilateral exchange of views. The Swiss ambassador disappointed his Swedish interlocutor regarding the two remaining Swedish areas of interest when he stated that his ministry did not believe that there was space for a neutral initiative on CBM or for substantial discussions in the fourth basket. With the struggle on the final drafting coming closer, there was a risk that the two blocs would try to use the N+N states, Bindschedler warned his Swedish colleague.[195] At Kloten, the N+N decided that they would take a common and final stand in the military subcommittee in late January 1975. Switzerland and Austria argued that the N+N should not abandon their own demands too early. The Swedish representatives objected, reiterating that their country had always been aware of the fact that it was impossible to fully accomplish objectives declared before the convocation of the conference.

They urged patience, since they did not expect the Soviet Union to make concessions in the near future and thought that further proposals could cause unnecessary irritation if presented too early. Gradually, the Swedes maintained, the N+N states would be forced to adopt a more realistic perspective. Åström stressed that the results achieved in the military field were already remarkable and that the N+N should seek a quick completion of the CSCE.

The Swedes added that the time was ripe for greater flexibility and an appropriate juncture to try to set a date for the presentation of a paper from February 1974 aiming at wrapping things up swiftly, in anticipation of 'that dramatic moment (which might come) when the USA and the Soviet Union decide that the CSCE must be concluded within a week'. The Swedes believed that the time aspect was crucial for the N+N and that it was a task for the group to present a realistic foundation for the final negotiations if they did not want them to be overrun by the course of events.[196] In Zürich it became clearer than ever that by the end of 1974, Sweden was the least ambitious and idealistic of the neutrals.

During the last weeks of 1974, some steps forwards were finally made. A compromise was reached on the reunification of families, and important sections on cultural exchange and the seventh principle on human rights could be registered. In the subcommittee on science and technology in the second basket, Sweden received praise for a proposal on the order that registered texts would be coded in the final declaration.[197] Such partial successes improved the mood of many in Geneva. The two blocs acknowledged the constructive role played by the N+N states and claimed they were hoping for further mediating efforts from them, although large package deals were not considered necessary anymore.[198] The completion of the seventh principle on human rights and fundamental freedoms was considered a historical achievement, although it was not certain whether or even how it would be implemented. For the first time, respect for human rights was defined as an essential element of the relations between states in an international agreement.

Up until then, the Soviet Union had always maintained that human rights belonged to the domestic sphere and were not an issue that should concern the international community. The text of the principle had expanded from three to thirty-eight lines since the original proposal of July 1974. The Swedish delegation considered its conclusion a success for the EC Nine, pointing to the fact that the steadfastness of the Western Europeans had forced the Soviets to make the necessary concessions.[199]

Due to earlier disappointments, and as much work remained to be done, this did not cause any euphoria among Swedish officials, however. Upcoming tasks, such as on the eighth principle on equal rights and the self-determination of peoples and the mutually acceptable conditions (MAC) in the third basket, looked problematic. Sweden still held ambitions regarding CBM and opened up for discussion on a common N+N position, but the Soviets refused to move. Unfortunately, once again the Swedes could not count on Finnish support, as Helsinki's focus was directed exclusively on the Kekkonen Plan for a Nordic nuclear-free zone.[200] As we have seen repeatedly, the relations between Stockholm and Helsinki were often characterized by disagreement on the most essential issues, and this was no different.

In order to move the tough bargaining forwards, major political leaders engaged more actively again. The CSCE occupied much space in the talks between the new French president Valéry Giscard d'Estaing and Leonid Brezhnev in Paris in December 1974, which brought closer together the positions of the Soviet Union and France.[201] Generally, the achievements of the previous weeks had created a new belief in a constructive last round of the exhausting second stage, although West Germany's adamant insistence on the peaceful change of frontiers remained a problem.[202] Therefore, the Swedish personnel carousel was set in motion again. With 1 January 1975 as commencement date, the delegation underwent several important changes. Axel Edelstam took over Richard Hichens-Bergström's position as head of the delegation and had Leif Leifland replace him as director of the Foreign Ministry's political department.[203] Through this replacement, the Swedish government made sure that its delegation would retain its pragmatic approach during the final phase.

Going Back to Normal during the War of Nerves: Swedish Minimalism

After returning to Geneva following the final Christmas break, the Swedes were surprised by a general lack of interest which significantly exceeded similar periods after earlier breaks. Despite the sobering atmosphere, and although no 'sensations' had occurred in either the third or the fourth basket, it was expected that negotiations could be concluded by April or May 1975 at the latest.[204] But, once again, several weeks passed without real progress. The N+N states supported West Germany's rejection of an amendment to the tenth principle, defining special responsibilities of the victorious powers after the end of World War II, as this established an unwelcome linkage to the status of Berlin.[205]

Further personnel joined the Swedish delegation in what was thought to be the last round and the final few months of the second stage. Gustaf Ekholm from the Swedish embassy of Vienna took over responsibility for the second basket, and Håkan Wilkens returned to his work in the subcommittee on human contacts and information in the third basket.[206]

These changes strengthened Axel Edelstam's position as the new head of delegation.

The Swedish Foreign Ministry's earlier analyses, suggesting a shift in the negotiations from a technical-diplomatic to a political character, proved correct. By late February 1975, everybody in Geneva was waiting for the outcome of top-level talks between the great powers, in particular between the United States and the Soviet Union. Referring to a day-long meeting between the Soviet delegation and Soviet foreign minister Andrei Gromyko, after the latter had met with Henry Kissinger, Edelstam noted that 'the near future will show whether this will result in new instructions'.[207] For the first time since the convocation of the first stage in July 1973, it was almost exclusively superpower instructions that set the course for the CSCE. This did not lift the spirits of the delegates, many of whom had arrived in 'a mood of dejection'.[208]

The Kremlin was well aware of the Swedish retreat and the country's efforts to lower ambitions in the neutral and Western camps. Soviet officials praised their Swedish colleagues in Geneva on several occasions; in *Pravda*, Sweden was applauded for its proposal on a special working group for the arrangement of the third stage.[209] Thus, the surprise was great when the Soviet diplomat Anatoly Kovalev criticized Axel Edelstam harshly for proposing yet another Easter break in early March 1975.[210] To Edelstam, the only explanation for what he called 'a personal attack' was that the Soviet delegation was under greater pressure from the Kremlin than it had been before. He was certain that Moscow had ordered its delegates to bring the CSCE to an end, and, instead of showing greater flexibility in military matters and on the remaining issues in the third basket, the Soviets now seemed to be losing their balance. Therefore, Edelstam reported to Stockholm that he expected the Soviet delegation to try to pressure the smaller states even harder during the remaining period.[211]

The non-European interests of two N+N states, Cyprus and Yugoslavia, were pointed out as further potential problems for Sweden and the other neutrals, to be dealt with if these two states were to maintain loyalty to the group.[212] In order to be able to cope with the fragmented and tense situation, the Swedish delegation once more requested additional personnel.[213] After the departure of the experts, the permanent delegation consisted of only five diplomats, whereas, one complaint held, all comparable states had between six and eight officials in Geneva. Shortly afterwards, Åke Berg and Mathias Mossberg were made available.[214]

Despite the conclusion of the seventh principle on respect for human rights and fundamental freedoms, human contacts were still perceived as *the* problem. Eager to secure the results in the military field, Sweden's irritation over the ongoing struggle on humanitarian concessions between

East and West finally grew considerably and would finally express itself publicly. Axel Edelstam and Göran Berg travelled to Stockholm and met with Foreign Minister Andersson on 18 March 1975.[215] The day after, a clear stand against the Western insistence on human rights concessions was pronounced in the annual foreign policy declaration of the Swedish government:

> Decisions on human contacts and increased information across national borders have not yet been finally approved by all participants. Sweden will be continuing its efforts to ensure that their content is in harmony with our democratic and humanitarian traditions. When judging the results possible in this field it must be borne in mind that the Conference cannot eliminate differences due to political, economic or social systems.[216]

Whereas this indicated to experts that Sweden was not playing the role of defender of the faith and values but actually criticizing the West, the government concealed its realpolitik prioritizing from the broader public by continuously referring to 'our democratic and humanitarian tradition'. As we have seen, these traditions never served as guiding principles for Sweden's CSCE policy. They were, nonetheless, viewed critically by the British Foreign Office:

> The Swedish performance at the CSCE has been depressingly wet. Unlike the Swiss and Austrians, with whom they co-ordinate closely, they do not have the courage to stand up to the East on the most important matters. They are eager to appear as conciliators in matters of procedure, but would clearly like to see the Conference finish as soon as possible ... Though at an early stage in the negotiations the Swedes were keen to obtain effective confidence-building measures, in particular notification of separate naval and small scale, land manoeuvres, they have of late made only token attempts to put pressure on the Warsaw Pact.[217]

At Geneva, Axel Edelstam held the fort in the military subcommittee, arguing that, although there was truth in the argument that the military field had a political rather than a military character and relevance, 'for a small neutral country like my own, the issues also have a direct bearing on national security'.[218]

In late March 1975, positions slowly opened up again and, although neither a package deal nor a breakthrough occurred this time, a conclusion in the summer seemed possible by mid-April.[219] But, as détente was petering out due to ongoing military conflict in different areas, the remaining issues turned out to be difficult to solve. In April 1975, the work on the tenth and last principle on the fulfilment obligations under international law was postponed indefinitely; instead, final clauses and introduction passages were drafted. The third basket remained completely deadlocked, and opposition parties even tended to fall back to more extreme positions.[220] Controversy also prevailed on the follow-up process. While the NATO states insisted on concessions on human contacts before moving on, the Soviets wanted to make a binding decision about the follow-up mechanism immediately and asked Sweden for support in this endeavour.[221]

At the Council of Europe, where the CSCE had been discussed since 1972, Sweden, in contrast to the other neutrals and a number of Western European states, refrained from making any statement. Austria supported Dutch proposals on the implementation of the final declaration, while Switzerland used the opportunity to stress the importance of the third basket.[222]

On 5 May 1975, the sixth anniversary of the Finnish initiative, Axel Edelstam presented in a lengthy memorandum the situation that had prevailed in the final weeks to Foreign Minister Andersson. Edelstam believed that, despite the excessive tactical manoeuvring and great uncertainty that had returned to the conference halls in Geneva, the CSCE was drawing to an end. The remaining question was whether it would be possible to conclude it in July, as most participants were hoping. The time schedule depended on the political will of the heads of state. It was commonly known that the prime ministers of the EC Nine countries had been ready to announce a final date at their meeting in Dublin in March but had been stopped by their diplomats. This last struggle was described as a 'war of nerves' and was endangered by questions outside of the East-West context, such as the Cyprus dispute; Malta's request for the participation of Mediterranean states at the third stage; and Romania's confrontational policy of the last month. In Edelstam's view, the ball was in the Kremlin's court.[223]

Among the issues still under negotiation, Sweden was only interested in CBM and the follow-up process. In the military subcommittee, Sweden and the other N+N states faced resistance from both blocs. The Soviets were struggling to avoid compromising their traditional secrecy in military matters, demanding that CBM be on a voluntary basis and reduced to a minimum level. The crucial point was how to define those zones in which military manoeuvres would have to be announced in advance. The West and the N+N states proposed that all of Europe should be included, while the Soviet Union proposed border zones of one hundred kilometres.

The latter proposal would have caused major problems to Sweden, as large portions of its territory would become part of such a zone, while the Soviet Union would not even have to make notifications for manoeuvres in the Baltic. Therefore, the Soviet proposal was completely unacceptable to Sweden from a military standpoint.[224] In talks with Lev Mendelevich, Edelstam tried to explain the problem that the Soviet position on CBM caused to Sweden. Edelstam proposed that the distance be calculated from the border of the concerned country and encompass three to four hundred kilometres. Mendelevich rejected this with reference to areas vital to Soviet security, such as the Crimea, but remained open to a special solution on the Baltic Sea. To Edelstam this was satisfactory, as it showed that positions were not completely locked.[225]

As regarded the follow-up process, the Western countries proposed a meeting of diplomats in 1977, whereas the group of the N+N hoped for a continuation of multilateral efforts on a broader basis and a commitment to the CSCE process beyond 1977.[226] In order to accomplish their goal, the N+N states worked on a document that brought together four separate but related proposals made by Finland, Yugoslavia, Czechoslovakia and Denmark.[227] At this point, the Swedes had almost completely lost interest and faith in the third basket, and few references were made to it. Human rights improvements in Eastern Europe were not vital to Sweden's national interest, despite the emphasis put on the issue by members of the government in official statements. There was no will to pay the political price for this, as Olof Palme and his ministers considered noninterference in the domestic affairs of Eastern European governments a guarantee for peace and stability in Europe and, therefore, untouchable. The course of negotiations at Helsinki and Geneva had strengthened this belief further.

As we have seen, the N+N countries were forced into the role of observers by May 1975. They had to wait for the meetings of Kissinger and Gromyko on 19 May, the EC Foreign Minister Meeting in Dublin on 26 May and the NATO summit on 29–30 May in Brussels to provide them with the necessary space for decisive decisions.[228] The outcome of the Kissinger-Gromyko meeting did not satisfy the Western Europeans, and now all eyes turned to the upcoming NATO meeting. Kissinger had pointed out to Gromyko that the tight schedule could only be kept to if Moscow understood that the time for substantial concessions had come.[229]

When the foreign ministers of the EC Nine states issued a critical public statement on the situation in Geneva the new 'crisis', as Axel Edelstam called it, was a fact. As a consequence, the Americans became as sceptical about concluding the CSCE as their transatlantic partners. The West was ready to pay the Soviets back in their own coin: 'We can only conclude that the conference has ended up in crisis. Only a quick and comprehensive Soviet retreat on the most vital issues, particularly regarding freer movement of information, could save the timetable. Otherwise, we believe there is a risk that the third stage will be delayed until the fall'.[230]

Sweden was still looked upon as an integral part of the N+N states, and their attempts to mediate between the blocs was considered vital, but its real focus had by now been restricted to its own national interests and a modification of the CBM zones. As had been the case for months, Sweden's performance was based on a set of roles comprising what Holsti defines as independent and isolate. Therefore, Swedish delegates rejected the possibility of a neutral mediation role in the Cyprus problem, pointing to the fact that the N+N countries had engaged in East-West issues for a reason.[231]

The Soviets finally retreated on several controversial points regarding human contacts shortly before the NATO summit in Brussels, which brought an end to the crisis at the eleventh hour.[232] During the first week of June 1975, discussions progressed in the third basket, where texts were agreed on and tabled for registration quickly.[233] As a response to urges from the other Nordic countries, Edelstam raised the issue of the schedule on 19 June 1975, one week before a decision would have to be made if the third stage was to take place on the last weekend of July. This was one of the very few occasions when the Swedes did not consult the N+N states before the Nordics, which provoked immediate criticism from Malta, Austria, Switzerland and Yugoslavia, who all pointed out that neither follow-up nor military questions had been solved yet.[234] Numerous bilateral talks, and the immense will to conclude the conference before the summer break and during the last week of June, helped to solve problems, and texts were finally registered on a daily basis.[235]

Despite internal criticism claiming that the rush served primarily the superpowers', rather than Swedish, interests, the Swedish delegation made efforts to prepare for the third stage on 26 June 1975 when it introduced the question of the schedule at the coordination committee.[236] While the Eastern bloc reacted positively, France and Denmark expressed reservations towards the Swedish proposal on behalf of the EC Nine.[237] A response to this criticism was then formulated by Sweden, together with Finland and Norway, and presented on 8 July 1975, with the aim of forcing the EC Nine to cooperate. It was only under 'dramatic conditions' that a compromise was reached two days later, after seventeen hours of uninterrupted negotiations. Finally, the participants agreed on 30 July 1975 as the target date for the third stage.[238]

Sweden's return to its pre-1971 reluctance did attract some resentment from the East. A strictly confidential memorandum from the Warsaw Pact states reveals that the Eastern Europeans thought 'the Danes were the worst offenders, but the Swedes did not come far behind'.[239] In essence, the CSCE had changed little of the general Swedish discomfort concerning the place of Europe in the country's foreign policy. When Poland suggested a draft text for a joint statement on the expansion of friendly relations between the two countries, this discomfort was reflected in the reaction of

Göran Berg: 'Another notable aspect in the Polish paper is the consequent focus on Europe . . . Is it, for example, of special importance that Sweden shall engage in Central European border issues in one way or another? Is it right on our behalf to emphasise Europe and virtually neglect the rest of the world?'[240]

When the final session ended in the morning of Monday 21 July 1975 at 4 a.m., the Swedish delegation at Geneva cabled that this was going to be its last weekly report, 'however impossible it may sound'. Over the weekend, final texts had been reviewed and translated. Negotiations on CBM had resulted in the parameters for mandatory notifications of military manoeuvres being set at 250 kilometres, 25,000 soldiers and 21 days.[241] In this context, a first draft of Olof Palme's speech at the third stage in Helsinki could be presented by Gustav Ekholm and consequently forwarded to Foreign Minister Sven Andersson and higher officials at the Swedish Foreign Ministry in Stockholm for review.[242]

The Swedes did not perceive as a problem the fact that the Final Act was not a legally binding document, since they believed that it would be of higher value than comparable UN resolutions, given that heads of governments would sign it. With the benefit of hindsight, this assessment proved to be correct. Edelstam explained to Foreign Minister Sven Andersson that the most important part was the establishment of an all-European framework, which could be used to deal with East-West issues in the future. Therefore, the overall result, Edelstam claimed, was satisfying. Naturally, high expectations before the conference had given place to more modest solutions over the course of the negotiations, but, most importantly, the CBM parameters had met Swedish minimum requirements and would be subject to review at the 1977 follow-up meeting in Belgrade.[243]

The settlements on human contacts were believed to provide a positive impulse to East-West relations. In this regard, the clause on the reunification of families was considered the most important achievement, together with provisions on cultural and educational exchange. All in all, results in all four baskets achieved more than the bottom line, and the contribution of the N+N states to this had been 'considerable'. Bizarrely, Edelstam also stated that 'Nordic cooperation has worked out very well during the whole conference' and claimed that the Finns had 'expressed their appreciation over this Nordic solidarity'. This was nothing but whitewashing the absence of common interests with Denmark and Norway, which was much cited by Swedish delegates during the second stage, and even more eliding the recurring tension between the Swedish and Finnish delegations. Edelstam's summation once more illustrated that Sweden's interest in Europe lay in maintaining the status quo and lacked any vision of long-term change:

The conference has been looked at as a necessary element of détente. All participants have been eager for the process to continue along the same lines as hitherto, i.e. based on the persistence of the military blocs, on continued American active engagement in European affairs, and on gradual rapprochement between all states ... If allowed to continue undisturbed, maybe one can speak of a sort of factual convergence between the systems as a consequence of this process, which should further contribute to a lasting stabilization of conditions in Europe.[244]

Edelstam was particularly critical of the methods applied by the Soviet delegation at Geneva and pointed to a 'certain disillusionment' overshadowing the conclusion of the CSCE.

He also described the efforts of the N+N states as having advanced the negotiations by playing 'a considerable role in bridging differences'.[245] Even here, Edelstam's assessment must be put into perspective on the basis of our examination, as it left out the numerous limitations to Sweden as a bridge or mediator-integrator at the CSCE. During most of the six and a half years between the Budapest Appeal and the signing of the Final Act, Sweden's role performance was that of an isolationist and an independent. All in all, the country had been considerably less active and constructive than portrayed by Edelstam. Still, his evaluation was natural enough, seeing as it was drafted at a time when international tensions were increasing again and the value of the negotiations seemed uncertain. Comparable countries such as Switzerland shared his thoughts.[246]

During the days prior to the signing of the Final Act, preparations started in Stockholm. Edelstam travelled to the Swedish capital and handed over relevant documents, which became the basis of Foreign Minister Andersson's consultations.[247] A compilation of documents was then sent from the Foreign Ministry to Prime Minister Palme and the leaders of the opposition parties: Gösta Bohman (Conservative Party, Moderata samlingspartiet), Thorbjörn Fälldin (Centre Party) and Gunnar Helén (Liberal Party).[248] In Helsinki, the Swedish delegation booked two suites and eighteen rooms at the Hotel Hesperia, which was less than a ten-minute walk to Finlandia Hall, the venue of the third stage.[249]

At the third stage of the CSCE, Sweden was represented by a delegation of nineteen members led by Prime Minister Olof Palme and Foreign Minister Sven Andersson. Other prominent members of the delegation were Sverker Åström, Anders Thunborg, Richard Hichens-Bergström, Göran Ryding, Leif Leifland and Axel Edelstam.[250] Foreign Minister Andersson and other members of the delegation travelled to Helsinki the day before the commencement of the third stage.[251] Palme himself arrived from Visby on 30 July at 10 a.m., just two hours before Finland's president Kekkonen opened the summit conference.[252]

The third stage of the CSCE was a major political event, broadly followed by international media. It was attended by 550 accredited delegation members and administrated by some 3,000 staff members.[253] For many of the participants it became an opportunity for interesting conversations. Palme, for instance, used the opportunity for a thirty-five-minute discussion with US secretary of state Henry Kissinger on a number of international issues.[254] After Urho Kekkonen's introductory speech, UN secretary-general Kurt Waldheim delivered a note. Then, the heads of states entered the stage for the following two days. Olof Palme gave his speech at Finlandia Hall the day after, as the twenty-second speaker on the list. The Swedish prime minister started off by thanking the Finnish host for the 'special role in initiating and carrying through this conference'. In contrast to statements made at Dipoli and at the first stage, West Germany was not mentioned. As we have seen, this was due to the second stage creating a new setting, leading to the decreasing importance of the FRG as a faithful friend.

Palme proceeded to point to the importance of continuing the chosen path of détente, to which, from a Swedish point of view, 'there is no alternative'. Notably, he put similar emphasis on the first and third baskets, arguing that military balance as a guarantee of peace could be maintained at a lower level if states overcame their mutual mistrust through providing extended information on military expenditures and manoeuvres. Essentially, Palme claimed that political détente without a military component was doomed to fail. This had been a long-standing Swedish position. With regard to respect for human rights and their role in the Final Act, Palme expressed Swedish hopes for an improved exchange of opinions over borders and greater freedom of expression in all of Europe on ideological, social and political questions. Acknowledging respect for the different social systems, he claimed that 'flagrant violations of these rights cannot but affect the climate of détente'.[255]

Palme also applied the then prominent Swedish Third Way rhetoric, maintaining, 'The conclusion of this European conference should increase our responsibility to work for peace and greater equality between the nations of the world and, not least, to establish more equitable relations between the poor and the rich countries in the spirit of a new economic world order'.[256] In his address, Palme stressed the idealistic aspects of the Final Act, while hardly referring to neutrality. His speech was also distinct in that it framed the CSCE and its aftermath from a global perspective.[257] In contrast to earlier speeches delivered by Ambassador Ryding at Dipoli and Foreign Minister Wickman at the first stage of the CSCE, it seems as though Palme drafted his speech himself.

There is little evidence to suggest that his strong emphasis on human contacts, and the rather unexpected reference to global politics, were attempts to attract the attention of the present leaders and point them in this direction. There had been awareness of the role of developing countries in the CSCE by Swedish diplomats for several years, but it was well known that the prospects in this regard were limited.[258] In March 1972, for instance, Thyberg's suggestion for a Swedish proposal on cooperation directed towards developing countries had gone unnoticed.[259] Thus, it must be concluded that Palme's speech was merely another conscious distortion of Sweden's profile by an advocate of realpolitik in European security affairs.

Conclusion

Sweden's role at the CSCE was the outcome of a complex structure which brought together the views and role perceptions of numerous diplomats, experts from different ministries and high-ranking politicians. Naturally, the latter defined the general framework, which set limits for the policy to be carried out on the ground by diplomats. Due to the complexity of the CSCE, however, diplomats and experts maintained a relatively high degree of freedom of action throughout the negotiations. As the daily negotiations were not subject to public controversy, room for manoeuvring was greater than in other foreign policy areas, where public opinion had to be taken into account.

Sweden's delegation to the CSCE used this additional space to engage actively in the institutionalization of the group of neutral and nonaligned states, which came to contribute to the progress of the conference in different ways. This engagement substituted for the role performance that Sweden usually carried out in multilateral negotiations at the United Nations together with the other Nordic states. The participation with the group of N+N states resulted in Sweden's role of mediator-integrator by early 1974, when expectations of other states and Swedish role conceptions finally corresponded.

During the second stage of the CSCE in Geneva, Nordic cooperation never exceeded the level of a courteous exchange of information and, where circumstances and loyalties permitted, mutual support for single positions. From a Swedish perspective, there was a significant difference between the positive relations maintained with Norway, the rather neutral ties with Denmark and the close, but often tense, relationship with Finland. Norway's NATO membership was not really a concern, as Sweden's connection with the military alliance was intimate and almost genuinely positive. Denmark's involvement with the EC Nine after the commencement of its membership in 1973, on the other hand, resulted in diverging interests once common Western European ambitions materialized. The low priority assigned to human contacts by Sweden came into sharp contrast with the maximalist stance of Denmark and the rest of the EC Nine.

Finally, Finland's troubled relationship with the Soviet Union created severe pressure on Swedish-Finnish relations in a context where security was at stake. In neither case can Sweden be said to have enjoyed a faithful friendship or even played the role of regional collaborator. Although Sweden wanted to give the impression of supporting Finland and maintained an interest in regional disarmament throughout the second stage, it cannot be ascribed the role of regional leader as defined by Holsti. This is interesting considering the otherwise strong Nordic character of Swedish foreign policy during this era.

Ultimately, most of the Swedish decision makers and diplomats viewed their own role in the political and diplomatic process leading towards the Helsinki Final Act as firm advocates of realpolitik. Swedish officials involved with the CSCE did not consider 'soft' issues, human rights or solidarity to be of essential significance. The only exceptions were Ambassador Tore Tallroth, who negotiated in the third basket, and, to a limited extent, Richard Hichens-Bergström, the head of delegation between July 1973 and the 1974/1975 turn of the year. Instead, focus was on disarmament, and CBM negotiated in the first basket. The reason for this was Sweden's belief in the maintenance of the strategic balance between the two military alliances as the best guarantee for peace.

The neutral and nonaligned cooperation, which emerged in late 1973 and flourished during the first half of 1974, resulted in a Swedish role performance best thought of as a blend of active independent and mediator-integrator. It served Swedish interests and was hardly ever carried out against the will of the two blocs. In the case of Sweden, it was both preceded and succeeded by passivity and reluctance – or, to again apply Holsti's typology to our analysis, by the roles of independent and isolate. The more that détente deteriorated after the outbreak of the Yom Kippur War in October 1973, the more Sweden fell back from active independence to the more modest role of an independent actor, with exclusive focus on its own interests. None of the developments of the second stage tempted the Swedes to seek more idealistic roles such as developer, defender of the faith or example, as one would expect based on their profile in global matters and the UN at the time.

On several occasions, internally and externally, the Swedes identified themselves as sharing the core values of the United States, the country with which they had no diplomatic relations during all of 1973, but they nevertheless refrained from actively defending these Western values because of the risk of paying a political price. The Swedes were too bound by realpolitik thinking to develop a more values-led strategy and role. This was, however, again de-emphasized in public statements, such as Olof Palme's speech at the third and final stage of the CSCE in Helsinki.

The one single moment when the Swedes tried to play a different tune was in summer 1974, when the government suggested proposing a meeting at a high political level to give renewed impetus to the tough bargaining. It was quickly abandoned – mainly due to resistance from the West but also because it did not receive any support from the other neutral states. Individuals who failed to adapt to the Swedish realist approach to the CSCE were rebuked or eventually weeded out. The replacement of Tallroth, and arguably of Hichens-Bergström, was grounded in similar motives to the charges brought against opposition leaders Jarl Hjalmarson in 1959 and Sven Wedén in 1968, or against Harald Edelstam, Sweden's ambassador in Chile, in 1973. The role performance of Sweden was based on the conceptions of the government and treated as a no go area for political opposition and diplomats alike.

Taken as a whole, the role played by Sweden during the second stage of the CSCE was a blend of different roles, as offered by Holsti's typology. Above all, Sweden was independent in the sense of making 'policy decisions according to the state's own interests rather than in support of the objectives of other states', but at the same time, and despite its reluctance regarding the Western demands on human contacts, it remained a close partner of the West – of NATO, but also, to a lesser extent, of the EC Nine. It can, just as during the years prior to the MPT, be defined as a faithful friend, since Sweden did support most of the policies of the West and maintained a clear distance from the East Europeans. It also sustained much more intimate ties with the Western camp than with the Warsaw Pact states. The most important faithful friendships during the second stage, however, were with Switzerland and, to a lesser extent, Austria. Eastwards, relations were much weaker than they had been during the bilateral preparatory stage prior to the MPT at Dipoli, and they never again reached a comparable level.

Notes

1. Ryding to Wickman, 'Slutrapport från FMÖ', 8 June 1973, File 40, Vol. 39, HP 79, UD, RA.
2. Bo Stråth, 'The Swedish Demarcation from Europe', in Mikael af Malmborg and Bo Stråth (eds.), *The Meaning of Europe: Variety and Contention within and among Nations* (Oxford: Berg, 2002), 141.
3. Ibid.
4. Gilde, *Österreich im KSZE-Prozess*, 131–33; Peter, *Die Bundesrepublik im KSZE-Prozess*, 91–94; Rosin, *Die Schweiz im KSZE-Prozeß*, 79–81.
5. Ibid. On the role of the EC Nine, see Möckli, *European Foreign Policy*, 94–110.
6. Sverker Åström, 'Kommentarer', 15 June 1973, File 40, Vol. 39, HP 79, UD, RA.
7. With the notable exception of the doctoral dissertation of Stefan Ekecrantz on the period between 1946 and 1959, very little has been written on the Advisory Council and its role in Swedish Cold War politics. Nyström, 'Anförande av utrikesministern', 21 June 1973, File 41, Vol. 39, HP 79, UD, RA; and Wickman to Alva Myrdal, Enclair telegram, 25 June 1973, File 41, Vol. 39, HP 79, UD, RA. Generally, the council was briefed on the conference by Foreign Minister Wickman on a regular basis.
8. Kaj Björk, 'Kommentarer till utkastet till Helsingfors-anförande den 21/6', 25 June 1973, File 41, Vol. 39, HP 79, UD, RA. Further changes were added by the Ministry of Industry, Ilmar Bekeris of the Ministry of Education, and Ambassador Göran Ryding. See Industridepartementet, 'Ny version av sid 7 2a stycket t o m sid 8 2a stycket i utkast 1973-06-21 till utrikesministerns anförande vid ESK:s första fas' i Ringborg to Nyström, 26 June 1973, File 41, Vol. 39, HP 79, UD, RA.
9. Ryding to Nyström, Telegram 354, 26 June 1973; Bekeris to Nyström, 'Anförande av utrikesministern vid ESK', 28 June 1973, File 41, Vol. 39, HP 79, UD, RA.
10. Berg to Swedish Embassy Helsinki, Enclair telegram 334, 20 June 1973, File 40, Vol. 39; Swedish Delegation Geneva to UD, 'Övers. deltagarförteckning från ESK:s första fas', 15 October 1973, File 49, Vol. 42, HP 79, UD, RA.
11. See attachment, 'Consultations de Helsinki sur la question de la Conférence sur la sécurité et la coopération en Europe', File 41, Vol. 39, HP 79, UD, RA.
12. Interestingly, the Austrians were excluded from the invitation.
13. Asp to Wachtmeister, Telegram 344, 21 June 1973, File 41, Vol. 39, HP 79, UD, RA.
14. The tactical relevance of the order is reflected by the fact that it was discussed in several memoranda issued shortly before the first stage commenced.
15. Clearly, this was a reaction to the joint communiqué of Richard Nixon and Leonid Brezhnev issued the week before. See 'Joint Communiqué Following Discussions with General Secretary Brezhnev', 25 June 1973, www.ena.lu/joint_communique_25_june_1973-03-11709 (accessed 1 December 2015). The text passages were part of the first draft and never commented upon by Björk, Ryding or any of the ministries.
16. UD Press Department, 'Speech by Mr. Krister Wickman, Swedish Minister for Foreign Affairs, at the Opening Session in Helsinki of the Conference on Security and Co-operation in Europe', 4 July 1973, File 42, Vol. 39, HP 79, UD, RA.
17. Ibid.
18. Ibid.
19. UD Press Department, 'Utrikesminister Krister Wickman i Radions P1 1973-07-04 om den europeiska säkerhetskonferensen', 5 July 1973, File 42, Vol. 39, HP 79, UD, RA.
20. Rune Nyström, 'ESK: Polens chargé d'affaires om utrikesministerns anförande', 5 July 1973; Wachtmeister, 'ESK 1', 10 July 1973, File 42, Vol. 39, HP 79, UD, RA.

21. Curt Ekholm, 'Balt- och tyskutlämningen 1945–1946: omständigheter kring interneringen i läger i Sverige och utlämningen till Sovjetunionen av f d tyska krigsdeltagare', PhD dissertation, 2 vols. (Uppsala University, 1984); Bjereld et al., *Sveriges säkerhet*, 72–79. For a broader background, see also Mikael Byström and Pär Frohnert (eds.), *Reaching a State of Hope: Refugees, Immigrants and the Swedish Welfare State, 1930–2000* (Lund: Nordic Academic Press, 2013) and Cecilia Notini Burch, *A Cold War Pursuit: Soviet Refugees in Sweden, 1945–54* (Stockholm: Santérus Academic Press, 2014).
22. Archer to Wickman, 29 June 1973, File 42, Vol. 39, HP 79, UD, RA.
23. Ryding to UD, Telegram 401, 11 July 1973, File 42, Vol. 39, HP 79, UD, RA.
24. Sverker Åström, 'Inför ESK 2', 9 July 1973, File 43, Vol. 40, HP 79, UD, RA.
25. Ibid.
26. Ibid.
27. Peter Landelius, 'Utrikesministerns samtal med den sovjetiske ambassadör Jakovlev', 16 July 1973, File 43, Vol. 40; Bundy to UD, Telegram 423, File 46, Vol. 41, HP 79, UD, RA.
28. Göran Berg, 'Sammanfattning av FMÖ och ESK I', 25 July 1973, File 46, Vol. 41, HP 79, UD, RA.
29. Hakkarainen, *State of Peace*, 213.
30. Björk, 'Utkast till svenskt papper om de militära frågorna vid ESK:s andra etapp', 12 July 1973; Edelstam, 'Nedrustningsfrågornas behandling under ESK II. Synpunkter från den svenska arbetsgruppens sida', 30 July 1973, File 46, Vol. 41, HP 79, UD, RA.
31. Edelstam, 'ESK:s andra fas; informations – och kulturfrågorna', 8 August 1973, File 46, Vol. 41, HP 79, UD, RA. On the EC countries at the CSCE, see Romano, *Détente*, 160–66, 169–73.
32. This once again signals how important the subject was to Sweden at the time.
33. Berg, 'Ombud m.m. vid konferensen om säkerhet och samarbete i Europa', 22 August 1973, File 47, Vol. 41; Berg to Vahlquist, Enclair telegram 721, 13 September 1973, File 48, Vol. 41, HP 79, UD, RA.
34. For a complete list, see Tallroth to Bergquist, 'ESK II', 19 March 1974, File 54, Vol. 43, HP 79, UD, RA.
35. Berg, 'ESK-möte den 17 augusti', 23 August 1973, File 47, Vol. 41, HP 79, UD, RA.
36. Patek, 'ESSK – fortsatta arbetet inom korg II'; and Ministry of Defence, 'Förtroendeskapande åtgärder', 23 August 1973, File 47, Vol. 41, HP 79, UD, RA. Swedish positions continued to be developed on a broad foundation. For discussions in the subcommittee on information, a memorandum on the working conditions of Swedish journalists in the Soviet Union was drafted by Olle Stenholm from Swedish Radio in cooperation with colleagues from *Dagens Nyheter* and the news agency TT. See Manfred Nilsson, 'Förtroligt arbetspapper', 14 November 1973, File 50, Vol. 42, HP 79, UD, RA.
37. 'Sveriges agerande vid ESK II' in Edelstam and Berg, 'ESK; Korg 1 – principer som styr relationer mellan stater', 14 September 1973, File 48, Vol. 41, HP 79, UD, RA.
38. It was originally labelled 'Swedish-Swiss-Austrian meeting', see Rune Nyström, 'Svenskt-schweiziskt-österrikiskt möte den 28 augusti i Genève', 16 August 1973, File 46, Vol. 41, HP 79, UD, RA.
39. Berg, 'ESK II:s organisation', 7 September 1973, File 47, Vol. 41, HP 79, UD, RA.
40. Wachtmeister, 'Samtal med Tjeckoslovakiens ambassadör', 5 September 1973, File 47, Vol. 41, HP 79, UD, RA.
41. Nilsson, *Hundra år*, 175–79.
42. Snyder, *Human Rights Activism*, 22.
43. Lagerfelt to Lundvik, Telegram 1133, 25 September 1973, File 49, Vol. 42, HP 79, UD, RA.

44. UD Press Department, 'Utdrag ur ambassadör Lennart Eckerbergs anförande vid konferensen om säkerhet och samarbete i Europa den 28 september 1973', File 49, Vol. 42, HP 79, UD, RA.
45. Eckerberg to Edelstam and Prawitz, Telegram 1311, 25 October 1973, File 50, Vol. 42, HP 79, UD, RA; Fischer, *Neutral Power,* 235; Rosin, *Die Schweiz im KSZE-Prozeß,* 114.
46. UD Press Department, 'Svenskt förslag i europeiska säkerhetskonferensen om ökad insyn i staternas försvarsbudgetar', 25 October 1973, File 50, Vol. 42, HP 79, UD, RA.
47. 'The Swedish Proposal' in Burns to Walden, 'CSCE: Confidence Building Measures', 3 October 1973, FCO 41/1331, TNA. See also Hildyard to FCO, 29 September 1973, FCO 41/1331, TNA.
48. Edelstam, 'Konferensen om säkerhet och samarbete i Europa (ESK)', 1 October 1973, File 49, Vol. 42, HP 79, UD, RA.
49. Millard to Bullard, 11 October 1973, FCO 41/1332, TNA.
50. Lagerfelt to UD, Telegram 1466, 26 November 1973, and Lagerfelt to UD, Telegram 1403, 12 December 1973, File 51, Vol. 42, HP 79, UD, RA.
51. Edelstam to Wachtmeister, 'ESK II: Några intryck', 7 November 1973, File 50, Vol. 42, HP 79, UD, RA.
52. Hichens-Bergström to Wachtmeister, Cipher telegram 41, 8 October 1973, File 49; Hichens-Bergström to Wachtmeister, Cipher telegram 47, 16 October 1973; Hichens-Bergström to Wickman, 'Säkerhetskonferensen efter fem veckor', 26 October 1973, File 50, Vol. 42, HP 79, UD, RA.
53. Lars Bergquist, 'Läget i säkerhetskonferensen: slutet på november 1973', 27 November 1973, File 51, Vol. 42, HP 79, UD, RA.
54. UD Press Department, 'Avsnitt ur utrikesministerns FN-tal', 11 October 1973; Edelstam to [Hichens-]Bergström, Enclair telegram, 18 October 1973, File 49, Vol. 42, HP 79, UD, RA.
55. Björn Elmér, 'Ombud och sakkunniga vid konferensen om säkerhet och samarbete i Europa', 9 October 1973; Tallroth to Mårtensson, 11 October 1973, File 49, Vol. 42, HP 79, UD, RA.
56. Lagerfelt to UD, Telegram 1189, 8 October 1973; Hichens-Bergström to UD, Telegram 1245, 15 October 1973, File 49, Vol. 42, HP 79, UD, RA.
57. Fischer, *Neutral Power,* 219–43.
58. Lagerfelt to UD, Telegram 1419, 14 November 1973, File 50; Berg to Blix, Telegram 1530, 10 December 1973, File 51, Vol. 42, HP 79, UD, RA.
59. Lagerfelt to UD, Telegram 1493, 3 December 1973, File 51, Vol. 42, HP 79, UD, RA.
60. Björn Elmér, 'Norge vid ESK II', 16 November 1973, File 50, 'De nios polchefsmöte i Köpenhamn', 21 November 1973; 'Finland och ESK', 29 November 1973, File 51, Vol. 42, HP 79, UD, RA. A document on the strategy of the Nine after the Copenhagen meeting of 13 November was handed over to the Swedes some five weeks later; see UD, 'De nios strategi för ESK (per den 13 november)', 20 December 1973, File 52, Vol. 43, HP 79, UD, RA.
61. Hichens-Bergström to Wachtmeister, Cipher telegram 71, 14 December 1973, File 51, Vol. 42, HP 79, UD, RA.
62. For a history of the group, see Klaus Misgeld, 'Die "Internationale Gruppe demokratischer Sozialisten" in Stockholm 1942–1945: Zur sozialistischen Friedensdiskussion während des zweiten Weltkrieges', PhD dissertation (Uppsala University, 1976).
63. Their continued discussions resulted in noted publications; see, for example, Brandt et al., *Briefe und Gespräche.* The history (and significance) of the relationship between

the three remains under-researched; see Rathkolb, 'Brandt, Kreisky and Palme', 152–75. See also Judt, *Postwar*, 360–89.
64. Arvidson to Åström, Telegram 1503, 5 December 1973, File 51, Vol. 42, HP 79, UD, RA.
65. Åström to Hichens-Bergström, Cipher telegram, 5 December 1973, File 51, Vol. 42, HP 79, UD, RA.
66. 'Öl ins Getriebe', *Die Zeit*, 7 December 1973, www.zeit.de/1973/50/oel-ins-getriebe (accessed 1 December 2015).
67. Backlund to UD, Cipher telegram 68, 11 December 1973; Hichens-Bergström to Wachtmeister, Cipher telegram 70, 13 December 1973, File 51, Vol. 42, HP 79, UD, RA.
68. Ibid.
69. Hichens-Bergström to Andersson, 'Säkerhetskonferensen tar julledigt: presentationsfasen avslutad', 14 December 1973, File 52, Vol. 43, HP 79, UD, RA.
70. Ibid.
71. See, for example, Arvidsson, 'ESK II – västtyska synpunkter', 29 December 1973; Backlund to UD, Cipher telegram 2, 11 January 1974, File 52, Vol. 43, HP 79, UD, RA.
72. Ulf Ericsson, 'Nytt utkast till säkerhetspolitiskt avsnitt i USA-gruppens rapport', 21 December 1973, File 52, Vol. 43, HP 79, UD, RA.
73. Leifland, *Frostens år*, 156.
74. Eckerberg to Wachtmeister, Telegram 33, 16 January 1974, File 53, Vol. 43, HP 79, UD, RA.
75. Elmér, 'ESK', 18 January 1974, File 53, Vol. 43, HP 79, UD, RA.
76. Maresca, *To Helsinki*, 88–94; Ferraris, *Report*, 109–12. See also Lagerfelt to UD, Telegram 90, 25 January 1974 and Lagerfelt to UD, Telegram 173, 11 February 1974, File 53, Vol. 43, HP 79, UD, RA.
77. Eckerberg to Wachtmeister, Cipher telegram 29, 15 January 1974, File 52; and Björn Elmér, 'Anteckningar från nordiskt samrådsmöte ang. ESK II i Oslo den 28 januari 1974', 31 January 1974, File 53, Vol. 43, HP 79, UD, RA.
78. Ibid.
79. Lagerfelt to UD, Telegram 241, 25 February 1974, File 53; and Colliander to UD, Telegram 375, 18 March 1974, File 54, Vol. 43, HP 79, UD, RA.
80. Lagerfelt to UD, Telegram 203, 18 February 1974, File 53, Vol. 43, HP 79, UD, RA.
81. Lagerfelt to UD, Cipher telegram 9, 13 February 1974, File 53, Vol. 43, HP 79, UD, RA.
82. Hichens-Bergström to Edelstam, Cipher telegram 17, 22 February 1974, File 53, Vol. 43, HP 79, UD, RA.
83. Leifland to Wachtmeister, Cipher telegram 69, 20 February 1974, File 53; Eng to UD, 'Kring andra ESK-etappen', 15 March 1974, File 54, Vol. 43, HP 79, UD, RA.
84. Hanhimäki, 'They Can Write It', 55.
85. Lagerfelt to UD, Cipher telegram 10, 13 February 1974, File 53, Vol. 43, HP 79, UD, RA.
86. The term was originally coined in Zielinski, *Die neutralen und blockfreien*, 231.
87. Fischer, *Neutral Power*, 246–50; Swedish Delegation Geneva to UD, 'ESK II. Förslag framlagt i militärkommittén', 20 February 1974, File 53, Vol. 43, HP 79, UD, RA.
88. Edelstam to Hichens-Bergström, 'Eventuellt nordiskt ESK-möte', 8 April 1974; Hichens-Bergström to Edelstam, Cipher telegram 31, 26 April 1974, File 54, Vol. 43, HP 79, UD, RA.
89. On the deadlocked negotiations between January and April 1974, see Gilde, *Österreich im KSZE-Prozess*, 151–59.
90. Lagerfelt to UD, Telegram 501, 8 April 1974; Colliander to UD, Telegram 561, 29 April 1974, File 54, Vol. 43, HP 79, UD, RA.

91. Bergquist to Eckerberg, Cipher telegram 4, 2 May 1974, File 55, Vol. 44, HP 79, UD, RA.
92. 'Utkast till anförande av utrikesministern i Europarådets ministerkommitté den 6 maj 1974', in Bergquist to Eckerberg, Enclair telegram 440, 3 May 1974, File 55, Vol. 44, HP 79, UD, RA.
93. Gilde, *Österreich im KSZE-Prozess*, 159–69.
94. Berg to Bergquist, Cipher telegram 33, 9 May 1974, File 55, Vol. 44, HP 79, UD, RA.
95. Loth, *Overcoming the Cold War*, 100–127; Jussi M. Hanhimäki, *The Flawed Architect: Henry Kissinger and American Foreign Policy* (Oxford: Oxford University Press, 2004), 350–52.
96. Hichens-Bergström to Edelstam, Cipher telegram 36, 9 May 1974; Berg to Bergquist, Cipher telegram 34, 10 May 1974, File 55, Vol. 44, HP 79, UD, RA.
97. Lagerfelt to UD, Telegram 634, 13 May 1974, File 55, Vol. 44, HP 79, UD, RA.
98. Hichens-Bergström to Edelstam, Cipher telegram 36, 15 May 1974, File 55, Vol. 44, HP 79, UD, RA.
99. Åström, 'Besök av polske ambassadören', 17 May 1974, File 55, Vol. 44, HP 79, UD, RA.
100. Hichens-Bergström to Edelstam, Cipher telegram 38, 17 May 1974, File 55, Vol. 44, HP 79, UD, RA.
101. UD Press Department, 'Pressammandrag av anförande av ambassadör Hichens-Bergström inför den europeiska säkerhets- och samarbetskonferensen i Genève', 17 May 1974, File 55, Vol. 44, HP 79, UD, RA.
102. Wachtmeister had been appointed ambassador to Washington in May 1974. This ended the diplomatic crisis between Sweden and the United States, which had persisted since Palme's harsh criticism of the Vietnam War in late 1972. Wachtmeister to UD, Cipher telegram 183, 20 May 1974, File 55, Vol. 44, HP 79, UD, RA.
103. Hichens-Bergström to Edelstam, Cipher telegram 40, 22 May 1974, File 55, Vol. 44, HP 79, UD, RA.
104. Lagerfelt to UD, Telegram 695, 27 May 1974, File 55, Vol. 44, HP 79, UD, RA.
105. Åström to Wachtmeister, Cipher telegram 146, 22 May 1974; Åström to Wachtmeister, Cipher telegram 192, 24 May 1974, File 55, Vol. 44, HP 79, UD, RA. See also Gilde, *Österreich im KSZE-Prozess*, 169–80.
106. Hichens-Bergström, Cipher telegram 42, 28 May 1974, File 55, Vol. 44, HP 79, UD, RA. For a full account of how the Swedish government perceived the deadlock and its eventual effects, see Åström to Swedish Embassies/Consulates, Enclair telegram, 30 May 1974, File 55, Vol. 44, HP 79, UD, RA.
107. Quote from Fischer, *Neutral Power*, 274.
108. Although Olof Palme is not mentioned in the correspondence, the extent and level of the plan indicates that he was privy to it or even the mastermind behind it. Åström to Ryding, Cipher telegram 22 and Åström to Eng, Cipher telegram, 28 May 1974, File 55, Vol. 44, HP 79, UD, RA.
109. Hichens-Bergström to Åström, Telegram, 29 May 1974, File 55, Vol. 44, HP 79, UD, RA; Karl Fritschi, 'Schweden und die KSZE: Besuch von Botschafter Sverker Astroem, Generalsekretär im Aussenministerium', 28 May 1974, 766, 1987/78, E 2001(E), BAR.
110. Hichens-Bergström to Edelstam, Telegram 724, 29 May 1974, File 55, Vol. 44, HP 79, UD, RA.
111. Eng to Åström, Cipher telegram 218, 30 May 1974, File 55, Vol. 44, HP 79, UD, RA.
112. 'Aufzeichnung des Gesprächs mit dem Generalsekretär des schwedischen Aussenministeriums, Sverker Astroem, in Bern am 29. Mai 1974', 29 May 1974, Handakten [HA] Bindschedler, 1, 1993/210, E 2814, BAR.

113. Åström to Swedish Embassies/Consulates, 30 May 1974; Åström to De Besche, Enclair telegram 158, 30 May 1974; Engfeldt, 'Samtal i Bern ang. ESK', 31 May 1974, File 55, Vol. 44, HP 79, UD, RA.
114. Åström to Ryding, Enclair telegram, 30 May 1974, File 55, Vol. 44, HP 79, UD, RA.
115. Eckerberg to UD, Cipher telegram 43, 31 May 1974, File 55, Vol. 44, HP 79, UD, RA.
116. Lagerfelt to UD, Telegram 732, 31 May 1974, File 55, Vol. 44, HP 79, UD, RA.
117. Malmaeus to Åström, Cipher telegram 23, 3 June 1974; Åkerren to UD, Cipher telegram 37, 5 June 1974; Ingemar Hägglöf to UD, Cipher telegram 53, 10 June 1974, File 56, Vol. 44, HP 79, UD, RA.
118. Möller to Åström, 'Norge och ESK', 4 June 1974; Finnmark to Åström, Cipher telegram 50, 6 June 1974, File 56, Vol. 44, HP 79, UD, RA.
119. Nuenlist, 'East-West dialog', 213.
120. Interestingly, Ryding refers to three neutrals rather than four, which indicates that Finland was not recognized by all officials as part of the N+N. See Ryding to UD, Cipher telegram 25, 5 June 1974, File 56, Vol. 44, HP 79, UD, RA.
121. On the origins of the package deal, see Reimaa, *Helsinki Catch*, 79–82.
122. Petri to Åström, Cipher telegram 68, 7 June 1974, File 56, Vol. 44, HP 79, UD, RA.
123. Eng till Åström, Cipher telegram 230, 9 June 1974, File 56, Vol. 44, HP 79, UD, RA.
124. Åström to Hichens-Bergström, Cipher telegram, 10 June 1974; Hichens-Bergström to Åström and Edelstam, Telegram 792, 12 June 1974, File 56, Vol. 44, HP 79, UD, RA.
125. Edelstam to Swedish Delegation Geneva, Enclair telegram, 12 June 1974, File 56, Vol. 44, HP 79, UD, RA.
126. Lundvik to Swedish Embassies, 12 June 1974, File 56, Vol. 44, HP 79, UD, RA.
127. Hichens-Bergström to Åström and Edelstam, Telegram 813, 13 June 1974, File 56, Vol. 44, HP 79, UD, RA.
128. Bergquist, 'PM angående sovjetiske ambassadören Jakovlevs samtal med utrikesminister Andersson den 17 juni 1974', 18 June 1974, File 56, Vol. 44, HP 79, UD, RA.
129. Hichens-Bergström to Åström, Cipher telegram 44, 19 June 1974, File 56, Vol. 44, HP 79, UD, RA.
130. DeBesche to Åström, 'ESK', 17 June 1974, File 56, Vol. 44, HP 79, UD, RA.
131. Reimaa, *Helsinki Catch*, 82–89.
132. Lagerfelt to Bergquist, Telegram 876, 26 June 1974, File 56, Vol. 44, HP 79, UD, RA.
133. Hichens-Bergström to Bergquist, Telegram 907, 1 July 1974, File 57, Vol. 44, HP 79, UD, RA.
134. Lagerfelt to Edelstam and Bergquist, Telegram 899, 1 July 1974, File 57, Vol. 44, HP 79, UD, RA.
135. Lagerfelt to UD, Telegram 921, 5 July 1974, File 57, Vol. 44, HP 79, UD, RA. For meticulous information on the development leading to the Swedish withdrawal, see telegrams 298, 480, 914, 926, 933, 946 and 962. See also Fischer, *Neutral Power*, 278–93.
136. Bergquist, 'Telefonsamtal Palme-Sorsa', 8 July 1974, File 57, Vol. 44, HP 79, UD, RA.
137. Hichens-Bergström to Bergquist and Blix, Cipher telegram 54, 12 July 1974, File 57, Vol. 44, HP 79, UD, RA.
138. Hichens-Bergström to UD, Telegram 972, 12 July 1974, File 57, Vol. 44, HP 79, UD, RA.
139. Berg, 'Samtal den 18 juli 1974 med medlem av sovjetiska delegationen vid ESK, K. Gribin', 20 July 1974, File 57, Vol. 44, HP 79, UD, RA.
140. Lagerfelt to UD, Telegram 1075, 31 July 1974, File 57, Vol. 44, HP 79, UD, RA. See also Reimaa, *Helsinki Catch*, 89–95.

141. Berg to Bergquist, 'ESK II – Paketlösningen', 1 August 1974, File 58, Vol. 45, HP 79, UD, RA.
142. Elliott to Callaghan, 'CSCE: The Long Haul', 29 July 1974, FCO 28/2456, TNA.
143. Hichens-Bergström to Andersson, 'Kring den europeiska säkerhetskonferensen, juli 1974', 29 July 1974; Berg to Bergquist, 'De neutralas paketlösning', 30 July 1974, File 58, Vol. 45, HP 79, UD, RA.
144. Badalassi, 'Mediterranean Stake', 65–66.
145. Romano, *Détente*, 182. See also Asp, 'ESK II. "General stock-taking" av de Nios positioner i korg 1 och korg 3', 31 July 1974, File 58, Vol. 45, HP 79, UD, RA.
146. Wenger and Mastny, 'New Perspectives, 183.
147. Berg, 'Möte om ESK den 22/8 1974 under kabinettssekreteraren Åströms ledning. Sammanfattning av diskussionen rörande Sveriges agerande under de fortsatta ESK–förhandlingarna', 27 August 1974, File 58, Vol. 45, HP 79, UD, RA.
148. Berg, 'Möte om ESK den 22 augusti 1974', 27 August 1974, File 58, Vol. 45, HP 79, UD, RA.
149. 'Besuch Aussenminister Anderssons in der Schweiz, 11.–13.9.1974 – schwedische Kommentare. Kurzauszug', II-Pol/Schweden, BMfaA, ÖStA/AdR.
150. Lagerfelt to UD, Telegram 1205, 16 September 1974, File 59, Vol. 45, HP 79, UD, RA.
151. Nils-Erik Schyberg, 'ESK II: sammanträde med den neutrala och alliansfria gruppen', 17 September 1974, File 59, Vol. 45, HP 79, UD, RA.
152. Backlund to UD, Cipher telegram 54, 20 September 1974, File 59, Vol. 45, HP 79, UD, RA.
153. Hägglöf to UD, Cipher telegram 95, 19 September 1974, Hellners to UD, 'ESK', 20 September 1974, File 59, Vol. 45, HP 79, UD, RA.
154. Lagerfelt to UD, Telegram 1252, 23 September 1974; Örn to UD, Cipher telegram 393, 26 September 1974, File 59, Vol. 45, HP 79, UD, RA.
155. Austrian embassy The Hague (Coreth), 'Olof Palme zu Besuch in Den Haag', 13 September 1974 and Austrian embassy Stockholm (Schober), 'Besuch Aussenminister Anderssons in der Schweiz – schwedische Kommentare', 24 September 1974, II-Pol/Schweden, BMfaA, ÖStA/AdR. See also 'Visite en Suisse de M. Sven Andersson, Ministre des affaires étrangères de la Suède du 11 au 13 septembre 1974', 20 September 1974, 766, 1987/78, E 2001(E), BAR.
156. Wollter, 'ESK; kommentar till cypriotiska och italienska förslagen till Medelhavsdeklaration', 24 September 1974, File 59, Vol. 45, HP 79, UD, RA.
157. Lagerfelt to UD, Telegram 1270, 26 September 1974, File 59, Vol. 45, HP 79, UD, RA.
158. Edelstam to Hichens-Bergström, Cipher telegram, 26 September 1974, File 59, Vol. 45, HP 79, UD, RA.
159. Edelstam to Åström, Cipher telegram, 26 September 1974, File 59, Vol. 45, HP 79, UD, RA.
160. Hichens-Bergström to Edelstam, Cipher telegram 73, 27 September 1974, File 59, Vol. 45, HP 79, UD, RA.
161. Edelstam to Åström, Cipher telegram 155, 27 September 1974, File 59, Vol. 45, HP 79, UD, RA.
162. Ibid.
163. Edelstam to Hichens-Bergström, Cipher telegram, 1 October 1974, File 59, Vol. 45, HP 79, UD, RA.
164. Hichens-Bergström to Edelstam, Cipher telegram 76, 4 October 1974, File 59, Vol. 45, HP 79, UD, RA.
165. Ibid.
166. Ibid.

167. Åström to Hichens-Bergström, Cipher telegram, 7 October 1974, File 59, Vol. 45, HP 79, UD, RA.
168. Hichens-Bergström to Edelstam, Cipher telegram 76, 4 October 1974, File 59, Vol. 45, HP 79, UD, RA.
169. Ibid.
170. Tallroth to Edelstam, 8 October 1974, File 60, Vol. 45, HP 79, UD, RA.
171. Mats Fors, *Svarta Nejlikan*.
172. Peter, *Die Bundesrepublik im KSZE-Prozess*, 101; Snyder, *Human Rights Activism*, 27–29.
173. Hichens-Bergström to Edelstam, Cipher telegram 67, 2 October 1974, File 59, Vol. 45, HP 79, UD, RA.
174. Hyltenius, 'Samtal i New York mellan Sveriges och Sovjetunionens utrikesministrar', 3 October 1974, File 59, Vol. 45, HP 79, UD, RA.
175. Lagerfelt to UD, Telegram 1358, 14 October 1974, File 60, Vol. 45, HP 79, UD, RA.
176. Lagerfelt to UD, Telegram 1396, 21 October 1974, File 60, Vol. 45, HP 79, UD, RA.
177. Gilde, *Österreich im KSZE-Prozess*, 181–86.
178. Hichens-Bergström to Åström and Edelstam, Cipher telegram 73, 23 October 1974, File 60, Vol. 45, HP 79, UD, RA.
179. Hichens-Bergström to Åström and Edelstam, Cipher telegram 74, 23 October 1974, File 60, Vol. 45, HP 79, UD, RA.
180. Hichens-Bergström to Åström and Edelstam, Cipher telegram 85 and Schyberg, Samtal med Kerstin Asp, 'Samtal med Kerstin Asp angående ESK', 25 October 1974, File 60, Vol. 45, HP 79, UD, RA.
181. Hamilton to Edelstam, Cipher telegram 76, 28 October 1974; Hichens-Bergström to Åström and Edelstam, Cipher telegram 77, 30 October 1974, File 60, Vol. 45, HP 79, UD, RA.
182. Åström to Swedish Delegation Geneva, 30 October 1974, File 60, Vol. 45, HP 79, UD, RA.
183. Ryding to UD, Cipher telegram 55, 14 November 1974; Bergquist and Schyberg, 'ESK II: svensk-finska meningsskiljaktigheter', 12 November 1974, File 60, Vol. 45, HP 79, UD, RA.
184. Drawing on public documents and interviews only, Leatherman naturally failed to include these recurring tensions between the Swedish and Finnish delegations in her narrative; see Leatherman, 'Engaging East and West', 448–81 and Zielinski, *Die neutralen und blockfreien*, 230–40.
185. See also introductory chapter and Makko, 'Sweden, Europe'.
186. Schyberg, 'ESK II. Kortfattad sammanfattning av läget', 1 November 1974, File 60, Vol. 45, HP 79, UD, RA.
187. Schyberg, 'ESK II: Sammanträde på UD under kabinettssekreterarens ordförandeskap den 4/11 1974', 4 November 1974, File 60, Vol. 45, HP 79, UD, RA.
188. Lagerfelt to UD, Telegram 1499, 11 November 1974, File 60, Vol. 45, HP 79, UD, RA.
189. Hichens-Bergström to Åström and Edelstam, Cipher telegram 80, 12 November 1974, File 60, Vol. 45, HP 79, UD, RA.
190. Hichens-Bergström to Åström and Edelstam, Cipher telegram 81, 15 November 1974, File 60, Vol. 45, HP 79, UD, RA.
191. Hichens-Bergström to Edelstam, Cipher telegram 82, 20 November 1974, File 60, Vol. 45, HP 79, UD, RA.
192. Åström to Swedish delegation Geneva and embassies Helsinki, Vienna, Berne, 25 November 1974, File 60, Vol. 45, HP 79, UD, RA.
193. The meeting was actually an offspring of the Swedish initiative in the summer; see Fischer, *Neutral Power*, 322.

194. Hichens-Bergström to Åström, Cipher telegram 84, 6 December 1974, File 61, Vol. 46, HP 79, UD, RA.
195. Hichens-Bergström to Åström, Telegram 1676, 16 December 1974; Hichens-Bergström to Edelstam, Telegram 1693, 21 December 1974, File 61, Vol. 46, HP 79, UD, RA.
196. Hichens-Bergström to Edelstam, Telegram 1693, 21 December 1974, File 61, Vol. 46, HP 79, UD, RA. See also Berg, 'ESK – Anteckningar från möte mellan statssekreterarna i Sveriges, Finlands, Österrikes och Schweiz' utrikesministerier i Zürich onsdagen den 18 december 1974 rörande de neutralas agerande i ESK', 20 January 1975, File 62, HP 79, UD, Regeringskansliets Arkiv (RegA).
197. Lagerfelt to UD, Telegram 1577, 25 November 1974, File 60, Vol. 45, HP 79, UD, RA.
198. Lagerfelt to UD, Telegram 1610, 2 December 1974, File 61, Vol. 46, HP 79, UD, RA.
199. Hichens-Bergström to Åström, 'Skuggor och dagrar på ESK-scenen', 29 November 1974, File 61, Vol. 46, HP 79, UD, RA.
200. Ibid. Contrary to expectations, these tasks were performed within a week. See Lagerfelt to UD, Telegram 1640, 7 December 1974, File 61, Vol. 46, HP 79, UD, RA.
201. Romano, *Détente*, 214; Ferraris, *Report*, 144; Boel, 'French Support', 233.
202. Örn to UD, Cipher telegram 534, 10 December 1974; Hichens-Bergström to Åström, Cipher telegram 87, 12 December 1974, File 61, Vol. 46, HP 79, UD, RA.
203. Åström to Hichens-Bergström, 2 December 1974, File 61, Vol. 46, HP 79, UD, RA.
204. Lagerfelt to UD, Telegram 92, 27 January 1975, File 62, HP 79, UD, RegA.
205. Bergquist, 'Förslag från Sovjet, Frankrike, USA och Storbritannien', 13 February 1975, File 62, HP 79, UD, RegA.
206. Edelstam to Leifland, 'Personalläget vid ESK-delegationen', 11 February 1975, File 62, HP 79, UD, RegA.
207. Edelstam to Leifland, Cipher telegram, 25 February 1975, File 62, HP 79, UD, RegA.
208. Lagerfelt to UD, Telegram 258, 3 March 1975, File 63, HP 79, UD, RegA.
209. The proposal had been a reaction to Finnish pushes towards a treatment of 'technicalities' related to the third stage, which had been presented to the Western delegations before, and ultimately included a Romanian proposal. Eng to UD, Telegram 200, 4 March 1975, File 63, HP 79, UD, RegA.
210. Edelstam, 'Sveriges agerande i fråga om påskpaus' and 'Sveriges förslag om en speciell arbetsgrupp för diskussion av ESK:s tredje fas', File 63, HP 79, UD, RegA.
211. Edelstam to Åström, Cipher telegram, 10 March 1975, File 63, HP 79, UD, RegA.
212. Edelstam to Leifland, Telegram 322, 12 March 1975, File 63, HP 79, UD, RegA.
213. Edelstam to Leifland, Telegram 313, 11 March 1975, File 63, HP 79, UD, RegA.
214. Edelstam to Leifland, Telegram 373, 20 March 1975, File 63, HP 79, UD, RegA.
215. Edelstam to Leifland, Telegram 356, and Leifland to Edelstam, Enclair telegram, 18 March 1975, File 63, HP 79, UD, RegA.
216. *FRUS* 1975, 21.
217. 'Visit of Minister of State at FCO to Sweden (Mr Hattersley)', 27 February 1975, FCO 33/2792, TNA.
218. Edelstam to UD, Telegram 376, 20 March 1975, File 63, HP 79, UD, RegA.
219. Lagerfelt to UD, Telegram 471, 14 April 1975, File 63, HP 79, UD, RegA.
220. Lagerfelt to UD, Telegram 561, 28 April 1975; Colliander to UD, Telegram 594, 5 May 1975, File 64, HP 79, UD, RegA.
221. Eng to UD, Cipher telegram 209, 5 May 1975, File 64, HP 79, UD, RegA.
222. Swedish Delegation Strasbourg to UD, 'Europarådets ministerkommitté diskuterar ESK', 23 April 1975, File 64, HP 79, UD, RegA.

223. Edelstam to Andersson, 'Läget vid den europeiska säkerhetskonferensen', 5 May 1975, File 64, HP 79, UD, RegA.
224. Ibid.
225. Edelstam to Åström, Cipher telegram 34, 16 May 1975; for a complete list of Swedish aims by late May 1975, Schyberg, 'ESK II: Sveriges ståndpunkt i några viktigare utestående frågor', 21 May 1975, File 64, HP 79, UD, RegA.
226. Ibid.
227. Lagerfelt to UD, Telegram 680, 16 May 1975, File 64, HP 79, UD, RegA.
228. Edelstam to UD, Cipher telegram 'Från ESK-delegationen: Spekulationer om tidtabellen', 14 May 1975, File 64, HP 79, UD, RegA.
229. Edelstam to UD, Cipher telegram 35, 21 May 1975; Cipher telegram 36, 23 May 1975; Lagerfelt to UD, Telegram 709, 26 May 1975, File 64, HP 79, UD, RegA.
230. Edelstam to UD, Cipher telegram 39, 27 May 1975, File 64, HP 79, UD, RegA.
231. Wachtmeister to Leifland, 'ESK', 17 June 1975, File 65, HP 79, UD, RegA. This also occurred in mid-July; see Lundvik, 'Besök av turkiske chargé d'affaires Kiciman', 14 July 1975 and Lundvik to Swedish Embassies Ankara, Geneva, Athens, New York, Cipher telegram, 15 July 1975, File 65, HP 79, UD, RegA.
232. Edelstam to UD, Cipher telegram 40, 27 May 1975 and Lagerfelt to UD, Telegram 748, 2 June 1975, File 64, HP 79, UD, RegA.
233. Lagerfelt to UD, Telegram 784, 9 June 1975, File 64, HP 79, UD, RegA.
234. Edelstam to Leifland, Telegram 830, 18 June 1975, File 65, HP 79, UD, RegA.
235. Lagerfelt to UD, Telegram 860, 23 June 1975, File 65, HP 79, UD, RegA.
236. Lagerfelt to Leifland, Telegram 892; Bergquist, 'Läget vid ESK', 26 June 1975, File 65, HP 79, UD, RegA.
237. Edelstam to Leifland, Cipher telegram 47, 2 July 1975; Swedish CSCE Delegation to Leifland, Telegram 931, 3 July 1975, File 65, HP 79, UD, RegA.
238. Edelstam to Leifland, Telegram 959, 8 July 1975; Edelstam to Leifland, Telegram 968, 9 July 1975; Edelstam to Åström and Leifland, Telegram 974, 10 July 1975, File 65, HP 79, UD, RegA.
239. Leifland to UD, Cipher telegram, 'Strängt förtroligt från Leifland. Endast för tjf polchefen', 11 July 1975, File 65, HP 79, UD, RegA.
240. Berg to Schyberg, Telegram 711, 27 May 1975, File 64, HP 79, UD, RegA.
241. Lagerfelt to UD, Telegram 1041, 21 July 1975, File 65, HP 79, UD, RegA.
242. Edelstam to Leifland, 'ESK III – utkast till statsministerns anförande', 11 July 1975, File 65; Thyberg to Edelstam, Enclair Telegram, 22 July 1975, File 66, HP 79, UD, RegA.
243. Edelstam to Andersson, 'Den europeiska säkerhetskonferensens förhandlingsfas avslutad', 21 July 1975, File 66, HP 79, UD, RegA.
244. Ibid.
245. Ibid.
246. Fischer, *Neutral Power*, 319.
247. Thyberg to Edelstam, Enclair telegram, 22 July 1975, File 66, HP 79, UD, RegA.
248. Thyberg to Palme, 'ESK', 24 July 1975, File 66, HP 79, UD, RegA.
249. Ryding to UD, Telegram 249, 22 July 1975, File 66, HP 79, UD, RegA.
250. See Appendix 3.
251. Gyllenhaal to Swedish Embassy Helsinki, Enclair telegram 241, 30 July 1975, File 68, HP 79, UD, RegA.
252. Rosenberg to Swedish Embassy Helsinki, Enclair telegram, 23 July 1975, File 66, HP 79, UD, RegA; Fischer, *Neutral Power*, 317–18.

253. Reimaa, *Helsinki Catch*, 142.
254. Anders Stephanson, 'Om samtalet mellan Palme och Kissinger', *Arkiv för studier i arbetarrörelsens historia*, 86–87, 2002, 35–43, available at the Labour Movement Archives and Library in Stockholm: 3 Minnesanteckningar, protokoll mm (1965), 1 Minnesanteckningar, protokoll mm (1953–1965), 2 Egna Verk (1944–1986), OPA, ARAB.
255. *FRUS* 1975, 52–57.
256. Ibid., 55–56.
257. This has been rightly observed in Fischer, *Neutral Power*, 320–21.
258. See, for example, Ryding to UD, 19 January 1973, File 30, Vol. 35; Wollter, 'Den europeiska säkerhetskonferensen och ECE:s framtida roll', 22 February 1973, File 36, Vol. 37; Berg, 'Rumänien och ESK', 26 June 1973, File 41, Vol. 39, HP 79, UD, RA.
259. Thyberg to Nyström, 'Bonn och säkerhetskonferensen', 14 March 1972, File 18, Vol. 31, HP 79, UD, RA.

Conclusion

It is fair to say that Sweden's approach to the CSCE and its contribution to the Helsinki Final Act were based on realpolitik thinking. The years between 1969 and 1975 were a turbulent period in the history of Sweden's foreign relations. The replacement of long-standing Prime Minister Tage Erlander by Olof Palme in October 1969 marked the culmination of a social, cultural and political transition which the country had been undergoing since the early 1960s. Three simultaneous developments – the success of the so-called Swedish model, four decades of sustained Social Democratic government majority and the liberation of numerous Third World countries – allowed the small Nordic country to establish itself in a new position in global affairs. The ruling party's outspoken internationalism appealed to young voters at home and among Third World representatives, and by the mid-1970s the Swedes received praise in the form of labels such as 'the good conscience of the world'.

With this new appellation, the armed isolationism that had been the cornerstone of Swedish neutrality in the 1950s was finally abandoned. The youthful Palme, to many a Swedish version of US president John F. Kennedy, was a genuine and well-connected internationalist who contributed greatly to the new 'active foreign policy', a blend of vociferous criticism of the superpowers, preservation of good offices at the UN and a strong commitment to development aid.

Given these characteristics, it seemed natural to the world that Sweden would fully embrace détente and welcome a conference on security in Europe, without any ifs, ands or buts. Yet the Swedish government and its officials at the Ministry for Foreign Affairs in Stockholm perceived the CSCE as problematic until the Four Power Agreement on Berlin and the breakthrough of Willy Brandt's *Neue Ostpolitik* in late 1971 and, after that, saw it at best as a tedious challenge. We have looked closely at this lack of enthusiasm and vision. Four reasons, originating in two overarching and reciprocal research questions, were presented in the introductory chapter.

Sweden's contribution to the process leading to the Helsinki Final Act, and the reasons behind the country's approach, were explored and contrasted with the broader Swedish active foreign policy. Furthermore, the perception of Swedish CSCE policy by other states and, to a lesser extent, the reactions of the public and the media were investigated in the four empirical chapters. The analysis of Sweden's performance was conducted with the help of Holsti's typology of national role conceptions. The following six roles proved particularly helpful in identifying the role performance of Sweden in the context of the CSCE: isolate, faithful friend, independent, active independent, bridge and mediator-integrator. Other roles, such as defender of the faith, regional subsystem collaborator, and example and developer are equally important, as they allow us to better understand the reasons for absent role conceptions.

Chapter 3 outlined why Sweden responded reluctantly to the establishment of the CSCE on the international agenda through the Budapest Appeal of the Warsaw Pact states issued on 17 March 1969. In addition to the fact that it saw the proposal as coming from the wrong side, Sweden was not under the same immediate Soviet pressure as Finland or Austria and, therefore, did not have any reason to shift focus away from global issues and the UN towards Europe.

In the earliest phase, between 1969 and 1971, Swedish interests at a security conference were not yet developed within the context of a generally cautious and sceptical approach to Europe. Therefore, Stockholm limited its action to supporting the policies of others, mainly of Finland and – due to the good relationship between Olof Palme and Willy Brandt – West Germany, and focused on the role of faithful friend to these countries in particular and the Western bloc more generally. Other than that, Sweden was much criticized for its unexpected isolationism, which looked odd in the eyes of both blocs and of the other European neutrals. Such role expectations were based on impressions created by Swedish activism, which, however, was not applicable in European affairs.

Thus, the reason for the early and persistent Swedish reluctance towards a security conference lay in the construction and nature of Sweden's Cold War foreign policy, which revolved around three spheres: national neutrality, Nordic cooperation and global commitment. Europe, on the other hand, remained an uncertain element, mainly for three reasons. First, the Old Continent had been the scene of an epic separation of the world into two blocs; second, the Soviet Union and its communist satellite states in Eastern Europe were perceived as a threat; third, (continental) Western Europe was viewed as capitalist, clerical, conservative and cartelistic, and thus incompatible with a progressive state such as Sweden. This image of Western Europe, based on the realities of the 1950s, persisted despite the rise to power of several social democratic parties in Western Europe in the late 1960s. In the West, with which Sweden shared its liberal and democratic societal model, the United States and the United Kingdom were looked at more positively than were the continental Europeans.

This general framework was questioned and reconsidered, but eventually accepted, by Olof Palme, resulting in the Swedish refusal to apply for full membership in the EC in March 1971, due to political incompatibility with Swedish neutrality. In the following years, neutrality between the blocs and Democratic Socialism were both praised as offering an alternative third way in a world divided between, as Palme described it, stable democracies and stable dictatorships. Sweden accepted the European checkmate and dismissed radical change against the background of the violent suppression of popular uprisings in East Germany in 1953, Hungary in 1956 and Czechoslovakia in 1968. In the Swedish view, change could pave the road to disaster, and therefore Swedish decision makers never viewed the CSCE as the appropriate scene for idealist policies and revolutionary reforms.

In matters of European security, Sweden preferred evolution to stability, peace to revolution. Therefore, the country adopted what I have called a 'strategy of adjustment' in order to bridge the time gap between the cooperative Prague Declaration of the Warsaw Pact states in October 1969 and the final breakthrough of European détente brought about by West Germany's reconciliation with Poland and the Soviet Union and the Four Power Agreement on Berlin two years later.

The fourth chapter examined how Sweden abandoned isolationism once continued rapprochement in East-West relations paved the way for détente and in its place assumed a more open and independent, yet very pragmatic, stance based on realpolitik thinking. A working group was established in the Ministry for Foreign Affairs in early December 1971. It was led by Wilhelm Wachtmeister, the director of the political department, and would soon coordinate a machinery involving up to thirty officials from five ministries and experts from several external institutes, such as scholars Nils Andrén and Karl Birnbaum.

The working group integrated the tasks performed in four study groups: on disarmament, relations between states, economic and scientific-technological cooperation, and cultural relations and freer communications. This working structure, in addition to the highly technical nature of the negotiations carried out at the Dipoli Congress Centre outside Helsinki and in Geneva, allowed for a combined top-down and bottom-up approach to decision making within the general boundaries laid down by the government and the highest officials of the Ministry for Foreign Affairs in Stockholm. It also allowed Sweden to reconsider its options.

As a result, Sweden developed ambitions in regional disarmament which, despite the continued support of Finland, never reached a level that caused decision makers in Stockholm to integrate roles such as regional leader or regional subsystem collaborator into their set of role conceptions. In terms of role analysis, focus thus remained on Sweden being a faithful friend to Finland and the Western bloc, in particular West Germany, until the commencement of the multilateral talks at Dipoli in November 1972. Stockholm refrained from taking up the task of becoming a defender of the faith by emphasizing values and soft power issues such as human rights in Eastern Europe. Instead, Swedish ideas surrounding the CSCE originated almost exclusively in balance-of-power thinking. Foreign Minister Krister Wickman also rejected as premature efforts which could have resulted in Sweden becoming what Holsti defines as bridge or mediator-integrator. Also, Sweden remained one of very few countries which did not launch its own initiative.

This pragmatic interpretation of Sweden's role in the early process and attitude to the CSCE did not meet the expectations of a number of leftist activists and intellectuals in Sweden, who argued that their country should carry out a more active policy, with specific focus on international solidarity. At the same time, diplomats such as Wachtmeister and Axel Edelstam maintained that the Western demands for greater freedoms in Eastern Europe could be understood as an attack on the core of the socialist system and were likely to be counterproductive. Yet, such disagreements provoked little criticism, as they were concealed by the active foreign policy rhetoric applied in official statements, which referred often to Sweden's humanitarian tradition and seldom to the strict realism that dominated the Swedish approach.

The rather unintentional adoption of the role of bridge was explained in the fifth chapter. On 22 November 1972, the preparations for the CSCE shifted from bilateral to multilateral with the commencement of the multilateral preparatory talks at the Dipoli Conference Centre in Otaniemi, near Helsinki. From a Swedish perspective, the intense negotiations during the following nine and a half months carried with them a shift between the two roles adopted earlier. During the bilateral preparatory phase, the faithful friendship with Finland and the Western bloc had been an almost predominant feature of the Swedish policy, due to the absence of its own prominent goals. During the MPT, these relations came to be subordinated to the role of independent. The Swedes continued to receive information on internal developments from the Western bloc.

On the diplomatic level, for instance, Sweden maintained its cooperation with the United States, despite the irritation caused by Olof Palme's famous Christmas speech in which the Swedish prime minister equalled the US war strategy in Vietnam with Nazi crimes committed during the Holocaust. But the Swedes also started defining more concrete goals of their own, making 'policy decisions according to the state's own interests rather than in support of the objectives of other states' (see Figure 3.1). This was largely due to the abovementioned CSCE working group and its four study groups. The way of thinking, however, remained untouched, as the almost exclusive focus on security matters and the so-called first basket persisted. The third basket, in which the Western states pushed for freer movements and other human rights–related concessions, remained a nonpriority.

Sweden was not concerned with the opportunities of the third basket but rather with its limitations. Thus, the role performance of Sweden during the MPT cannot be linked to the roles of defender of the faith, liberation supporter or any other of the more idealistic and altruistic roles offered by Holsti. The MPT also forged the adoption of a central role within the N+N group, consisting of four neutral and five nonaligned states, which moved from loose collaboration to institutionalized cooperation by 1974. The N+N states tried to avoid becoming a third bloc but, nevertheless, performed a 'communication function', that is, acting as a 'translator or conveyor of messages and information', which is how Holsti defines the role of a bridge (see Figure 3.1).

One of the tasks that changed the individual orientation of the neutrals was the role of chair of the so-called minigroups, in which the different tasks of the conference agenda were discussed. Within the N+N group, Sweden and Switzerland enjoyed the greatest appreciation as 'honest brokers' from the Eastern and Western camps. During the Helsinki Tea Party, as the MPT was called by some, the efforts of Ambassador Göran Ryding, Hans Blix and Axel Edelstam and their contributions to the catalogue of principles and discussions on military security and disarmament, as well as other compromise formulas, earned Sweden a good reputation.

The sixth and last chapter analysed the Swedish performance at the three stages of the CSCE proper in Geneva and Helsinki between September 1973 and August 1975. During these two years, Sweden's role performance shifted before and after the summer of 1974. As a result of the cooperation between the neutral and nonaligned participants of the CSCE, Sweden became a respected mediator during the first year of negotiations in Geneva. The country's own interests were presented and advocated in a fashion that corresponds well with Holsti's active independence role, defined as 'self-determination, possible mediation functions, and active programs to extend diplomatic and commercial relations to diverse areas of the world'. Notably, the cooperation between the N+N states played a role almost similar to that of Nordic cooperation in the United Nations. The Swedes were on friendly terms with the Norwegians, who ultimately coordinated their positions within NATO.

Denmark, having joined the EC at the beginning of 1973, immediately took a maximalist stance on human rights, the most controversial issue at Geneva, and the debate on which Sweden became one of the most reserved non–Warsaw Pact states. Finland's self-centredness, caused by its troublesome relationship with the Soviet Union, resulted in continuing tension with Sweden. In contrast to the earlier years, Sweden therefore did not fully maintain the faithful friend role towards Finland. This expressed itself in the Swedish reservations towards the so-called Package Deal of July 1974 and resulted in several complaints against each other's policies. After the complete failure of Sweden's single major initiative at the CSCE in June 1974, the country fell back on its former isolationist behaviour. The major obstacle during the rest of the second stage was how to secure the results achieved in relation to military security in the first basket, the so-called confidence-building measures.

As had been the case since 1969, none of the more idealist roles offered in Holsti's typology – such as developer, defender of the faith or liberation supporter – were even considered throughout the three stages of the CSCE. With the exception of Richard Hichens-Bergström, the head of the Swedish delegation between the first stage and the end of 1974, and ambassador Tore Tallroth, the negotiator in the third basket, the Swedes advocated a strict realpolitik, with focus on security. Again, this was successfully concealed in speeches delivered by Prime Minister Olof Palme and Foreign Minister Sven Andersson.

Their addresses must be viewed as conscious attempts to create a convergence between Sweden's CSCE policy and the general image of their country's foreign policy during this era. With the CSCE negotiated behind closed doors and quickly becoming highly technical and specific, the dissonance between declared and real foreign policy was not obvious to the public eye. This allowed the decision makers to impede eventual debates about a moral dilemma. Few scholars studied the CSCE, and not too many newspapers and magazines reported regularly from it, either. Therefore, the public interest remained at a rather modest level until the Helsinki Summit of Heads of State on 1 August 1975.

On the whole, Sweden never developed a genuine belief in the opportunities offered by the CSCE. With the benefit of hindsight, one might rush to the conclusion that this was a failure in itself, as it proved a historical misjudgement. But few Western politicians and diplomats really expected the CSCE to have the kind of effect it eventually did. Still, if sometimes for tactical reasons, the Western states stood by their positions on freer movements and other items controversial to the communist states.

There are, however, several additional reasons Sweden's role during the early CSCE process does not stand out as another chapter in the success story of Swedish active foreign policy in the 1970s. Generally, the country's contribution to the making of the Helsinki Final Act was less significant than that of comparable states, such as Finland or Switzerland. Sweden did indeed engage in neutral and nonaligned efforts to mediate between the East and West, which brought about breakthroughs on several occasions – most notably in July 1974 through the Package Deal. But it never actually brought about any substantial initiative and remained the only neutral country not to bring forward a prominent diplomat to be highlighted in the historiography of the CSCE. During the years of détente, Sweden never sought to become the 'good conscience' of Europe.

This brings us to the point where the results of our enquiry must be put in perspective in order to move on to a discussion of the second question presented in the introduction. What do the findings presented here imply for the historical assessment of Sweden's active foreign policy, the *Palmelinjen*? It has been demonstrated that Sweden was as reluctant to carry out an active European security policy as it had been to participate in the European integration process. Generally, the Swedish government preferred stability and status quo to uncertainty, involvement and change, for which it was not willing to pay a political price. During the early CSCE process, Sweden never developed any faith in the value of freer movements and other extended rights for Eastern European citizens. Viewing the development in Europe from a strictly geostrategic and state-centred perspective, with focus on states and power balance, Stockholm was mainly concerned with political and military stability.

This left little space for concern about human rights violations committed by the communist regimes of Eastern Europe or any consideration of the applicability of Sweden's humanitarian tradition. Thus, Sweden's foreign policy identity in the 1970s must be thought of as containing a blend of pragmatic realpolitik thinking, particularly in the European realm, and active internationalist solidarity. This explains why Sweden criticized the far-reaching Western demands in the third basket when it believed they threatened the conclusion of the CSCE and the modest but relevant military results already achieved.

Taken together, this puts a question mark on the established notion of *aktiv utrikespolitik* as an internationalist policy centring on solidarity in the first place, as it is still seen by many. According to Swedish historian Bo Stråth, Olof Palme introduced moralism to foreign policy and led the transformation from armed isolationism to internationalist solidarity, as put forward by Bjereld, Johansson and Molin. But in Europe, at the heart of the Cold War division, Sweden's foreign policy contained very little of either moralism or solidarity. As a consequence, the traditional narrative must be considered as flawed, if not insupportable.

There is, nevertheless, little evidence to suggest that Palme's internationalism and that of his party were merely disingenuous attempts to win elections. Social democrats such as Hjalmar Branting and liberals such as Bertil Ohlin had introduced internationalism to Swedish foreign policy during the interwar period. With this historical heritage as a background, the introduction of moralism and solidarity as a reaction to a changing international environment was a meaningful and profitable move. In certain areas, however, security set boundaries for altruistic principles; and in the European sphere, these boundaries were particularly narrow.

Appendices

Register of Persons

Sven **Andersson** (1910–1987), Social Democrat, foreign minister from 1973 to 1976.
Bertil **Arvidson** (1921–2004), head of the Negotiation Committee (*förhandlingsgrupp*) at the Ministry for Foreign Affairs from 1972 to 1978.
Kerstin **Asp (Johnsson)** (*1942), secretary of embassy and member of delegations to the MPT and CSCE.
Sverker **Åström** (1915–2012), permanent representative to the UN from 1964 to 1970, chief negotiator with the EC between 1970 and 1972 and state secretary for foreign affairs from 1972 to 1977.
Ilmar **Bekeris** (1910–1990), undersecretary at the Ministry of Education, member of the Study Group on Cultural Relations and Freer Communications, expert for Basket III.
René **Belding** (1917–1993), embassy counsellor in Copenhagen between 1966 and 1974.
Leif **Belfrage** (1910–1990), ambassador in London from 1967 to 1972 and head of delegation to the OECD in Paris between 1972 and 1976.
Göran **Berg** (*1940), first secretary to the CSCE delegation and representative in the Subcommittee on Principles Guiding the Relations between States (A).
Kaj **Björk** (1918–2014), Social Democrat, director-general for trade policy and expert at the Ministry for Foreign Affairs.
Hans **Blix** (*1928), Liberal, expert on international law, foreign minister from 1978 to 1979 and member of the delegation to the CCD.
Hubert **De Besche** (1911–1997), ambassador in Washington from 1964 to 1973 and in Copenhagen between 1973 and 1977.
Lennart **Eckerberg** (*1928), member of the delegation to the CCD and negotiator in Basket I.

Axel **Edelstam** (1924–2012), deputy director of the Political Section at the Ministry for Foreign Affairs between 1972 and 1975 and head of delegation to the CSCE between January and July 1975.

Brynolf **Eng** (1910–1988), ambassador in Rome from 1966 to 1973 and in Moscow and Ulan Bator between 1973 and 1975.

Ulf **Ericsson,** Ministry for Foreign Affairs and member of the Study Group on Disarmament.

Hans **Ewerlöf** (*1929), Ministry for Foreign Affairs, head of the Study Group on Economic, Industrial, Commercial and Technical-Scientific Cooperation.

Kaj **Falkman** (*1934), member of the CSCE Working Group and first secretary to the CSCE delegation (Basket III).

Per Olof **Forshell** (1928–1991), member of the Study Group on Disarmament.

Gunnar **Hägglöf** (1904–1994), permanent representative to the UN in 1947–1948, ambassador in London between 1948 and 1967 and in Paris from 1967 to 1971.

Ingemar **Hägglöf** (1912–1995), ambassador in Helsinki between 1964 and 1971 and in Paris from 1971 to 1978.

Gustaf **Hamilton** af Hageby (*1921), member of the CSCE delegation (Basket I).

Richard (Dick) **Hichens-Bergström** (1913–1989), head of the CSCE delegation from September 1973 to December 1974.

Claes **Huldtgren** (1922–1973), counsellor at the embassy in Helsinki between 1968 and 1973.

Gunnar **Jarring** (1907–2002), permanent representative to the UN from 1956 to 1958, ambassador in Washington between 1958 and 1964 and in Moscow from 1964 to 1973.

Ole **Jödahl** (1910–1982), state secretary for foreign affairs between 1967 and 1972 and ambassador in London between 1972 and 1976.

Leif **Leifland** (1925–2015), chargé d'affaires in Washington in 1973–1974 and director of the Political Section between 1975 and 1977.

Nils Börje **Leuf** (1918–1998), Ministry of Trade and member of the Study Group on Economic, Industrial, Commercial and Technical-Scientific Cooperation.

Sigge **Lilliehöök** (1913–2004), ambassador in Budapest between 1969 and 1973.

Dag **Malm** (1923–1990), head of Second Bureau of the Political Section between 1967 and 1970.

Cai **Melin** (1925–2013), member of the Study Group on Economic, Industrial, Commercial and Technical-Scientific Cooperation.

Nils **Montan** (1916–1986), ambassador in Bonn between 1967 and 1972.

Alva **Myrdal** (1902–1986), Social Democrat, head of CCD delegation between 1962 and 1973 and 1982 Nobel Peace Prize laureate.

Gunnar **Myrdal** (1898–1987), Social Democrat, ECE executive secretary from 1947 to 1957, president of SIPRI between 1967 and 1973, 1974 Nobel Memorial Prize in Economics laureate.

Manfred **Nilsson** (1915–2000), ministry for foreign affairs, member of the Study Group on Cultural Relations and Freer Communications.

Torsten **Nilsson** (1905–1997), Social Democrat, foreign minister between 1962 and 1971.

Rune **Nyström** (1925–2004), Ministry for Foreign Affairs, member of the CSCE Working Group.

Jan **Olsson,** press attaché, member of the delegation to the CSCE.

Olof **Palme** (1927–1986), prime minister between 1969 and 1976 and from 1982 to 1986.

Lennart **Petri** (1914–1996), ambassador in Vienna between 1969 and 1976.

Ulf **Reinius** (1918–1985), defence staff, expert on military issues (Basket I).

Mats **Ringborg** (*1945), first secretary in the delegation to the CSCE (Basket II).

Agda **Rössel** (1910–2001), ambassador in Prague between 1969 and 1973.

Lennart **Rydfors** (1922–1999), head of Trade Section at the Ministry for Foreign Affairs in 1972 and member of the Swedish delegation to the MPT.

Göran **Ryding** (1916–2007), deputy state secretary for foreign affairs from 1967 to 1971, ambassador in Helsinki from 1971 to 1975 and in Moscow between 1975 and 1979.

Tore **Tallroth** (1912–1992), cultural attaché and negotiator in Basket III in 1973–1974.

Inga **Thorsson** (1915–1994), Social Democrat, head of CCD delegation between 1974 and 1982.

Magnus **Vahlquist** (*1938), first secretary to the CSCE delegation (Basket II).

Wilhelm **Wachtmeister** (1923–2012), director of the Political Section between 1968 and 1974 and ambassador in Washington from 1974 to 1989.

Krister **Wickman** (1924–1993), Social Democrat, foreign minister between 1971 and 1973.

Karl-Anders **Wollter** (*1927), consul general in Leningrad in 1972 and deputy head of department and expert on Basket II issues.

Torgil **Wulff** (1916–1986), defence ministry, member of the Study Group on Principles for Relations between States.

The Helsinki Final Act's Declaration on Principles Guiding Relations between Participating States

I. Sovereign equality, respect for the rights inherent in sovereignty
II. Refraining from the threat or use of force
III. Inviolability of frontiers
IV. Territorial integrity of states
V. Peaceful settlement of disputes
VI. Nonintervention in internal affairs
VII. Respect for human rights and fundamental freedoms, including the freedom of thought, conscience, religion or belief
VIII. Equal rights and self-determination of peoples
IX. Cooperation among states
X. Fulfilment in good faith of obligations under international law

Swedish delegations to the MPT and the CSCE (including experts)

Multilateral Preparatory Talks at the Dipoli Congress Centre in Otaniemi, 22 November 1972–8 June 1973

Permanent: Göran Ryding, Kerstin Asp, Göran Berg, Jan Olsson; *Other:* Wilhelm Wachtmeister, Axel Edelstam, Rune Nyström, Lennart Rydfors, Torgil Wulff, Jan Prawitz, Hans Blix, Tore Tallroth, Manfred Nilsson, Hans Ewerlöf, Nils Börje Leuf, Sten Niklasson, Ilmar Bekeris, Desirée Edmar

First Stage of the CSCE in Helsinki, 3–7 July 1973

Krister Wickman, Sverker Åström, Göran Ryding, Kaj Björk, Wilhelm Wachtmeister, Tore Tallroth, Axel Edelstam, Rolf Ekéus, Göran Berg, Kerstin Asp, Jan Olsson

Second Stage of the CSCE in Geneva, 18 September 1973–21 July 1975[1]

Head of Delegation: Richard Hichens-Bergström (–December 1974), Axel Edelstam (January 1975–); *Basket I:* Lennart Eckerberg, Gustaf Hamilton af Hageby (October 1973–) [Hans Blix, Ulf Reinius, Jan Prawitz, Torgil Wulff]; *Basket II:* Bertil Arvidson (1975), Gustav Ekholm (February 1975–) [Karl-Anders Wollter, Stanislaw Patek, Mats Ringborg, Lennart Watz]; *Basket III:* Tore Tallroth, Håkan Wilkens (February–April 1975) (Ilmar Bekeris); *Secretaries:* Göran Berg (I), Magnus Vahlquist (II), Mathias Mossberg (II, July 1974–), Kerstin Asp (III), Desirée Edmar (III), Kaj Falkman (III), Nils-Erik Schyberg, Jan Söderberg (August 1974–), *Press Attaché:* Jan Olsson

Third Stage of the CSCE in Helsinki, 30 July 1975–1 August 1975

Olof Palme, Sven Andersson, Sverker Åström, Anders Thunborg, Richard Hichens-Bergström, Göran Ryding, Bertil Arvidson, Leif Leifland, Axel Edelstam, Torgil Wulff, Ulf Reinius, Ilmar Bekeris, Manfred Nilsson, Pierre Schori, Göran Berg, Hans Dahlgren, Nils-Erik Schyberg, Kerstin Asp, Jan Olsson

Notes

1. Experts in brackets. Some officials and experts alternated between different roles; the majority of them were not permanently in Geneva.

Bibliography

Archival Sources

Austria

Bruno Kreisky Archives Foundation, Vienna, Austria (BKAF)
    Bestand VII.1 Länderboxen
    Länderbox Schweden
Österreichiches Staatsarchiv/Archiv der Republik, Vienna (ÖStA/AdR),
    Bundesministerium für auswärtige Angelegenheiten (BMfaA)
    II-Pol/Schweden 1969
    II-Pol/Schweden 1970
    II-Pol/Schweden 1971
    II-Pol/Schweden 1972
    II-Pol/Schweden 1973
    II-Pol/Schweden 1974
    II-Pol/Schweden 1975

Germany

Politisches Archiv des Auswärtigen Amtes, Berlin (PAAA)
    Bestand 31
    Bestand 32
    ZA 111518 (KSZE)
Willy-Brandt-Archiv im Archiv der sozialen Demokratie, Friedrich-Ebert-
    Stiftung, Bonn (WBA)

Sweden

Arbetarrörelsens arkiv och bibliotek, Stockholm (ARAB)
  Olof Palmes Arkiv (OPA)
Regeringskansliets arkiv, Stockholm (RegA)
  Utrikesnämndens memorialprotokoll, 1968–1972
  UD, HP 79, Mål: A 30/6 allmänt. Konferenser och kongresser. Europeisk säkerhetskonferens (ESK), 67–68
  UD, HP 79, Mål: A 30/6 Korg 1. Konferenser och kongresser. Europeisk säkerhetskonferens (ESK), 7–8
  UD, HP 79, Mål: A 30/6 Korg 2. Konferenser och kongresser. Europeisk säkerhetskonferens (ESK), 1–8
  UD, HP 79, Mål: A 30/6 Korg 3. Konferenser och kongresser. Europeisk säkerhetskonferens (ESK), 8–9
  UD, HP 79, Mål: A 30/6 Korg 4. Konferenser och kongresser. Europeisk säkerhetskonferens (ESK), 2–3
Riksarkivet Arninge, Stockholm (RA)
  Utrikesdepartementets arkiv (UD), 1920 års dossiersystem, HP (Politiska ärenden 1953–1974), 79 (Konferenser och kongresser 1953––1974), 26–50

Switzerland

Schweizerisches Bundesarchiv, Berne (BAR)
  E 2001 (E) 1980/83, EPD, Abteilung für politische Angelegenheiten, 1968–1970
  E 2001 (E) 1987/78, EPD, Politische Direktion, 1973–1975
  E 2200.53 (-) 1997/83, Legation Vienna, 1969–1975
  E 2200.148 (-) 1988/70, Legation Stockholm, 1969–1975
  E 2814 1993/210, Handakten Bindschedler, 1973–1975

United Kingdom

The National Archives, Kew, Richmond, Surrey (TNA)
  FCO, 28, Northern Department and East European and Soviet Department, 1972–1975
  FCO, 33, Western European Department, 1970–1975
  FCO, 41, Western Organisations Department, 1970–1975

Published Primary Sources

Sweden

Documents on Swedish Foreign Policy (DSFP)
New Series 1:C:19. *Documents on Swedish Foreign Policy 1969.* Stockholm: Ministry for Foreign Affairs, 1970.
New Series 1:C:20. *Documents on Swedish Foreign Policy 1970.* Stockholm: Ministry for Foreign Affairs, 1971.
New Series 1:C:21. *Documents on Swedish Foreign Policy 1971.* Stockholm: Ministry for Foreign Affairs, 1972
New Series 1:C:22. *Documents on Swedish Foreign Policy 1972.* Stockholm: Ministry for Foreign Affairs, 1974.
New Series 1:C:23. *Documents on Swedish Foreign Policy 1973.* Stockholm: Ministry for Foreign Affairs, 1975.
New Series 1:C:24. *Documents on Swedish Foreign Policy 1974.* Stockholm: Ministry for Foreign Affairs, 1976.
New Series 1:C:25. *Documents on Swedish Foreign Policy 1975.* Stockholm: Ministry for Foreign Affairs, 1977.

United States of America

Foreign Relations of the United States (FRUS) *1969–1976,* available online at www.history.state.gov/historicaldocuments.
Vol. XXXIX, *European Security,* edited by Douglas E. Selvage. Washington, DC: US Government Printing Office, 2007.

Interviews

Birnbaum, Karl Edvard, 18 May 2010
Björk, Kaj, 12 May 2010

Printed Secondary Sources

Aggestam, Lisbeth. *European Foreign Policy and the Quest for a Global Role: Britain, France and Germany*. London: Routledge, 2012.

———. 'A European Foreign Policy? Role Conceptions and the Politics of Identity in Britain, France and Germany'. PhD dissertation. Stockholm University, 2004.

———. 'Role Theory and European Foreign Policy'. In *The European Union's Roles in International Politics: Concepts and Analysis*, edited by Ole Elgström and Michael Smith. Routledge/ECPR Studies in European Political Science, Vol. 45. London: Routledge, 2006, 11–29.

Agius, Christine. *The Social Construction of Swedish Neutrality: Challenges to Swedish Identity and Sovereignty. New Approaches to Conflict Analysis*. Manchester: Manchester University Press, 2006.

Agrell, Wilhelm. *Den stora lögnen: Ett säkerhetspolitiskt dubbelspel i alltför många akter* [The Whopping Lie: A Security-Political Double Game in All Too Many Acts]. Stockholm: Ordfront, 1991.

———. *Fred och fruktan: Sveriges säkerhetspolitiska historia 1918–2000* [Peace and Fear: The History of Sweden's Security Politicy, 1918–2000]. Lund: Historisk media, 2000.

Almqvist, Kurt (ed.). *Betydelsen av revolutionsåret 1968: Kårhusockupationen 40 år* [The Meaning of the Revolutionary Year 1968: 40 Year Student Centre Occupation]. Stockholm: Atlantis, 2008.

Altrichter, Helmut and Hermann Wentker (eds.). *Der KSZE-Prozess: vom Kalten Krieg zu einem neuen Europa 1975 bis 1990*. Zeitgeschichte im Gespräch, Vol. 11. Munich: Oldenbourg, 2011.

Andrén, Nils. *Maktbalans och alliansfrihet: svensk utrikespolitik under 1900-talet* [Balance of Power and Nonalignment. Swedish Foreign Policy in the 20th Century]. Stockholm: Norstedts juridik, 1996.

———. *Säkerhetspolitik: Analyser och tillämpningar* [Security Policy: Analyses and Application]. 2nd ed. Stockholm: Norstedts juridik, 2002.

Andrén, Nils and Yngve Möller. *Från Undén till Palme: Svensk utrikespolitik efter andra världskriget* [From Undén to Palme: Swedish Foreign Policy after the Second World War]. Stockholm: Norstedt, 1990.

Appelqvist, Örjan. *Bruten brygga: Gunnar Myrdal och Sveriges ekonomiska efterkrigspolitik 1943–1947* [Broken Bridge: Gunnar Myrdal and Sweden's Economic Post-War Politics 1943–1947]. Stockholm: Santérus, 2000.

Apunen, Osmo. 'Three "Waves" of the Kekkonen Plan and Nordic Security in the 1980s'. *Security Dialogue* 11(1), 2012, 16–32.

Aras, Bülent and Aylin Gorener. 'National Role Conceptions and Foreign Policy Orientation: the Ideational Bases of Justice and Development Party's Foreign Policy Activism in the Middle East'. *Journal of Balkan and Near Eastern Studies*, 12(1), 2010, 73–92.

Artéus, Gunnar and Leifland, Leif (eds.). *Svenska diplomatprofiler under 1900-talet*. Stockholm: Probus, 2001.

Arvidsson, Claes. *Olof Palme: Med verkligheten som fiende* [Olof Palme: With Reality as an Enemy]. Stockholm: Timbro, 2007.

Åselius, Gunnar. *The Russian 'Menace' to Sweden: The Belief System of a Small Power Security Elite in the Age of Imperialism*. Stockholm: Almqvist & Wiksell International, 1994.

Aunesluoma, Juhana. *Britain, Sweden and the Cold War, 1945–54: Understanding Neutrality*. St. Antony's Series. Basingstoke: Palgrave Macmillan, 2003.

Aunesluoma, Juhana, Magnus Petersson and Charles Silva. 'Deterrence or Reassurance: Nordic Responses to the First Détente, 1953–1956'. *Scandinavian Journal of History*, 32(2), 2007, 183–208.

Badalassi, Nicolas. *En finir avec la guerre froide: la France, l'Europe et le processus d'Helsinki*. Rennes: Presses universitaires de Rennes, 2014.

———. 'The Mediterranean Stake of the CSCE, 1972–1975'. In *Détente in Cold War Europe: Politics and Diplomacy in the Mediterranean and the Middle East*, edited by Elena Calandri, Daniele Caviglia and Antonio Varsori. International Library of Twentieth Century History. London: I.B. Tauris, 2011, 61–73.

Bange, Oliver and Gottfried Niedhart (eds.). *Helsinki 1975 and the Transformation of Europe*. New York; Oxford: Berghahn Books, 2008.

Békés, Csaba. 'The Warsaw Pact, the German Question and the CSCE Process'. In *Helsinki 1975 and the Transformation of Europe*, edited by Oliver Bange and Gottfried Niedhart. New York: Berghahn Books, 2008, 113–28.

Bender, Thomas (ed.). *Rethinking American History in a Global Age*. Berkeley: University of California Press, 2002.

Berenskoetter, Felix and Michael J. Williams (eds.). *Power in World Politics*. London: Routledge, 2007.

Berggren, Håkan and Magnus Bard. *Första försvar: Diplomati från ursprung till UD* [First Line of Defence: Diplomacy from Beginning to UD]. Stockholm: Atlantis, 2008.

Berggren, Henrik. *Underbara dagar framför oss: en biografi över Olof Palme* [Wonderful Days Ahead of Us: A Biography of Olof Palme]. Stockholm: Norstedt, 2010.

Bergman, Johan. *Kulturfolk eller folkkultur? 1968, kulturarbetarna och demokrating* [Cultural Folk or Folk Culture? 1968, Cultural Workers and Democracy]. Umeå: Boréa, 2010.

Birnbaum, Karl E. and Hanspeter Neuhold (eds.). *Neutrality and Non-Alignment in Europe*. The Laxenburg Papers, Vol. 4. Vienna: Braumüller, 1981.

Bischof, Günter, Stefan Karner and Peter Ruggenthaler (eds.). *The Prague Spring and the Warsaw Pact Invasion of Czechoslovakia*. Harvard Cold War Studies Book Series, Vol. 15. Lanham, MD: Lexington Books, 2010.

Bjereld, Ulf. 'Critic or Mediator?: Sweden in World Politics, 1945–90'. *Journal of Peace Research*, 32(1), 1995, 23–35.

Bjereld, Ulf and Marie Demker. 'Foreign Policy as Battlefield: A Study of National Interest and Party Motives'. *Scandinavian Political Studies*, 23(1), 2000, 17–36.

Bjereld, Ulf and Marie Demker. *I Vattumannens tid?: en bok om 1968 års auktoritets-uppror och dess betydelse i dag* [Under the Star of Aquarius?: A Book on the Anti-authoritarian Revolts of 1968 and Their Contemporary Significance]. Stockholm: Nerenius & Santérus, 2005.

———. *Utrikespolitiken som slagfält: De svenska partierna och utrikesfrågorna* [Foreign Policy as Battlefield: The Swedish Parties and Foreign Policy Issues]. Stockholm: Nerenius & Santérus, 1995.

Bjereld, Ulf and Ann-Marie Ekengren. 'Cold War Historiography in Sweden'. In *The Cold War and the Nordic Countries. Historiography at a Crossroads*, edited by Thorsten B. Olesen. Odense: University Press of Southern Denmark, 2004, 143–75.

Bjereld, Ulf, Alf W. Johansson and Karl Molin. *Sveriges säkerhet och världens fred: svensk utrikespolitik under kalla kriget* [Sweden's Security and World Peace: Swedish Foreign Policy during the Cold War]. Sverige under kalla kriget [Sweden during the Cold War], Vol. 16. Stockholm: Santérus, 2008.

Boel, Bent. 'French Support for Eastern European Dissidence, 1968–1989'. In *Perforating the Iron Curtain: European Détente, Transatlantic Relations, and the Cold War*, edited by Poul Villaume and Odd Arne Westad. Copenhagen: Museum Tusculanum Press, 2010, 215–41.

Bozo, Frédéric, Université de Paris I: Panthéon-Sorbonne and Université de Paris III (eds.). *Europe and the End of the Cold War: A Reappraisal*. Cold War History Series, Vol. 19. London: Routledge, 2008.

Brandt, Willy, Bruno Kreisky and Olof Palme. *Briefe und Gespräche 1972 bis 1975*. Cologne: Europäische Verlagsanstalt, 1975.

Bredow, Wilfried von. *Der KSZE-Prozess von der Zähmung zur Auflösung des Ost–West-Konflikts* [The CSCE Process from the Taming to the Dissolution of the East–West Conflict]. Darmstadt: Wiss. Buchgesellschaft, 1994.

Breitenmoser, Christoph. *Sicherheit für Europa: Die KSZE-Politik der Schweiz bis zur Unterzeichnung der Helsinki-Schlussakte zwischen Skepsis und aktivem Engagement* [Security for Europe: The CSCE Policy of Switzerland until the Ratification of the Helsinki Final Act between Scepticism and Active Engagement]. Zürcher Beiträge zur Sicherheitspolitik und Konfliktforschung, Vol. 40. Zurich: Forschungsstelle für Sicherheitspolitik und Konfliktanalyse, 1996.

Breuning, Marijke. 'Role Theory Research in International Relations: State of the Art and Blind Spots'. In *Role Theory in International Relations: Approaches and Analyses*, edited by Sebastian Harnisch, Cornelia Frank and Hanns W. Maul. Routledge Advances in International Relations and Global Politics, Vol. 90. London: Routledge, 2011, 16–35.

Brommesson, Douglas. *Från Hanoi till Bryssel: Moralsyn i deklarerad svensk utrikes-politik 1969–1996* [From Hanoi to Brussels: Moral Beliefs in Declared Swedish Foreign Policy 1969–1996]. Sverige under kalla kriget [Sweden during the Cold War], Vol. 15. Stockholm: Santérus, 2007.

Brundtland, Arne Olav. 'The Nordic Balance. Past and Present'. *Cooperation and Conflict*, 1(4), 1965, 30–65.

Bynander, Fredrik. 'Utrikes- och säkerhetspolitik' [Foreign and Security Policy]. In *Svensk politik och den europeiska unionen* [Swedish Politics and the European Union], edited by Tom Bryder, Daniel Silander and Charlotte Wallin. Stockholm: Liber, 2004, 195–214.

Byström, Mikael and Pär Frohnert (eds.). *Reaching a State of Hope: Refugees, Immigrants and the Swedish Welfare State, 1930–2000*. Lund: Nordic Academic Press, 2013.

Campbell, Kurt M. and Michael E. O'Hanlon. *Hard Power: The New Politics of National Security*. New York: Basic Books, 2006.

Cole, Paul Marion. 'Neutralité du Jour: The Conduct of Swedish Security Policy since 1945'. PhD dissertation. Johns Hopkins University, 1990. Ann Arbor, MI: University Microfilms International, 1992.

Craig, Gordon A. 'The Historian and the Study of International Relations'. *American Historical Review*, 88(1), 1983, 1–11.

Creuzberger, Stefan. *Westintegration und Neue Ostpolitik. Die Außenpolitik der Bonner Republik* [Western Integration and New Ostpolitik. The Foreign Policy of the Bonn Republic]. Deutsche Geschichte im 20. Jahrhundert [German History in the 20th Century], Vol. 14. Berlin: be.bra verlag, 2009.

Daddow, Oliver J. (ed.). *Harold Wilson and European Integration: Britain's Second Application to Join the EEC*. London; Portland, OR: Frank Cass, 2003.

Dalsjö, Robert. 'The Hidden Rationality of Sweden's Policy of Neutrality during the Cold War'. *Cold War History*, 14(2), 2014, 175–94.

———. *Life-Line Lost: The Rise and Fall of 'Neutral' Sweden's Secret Reserve Option of Wartime Help from the West*. Stockholm: Santérus Academic Press, 2006.

Dedman, Martin J. *The Origins and Development of the European Union 1945–95: A History of European Integration*. London: Routledge, 1996.

Ekecrantz, Stefan. *Hemlig utrikespolitik: Kalla kriget, utrikesnämnden och regeringen* [Secret Foreign Policy: The Cold War, the Advisory Council on Foreign Affairs, and the Government]. Sverige under kalla kriget [Sweden during the Cold War], Vol. 12. Stockholm: Santérus, 2003.

Ekengren, Ann-Marie. *Av hänsyn till folkrätten? Svensk erkännandepolitik 1945–1995* [Out of Consideration for International Law? Swedish Policy of Recognition 1945–1995]. Sverige under kalla kriget [Sweden during the Cold War], Vol. 6. Stockholm: Nerenius & Santérus, 1999.

———. 'How Ideas Influence Decision-Making: Olof Palme and Swedish Foreign Policy, 1965–1975'. *Scandinavian Journal of History*, 36(2), 2011, 117–34.

———. *Olof Palme och utrikespolitiken: Europa och tredje världen* [Olof Palme and Foreign Policy: Europe and the Third World]. Umeå: Boréa, 2005.

———. *Sverige under kalla kriget 1945–1969: en forskningsöversikt* [Sweden during the Cold War 1945–1969: A Research Overview]. Gothenburg: Grafikerna i Kungälv, 1997.

Ekholm, Curt. 'Balt- och tyskutlämningen 1945–1946: omständigheter kring interneringen i läger i Sverige och utlämningen till Sovjetunionen av f d tyska krigsdeltagare'. PhD dissertation, 2 volumes. Uppsala University, 1984.

Elman, Colin and Miriam Fendius Elman. 'Diplomatic History and International Relations Theory: Respecting Difference and Crossing Boundaries'. *International Security*, 22(1), 1997, 5–21.
Engelbrekt, Kjell. 'Den sjuttonde alliansmedlemmen?' [The Seventeenth NATO Member?]. *Internationella Studier*, 4, 1999, 61–72.
——. 'En bättre återförsäkring än vi anade?' [A Better Reinsurgency Policy than We Suspected?]. *Internationella Studier*, 1, 2003.
Engh, Sunniva. 'The Conscience of the World? Swedish and Norwegian Provision of Development Aid'. *Itinerario*, 33(2), 2009, 65–82.
Ferraris, Luigi Vittorio (ed.), *Report on a Negotiation: Helsinki–Geneva–Helsinki, 1972–1975*. Collection de relations internationales, Vol. 7. Alphen aan den Rijn: Sijthoff & Noordhoff, 1979.
Finney, Patrick (ed.), *Palgrave Advances in International History*. Basingstoke: Palgrave Macmillan, 2004.
Fischer, Thomas. 'Bridging the Gap between East and West: The N+N as Catalysts of the CSCE Process, 1972–1983'. In *Perforating the Iron Curtain: European Détente, Transatlantic Relations, and the Cold War*, edited by Poul Villaume and Odd Arne Westad. Copenhagen: Museum Tusculanum Press, 2010, 143–78.
——. *Die Grenzen der Neutralität: Schweizerisches KSZE-Engagement und gescheiterte UNO-Beitrittspolitik im Kalten Krieg, 1969–1986* [The Boundaries of Neutrality: Swiss CSCE Engagement and Failed Accession Negotiations during the Cold War, 1969–1986]. Schweizer Beiträge zur internationalen Geschichte – Contributions suisses à l'histoire internationale [Swiss Contributions to International History], Vol. 7. Zurich: Chronos, 2004.
——. '"A Mustard Seed Grew into a Bushy Tree": The Finnish CSCE Initiative of 5 May 1969'. *Cold War History*, 9(2), 2009, 177–201.
——. *Neutral Power in the CSCE. The N+N States and the Making of the Helsinki Accords 1975*. Wiener Schriften zur Internationalen Politik [Viennese Contributions to International Politics], Vol. 12. Baden Baden: Nomos Verlagsgesellschaft, 2009.
Førland, Tor Ergil. 'En empirisk bauta, et intellektuelt gjesp. Kritisk blikk på Norsk utenrikspolitikks historie 1–6', *Historisk Tidsskrift*, 78(2), 1999, 214–36.
Fors, Mats. *Svarta Nejlikan: Harald Edelstam—en berättelse om mod, humanitet och passion* [The Black Pimpernel: Harald Edelstam – A History of Courage, Humanity and Passion]. Stockholm: Prisma, 2009.
Fukuyama, Francis. *The End of History and the Last Man*. New York: Free Press; Toronto: Maxwell Macmillan Canada; New York: Maxwell Macmillan International, 1992.
Gaddis, John Lewis. *The Cold War: A New History*. New York: Penguin Press, 2005.
——. 'History, Theory, and Common Ground'. *International Security*, 22(1), 1997, 75–85.
——. *We Now Know: Rethinking Cold War History*. Oxford: Clarendon Press, 1997.

Garavini, Guliano. *After Empires: European Integration, Decolonization, and the Challenge from the Global South 1957–1986*. Oxford Studies in Modern European History. Oxford: Oxford University Press, 2012.

Gardner, Philip. *Hermeneutics, History and Memory*. Abingdon: Routledge, 2010.

Garthoff, Raymond L. *Détente and Confrontation: American-Soviet Relations from Nixon to Reagan*. Rev. ed. Washington, DC: Brookings Institution, 1994.

George, Alexander L. 'Knowledge for Statecraft: The Challenge for Political Science and History'. *International Security*, 22(1), 1997, 44–52.

Gilde, Benjamin, *Österreich im KSZE-Prozess 1969–1983: Neutraler Vermittler in humanitärer Mission*. Quellen und Darstellungen zur Zeitgeschichte, Vol. 98. Munich: Oldenbourg, 2013.

Goldstein, Judith and Robert Keohane (eds.). *Ideas and Foreign Policy: Beliefs, Institutions, and Political Change*. Cornell Studies in Political Economy. Ithaca: Cornell University Press, 1993.

Götz, Norbert. *Deliberative Diplomacy: The Nordic Approach to Global Governance and Societal Representation at the United Nations*. International Relations Studies Series 11. Dordrecht: Republic of Letters, 2011.

Götz, Norbert and Heidi Haggrén (eds.). *Regional Cooperation and International Organizations: The Nordic Model in Transnational Alignment*. Routledge Advances in International Relations and Global Politics, Vol. 70. London: Routledge, 2009.

Grachev, Andrei. *Gorbachev's Gamble: Soviet Foreign Policy & the End of the Cold War*. Cambridge: Polity Press, 2008.

Graebner, Norman A., Richard Dean Burnes and Joseph M. Siracusa. *Reagan, Bush, Gorbachev: Revisiting the End of the Cold War*. Westport, CT: Praeger Security International, 2008.

Gstöhl, Sieglinde. *Reluctant Europeans: Norway, Sweden, and Switzerland in the Process of Integration*. Boulder: Lynne Rienner, 2002.

Gustavsson, Jakob. 'The Politics of Foreign Policy Change: Explaining the Swedish Reorientation on EC Membership'. PhD dissertation. Lund University, 1998.

Gussarsson Wijk, Maria. *Europeiska visioner och nationellt egenintresse: framväxten av den europeiska unionen 1945–2000* [European Visions and National Self-Interest: The Evolution of the European Union 1945–2000]. Lund: Studentlitteratur, 2005.

———. 'Realpolitik, ideologi, samarbete: Sveriges EEC-ansökningar 1961 och 1967 ur tre olika tolkningsperspektiv' [Realpolitik, Ideology, Cooperation: Three Interpretations of Sweden's EEC applications 1961 and 1967]. In *Samtidshistoria och politik: vänbok till Karl Molin* [Contemporary History and Politics: Festschrift for Karl Molin], edited by Ragnar Björk and Alf W. Johansson. Stockholm: Hjalmarson & Högberg, 2004, 123–43.

———. 'The Swedish Social Democracy, the Plans on West European Economic Cooperation, and International Party Cooperation, 1955–58'. *Journal of European Integration History*, 11(1), 2005, 85–101.

Haber, Stephen H., David M. Kennedy and Stephen D. Krasner. 'Brothers under the Skin: Diplomatic History and International Relations'. *International Security*, 22(1), 1997, 34–43.

Haftendorn, Helga. 'The Link between CSCE and MBFR: Two Sprouts from One Bulb'. In *Origins of the European Security System. The Helsinki Process Revisited, 1965–75*, edited by Andreas Wenger, Vojtech Mastny and Christian Nuenlist. London: Routledge, 2008, 237–58.

Hakkarainen, Petri. *A State of Peace in Europe: West Germany and the CSCE, 1966–1975*. Studies in Contemporary European History, Vol. 10. New York: Berghahn Books, 2011.

Hakovirta, Harto. *East–West Conflict and European Neutrality*. Oxford: Clarendon Press; New York: Oxford University Press, 1988.

Hanhimäki, Jussi. 'Conservative Goals, Revolutionary Outcomes: The Paradox of Détente'. *Cold War History*, 8(4), 2008, 503–12.

———. 'Détente in Europe, 1962–1975'. In *The Cambridge History of the Cold War. Volume II. Crises and Détente*, edited by Melvyn P. Leffler and Odd Arne Westad. Cambridge: Cambridge University Press, 2010, 198–218.

———. *The Flawed Architect: Henry Kissinger and American Foreign Policy*. Oxford: Oxford University Press, 2004.

———. *The Rise and Fall of Détente: American Foreign Policy and the Transformation of the Cold War*. Issues in the History of American Foreign Relations. Washington, DC: Potomac Books, 2013.

———. '"They Can Write It in Swahili": Kissinger, the Soviets, and the Helsinki Accords, 1973–1975'. *Journal of Transatlantic Studies*, 1(1), 2003, 37–58.

Hanhimäki, Jussi and Odd Arne Westad (eds.). *The Cold War. A History in Documents and Eyewitness Accounts*. Oxford: Oxford University Press, 2003.

Hanisch, Anja, *Die DDR im KSZE-Prozess 1972–1985: Zwischen Ostabhängigkeit, Westabgrenzung und Ausreisebewegung*. Quellen und Darstellungen zur Zeitgeschichte, Vol. 91. Munich: Oldenbourg, 2012.

Harnisch, Sebastian. 'Role Theory: Operationalization of Key Concepts'. In *Role Theory in International Relations: Approaches and Analyses*, edited by Sebastian Harnisch, Cornelia Frank and Hanns W. Maul. Routledge Advances in International Relations and Global Politics, Vol. 90. London: Routledge, 2011, 7–15.

Haslam, Jonathan. *No Virtue Like Necessity: Realist Thought in International Relations since Machiavelli*. New Haven: Yale University Press, 2002.

Haunt, Lynn. 'Where Have All the Theories Gone?' *Perspectives*, 40(3), 5–7.

Hebel, Kai. 'Britain's Contribution to Détente: The Conference on Security and Cooperation in Europe, 1972–1975'. PhD dissertation. University of Oxford, 2012.

Hentilä, Seppo. 'Finland and the Two German States: Finland's German Policy in the Framework of European Détente'. In *The Making of Détente: Eastern and Western Europe in the Cold War, 1965–75*, edited by Wilfried Loth and Georges-Henri Soutou. London; New York: Routledge, 2008, 183–200.

Heraclides, Alexis. *Security and Co-operation in Europe: The Human Dimension, 1972–1992*. London: Frank Cass, 1993.

Hobsbawm, Eric. *Age of Extremes: The Short Twentieth Century*. London: Joseph, 1994.
Hofmann, Arne. *The Emergence of Détente in Europe: Brandt, Kennedy and the Formation of Ostpolitik*. London: Routledge, 2007.
Hogan, Michael J. 'SHAFR Presidential Address: The "Next Big Thing": The Future of Diplomatic History in a Global Age'. *Diplomatic History*, 28(1), 2004, 1–21.
Hogan, Michael J. and Thomas G. Paterson (eds.). *Explaining the History of American Foreign Relations*. 2nd ed. Cambridge; New York: Cambridge University Press, 2004.
Holbraad, Carsten. *Internationalism and Nationalism in European Political Thought*. Palgrave Macmillan Series on the History of International Thought. New York: Palgrave Macmillan, 2003.
Hollerbach, Alexander. 'Religions- und Kirchenfreiheit im KSZE-Prozeß'. In *Grundrechte, soziale Ordnung und Verfassungsgerichtsbarkeit: Festschrift für Ernst Benda zum 70. Geburtstag*, edited by Eckart Klein. Heidelberg: Müller, 1995, 117–33.
Holmberg, Susan L. 'Welfare Abroad: Swedish Development Assistance'. In *The Committed Neutral. Sweden's Foreign Policy*, edited by Bengt Sundelius. Boulder, CO: Westview Press, 1989.
Holmström, Mikael. *Den dolda alliansen: Sveriges hemliga NATO-förbindelser* [The Hidden Alliance: Sweden's Secret Relations with NATO]. Försvaret och det kalla kriget (FOKK) [Defence and the Cold War], Vol. 28. Stockholm: Atlantis, 2011.
Holsti, Kalevi Jaakko. 'National Role Conceptions in the Study of Foreign Policy'. *International Studies Quarterly*, 14(3), 1970, 233–309.
———. 'National Role Conceptions in the Study of Foreign Policy'. In *Role Theory and Foreign Policy Analysis*, edited by Stephen G. Walker. Duke Press Policy Studies. Durham, NC: Duke University Press, 1987.
Hudson, Valerie. 'The History and Evolution of Foreign Policy Analysis'. In *Foreign Policy: Theories, Actors, Cases*, edited by Steve Smith, Amelia Hadfield and Tim Dunne. Oxford: Oxford University Press, 2008, 11–29.
Hugemark, Bo. 'Säkerhetspolitikens Grand Old Man—Still Going Strong [The Grand Old Man of Security Policy—Still Going Strong]'. *Vårt försvar*, 112(2), 2001.
Ingram, Edward. 'The Wonderland of the Political Scientist'. *International Security*, 22(1), 1997, 53–63.
Ionescu, Mihail E. 'Romania, Ostpolitik and the CSCE, 1967–1975'. In *Helsinki 1975 and the Transformation of Europe*, edited by Oliver Bange and Gottfried Niedhart. New York: Berghahn Books, 2008, 129–43.
Iriye, Akira. 'Internationalizing International History'. In *Rethinking American History in a Global Age*, edited by Thomas Bender. Berkeley: University of California Press, 2002, 47–62.
Jacobsen, Hans-Adolf (ed.). *Sicherheit und Zusammenarbeit in Europa (KSZE): Analyse und Dokumentation*. Cologne: Verlag Wissenschaft und Politik, 1973.

Jarzabek, Wanda. 'Hope and Reality: Poland and the Conference on Security and Cooperation in Europe, 1964–1989'. Cold War International History Project, Working Paper Number 56. Washington, DC: Woodrow Wilson International Center for Scholars, 2008.

———. 'Preserving the Status Quo or Promoting Change: The Role of the CSCE in the Perception of Polish Authorities'. In *Helsinki 1975 and the Transformation of Europe*, edited by Oliver Bange and Gottfried Niedhart. New York: Berghahn Books, 2008, 144–59.

Johansson, Alf W. 'Kampen om hjärtan och sinnen. Nyare forskning om kalla kriget' [The Struggle for the Heart and the Mind. New Research on the Cold War]. In *Samtidshistoria och politik: vänbok till Karl Molin* [Contemporary History and Politics: Festschrift for Karl Molin], edited by Ragnar Björk and Alf W. Johansson. Stockholm: Hjalmarson & Högberg, 2004, 195–216.

Josefsson, Sven-Olof. 'Året var 1968: universitetskris och studentrevolt i Stockholm och Lund' [The Year Was 1968: University Crisis and Student Revolt in Stockholm and Lund]. PhD dissertation. University of Gothenburg, 1996.

Judt, Tony. *Postwar: A History of Europe Since 1945*. 2nd ed. New York: Penguin Press, 2005.

Karlsson, Birgit. *Att handla neutralt: Sverige och den ekonomiska integrationen i Västeuropa 1948–1972* [To Trade Neutrally: Sweden and the Economic Integration in Western Europe 1948–1972]. Gothenburg: School of Business, University of Gothenburg, 2001.

———. 'Handelspolitik eller politisk handling: Sveriges handel med öststaterna 1946–1952' [Trade Policy or Political Action: Sweden's Trade with Eastern Europe 1946–1952]. PhD dissertation. University of Gothenburg, 1992.

Khudoley, Konstantin. 'Soviet Foreign Policy during the Cold War: The Baltic Factor'. In *The Baltic Question during the Cold War*, edited by John Hiden, Vahur Made and David J. Smith. London: Routledge, 2008, 56–72.

Kieninger, Stephan. 'Transformation or Status Quo: The Conflict of Stratagems in Washington over the Meaning and Purpose of the CSCE and MBFR, 1969–1973'. In *Helsinki 1975 and the Transformation of Europe*, edited by Oliver Bange and Gottfried Niedhart. New York: Berghahn Books, 2008, 67–78.

Kirste, Knut and Hanns W. Maull. 'Zivilmacht und Rollentheorie' [Civil Power and Role Theory]. *Zeitschrift für internationale Beziehungen*, 3(2), 1996, 283–312.

Korey, William. *The Promises We Keep: Human Rights, the Helsinki Process, and American Foreign Policy*. New York: St. Martin's Press, in association with the Institute for EastWest Studies, 1993.

Krohn, Johannes. 'Karl-Anders Wollters samling på filmarkivet i Grängesberg'. MA thesis. Uppsala University, 2010.

Kronvall, Olof and Magnus Petersson. 'Den bräckliga barriären: Finland i svensk säkerhetspolitik 1948–1962'. PhD dissertation. Swedish National Defence College, 2003.

———. *Svensk säkerhetspolitik i supermakternas skugga 1945–1991* [Swedish Security Policy in the Shadow of the Superpowers]. 2nd ed. Stockholm: Santérus, 2012.

Krotz, Ulrich. 'National Role Conceptions and Foreign Policies: France and Germany Compared'. Unpublished Manuscript. Cambridge, MA: Minda de Gunzburg Center for European Studies at Harvard University, 2002.

Kunter, Katarina. *Die Kirchen im KSZE-Prozeß 1968–1978*. Konfession und Gesellschaft, Vol. 20. Stuttgart: Kohlhammer, 2000.

Leatherman, Janie. 'Engaging East and West beyond the Bloc Division: Active Neutrality and the Dual Role of Finland and Sweden in the CSCE'. PhD dissertation. University of Denver, 1991.

———. *From Cold War to Democratic Peace: Third Parties, Peaceful Change, and the OSCE*. Syracuse Studies on Peace and Conflict Resolution. Syracuse, NY: Syracuse University Press, 2003.

Leffler, Melvyn P. and Odd Arne Westad (eds.). *The Cambridge History of the Cold War, Vol. 1, Origins*. Cambridge: Cambridge University Press, 2010.

—— (eds.). *The Cambridge History of the Cold War, Vol. 2, Crises and Détente*. Cambridge: Cambridge University Press, 2010.

—— (eds.). *The Cambridge History of the Cold War, Vol. 3, Endings*. Cambridge: Cambridge University Press, 2010.

———. *For the Soul of Mankind: The United States, the Soviet Union, and the Cold War*. New York: Hill and Wang, 2007.

Levy, Jack S. 'Too Important to Leave to the Other: History and Political Science in the Study of International Relations'. *International Security*, 22(1), 1997, 22–33.

Lindholm, Rolf H. *Kalla kriget och Sverige* [The Cold War and Sweden]. Vätö: Rolf H. Lindholm, 2008.

———. *Sverige under kalla kriget: Dokumentsamling om neutralitetspolitiken* [Sweden during the Cold War: Document Collection on Neutrality Policy]. Sverige under kalla kriget [Sweden during the Cold War], Vol. 9. Stockholm: Santérus, 2000.

Lödén, Hans, *'För säkerhets skull': ideologi och säkerhet i svensk aktiv utrikespolitik 1950–1975* ['Just to Be on the Safe Side': Ideology and Security in Swedish Active Foreign Policy 1950–1975]. Göteborg Studies in Politics, Vol. 61. Sverige under kalla kriget [Sweden during the Cold War], Vol. 5. Stockholm: Nerenius & Santérus, 1999.

Loth, Wilfried and Georges-Henri Soutou (eds.). *The Making of Détente: Eastern and Western Europe in the Cold War, 1965–75*. Cold War History Series, Vol. 20. London; New York: Routledge, 2008.

———. *Overcoming the Cold War: A History of Détente*. Basingstoke: Palgrave, 2002.

Ludlow, N. Piers. 'European Integration and the Cold War'. In *The Cambridge History of the Cold War. Volume II. Crises and Détente*, edited by Melvyn P. Leffler and Odd Arne Westad. Cambridge: Cambridge University Press, 2010, 175–97.

Lundestad, Geir. *East, West, North, South: Major Developments in International Politics since 1945*. Rev. 6th ed. Los Angeles: SAGE, 2010.

Luxmoore, Jonathan. *The Helsinki Agreement: Dialogue or Delusion?* London: Alliance Publishers for the Institute for European Defence & Strategic Studies, 1986.

Magnusson, Erik. 'Den egna vägen: Sverige och den europeiska integrationen 1961–1971'. PhD dissertation. Uppsala University, 2009.
Maier, Charles S. 'Marking Time: The Historiography of International Relations'. In *The Past Before Us: Contemporary Historical Writing in the United States*, edited by Michael G. Kammen. Ithaca, NY: Cornell University Press, 1980, 355–87.
Makko, Aryo. 'Arbitrator in a World of Wars: The League of Nations and the Mosul Dispute, 1924–1925'. *Diplomacy & Statecraft*, 21(4), 2010, 631–49.
———. 'Das schwedische Interesse an Vertrauensbildenden Maßnahmen und Abrüstungsfragen'. In *Die KSZE im Ost–West-Konflikt: Internationale Politik und gesellschaftliche Transformation 1975–1990*, edited by Matthias Peter and Herman Wentker. Munich: Oldenbourg, 2012, 191–202.
———. 'Multilateralism and the Shaping of an "Active Foreign Policy": Sweden during the Preparatory Phase of the CSCE'. *Scandinavian Journal of History*, 35(3), 2010, 310–29.
———. 'Sweden, Europe, and the Cold War: A Reappraisal'. *Journal of Cold War Studies*, 14(2), 2012, 68–97.
Malmborg, Mikael af. 'Den ståndaktiga nationalstaten: Sverige och den västeuropeiska integrationen 1945–1959' [The Persistent National State: Sweden and Western European Integration 1945–1959]. PhD dissertation. Lund University, 1994.
———. *Neutrality and State-Building in Sweden*. St Antony's Series. Basingstoke: Palgrave, 2001.
Maresca, John J. *To Helsinki: The Conference on Security and Cooperation in Europe 1973–1975*. Duke Press Policy Studies. Durham, NC: Duke University Press, 1985.
Maruzsa, Zoltán. 'Denuclearization in Central Europe? The Rapacki Plan during the Cold War'. In *Öt kontinens. Eötvös Loránd Tudományegyetem*.Budapest, 2008, 225–64.
Mastny, Vojtech. *Helsinki, Human Rights, and European Security: Analysis and Documentation*. Durham, NC: Duke University Press, 1986.
Merseburger, Peter. *Willy Brandt: 1913–1992: Visionär und Realist*. Munich: DVA, 2006.
Misgeld, Klaus. 'Den svenska socialdemokratin och Europa – från slutet av 1920-talet till början av 1970-talet. Attityder och synsätt i centrala uttalanden och dokument'. In *Socialdemokratin och svensk utrikespolitik: från Branting till Palme*, edited by Bo Huldt and Klaus Misgeld. Stockholm: Utrikespolitiska institutet, 1990.
———. 'Die "Internationale Gruppe demokratischer Sozialisten" in Stockholm 1942–1945: zur sozialistischen Friedensdiskussion während des zweiten Weltkrieges'. PhD dissertation. Uppsala University, 1976.
Möckli, Daniel. *European Foreign Policy during the Cold War: Heath, Brandt, Pompidou and the Short Dream of Political Unity*. London: I.B. Tauris, 2009.

Molin, Karl. 'The Central Issues of Swedish Neutrality Policy'. In *Die neutralen und die europäische Integration, 1945–1995 = The Neutrals and the European Integration, 1945–1995*, edited by Michael Gehler and Rolf Steiniger. Historische Forschungen: Veröffentlichungen [Historical Research: Publications]/Institut für Zeitgeschichte der Universität Innsbruck, Arbeitskreis Europäische Integration, Vol. 3. Vienna: Böhlau, 2000.

Möller, Yngve. *Östen Undén: En biografi* [Östen Undén: A Biography]. Stockholm: Norstedt, 1986.

———. *Sverige och Vietnamkriget: ett unikt kapitel i svensk utrikespolitik* [Sweden and the Vietnam War: A Unique Chapter in Swedish Foreign Policy]. Stockholm: Tiden, 1992.

Moores, Simon Robert, '"Neutral on Our Side": US–Swedish Military and Security Relations during the Eisenhower Administration'. PhD dissertation. London School of Economics and Political Science, 2005.

Moores, Simon Robert and Jerker Widén, 'Sverige under det kalla kriget–den amerikanska underrättelsetjänstens perspektiv, mars 1952'. *Kungliga Krigsakademiens handlingar och tidskrift*, 5, 2003, 78–92.

Morgan, Michael Cotey. 'The United States and the Making of the Helsinki Final Act'. In *Nixon in the World: American Foreign Relations, 1969–1977*, edited by Fredrik Logevall and Andrew Preston. New York: Oxford University Press, 2008, 164–82.

Muschik, Alexander. *Die beiden deutschen Staaten und das neutrale Schweden: eine Dreiecksbeziehung im Schatten der offenen Deutschlandfrage 1949–1972*. Münster: Lit, 2005.

Nabers, Dirk. 'Identity and Role Change in International Politics'. In *Role Theory in International Relations: Approaches and Analyses*, edited by Sebastian Harnisch, Cornelia Frank and Hanns. W. Maul. Routledge Advances in International Relations and Global Politics, Vol. 90. London: Routledge, 2011, 74–92.

Neuhold, Hanspeter. *CSCE: N+N Perspectives: The Process of the Conference on Security and Co-operation in Europe from the Viewpoint of the Neutral and Nonaligned Participating States*. The Laxenburg Papers, Vol. 8. Vienna; Laxenburg: Braumüller; Öiip, 1987.

Neumann, Iver B. 'Norsk utenrikspolitikks historie–en kritikk: del 1'. *Kungliga Krigsakademiens handlingar och tidskrift*, 5, 1999, 119–44.

———. 'Norsk utenrikspolitikks historie–en kritikk: del 2'. *Kungliga Krigsakademiens handlingar och tidskrift*, 6, 1999, 147–74.

Nilsson, Mikael. *Tools of Hegemony. Military Technology and Swedish–American Security Relations, 1945–1962*. Trita-HOT. Stockholm Papers in the History and Philosophy of Technology. Stockholm: Santérus Academic Press, 2007.

Nilsson, Torbjörn. *Hundra år av svensk politik* [Hundred Years of Swedish Politics]. Malmö: Gleerups utbildning, 2009.

Njølstad, Olav (ed.). *The Last Decade of the Cold War: From Conflict Escalation to Conflict Transformation*. Nobel Symposium. Cass Series: Cold War History, Vol. 5. London: Frank Cass, 2004.

Noreen, Erik. *Brobygge eller blockbildning?: de norska och svenska utrikesledningarnas säkerhetspolitiska föreställningar 1945–1948* [Bridge Building or Alignment?: Security Policy Beliefs in Norway and Sweden 1945–1948]. Stockholm: Carlsson, 1994.

Norlin, Annika. *Undénplanen: Ett lyckat misslyckande* [The Undén Plan: A Successful Failure]. Gothenburg: Department of Political Science, University of Gothenburg, 1998.

Notini Burch, Cecilia. *A Cold War Pursuit: Soviet Refugees in Sweden, 1945–54*. Stockholm: Santérus Academic Press, 2014.

Notini Burch, Cecilia, Karl Molin and Magnus Petersson (eds.), *Svensk säkerhetspolitik under det kalla kriget–öppen för olika tolkningar?* Stockholm: Stockholm University, 2011.

Nuenlist, Christian. 'Expanding the East-West Dialog beyond the Bloc Division. The Neutrals as Negotiators and Mediators, 1969–75'. In *Origins of the European Security System. The Helsinki Process Revisited, 1965–75*, edited by Andreas Wenger, Vojtech Mastny and Christian Nuenlist. London: Routledge, 2008, 201–21.

Nye, Joseph S. Jr. *The Powers to Lead*. Oxford: Oxford University Press, 2008.

———. *Soft Power: The Means to Success in World Politics*. New York: Public Affairs, 2004.

Östberg, Kjell. *1968 när allting var i rörelse: sextiotalsradikaliseringen och de sociala rörelserna* [1968, When Everything Was in Movement: The Radicalization of the Sixties and the Social Movements]. Stockholm: Leopard, 2008.

———. *I takt med tiden: Olof Palme 1927–1969* [With the Times: Olof Palme 1927–1969]. Stockholm: Leopard, 2008.

———. *När vinden vände: Olof Palme 1969–1986* [When the Wind Changed: Olof Palme 1969–1986]. Stockholm: Leopard, 2009

Ottosson, Sten. *Svensk självbild under kalla kriget: En studie av stats- och utrikesministrarnas bild av Sverige 1950–1989* [Swedish Self-Perception during the Cold War: A Study of Prime and Foreign Minister's Picture of Sweden 1950–1989]. Research report/Utrikespolitiska institutet, Vol. 34. Stockholm: Utrikespolitiska institutet, 2003.

———. *Sverige mellan öst och väst: Svensk självbild under kalla kriget* [Sweden between East and West: Swedish Self-Perception during the Cold War]. Research report/SUKK, Vol 11. Gothenburg: University of Gothenburg, 2001.

Parmar, Inderjeet and Michael Cox (eds.). *Soft Power and U.S. Foreign Policy: Theoretical, Historical and Contemporary Perspectives*. Routledge Studies in U.S. Foreign Policy. London: Routledge, 2010.

Paterson, Thomas G. 'Defining and Doing the History of American Foreign Relations: A Primer'. *Diplomatic History*, 14(4), 1990, 584–601.

Peter, Matthias, *Die Bundesrepublik im KSZE-Prozess: Die Umkehrung der Diplomatie, 1975–1983*. Quellen und Darstellungen zur Zeitgeschichte, Vol. 105. Berlin: De Gruyter Oldenbourg, 2015.

Peter, Matthias and Hermann Wentker (eds.). *Die KSZE im Ost–West-Konflikt: Internationale Politik und gesellschaftliche Transformation 1975–1990*.

Schriftenreihe der Vierteljahrshefte für Zeitgeschichte, Sondernummer. Munich: Oldenbourg, 2012.
Peterson, Thage G. *Olof Palme som jag minns honom* [Olof Palme as I Remember Him]. Stockholm: Bonnier, 2002.
Petersson, Magnus. *'Brödrafolkens väl': Svensk-norska säkerhetsrelationer 1949–1969* ['The Welfare of the Brother Peoples': Swedish-Norwegian Security Relations 1949–1969]. Stockholm: Santérus, 2003.
Plokhy, Serhii. *The Last Empire: The Final Days of the Soviet Union*. New York: Basic Books, 2014.
Rathkolb, Oliver. 'Brandt, Kreisky and Palme as Policy Entrepreneurs: Social Democratic Networks in Europe's Policy towards the Middle East'. In *Transnational Networks in Regional Integration: Governing Europe 1945–83*, edited by Wolfram Kaiser, Brigitte Leucht and Michael Gehler. Palgrave Studies in European Union Politics. Basingstoke: Palgrave Macmillan, 2010, 152–75.
Reimaa, Markku. *Helsinki Catch: European Security Accords*. Helsinki: Edita, 2009.
Renk, Hans-Jörg. *Der Weg der Schweiz nach Helsinki: Der Beitrag der schweizerischen Diplomatie zum Zustandekommen der Konferenz über Sicherheit und Zusammenarbeit in Europa (KSZE), 1972 – 1975* [Switzerland's Road to Helsinki: The Contribution of Swiss Diplomacy to the Realisation of the Conference on Security and Co-Operation in Europe (CSCE)]. Bern u.a.: Haupt, 1996.
Rey, Marie-Pierre. 'The USSR, and the Helsinki Process, 1969–75: Optimism, doubt, or defiance?' In *Origins of the European Security System. The Helsinki Process Revisited, 1965–75*, edited by Andreas Wenger, Vojtech Mastny and Christian Nuenlist. London: Routledge, 2008, 65–82.
Reynolds, David. 'International History, the Cultural Turn and the Diplomatic Twitch'. *Cultural and Social History*, 3(1), 2006, 75–91.
Rogers, John. 'The Foreign Policy of Small States: Sweden and the Mosul Crisis, 1924–1925'. *Contemporary European History*, 16(3), 2007, 349–69.
Romano, Angela. *From Détente in Europe to European Détente: How the West Shaped the Helsinki CSCE*. Euroclio. Brussels: PIE Peter Lang, 2009.
Rosenau, James. 'Pre-theories and Theories of Foreign Policy'. In *Approaches to Comparative and International Politics*, edited by Barry Robert Farrell. Evanston, IL: Northwestern University Press, 1966.
Rosin, Philip, *Die Schweiz im KSZE-Prozeß 1972–1983: Einfluß durch Neutralität*. Quellen und Darstellungen zur Zeitgeschichte, Vol. 99. Munich: Oldenbourg, 2013.
Rother, Bernd. 'Willy Brandts Außenpolitik: Grundlagen, Methoden und Formen'. In *Willy Brandts Außenpolitik*, edited by Bernd Rother. Wiesbaden: Springer, 2014.
Saal, Yuliya von, Die *KSZE-Prozess und Perestroika in der Sowjetunion: Demokratisierung, Werteumbruch und Auflösung 1985–1991*. Quellen und Darstellungen zur Zeitgeschichte, Vol. 100. Munich: Oldenbourg, 2013.
Sarotte, Mary E. *1989: The Struggle to Create Post-Cold War Europe*. Princeton Studies in International History and Politics. Princeton, NJ: Princeton University Press, 2009.

Sarotte, Mary E. *The Collapse. The Accidental Opening of the Berlin Wall*. New York: Basic Books, 2014.

———. *Dealing with the Devil: East Germany, Détente, and Ostpolitik, 1969–1973*. The New Cold War History. Chapel Hill: University of North Carolina Press, 2001.

Savranskaya, Svetlana. 'Unintended Consequences: Soviet Interests, Expectations and Reactions to the Helsinki Final Act'. In *Helsinki 1975 and the Transformation of Europe*, edited by Oliver Bange and Gottfried Niedhart. New York: Berghahn Books, 2008, 175–90.

Schlotter, Peter. *Die KSZE im Ost–West-Konflikt: Wirkung einer internationalen Institution*. Studien der Hessischen Stiftung Friedens- und Konfliktforschung, Vol. 32. Frankfurt, A.M.; New York: Campus Verlag, 1999.

Schmidt, Gustav (ed.). *A History of NATO—The First Fifty Years*. Vol. III. Basingstoke: Palgrave, 2001.

Schramm, Karl-Friedrich (ed.), *Sicherheitskonferenz in Europa: Dokumentation 1954–1972: die Bemühungen um Entspannung und Annäherung im politischen, militärischen, wirtschaftlichen, wissenschaftlich-technologischen und kulturellen Bereich*. Frankfurt A.M.: Metzner, 1972.

Schroeder, Paul W. 'History and International Relations Theory: Not Use or Abuse, but Fit or Misfit'. *International Security*, 22(1), 1997, 64–74.

Schweizer, Karl W. and Matt J. Schumann. 'The Revitalization of Diplomatic History: Renewed Reflections'. *Diplomacy & Statecraft*, 19(2), 2008, 149–86.

Senoo, Tetsuji. *Ein Irrweg zur deutschen Einheit? Egon Bahrs Konzeptionen, die Ostpolitik und die KSZE, 1963–1975*. Europäische Hochschulschriften, Vol. 588. Frankfurt A.M.: Peter Lang, 2011.

Silva, Charles. 'Keep Them Strong, Keep Them Friendly: Swedish–American Relations and the Pax Americana, 1948–1952'. PhD dissertation. Stockholm University, 1999.

Smith, Michael Eugene. *Europe's Foreign and Security Policy: The Institutionalization of Cooperation*. Cambridge: Cambridge University Press, 2004.

Smith, Steve, Amelia Hadfield and Tim Dunne (eds.). *Foreign Policy: Theories, Actors, Cases*. Oxford: Oxford University Press, 2008.

Snyder, Richard Carlton, Henry W. Bruck and Burton M. Sapin; with new chapters by Valerie M. Hudson, Derek H. Chollet and James M. Goldgeier. *Foreign Policy Decision-Making (Revisited)*. New York: Palgrave Macmillan, 2002.

Snyder, Sarah B. 'The Helsinki Process, American Foreign Policy, and the End of the Cold War'. PhD dissertation. Georgetown University, 2006.

———. *Human Rights Activism and the End of the Cold War: A Transnational History of the Helsinki Network*. Human Rights in History, Vol. 2. Cambridge: Cambridge University Press, 2011.

———. '"Jerry, Don't Go": Domestic Opposition to the 1975 Helsinki Final Act'. *Journal of American Studies*, 44(1), 2010, 67–81.

Sprout, Harold Hance and Margaret Tuttle Sprout. *The Ecological Perspective on Human Affairs: With Special Reference to International Politics*. Princeton, NJ: Princeton University Press, 1965.

Steiner, Zara. 'On Writing International History: Chaps, Maps and Much More'. *International Affairs*, 73(3), 1997, 531–46.
Stråth, Bo. *Folkhemmet mot Europa: ett historiskt perspektiv på 90-talet* [The People's Home toward Europe: A Historical Perspective on the 90s]. Stockholm: Tiden, 1993.
——. 'The Swedish Demarcation from Europe'. In *The Meaning of Europe: Variety and Contention within and among Nations*, edited by Mikael af Malmborg and Bo Stråth. Oxford: Berg, 2002.
Suri, Jeremi. *Power and Protest: Global Revolution and the Rise of Détente*. Cambridge, MA: Harvard University Press, 2003.
Sverige, Säkerhetspolitiska utredningen. *Fred och säkerhet: Svensk säkerhetspolitik 1969–89*. Stockholm: Fritzes offentliga publikationer, 2002.
——. *Om kriget kommit . . . Förberedelser för mottagande av militärt bistånd 1949–1969 (SOU 1994:11)* [Had There Been a War . . . Preparations for the Reception of Military Assistance 1949–1969]. Stockholm: Fritzes offentliga publikationer, 1994.
——. *Peace and Security: Swedish Security Policy 1969–89: Abridged Version and Translation of SOU 2002:108: Report from the Inquiry on Security Policy*. Stockholm: Fritzes offentliga publikationer, 2004.
Thomas, Daniel C. *The Helsinki Effect. International Norms, Human Rights, and the Demise of Communism*. Princeton, NJ: Princeton University Press, 2001.
Thorsell, Staffan. *Sverige i vita huset* [Sweden in the White House]. Stockholm: Bonnier fakta, 2004.
Torstendahl, Rolf. 'Thirty-Five Years of Theories in History. Social Science Theories and Philosophy of History in the Scandinavian Debate'. *Scandinavian Journal of History*, 25(1–2), 2000, 1–26.
Undén, Östen. *Anteckningar. 1952–1966* [Notes. 1952–1966], edited by Karl Molin. Handlingar/Kungl. samfundet för utgivande av handskrifter rörande skandinaviens historia [Documents/Royal Society for the Publication of Handwritings on Scandinavia's History], Vol. 25. Stockholm, Uppsala: Swedish Science Press, 2002.
Van Oudenaren, John. *Détente in Europe: The Soviet Union and the West since 1953*. Durham, NC: Duke University Press, 1991.
Von Dannenberg, Julia. *The Foundations of Ostpolitik: The Making of the Moscow Treaty between West Germany and the USSR*. Oxford Historical Monographs. Oxford; New York: Oxford University Press, 2008.
Wahlbäck, Krister. *Jättens andedräkt: Finlandsfrågan i svensk politik 1809–2009* [The Breath of the Giant: The Finnish Question in Swedish Politics 1809–2009]. Stockholm: Atlantis, 2011.
Wenger, Andreas and Vojtech Mastny. 'New Perspectives on the Origins of the CSCE Process'. In *Origins of the European Security System. The Helsinki Process Revisited, 1965–75*, edited by Andreas Wenger, Vojtech Mastny and Christian Nuenlist. London: Routledge, 2008, 3–22.
Westad, Odd Arne (ed.). 'A "New", "International" History of the Cold War?' *Journal of Peace Research*, 32(4), 1995, 483–87.
—— (ed.). *Reviewing the Cold War: Approaches, Interpretations, Theory*. Nobel Symposium. Cass Series: Cold War History, Vol. 1. London: Frank Cass, 2000.

Westberg, Jacob. 'Den nationella drömträdgården. Den stora berättelsen om den egna nationen i svensk och brittisk Europadebatt' [The National Dream Garden. The Great Story about the Nation in the Swedish and British Debates on Europe]. PhD dissertation. Stockholm University, 2003.

Widén, Jerker. *Väktare, ombud, kritiker: Sverige i amerikanskt säkerhetstänkande 1961–1968* [Guardian, Ombudsman, Critic: Sweden in American Security Thinking]. Stockholm: Santérus Academic Press Sweden, 2009.

Winkler, Heinrich August. *Germany: The Long Road West 1789–1933 [Vol 1]*. Oxford: Oxford University Press, 2006.

Yamamoto, Takeshi. 'The Road to the Conference on Security and Cooperation in Europe, 1969–1973: Britain, France and West Germany'. PhD dissertation. London School of Economics and Political Science, 2007.

Zetterberg, Kent. 'Introduktion'. In *Hotet från öster: tre studier om svensk säkerhetspolitik, krigsplanering och strategi i det kalla krigets första fas 1945–1958* [The Menace from the East: Three Studies about Swedish Security Policy, War Plans and Strategy during the First Phase of the Cold War 1945–1958], edited by Kent Zetterberg. Stockholm: National Defence College, 1997.

Zielinski, Michael. *Die neutralen und blockfreien Staaten und ihre Rolle im KSZE-Prozess* [The Neutral and Nonaligned States and Their Role in the CSCE Process]. Baden Baden: Nomos Verlagsgesellschaft, 1990.

Zubok, Vladislav Martinovich. *A Failed Empire: The Soviet Union in the Cold War from Stalin to Gorbachev*. The New Cold War History. Chapel Hill: University of North Carolina Press, 2007.

———. 'The Soviet Attitude towards the European Neutrals'. In *Die neutralen und die europäische Integration=The Neutrals and the European Integration*, edited by Michael Gehler and Rolf Steininger. Vienna: Böhlau, 2000, 29–43.

Memoirs

Åström, Sverker. *Ögonblick: från ett halvsekel i UD-tjänst* [Moment: From Half a Century of UD Service]. Stockholm: Bonnier Alba, 1992.
Leifland, Leif. *Frostens år: om USA:s diplomatiska utfrysning av Sverige* [The Year of the Frost: On the United States' Diplomatic Ostracism of Sweden]. Sverige under kalla kriget [Sweden during the Cold War], Vol. 2. Stockholm: Nerenius & Santérus, 1997.
Nilsson, Torsten. *Lag eller näve* [Law or Fist]. Stockholm: Tiden, 1980.
Petri, Lennart. *Sverige i stora världen: minnen och reflexioner från 40 års diplomattjänst* [Sweden in the Wide World: Memories and Reflections from 40 Years of Diplomatic Service]. Stockholm: Atlantis, 1996.
Wachtmeister, Wilhelm. *Som jag såg det: händelser och människor på världsscenen* [As I Saw It: Events and People on the World Stage]. Stockholm: Norstedt, 1996.

Newspapers and Journals

Dagens Nyheter
Die Zeit
New York Times
TIME Magazine
The Washington Post

Websites

American Historical Association, www.historians.org
European Navigator, www.ena.lu
H–Net Humanities and Social Sciences Online, www.h-net.org
Institut für Zeitgeschichte München-Berlin, http://ifz-muenchen.de
Institute of Historical Research, www.history.ac.uk
Internet Portal on German and European Foreign Policy, Trier University, www.deutsche-aussenpolitik.de
North Atlantic Treaty Organization, www.nato.in
United Nations, www.un.org

INDEX

Aftonbladet, 108
Agrell, Wilhelm, 7
Allard, Henry, 114
Andersson, Sven, 171, 183, 194, 200, 201, 204–6, 209, 216, 218, 220, 222, 226–27, 230–31, 252, 255, 259
Andrén, Nils, 116, 137, 141–42, 249
Archer, Peter, 188
Arms Control and Disarmament Research Unit, 128
Arvidson, Bertil, 191, 255, 259
Arvidsson, Stellan, 71, 115, 124
Asp, Kerstin, 136, 186, 213, 219–20, 255, 258–59
Åström, Sverker, 58, 76, 88, 135, 155–56, 167, 174, 186, 189, 191–93, 196–99, 205, 207–10, 213, 216, 220, 223, 231, 255, 258–59
Austria, 38, 48, 50, 53–54, 57, 59–60, 66, 71–75, 82, 84, 88–89, 91, 93, 98, 110, 112, 115, 117, 130, 137, 150, 155, 164, 166–68, 171, 174, 187, 189, 199, 201, 203, 209, 212, 216, 219, 222, 227, 229, 235, 248
Auswärtiges Amt (AA), 50, 52, 113, 118, 129–30, 159

Backlund, Sven, 130, 214
Basic Treaty (Grundlagenvertrag), 106, 125
Basket III, 7, 196, 216, 219. See also Third Basket
Bekeris, Ilmar, 123–24, 137, 139, 191, 213, 236, 255, 258–59
Belding, René, 87, 255
Belfrage, Leif, 59, 68, 79, 255

Bengtsson, Nils, 124
Berg, Åke, 225
Berg, Göran, 112, 123, 136, 139, 171, 186, 220, 226, 230, 255, 258–59
Bergmark, Torsten, 115
Bergquist, Lars, 197
Berlin Agreement, 105, 111, 116. See also Four Power Agreement and Quadripartite Agreement
Berlin Wall, 1, 6, 106
Berne, 35, 48–49, 60, 64, 108, 111–12, 184, 192–93, 198, 207, 214
Berührungsangst 4, 108. See also fear of contact
Bindschedler, Rudolf, 82–83, 108, 112, 134, 222
biological weapon-free zone, 129
Birnbaum, Karl, 137, 249
Bjereld, Ulf, 9, 10, 12–13, 254
Björk, Kaj, 35, 63, 148–49, 157–58, 176, 185–86, 190, 192, 213, 255, 258
Blix, Hans, 83, 112–13, 123, 133–34, 136–39, 164, 167, 172–73, 175, 186, 191–92, 196, 210, 251, 255, 258–59
Blue Book, 172, 174, 188, 221
Bonn, 50, 52, 61–62, 67–70, 76, 80, 83–86, 94, 97, 106, 113, 118–19, 122–23, 126, 129, 143, 151, 159, 166, 184, 191, 199, 214, 256
Börje Leuf, Nils, 123, 139, 256, 258
Brandt, Willy, 39–40, 50, 52, 54, 59, 66–69, 76, 84–85, 88–90, 92, 105–6, 114, 117, 122, 137, 199, 205, 218, 247–48
Brezhnev Doctrine, 61, 63, 70, 79, 91, 110, 115, 133, 136, 157, 169, 173, 193, 213

Brezhnev, Leonid, 7–8, 41, 86, 96, 107, 129–30, 197, 207, 224, 236
Brosio, Manlio, 109, 112
Brunner, Edouard, 169, 172, 221
Budapest Appeal, 4, 49–51, 53–54, 58, 62, 107, 147, 231, 248
Bundesministerium für auswärtige Angelegenheiten (BmfaA), 73
Bundestag, 114

Campiche, Samuel, 149, 155, 175,
Carl XVI Gustaf, 220
Carlsson, Bernt, 124
Ceausescu, Nicolae, 157
Conference of the Committee on Disarmament (CCD), 107, 116, 131, 139, 160, 163, 166–67, 179–80, 255, 257
Communist Party of the Soviet Union (CPSU), 57, 202
Conférence pour la Sécurité et la Coopération Européennes, 71, 120
confidence-building measures, 9, 121–22, 136, 142, 154, 158, 160, 168–69, 171, 173, 190, 192–93, 195, 212, 214, 218, 221–22, 224, 226–27, 229–30, 234, 252
Council of Europe, 35–36, 56, 76, 82, 86, 201, 204, 227
Czechoslovakia, 2, 41, 50, 53, 57–58, 60, 62–63, 65, 73, 152, 167, 194, 228, 249

Dahlén, Olle, 120
Davignon Committee, 127
De Besche, Hubert, 59, 135, 210, 255
De Margerie, Emmanuel, 214
Diesel, Jürgen, 113
Dipoli, 82, 89, 113, 135, 138, 147–77, 184, 186, 189–90, 195, 197, 203, 221, 232, 235, 249–50, 258. *See also* multilateral preparatory talks (MPT) and *Salon des Ambassadeurs*
Dobrynin, Anatoly, 200, 221–22
Douglas-Home, Alec, 186
Dzunov, Risto, 154

Eastern treaties, 82, 84, 88, 90, 106, 109, 116, 123, 125, 151
EC Nine, 8, 150, 155, 168, 176, 184–85, 190, 199–200, 203, 207, 212, 214, 218, 221, 223, 227–29, 234–35, 238
Eckerberg, Lennart, 166, 191, 195, 207, 255, 259

Economic Commission for Europe (ECE), 110, 116–17, 127, 132, 136, 165, 257
Economic Recovery Plan (ERP), 34
Edelstam, Axel, 111, 116–17, 123–24, 126, 128–29, 131–32, 136–39, 148, 154, 161–64, 166–67, 169, 173, 175, 186, 190–91, 195–98, 202, 205, 209, 213, 216–17, 220, 224–31, 250–51, 256, 258–59
Edelstam, Harald, 217, 235
Edmar, Désirée, 186, 191, 258–59
Ekéus, Rolf, 1–3, 23, 186, 258
Ekholm, Gustaf, 224, 230, 259
Ekström, Tord, 124
Eliasson, Jan, 119, 134, 161
Eng, Brynolf, 112, 256
Enquist, Per Olov, 124
Ericsson, Ulf, 123, 129, 139, 256
European Coal and Steel Community (ECSC), 36–37, 45
European Communities (EC), 8, 14, 40–41, 44–45, 76, 127, 150, 189, 206, 216, 228, 249, 252, 255
European Defence Community (EDC), 36
European Economic Community (EEC), 29, 36–38, 40, 45, 87, 116, 125, 189
European Free Trade Association (EFTA), 37–38, 40, 125
European Political Cooperation (EPC), 8
European Security Conference (ESC), 14, 42, 49, 52, 54, 60–61, 63–65, 67–77, 79–85, 87–89, 91, 98, 108
Ewerlöf, Hans, 123, 137, 139, 175, 256, 258

Falkman, Kaj, 50, 73, 81, 84, 91, 105, 111, 113, 116–17, 123–24, 139, 191, 256, 259
fear of contact, 4. *See also* Berührungsangst
Final Accords, 2. *See also* Final Act
Final Act, 1–5, 7–8, 16, 22, 183, 230–32, 234, 247–48, 253, 258. *See also* Final Accords
Finland, 9, 28, 36, 40, 43, 45, 48, 50, 54–57, 60–61, 64–66, 68–71, 73, 75, 82–95, 108–110, 112, 114–15, 117, 119, 123–24, 129, 131, 135, 137–38, 143, 147–48, 151, 154–57, 161–62, 167–68,

171, 175, 181, 185–86, 193–94, 198, 203, 207–8, 210–12, 216–17, 219–20, 222, 228–29, 231–34, 241, 248, 250, 252–53
Finlandia Hall, 2, 185–86, 231–32
Finnish Initiative, 55–57, 59–60, 62–66, 72, 82, 208, 227
Finnmark, Lennart, 87, 208, *Folkpartiet*, 41. *See also* Liberal Party
Forshell, Per Olof, 123, 139, 175, 256
Four Power Agreement, 88, 90, 105, 111, 125, 215, 247, 249. *See also* Berlin Agreement and Quadripartite Agreement
Freedom of action, 5, 37, 74, 83, 193, 195, 233
FRG (Federal Republic of Germany), 76, 88, 90, 118, 232. *See also* West Germany

Gantchev, Gantcho, 114
Gardiner, Gerald, 120
General Agreement on Tariffs and Trade (GATT), 35, 192
German Question, 51, 56, 61–62, 68, 74, 82, 86, 213
Giron, Marc, 73–74, 124, 139
Giscard d'Estaing, Valéry, 205, 224
Gomulka Plan, 128
Graber, Pierre, 207
Gromyko, Andrei, 8, 124, 127, 202, 214, 218, 225, 228
Gustaf VI Adolf, 56, 127

Hagen, Tord, 168
Hägglöf, Gunnar, 68, 256
Hägglöf, Ingemar, 60, 65–66, 88, 95, 208, 256
Hallstein Doctrine, 90, 114, 118
Hamilton af Hageby, Gustaf, 130, 217–18, 220, 256, 259
Helsinki Effect, 5. *See also* Spirit of Helsinki
Helsinki Process, 3, 6, 8–9, 90–91
Hichens-Bergström, Richard, 191, 197–98, 200, 202, 205–6, 209, 211, 213, 216–18, 222, 224, 231, 234–35, 252, 256, 259
Hjalmarson, Jarl, 235
Hogan, Michael, 15
Holsti, Kalevi Jaakko, 16–17, 19–21, 32, 47, 56, 58, 69, 72, 75, 78, 89, 92, 100, 107, 113, 117, 126, 136, 138, 151, 165, 174–76, 184, 200, 218, 221, 229, 234–35, 248, 250–52
Huldtgren, Claes, 55, 95, 256
Hungary, 50, 57, 64, 72–73, 75–76, 81, 86, 93, 168, 249

IB Affair, 194
Iloniemi, Jaakko, 149, 199, 216, 219–20, 222
Inner Six, 37, 40, 44, 127
Inner-German Transit Agreement, 125

Jakobson, Max, 55, 155, 167, 207, 220
Jarring, Gunnar, 67, 69, 73, 120, 256
Jödahl, Ole, 54, 56, 74–76, 78–79, 84–85, 109, 114, 116, 126, 130, 256

Karjalainen, Ahti, 55, 71, 86, 95, 97, 208, 222
Kekkonen plan, 128, 131, 224
Kekkonen, Urho, 50, 55–57, 60–61, 64–65, 70, 83, 95, 156, 203, 207, 222, 231–32
Kissinger, Henry, 59, 90, 129, 135, 194, 203, 212, 218, 225, 228, 232
Klaus, Josef, 72
Kovalev, Anatoly, 205, 214, 225
Kreisky, Bruno, 40, 74, 82, 89, 98, 150, 187, 199, 207, 222
Kremlin, 2, 7, 34, 41, 49–52, 55, 57, 60, 65–66, 70, 74, 76, 83, 148, 156, 161, 204, 221, 225, 227
Kronvall, Erik, 165

League of Nations, 33
Leifland, Leif, 119, 121, 123, 132, 134, 161, 201, 203, 224, 231, 256, 259
Lewis, Flora, 154
Liberal Party, 41, 120, 231. *See Folkpartiet*
Liechtenstein, 210
Lilliehöök, Sigge, 81, 256
Lloyd, R. E., 128
Lo-Johansson, Ivar, 115
Lönnqvist, Ulf, 165

Maltsev, Viktor, 51–53, 69, 79, 151, 156, 158
McCloy–Zorin Accords, 166, 180
Melin, Cai, 123, 139, 256
Mendelevich, Lev, 156, 160–61, 164, 172, 207, 227–28

Mevik, Leif, 218
Mitterrand, François, 205
Moro, Aldo, 202
Mossberg, Mathias, 225, 259
Motjalov, Georgij, 128
multilateral preparatory talks (MPT), 22, 89, 117, 121–22, 127–30, 135–36, 138, 147–77, 184–89, 235, 250–51, 258. See also Dipoli and *Salon des Ambassadeurs*
Mutual and Balanced Force Reductions (MBFR), 69, 82, 88, 92, 109–10, 112, 116, 119, 121–23, 125–30, 135, 148, 151, 157–61, 168–69, 171, 173, 192–93, 206
mutually acceptable conditions (MAC), 223
Myrdal, Alva, 160–61, 163, 166, 185, 257
Myrdal, Gunnar 34, 127–28, 137, 179, 257

national role conception (NRC), 16–21, 30, 47, 92, 131, 138, 163, 175, 184, 248
Neutral and Nonaligned States (N+N), 8–9, 158, 169, 174–75, 193, 201–3, 208–10, 213–15, 219, 221–25, 227–31, 233, 251–52
Niklasson, Sten, 123–24, 137, 139, 258
Nilsson, Manfred, 123, 139, 257–59
Nincic, Djuro, 70, 87, 175
Nixon, Richard, 47, 90, 107, 109, 121, 124, 205–6, 209, 212, 236
North Atlantic Treaty, 11, 35, 133
North Atlantic Treaty Organization (NATO), 8, 10–13, 28, 37, 49–50, 52–54, 59, 64–65, 67–71, 73–75, 78–81, 86–88, 90, 92, 97, 106, 109–13, 116–17, 119, 121–23, 126, 130–31, 147, 155, 157, 161–62, 168, 173, 176, 185, 194, 199–200, 205–6, 209–10, 227–29, 233, 235, 252
Novikov, Vladimir, 106
Nuclear Weapon-Free Zones, 128
Nyström, Rune, 49–50, 123–24, 126, 137, 139, 167, 257–58

Olsson, Jan, 136, 186, 257–59
Organization for European Economic Co-operation (OEEC), 34–35, 37
Ostpolitik, 39, 66, 68–69, 76, 81, 83, 85, 89–90, 92, 106, 114, 120, 137–38, 221, 247

Palm, Göran, 115
Palme, Olof, 3, 5, 12, 21, 39–42, 47–48, 65, 68, 75–77, 79, 87–92, 105–7, 109, 116, 127, 131, 134, 137–38, 147, 152, 162, 176, 183–84, 193–94, 196–97, 199, 201, 206, 211, 228, 230–33, 235, 240, 247–54. See also Palmelinjen
Palmelinjen, 75, 253. See also Palme, Olof
Patek, Stanislaw, 191, 259
Petri, Lennart, 57, 72, 74, 78, 208, 257
Pompidou, Georges, 41, 68, 84, 205
Prace, 152
Pravda, 8, 66, 71, 98, 108, 120, 225
Prawitz, Jan, 116, 123–24, 137, 139, 171–72, 175, 186, 258–59

Quadripartite Agreement, 90, 134. See also Berlin Agreement and Four Power Agreement
Quai d'Orsay, 59, 130, 214

Rapacki Plan, 126, 128
Reinius, Ulf, 128, 191, 257, 259
Riksdag (Swedish Parliament), 3, 35, 71, 78, 114, 119
Ringborg, Mats, 191–92, 257, 259
Rogers, William P., 70, 122, 126
Rössel, Agda, 46, 57–58, 152, 257
Rudé Právo, 152
Rustningskontroll, 162
Rydfors, Lennart, 186, 192, 257–58
Ryding, Göran, 88, 119, 122, 136, 147, 149–52, 155–64, 167, 170–71, 173–75, 184, 186, 189, 191, 208, 220, 231–32, 236, 241, 251, 257–59
Ryding, Gunvor, 124

Salon des Ambassadeurs, 81, 109, 130, 172. See also Dipoli and multilateral preparatory talks (MPT)
Scheel, Walter, 67, 123, 174
Schlangenbad, 199
Schmidt, Helmut, 214
Sharp, Mitchell, 123, 162, 175
Shenstone, Michael, 211
Social Democratic Party (*Sveriges socialdemokratiska arbetarpartiet*, SAP), 36, 38, 41, 43, 62, 247, 254
Social Democratic Youth League (*Sveriges socialdemokratiska ungdomsförbund*, SSU), 79

Solzhenitsyn, Alexander, 209
Sorsa, Kalevi, 211
Spirit of Helsinki, 1–2. *See also* Helsinki Effect
Springsteen, George S., 134
Steglich, Peter, 118
Strategic Arms Limitation Talks (SALT), 61, 83, 121, 123, 127, 129, 152, 160, 167, 206
Svanström, Bertil, 115
Svenska Vietnamkommittén (Swedish Committee for Vietnam), 115
Svensson, Evert, 188
Swedish Defence Research Agency (*Försvarets forskningsanstalt*), 124
Switzerland 21, 35–36, 38, 48, 54, 59–60, 75, 82–83, 89, 108, 112, 114–15, 117, 119, 121–22, 129, 137, 149, 156, 158–59, 164, 166, 169–71, 174, 180, 189, 193, 203, 207, 209, 212, 214–15, 219, 222, 227, 229, 231, 235, 251, 253
Synnergren, Stig, 172
System for the Peaceful Settlement of Disputes (SRPD), 83, 89, 108, 112, 136, 168, 192, 198

Tallroth, Tore, 130, 186, 191, 198, 213, 215–17, 219, 234–35, 252, 257–59
TASS, 57, 106, 108
Third basket, 7–8, 161, 164–66, 168, 170–73, 188, 190, 193–94, 196–98, 201–6, 208–29, 232, 234, 251–53. *See* Basket III
Thorén, Marianne, 123, 139
Thorsson, Inga, 164–65, 180, 257
Thyberg, Knut, 118, 233
Tickell, Crispin, 126, 128, 174
Tötterman, Richard, 128, 149
Treaty of Moscow, 84, 111, 123 *See also* Eastern treaties
Treaty of Warsaw, 85, 123. *See also* Eastern treaties
Tuovinen, Matti, 156
Turco–Greek conflict, 212

Vahlquist, Magnus, 191, 257, 259
Von Groll, Götz, 113, 199
Von Staden, Berndt, 118

Wachtmeister, Wilhelm, 47, 51, 54, 58–60, 63–64, 67, 70, 73–74, 77, 80, 84, 87, 108–9, 111–12, 116–18, 121–22, 124, 134, 137–39, 154, 168, 174, 186, 188, 194, 196–98, 205–6, 240, 249–50, 257–58
Waldheim, Kurt, 50, 63–64, 72, 232
Warsaw Pact, 4, 7–8, 13, 49–50, 53, 58, 62–63, 65–66, 68–70, 72–76, 79–81, 86–87, 89, 107, 110–11, 114, 116–17, 122, 130–31, 135, 153, 155, 157–58, 161–62, 168, 191, 204, 215, 219, 226, 229, 235, 248–49, 252
Watz, Lennart, 191, 259
Wedén, Sven, 41, 235
West Germany, 9, 35, 39, 50, 52, 54, 59, 61–64, 66–69, 71, 76, 82, 84–85, 88, 90, 92, 98, 105, 109–11, 113–14, 122, 125, 130, 135, 138, 151, 153, 162, 186, 188, 199–200, 205, 217, 224, 232, 248–50. *See also* FRG
Wickman, Krister, 14, 83, 88, 106, 109, 112, 115, 119–20, 122, 127, 135–36, 138, 148, 156, 160, 162, 167, 174–76, 185–90, 193–94, 198, 213, 232, 250, 257–58
Wilkens, Håkan, 216, 224, 259
Willman, Adam, 76, 80, 114
Wodak, Walter, 73, 85, 130
Wollin, Claes, 65, 76–78
Wollter, Karl Anders, 53, 161, 191, 257, 259
Wulff, Torgil, 123, 137, 139, 172, 186, 191, 257–59

Yakovlev, Mikhail, 190, 209
Yom Kippur War, 197, 199, 234

Zorin, Valerian, 135, 156, 166

www.ingramcontent.com/pod-product-compliance
Lightning Source LLC
Chambersburg PA
CBHW072146100526
44589CB00015B/2112